Consumer Behaviour

The author has prepared files and programs to accompany this disk. These are supplied via teaching staff on an Instructor's disk. Any purchaser of the book who cannot obtain access to this software via teaching staff should write to:

Julia Helmsley
Prentice Hall
Campus 400
Maylands Avenue
Hemel Hempstead
Herts HP2 7EZ

Telephone: 01442 881900
Fax: 01442 252544
email: julia_helmsley@prenhall.co.uk

Consumer Behaviour:
Advances and Applications in Marketing

Robert East
Kingston University

PRENTICE HALL

London   New York   Toronto   Sydney   Tokyo   Singapore
Madrid   Mexico   Munich   Paris

First published 1997 by
Prentice Hall Europe
Campus 400, Maylands Avenue
Hemel Hempstead
Hertfordshire, HP2 7EZ
A division of
Simon & Schuster International Group
© Prentice Hall 1997

Photographs by Ben Hammond

Typeset in 10/12 Palatino
by PPS, London Road, Amesbury, Wilts.

Printed and bound in Great Britain by
Biddles Ltd, Guildford and King's Lynn

Library of Congress Cataloging-in-Publication Data

Available from the publisher

British Library Cataloguing in Publication Data

A catalogue record for this book is available from
the British Library

ISBN 0–13–359316–9

1 2 3 4 5   01 00 99 98 97

Contents

List of figures

List of tables

List of exercises

Preface

Readership

Consumer Behaviour: Advances and Applications in Marketing is designed as a textbook for a consumer behaviour elective or for a second-level marketing course. The book addresses a range of problems raised in marketing and should also assist students specialising in services, retailing and advertising as well as those with wider concerns in business strategy, economics and psychology.

Scope

This book describes the theories, research methods and interventions that help us to predict, understand and bring about change in consumer behaviour. Most textbooks in consumer behaviour are comprehensive and well illustrated but they often present the subject in a rather uncritical manner. In practice there are competing methods and explanations, and the existing textbooks usually understate the uncertainties about many of our explanations of consumer behaviour. I have tried to treat issues in some depth and to show where theories and evidence are in question. This approach is very demanding and in the earlier *Changing Consumer Behaviour*, I left out a number of topics; *Consumer Behaviour: Advances and Applications in Marketing* fills many of these gaps with new material on brand loyalty, brand equity, the response to prices, customer satisfaction and complaining, quality perception, the use of retail facilities and also some of the implications of this work for consumer policy. I have also included an appendix on aspects of research, measurement, dissertation writing and the presentation of data. I have found that students often draw on consumer behaviour when preparing dissertations and it seemed useful to provide this material.

Approach

The sub-title *Advances and Applications in Marketing* reflects a belief that the focus of consumer research should be directed mainly by problems in marketing and not by theories drawn from psychology and the social sciences. I am not discounting such theories, rather I am arguing that their relevance is determined by the problems raised by marketing. For this reason the content of the book emphasizes topics that concern marketers.

But while I believe that marketing questions should set the agenda I do not believe that marketing analyses should define the way in which those questions are answered. Consumer behaviour is based on investigation and not on the conventions of practitioners. The remit of consumer behaviour is to provide systematic evidence on consumer responses that will help us to improve marketing practice and consumer policy. For this reason I distrust the rather seamless mix of marketing and consumer behaviour that is to be found in many textbooks. This approach leads too easily to a subservient role for consumer behaviour in which instances are found which fit the marketing thinking. There will always be instances that fit assumptions, and such examples have a place in teaching, but a scientific approach needs systematic verification. This means that a textbook on consumer behaviour must draw on the research literature to answer problems; if it fails to do this it is simply an extension of marketing thinking. I hope that in this book the reader can clearly distinguish the reporting of marketing ideas from the more scientific account of work in consumer behaviour.

This touches on a problem familiar to those who teach marketing students. Some business students find the argument from evidence quite unfamiliar: they may provide fluent accounts of current marketing practice, reporting practitioner thinking as though it were reliably true and omitting any details of research findings. In so doing they fail to see that the evidence is sometimes at odds with practitioner beliefs and they do not understand how marketing may progress by objective study; those who learn to use evidence when they are students may continue to question assumptions and to look for empirical support later when they become practitioners.

One hazard of research-based texts is the sheer weight of evidence. I have noticed some tendency to omit the work of early researchers in published articles and I believe that this should be resisted; I fear that those who forget the original research in their subjects are destined to repeat it and this seems wasteful and unscholarly. I therefore make no apology for some of the more ancient citations in this book that describe the origins of problem areas. I have also tried to emphasize the most recent work and key papers on topics.

As subjects get more fragmented, the textbook can acquire an importance as an integrator of different perspectives. In our field we can discern two rather different approaches to research. On the one hand, there is the tradition that dominates in the large conferences of the *Association for Consumer Research*. Put baldly, this is an approach that endorses theorizing and hypothesis-testing, often within experimental designs, and that tends to emphasize explanations in terms of the beliefs, preferences and culture of consumers – a cognitive orientation. Contrasted with this is the approach of those who belong to the *Marketing Science* grouping, who place emphasis on behaviour, measures rather than concepts, generalization from an accumulation of findings rather than testing hypotheses, and on the use of mathematical models rather than psychological theories for explanation. Many of us, including myself, have sympathy for both approaches but textbooks have generally emphasized the cognitive tradition. I have given more space than usual to the marketing science orientation in this textbook; in particular, I have emphasized behavioural explanations, the role of habit and the modelling of stationary markets. At the same time I have given a very full treatment to attitudes and to the techniques and theory that help us to predict and explain behaviour from reported beliefs. This balanced approach was appreciated by users of *Changing Consumer Behaviour* and I have extended it here.

Consumer behaviour is an exciting field. New techniques are giving answers to questions of major importance and will, in due course, give rise to a new breed of professional marketer. At the same time, the academic advance of consumer behaviour is raising issues in psychology and other disciplines and is contributing to the development of these subjects. I have conducted research in several fields which I use in this book; I hope that, in doing so, I manage to convey the interest of such research which often produces surprising findings.

Exercises

Good education gives students a confidence about using and criticizing ideas. I try to enlarge this confidence by the use of appropriate exercises that help students to approach consumer behaviour from a practical standpoint. The exercises require self-appraisal, calculation, observation, the measurement of attitudes and the use of computer programs, and are placed where they will amplify the text. In many cases they are quickly done and the reader will benefit by doing them as they occur.

Plan of the book

Part I (Chapter 1) introduces the reader to a classification of different forms of consumption based on frequency, importance and freedom of action. The reader is introduced to the different cognitive and behavioural explanations of consumer behaviour. More specific theories are introduced which relate to frequent purchase, important choices and consumption where freedom of choice is lacking.

Part II (Chapters 2, 3 and 4) focuses on the patterns that can be seen in frequent purchase and the way these help us to understand loyalty, stationary markets and the effects of market interventions such as price changes.

Part III (Chapters 5 and 6) is concerned with voluntary actions where attitude can be used to explain decisions and where we can identify reasons for action that can be used to influence consumers.

Part IV (Chapters 7 and 8) covers the mechanisms involved in perception, thought and judgement and the processes that are involved in the post-purchase phase of consumption.

Part V covers a number of applications: the use of retail services (Chapter 9), the response to advertising (Chapter 10), and in Chapter 11 I give a postscript on wider policy implications of consumer behaviour.

Acknowledgements

This book has evolved from *Changing Consumer Behaviour* and I am indebted to those who assisted me then and subsequently: Tim Ambler, Icek Ajzen, Alison Assiter, Neil Barnard, Patrick Barwise, John Bateson, Simon Broadbent, Maria Clemente, Pratibha Dabholkar, Andrew Ehrenberg, Richard Elliott, Allison Faehse, Gian Fulgoni, Jules Goddard, Gerald Goodhardt, Kathy Hammond, Patricia Harris, Annik Hogg, Keith Hunt, Stavros Kalafatis, Darryl Kirk, Stephen Lea, Wendy Lomax, Neil Mason, Debra Perkins, John Rossiter, Byron Sharp, Jan-Benedict Steenkamp, Phil Stern, Mark Uncles and Gill Willson.

Finally, I greatly appreciate the comments of my first degree and postgraduate students at Kingston University. With them in mind I have tried to be relevant and clear, but any failure is entirely mine.

Part I

Introduction

Chapter 1

Ideas and explanations in consumer research

Introduction

From a marketing standpoint, consumer behaviour is about human responses in a commercial world: how and why people buy and use products,[1] how they react to prices, advertising and other promotional tools, and what underlying mechanisms operate to help and hinder consumption. In this book I try to report the theory and research on these issues in a way that helps marketers to adopt realistic strategies and to make *wise decisions* between alternative actions.

This book is not an elementary text; some understanding of marketing and research methods is assumed and for this reason it is more demanding and takes a rather more critical approach than most texts. Our knowledge of how people buy and use products has grown rapidly and I have tried to describe some of this work in detail. But there are also many areas of consumer behaviour where we have limited knowledge and we have to make a judgement on the facts available. Where appropriate I have tried to convey worries about the evidence because doubt is at the centre of any subject that is founded on investigation; it is this doubt that propels research. Doubt is also relevant to good education; students who see the uncertainties in consumer behaviour will be better placed to understand and adapt to new findings when these emerge. These considerations lead to a rather different selection of material from that found in first-year texts.

In this chapter the following are introduced:

■ The sort of *questions* raised, and the *answers* offered, in consumer behaviour.

■ The role of *facts, theories, explanations* and *classifications of consumption* in consumer behaviour.

■ Types of consumption. The way consumer behaviour can be classified by reference to *importance, frequency, freedom* and susceptibility to *group influence.*

[1] Throughout this book the term 'product' is used to cover both goods and services.

■ Three ways of thinking about consumer action: the *cognitive approach*, which treats purchase decisions as *problem-solving*; the *reinforcement approach*, which treats consumption as *learned behaviour*; and the approach via *habit*, where we focus on the routine production of behaviour in particular contexts.

■ Some key concepts: *involvement, freedom, frustration, attribution* and *social influence*.

Questions and answers

There is a close affinity between marketing and consumer behaviour; in a sense marketing is a client to consumer behaviour with the marketers wanting answers to a number of problems raised by their practices. Examples of marketing practices are:

■ Use of price incentives.
■ Advertising.
■ Launching new products using existing brand names (brand extensions).

These practices are used because it is believed that consumers will respond in particular ways, for example, that price discounts will stimulate purchase. But the success of a discount depends on the amount of extra sales generated by, say, a 10% price reduction and here common sense does not supply an accurate answer. For informed action we need to conduct systematic research which helps us to *estimate the size* of any effect and to *explain* how it comes about. So our questions might be:

■ How much do sales change when price cuts are run with special displays? What happens to sales after a price cut has finished? Why do these effects occur?
■ How much do advertising campaigns affect sales and for how long do the effects last? What underlying mechanisms explain these effects?
■ When a new product is launched under an old brand name, how much does the old name affect purchase of the new product? What is the basis for any advantage conferred on the new product by the old brand name?

Another set of questions comes from those who control markets, governments and regulators, who have to set rules on labelling, honesty in advertising, package design etc. Examples of such questions are:

■ How do consumers use information on packages? What explains their behaviour?
■ What is the effect of corrective advertising? Why so?
■ Do child-proof packs save lives? How are such packs used?

These questions posed by marketers and legislators can only be answered by gathering evidence about the way people behave. Notice that although we let marketing and government set the questions, we do not let these fields dictate the way in which we discover answers to these questions; for this purpose the methods of market research, data analysis, psychology and the social sciences are used.

In any applied subject, practitioners need to use their judgement and make assumptions when evidence is lacking. Those who have to take decisions cannot delay until issues have been fully researched, but it is important that marketing practitioners do accept new evidence when it becomes available. Some apparently sensible practices may need to be changed as a result of new findings. For example, it has been assumed that the child-proof packs for pharmaceuticals increase safety, but this may be illusory. Viscusi (1984) found evidence that child-resistant bottle caps were associated with an *increase* in fatal child poisonings, possibly because parents left medicines accessible when they thought the cap was child-proof, or because the closure was so much trouble that the container was left open. There may be doubts about aspects of Viscusi's work, but his research obliges some reappraisal of safety assumptions.

Improving Safety?

A cautionary tale comes from the field of road safety. It appears that people may take advantage of improvements in safety by taking more risks: if the car is safer, then you drive a little faster. This effect is called *risk compensation*. Supporting this effect, Peltzman (1983) found in the United States that the introduction of standard safety devices in cars showed no impact on fatal and serious injuries to motorists. In Britain, Davis (1992) reports that legislation enforcing the use of seat belts has similarly failed to show the expected reductions in serious injury; it seems that drivers go faster when they are wearing seat belts and, as a result, have more accidents. In Britain, corroborating this, there was an increase in pedestrian and cycling accidents involving a car *after* seat belts became compulsory.

Facts, theories, explanations and classifications

The value of information depends upon its range of application. Some facts can be very useful because they cover many different situations. For example Ehrenberg, Hammond and Goodhardt (1994) have found from an analysis of a large body of market research data that, when a price discount has finished and the product is offered again at the normal price, sales return to the pre-promotion level. This is a useful fact for anyone who has to spend the advertising and promotion budget, but most of us would be happier if we had some form of *explanation* that related this fact to other ideas: how is it that promotions that raise sales by 50 per cent or more while they are running have no lasting effects? Surely a promotion introduces new buyers, some of whom stay with the brand? In this case the authors provided an explanation. When they examined the sales figures they found that 93 per cent of those responding to price-cutting promotions for major brands had bought the brand in the previous $2\frac{1}{2}$ years so that very few genuinely new buyers were introduced to the brand by such sales promotions.

Explanations allow us to use facts better and to raise further questions. In the case of sales promotions we can hypothesize that small brands might show some residual effect from the promotion because a larger proportion of new purchasers are likely to be introduced to a brand that has fewer buyers to start with. So far this hypothesis has not been examined, but if we find that there is no relationship between the proportion of new buyers raised by a promotion and the post-promotion sales, we shall have to think again about the explanation offered by Ehrenberg, Hammond and Goodhardt.

Facts can be explained in a variety of ways, and because different explanations carry different implications, we can test one against the other. For example, another explanation for the Ehrenberg, Hammond and Goodhardt findings is that any reinforcing effect of the sales promotion is cancelled out by a tendency for people to associate low price with low quality. The idea that discounts affect the perception of brand quality is a widely held view which is discussed in Chapter 4.

Explanations drive research because they build a network of concepts, or *theories*, within which a range of phenomena can be interpreted and from which new hypotheses can be drawn. Such theories explain how people learn, take decisions, change their minds, seek consistency between thought and action, etc. Theories do not respect arbitrary boundaries, and we find that the theory that explains why people buy a dishwasher may also be used to explain why people buy shares or how they vote. The specific reasons are different in each case, but the form of the explanation can be the same. In this book we draw on a range of theories and some of these are described briefly in this chapter. The evidence that is explained by a theory has to be organized or classified in some way. Thus an initial task is to distinguish some of the different types of consumption that occur.

Types of consumption

Important purchases
Important purchases are usually novel or infrequently performed and may demand time and effort on the part of the decision-maker because there is little experience on which to base the decision. As such, these purchases are *high involvement*. Actions of this sort may cover the purchase of a new car, where to go on holiday, whether to go to a new restaurant and what company to buy shares in. This type of action also includes serious life-choices outside the field of consumer behaviour, such as what job to take and whether to have children.

Repetitive consumption
Some purchases are made again and again; if we look at the items purchased on the last trip to the supermarket, we see that we have bought most of them many times before. Learning theory is concerned with repeated behaviour and is therefore relevant to frequent purchase. Generally, frequent purchase requires little conscious attention and because of this it is usually described as *low involvement*.

Involuntary consumption

Some actions are freely performed, while others are done with little or no choice. Involuntary consumption has individual and social forms. Individually, we have to buy petrol if we use a car, and we may find it difficult to manage without such conveniences as cheque accounts and telephones. Although we have to buy the *category* (or product type) there is a choice between *brands* of petrol, banking services and telephone companies, but when the choice is trivial (e.g. the brand of petrol) or troublesome to implement (e.g. changing bank accounts), even this freedom of action is reduced.

The social form of involuntary consumption occurs when products are collectively, rather than individually, provided. Many of the services that we use are of this form – for example, the repair of roads and the supply of passports. Here there is no market, we cannot switch suppliers, and the control of product quality can only be achieved by influencing the supplying organization.

Group consumption

A fourth distinction is between purchases that are individually made and those that are based on some group influence process. Much consumer expenditure in the family reflects the preferences of different family members and many industrial decisions are similarly based on the views of a decision-making unit (DMU) composed of a few key personnel.

Purchase paradigms

A paradigm is a perspective or framework within which theories may be cast. In philosophy of science, paradigms were presented as restrictive so that scientific advance was held back until the dominant paradigm was overthrown and scientific problems were redescribed within the framework of the new paradigm. In modern research, paradigms are treated rather differently and researchers may respect more than one framework for the definition of knowledge (although we tend to have our preferences). Some parallel thinking of this type is needed because paradigms are not mutually exclusive in the sense that one is right and the others wrong, but one paradigm may be more appropriate than another for particular conditions. When we look at the different theories about purchase we find that they fit within three paradigms. These are:

1. The *cognitive* approach, treating purchase as the outcome of *decision processes* or *problem-solving*.
2. The *reinforcement* approach, treating purchase as behaviour learned in response to aspects of the consumer's situation.
3. The *habit* approach, treating purchase as a pre-established pattern of behaviour, which is elicited by particular situations.

Paradigms of purchase and managerial control

The *cognitive paradigm* focuses on consumer decisions which rest on ideas, information, evaluation, etc.; thus managerial control is achieved by providing information and persuasion. Systematic decision-making among consumers may be less common than is generally assumed, and this limits the value of this approach. It seems more suitable for one-off decisions than repetitive purchasing.

The *reinforcement paradigm* focuses on the way behaviour is modified by the environment; therefore, managerial control is achieved by changing the consumer's situation. It is less useful for explaining complex behaviour built upon a great variety of past experience which cannot be traced.

The *habit paradigm* focuses on established patterns of behaviour which are rapidly mobilized in response to relevant stimuli in the situation. Here managers benefit from studying the way behaviour is associated with particular stimuli; once identified, these stimuli can be used to elicit the behaviour and this is important in fields such as pack design and advertising.

All paradigms have value in helping us to frame our ideas about purchase behaviour, but there is debate about the emphasis that should be accorded to each. In practice the cognitive paradigm has been the most influential and pervades most American textbooks on consumer behaviour (e.g. Engel, Blackwell and Miniard, 1995; Howard, 1994). In Britain, there has been some support for reinforcement approaches and Foxall (1990) has argued that much of consumer behaviour fits learning principles established by experimental research. Other marketing researchers (e.g. Ehrenberg, 1988) have examined the data gathered by market research agencies and have shown regularities, which they describe in mathematical terms, that are consistent with the habit paradigm. In the following pages we look in greater detail at the research traditions that underlie these different paradigms.

The cognitive approach

When an important purchase is made for the first time people may investigate options, discuss pros and cons and reflect on alternatives; thus the action is preceded by decision-making, or planning, designed to seek particular benefits and to avoid particular costs. Foxall (1992a) describes this decision-making paradigm:

> Consumer behaviour is widely understood as a problem solving and decision-making sequence, the outcome of which is determined by the buyer's goal directed processing of information. The 'cognitive consumer' is credited with the capacity to receive and handle considerable quantities of information, to engage actively in the comparative evaluation of alternative products and brands, and to select rationally among them. Belief in the cognitive consumer underpins not only marketing but a great deal of economic analysis. It is also central to the analysis of managerial strategy.

Despite the popularity of decision-making as an explanation for consumer behaviour, there are doubts about whether it covers much of the field. One review by

Olshavsky and Granbois (1979: 98 and 99) noted: 'that for many purchases a decision never occurs, not even on the first purchase. ... even when purchase behaviour is preceded by a choice process, it is likely to be very limited. It typically involves the evaluation of few alternatives, little external search, few evaluative criteria, and simple evaluation process models.'

The reader may find these comments puzzling, but remember that behaviour may be drawn from past experience and cued by features of the consumer's situation, and these processes may pre-empt decision-making. Consumer theorists can agree that some consumer behaviour is controlled by factors in the consumer's situation while other behaviour is deliberate and preceded by planning, but there is disagreement about the extent to which each type of explanation is useful. Most texts on consumer behaviour use active consumer decision-making as the prime explanation of consumer choice and do not give enough attention to more habitual aspects of purchase. This is exemplified by Engel, Blackwell and Miniard (1995), who try to accommodate all the different perspectives within a *decision process continuum*. They state that new and important purchases elicit *extended problem-solving* (EPS) with problem recognition, search for different alternatives and for information about each one, evaluation of alternatives, then purchase and, finally, post-purchase activities such as recommending the product to others. Engel *et al.* agree that even in new purchase situations consumers often do not have the time, resources or the motivation to conduct EPS and engage instead in more *limited problem-solving* (LPS), which omits many of the stages of EPS. For repeat purchases Engel *et al.* argue that people use *habitual decision-making*, which may be based on either high loyalty to the brand or inertia when the brand meets a need but the consumer has no special interest in it. This account is plausible and seems to accommodate habitual action, but there is a contradiction in the idea of habitual decision-making; if it is habitual, then there is no decision in the sense of conscious cognitive processing before action. Habits, if they account for much of consumption, need a better explanation than absence of thought.

Extended problem-solving is represented in Figure 1.1 where we see that the focus is on the internal processes of the consumer (in contrast to the reinforcement and habit paradigms, which emphasize features of the consumer's situation). This predominantly cognitive model of consumer action is widely supported and is an enduring idea which first appeared in a somewhat different form in Engel, Kollat and Blackwell (1968); a similar model is found in Howard and Sheth (1969), and in one form or another this approach has been the centrepiece of many textbooks of consumer behaviour since then. Cognitive models such as these have been criticized by Ehrenberg (1988) because the concepts lack agreed methods of measurement and the relationships between these concepts are poorly specified.

It is quite hard to identify behaviour that approximates to the coherent and elaborate sequences of extended problem-solving. We know from work by Beales *et al.* (1981) that few people consult *Consumer Reports* (the publication of the US Consumers' Association) before they buy expensive items; also Beatty and Smith (1987) found little search before the purchase of durables. Sometimes people do not consider alternatives; Lapersonne, Laurent and Le Goff (1995) found that 17 per cent of car buyers took account only of the brand they last bought. We may recognize such restrictions in our

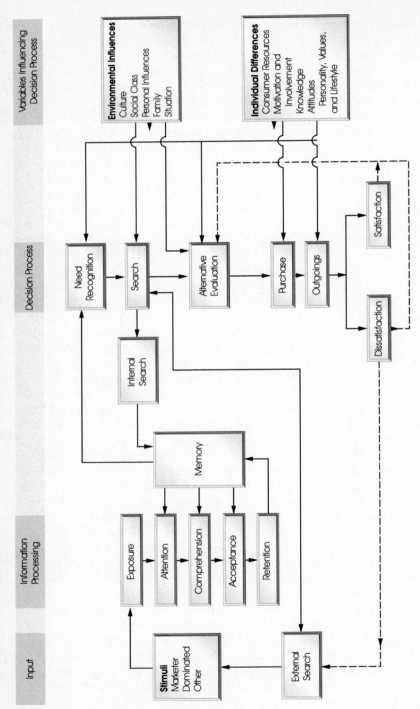

Figure 1.1 A complete model of consumer behaviour showing purchase and its outcomes (*Source: Engel et al.,* 1995)

own decision-making; even important purchases are often made without much investigation. Full decision-making seems most relevant to first purchases but, even in consumer durable markets, these are rare since most purchasers are either buying a replacement for an existing product or making an additional purchase. A study of white goods purchases in the United States by Wilkie and Dickson (1985) found that two-thirds of the purchasers had bought the appliance before, and Bayus (1991), quoting US industry sources, gives the following replacement percentages for consumer durables:

Refrigerators	88%
Washing machines	78%
Cars	70%
Colour TVs	53%

Those purchases that are not replacements are often second or third purchases, particularly in the case of cars and TVs. Thus genuine new buyers are uncommon but, none the less, they are important since the first purchase may determine the brand chosen in later purchases.

Do savers make decisions?

Savers are failing to make the most of their tax concessions according to a survey by the Woolwich Building Society.

Four out of ten non-taxpayers have not registered with their bank or building society to receive gross interest on their savings.

More than half did not even know whether they were registered to receive gross interest on their accounts. Of those that had failed to register, 40% said they were not aware of their entitlement to receive gross interest, and many said that they did not know how to register.

The Inland Revenue estimates that only a third of those eligible to receive gross interest have registered. A spokesman said that these savers are eligible to claim back around £800m unnecessary tax paid during the last two years.

Source: Daily Telegraph, 11 September 1993.

Even decisions that one might expect to be well thought out seem often to be made in a fairly summary manner. For example, it might be thought that people would be quite rigorous about avoiding unnecessary tax yet the evidence is against this (see box, above). Similarly, we might expect industrial decision-making to have much in common with extended problem-solving, yet Simon (1957) has noted that much decision-making at work is based on limited information search. Executives tend to accept the first option which is 'good enough' to solve a problem so that better solutions may be missed. Simon called this *satisficing* behaviour; everyday examples are provided in

Mintzberg (1979). One study of investment decisions in British industry revealed that proposals were subjected to second guessing, faulty financial analysis and lack of coherence with stated strategic objectives (Marsh *et al.*, 1988). A comment on this work in the *Economist* (9 July 1988) described this decision-making as *retrofitted* to the corporate strategy.

Klein (1989) has found that many decisions in operational settings follow a pattern that is consistent with Simon's ideas. Typically, people assess the situation and generate a prospective action or option based on this assessment, then they evaluate this option to see whether it will provide a satisfactory solution. If it fails, they generate another option and evaluate this, but they *do not compare* old and new options. Consumer problem-solving may also follow this pattern. People begin with a problem – for example, that the freezer needs to be replaced – and if preliminary enquiry establishes that there is an appropriate model in a convenient shop they may well buy it. If not, they may try other stores and other models, but if they fit Klein's model they will *not* generate a set of alternatives and make comparisons between them. If many consumer choices fit this model, the order in which products are evaluated is important since the first satisfactory solution will be the one adopted. Although satisficing approaches may not result in the *optimal* solution, they may be an efficient way of using time; many people cannot afford to give the time required for careful decision-making and, by satisficing, they leave themselves with more time to deal with other problems.

Diagnosis

Klein's (1989) description of decision-making reminded me of a description I once heard of the way doctors make diagnoses. The presenting symptoms are assessed and a preliminary diagnosis made; then other symptoms are checked to see whether they confirm this diagnosis. Only if they fail to support the first diagnosis is a second one considered. It is easy to see that this procedure may lead to the over-diagnosis of common illnesses. My informant lectured to medical students and was unable to get them to begin with more than one possibility. It seems that normal problem-solving is often serial hypothesis-testing.

Engel, Blackwell and Miniard have claimed that their model has a normative function, indicating to managers what they need to find out about consumers, but this rather depends on whether it accurately depicts how consumers operate. If consumers rarely give extended thought to problems, and use a satisficing mode of analysis when they do, we should be careful about treating the EPS model as the norm for identifying the kinds of information needed to influence consumer behaviour. In Chapter 7 we return to extended decision-making with a review of work that focuses on the moment-by-moment processes involved in choice.

> ## Managerial decision-making
>
> If managers, like consumers, rarely make fully analyzed decisions, we should allow for this in management education. Simply supplying evidence is no guarantee that it will be used to make better decisions. To some extent we already take this into account when we use exercises and case studies to train people in the use of evidence and the practice of decision-making. We can also try to train habits of mind that will improve decision-making, for example, to identify and evaluate a second alternative to a proposed course of action.
>
> In business, there are practices that will support well thought-out decisions, e.g. brainstorming to create new ideas, ensuring that decisions are routinely reviewed, and the specification of guidelines from senior management that will identify the most important issues for wider discussion.

Exercise 1.1   Decision-making

Identify a purchase that you have made which was important to you.

- Did you know what alternatives were available and how to evaluate them?
- Did you have a clear idea of what you wanted?
- How much investigation did you do before purchase and how much afterwards?
- Did you consider one option and move on to others if it was unsuitable, or did you compare several alternatives?
- Do you think you made the right choice?

It is likely that, in retrospect, you can see defects in your decision-making *process*, even if you made the best choice. Often we lack enough prior experience, knowledge, time or motivation to fully explore the options.

Purchase as learned behaviour

We *learn* from our past behaviour and may use this learning to modify later behaviour. If a purchase brings unsatisfactory outcomes it may be avoided in the future; conversely, satisfaction with a product may increase the likelihood that it will be selected next time. *Learning theory* is a systematic description of the relationship between experience and subsequent behaviour, which is relevant to both the reinforcement and habit paradigms.

Classical conditioning
One type of learning, called classical conditioning, was studied by the Russian physiologist Pavlov (1927). Pavlov noticed that dogs started to salivate at the sight of the persons who fed them. The older dogs showed this trait most and Pavlov thought that, over time, the salivation reflex had become associated with or conditioned to the new stimulus, that is, that a dog associated its handler with food so that salivation

Starting with:

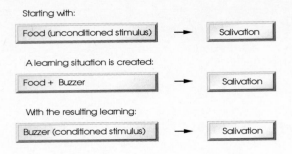

Figure 1.2 Classical conditioning – Pavlov's experiment

was now stimulated by the sight of this person. In this sort of learning a new stimulus is paired with the stimulus in an existing stimulus–response sequence so that after a while the new stimulus alone creates the response. Pavlov set up a series of experiments to demonstrate this process of classical conditioning using the sound of a buzzer as the conditioned stimulus instead of the dog's handler (see Figure 1.2).

Pavlov's work was taken up by J.B. Watson, a psychologist at Johns Hopkins University, who later became a vice-president of the J. Walter Thompson advertising agency. Watson and his colleague R. Rayner experimented on a child known as 'Little Albert'. Watson and Rayner (1920) used the distress on hearing unexpected loud noises as the initial stimulus–response sequence; a white rat was the conditioned stimulus. Whenever the white rat came into Albert's sight, Watson frightened the child by striking an iron bar behind him. Initially, the white rat evoked no fear in the child, but after a number of trials the appearance of the rat caused Albert to react with the distress previously associated with the loud noise, even when no noise was produced. Watson noted that fear was also exhibited when the boy saw other white furry objects, showing that the learning was *generalized*. Watson and Rayner's work has been critically reviewed by Samelson (1980) and is described here only to illustrate the idea of conditioning; others (e.g. Hilgard and Marquis, 1940) have had difficulty in reproducing the key features of Watson's work. A direct application of generalization in marketing, cited earlier, is the use of an existing brand name for a new product. By this process of *brand extension* some of the buying propensity for the old brand may attach to the new brand; for example, when liquid detergents were introduced many of them used the name of an established detergent powder.

Classical conditioning has considerable relevance in consumer behaviour. Packaging, brand names, colours, smells, music and the context of purchase and consumption may become associated with the buying of particular products. Some advertising is clearly intended to forge associations between brands and stimulus features, e.g. Marlboro and cowboys, McDonalds and the big 'M' sign and more generally a variety of logos and their respective companies. The idea here is that the conditioned stimulus may help in identification and add to purchasing tendency. It is also noticeable that, to compete in some markets, manufacturers have to adopt the colours and pack shape

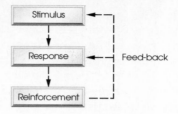

Figure 1.3 Reinforcement learning

that is conventional for that type of product. The power of such product type associations is revealed by a trip to an unfamiliar country. The absence of familiar signs and colour codings makes the high street confusing so that a simple task, like posting a letter, requires investigation and effort in order to identify the colour, shape and location of the post box.

Reinforcement learning

A rather different approach to learning focuses on the immediate consequences of action. Early research in this tradition was done by Thorndike (1911), who confined a hungry cat to a cage and placed food outside. The erratic movements of the cat eventually released a simple catch and the cat escaped. The cat took less time on subsequent trials and eventually it released the catch immediately when it was placed in the cage. Thorndike called this *trial and error learning* and it has some relevance to consumption. People entering new markets are faced with a range of brands and may make near-random trials of alternatives until they come upon a brand that they like.

In Thorndike's work the cat's actions were driven by the results: the gaining of food and freedom. Such outcomes were later called *reinforcers* by B.F. Skinner. Skinner (1938; 1953) defined a reinforcer as an experience that raises the frequency of responses associated with it, while a punisher reduces the frequency of such responses (see Figure 1.3). Reinforcers are typically rewards or reductions in cost, while punishers are costs or reductions in reward. Reinforcement has most effect when it occurs at the same time or just after the response. Although Skinner placed emphasis on the way in which reinforcement changes the frequency of the response, the reinforcement also strengthens the association between stimulus and response, and this is important for the habit paradigm.

The principles of response conditioning can be seen at work in many sales promotions which reinforce purchase or product use, for example, *Airmiles* for using particular products, or 'cash backs' when certain goods are bought.

Skinner also introduced the idea of *shaping*, the process whereby behaviour is moved from one form to another by selectively reinforcing the performances that show change in the desired direction. Shaping is sometimes apparent in sales techniques where the salesperson moves the prospect towards the sales goal by reinforcing movements in the preferred direction with nods, agreement and approval. Products also shape us; we become more expert at using computers and driving cars, partly because of the reinforcers that the product delivers. As a result we may seek more sophisticated models. The evolution of products in recent years may also involve shaping. A large number of brands have been positioned with specialized benefits that are likely to appeal only to those who are already familiar with the more basic versions of the product. An early example of this sort of brand development was the subdivision of shampoo into varieties for dry, normal and greasy hair. These varieties are now commonplace, but when they were first used by Elida Gibbs they helped *All Clear* shampoo to take a significant share of the market in Britain (see Broadbent, 1981). More recently, the market has been subdivided again into regular and frequent wash, and by the addition of preparations that combine shampoo and conditioner, e.g. *Wash and Go.*

Skinner noted that reinforcers can lose their power to affect behaviour if they were heavily used. This *satiation effect* provides an explanation for *wearout*, the loss of effectiveness of advertisements after extended use. The power of a reinforcer returns when it is not used for a while and advertisers use this effect when they 'rest' advertisements and then reintroduce them.

A satiation effect also occurs when stimuli are frequently presented so that they lose their power to elicit a response. Stimulus satiation, or *desensitization*, helps people to put up with recurring unpleasant experiences. It is because the stimulus loses its power to evoke a response that surgeons suffer no qualms as they make an incision for the hundredth time. An important effect of desensitization in consumer behaviour is the way in which people get used to conditions that are inadequate or unpleasant and, as a result, rarely complain or demand compensation. Examples of this are the way people tolerate queues in banks, litter in streets and overcrowding on metropolitan transport.

Learning can be reinforced each time a response is produced, i.e. *continuously*, or the reinforcement may be *intermittent*. Learning is faster if the reinforcement schedule is continuous, but the final effect of a given amount of reinforcement is greater when it is used intermittently. Reinforcement schedules explain why people are prepared to lose money by gambling on fruit machines. The cost of playing a one-armed bandit (slot machine) is fairly continuous punishment, but the machine pays out intermittently. Over time the payout is less than the amount paid in, but the effect on behaviour of the irregular reward is greater than the effect of the regular cost.

When reinforcement stops there is a gradual *extinction* of the response; this extinction period is extended if the learning occurs under an intermittent rather than a continuous schedule of reinforcement.

Punishment discourages action and drives people away from the context in which it occurs. Unpleasant experiences with products – for example, a 'chemical' smell on a soap, or nausea after a meal at a restaurant – reduce the likelihood of a further purchase of the product. Learning of this sort can result in a product being avoided and any later improvement or other redeeming features may then remain undiscovered. This sort of learning can be very costly to a supplier; just one failure in a product may deter customers for a long time.

Using reinforcement

Managers can control stimuli and reinforcement in the environment so that customers are directed towards behaviour that produces more profit. Foxall (1992a, 1992b) has proposed that learning theory should be used more systematically to define and control the setting. Foxall notes that consumer environments differ in their *openness* with the *closed–open* continuum defining the range of activities available to the consumer. Environments also differ in the amount and type of reinforcement that they offer and Foxall distinguishes between two sorts of reinforcer: *pleasure* and *information*.

Foxall discusses how, sometimes, it is in a management's interest to reduce openness; casino owners use dim lighting and have no clocks, so that people lose track of time and stay longer. Control on behaviour is further enhanced by rules and conventions, for example, a minimum bet in the casino. Pleasure can be raised by various additions to a service – free drinks on flights, for example – while information on flights includes expected arrival times, the weather and time of day at the destination, as well as pointing out interesting aspects of the terrain below and the facilities available on board. Many airlines now project journey information on the video screens.

Open environments can be profitable

Managements may serve their customers better by raising openness. We tend to forget how a revolution in retailing was made possible by the move to self-service. Before the advent of the self-service supermarket, customers had to queue at several counters in order to get their different groceries and it was difficult to introduce new lines because these were stored behind the counter where they could not be easily examined. The introduction of self-service made the modern supermarket possible.

A value of Foxall's thinking is that he makes us consider with care the elements in a consumer's situation that affect behaviour. This meticulous attention to detail is a feature of other applications of learning theory; pick up a book on how to lose weight, avoid insomnia or give up cigarettes and you will find advice that is largely concerned with controlling your environment, e.g. for weight loss: buy no prepared foods; always eat in the same room; never associate eating with other aspects of the environment such as television; keep the food fairly boring. Thus, instead of resisting temptation – a form of internal control – the behaviour therapist changes the external control on behaviour by altering the cues and reinforcers in the environment. Individuals who understand how their environment affects their behaviour can be their own behaviour therapists.

Habits of purchase

The cognitive and reinforcement paradigms emphasize the *modification* of consumer behaviour and thus may explain the *changes* that occur in our purchasing. However, if we consider consumers in aggregate, markets are often very stable. Much of this constancy comes from the relatively unchanging behaviour of consumers, who tend to buy the same brands and to use the same stores over long periods of time. This habitual aspect of consumption is of major economic importance and is discussed in more detail in Chapters 2, 3 and 9.

We say that people have habits when they regularly produce much the same behaviour in similar situations. The context provides a stimulus which elicits previously established behaviour; for example, the sight of the brand reminds consumers to buy it again. By calling on habits we simplify our behaviour; habits side-step decision-making and allow us to ignore minor changes in the reinforcement relating to the behaviour. Thus habits leave us free to concentrate on the relatively few problems where our past experience provides us with no ready response. But even in novel situations people may trade on already acquired habits. Consider the person who is on the point of buying a car for the first time. Most first-time car purchasers are familiar with cars, they may have visited car showrooms, they will often have bargained for goods before, and they are likely to be knowledgeable about the ways of sales staff and credit arrangements. Thus their car purchasing behaviour may owe much to habits established in related contexts. From this standpoint the basic form of all behaviour is habitual and in unusual situations we may try out, modify and reassemble the habitual behaviours in our repertoire.

The habit paradigm excludes problem-solving or planning before action, but does not imply that consumers are irrational or even unreflecting. People may think about their actions *after the event* rather than before as in decision-making. People do not continue to buy a brand that persistently disappoints; instead, they break their habit and try something else. This means that most repeated purchase settles on satisfactory brands. But although people do have good reasons for their purchases, these may not be *the best* reasons. It is in the nature of habit that it restricts experimentation so that consumers may be unaware of improvements in product ranges from which they could benefit.

Exercise 1.2 Habits

It is hard to detect habits that work against your own interests but consider two areas:

1. Adding sugar to tea and coffee is a habit that adds to bodyweight and contributes to tooth decay. When people give up sugar they soon get used to the taste, and after a few weeks may prefer unsweetened tea or coffee. Is this not a habit worth changing?

2. If you make a regular journey, is the route optimal? People often discover journey improvements after years of using a less suitable route.

Questions:

1. What are the goods and services that you use habitually?

2. Are these patterns of consumption efficient? Are they optimal?

3. How should marketers present their brands when purchase is strongly habitual?

When purchase is habitual a new and superior brand should jolt consumers enough to get them to try it out. This is not easily achieved. Advertising may be ignored, while discounts and free samples may be used without thought. Most of the time consumers carry on buying what they bought before. But no one said that marketing was easy.

Some key concepts

Involvement

Involvement in product purchase is related to the importance of the purchase, the risks involved and the type of cognitive processing that is generated. Krugman (1965) popularized the idea of involvement as a way of explaining the different levels of cognitive activity created by advertising and purchase situations. He argued that when people had low involvement in a product, advertising could still affect their behaviour by strengthening recognition and recall of brand-relevant stimuli. Engel, Blackwell and Miniard (1995) also identify involvement as one of the factors that affect the level of cognitive activity so that EPS is more likely when the product is highly involving. Other factors that may increase EPS are the degree of difference between alternatives and the time available.

Engel, Blackwell and Miniard treat involvement as a matter of degree, but this is questionable. Using the definitions in this chapter, low involvement is habitual whereas high involvement requires planning, and there is probably no smooth transition from one to the other as conditions become more complicated. Instead, people probably accommodate small departures from what they are used to and continue to react habitually up to a point at which they suddenly realize that conditions have changed and they must reassess the situation. There is some support for this thinking in the early work by Weber (see Fechner, 1860) who introduced the notion of a 'just noticeable difference' (JND) in perception; a change in a stimulus that fell below the level of the JND was not responded to. Fechner showed that the JND was in proportion to the size of the stimulus.

Purchase risk raises potential costs and therefore affects involvement; it is often associated with the irreversibility of the decision and with those decisions that affect the way in which the purchaser is regarded by others. Some purchases display judgement or indicate a particular style of living and, for this reason, many people would think carefully before they buy flowers for a partner or select a wine to take to a dinner engagement.

This indicative function of purchases and possessions was first documented by Veblen (1899/1963) in his book *The Theory of The Leisure Class*. Veblen used the term *conspicuous consumption* to describe expenditure that showed others what sort of person the consumer was. In particular, Veblen drew attention to the vast houses built by successful businessmen, which served to exhibit their success to others. In his book *The Presentation of Self in Everyday Life* (1959), Goffman extended this analysis and suggested that people manage the impression that others have of them by their choice of what they do, say and wear. Personal possessions can convey a variety of impressions: Levi 501s say one thing, Armani jeans another; a BMW suggests someone different from a Ford owner; a single malt something different from J & B whisky. Often the possessions indicate social status or wealth, but some reflect other distinctions: old stripped pine rather than new furniture says something about the owners' values, and their music collection may be equally informative. In some sense we are what others think we are, and thus our purchases provide information to others and so contribute to our identity. Clothes, footwear and other personal accessories are particularly indicative.

Menu matching

After a press release about a supermarket report I was rung up by a journalist. Could I tell him anything about the way in which supermarkets are used for making sexual contacts? I had no knowledge about this. 'Oh yes,' he said. 'It's common in the US and now here in the UK; particular stores on particular days are used for straight or gay pick-ups.'

It occurred to me that supermarkets have merit here; people can check on what the others are buying and can start to form an impression of their lifestyle and its compatibility with their own. Were they buying olives, Chianti and a leg of lamb, or was it peanuts, Blue Nun and turkey mince? Perhaps the dating agencies should start by asking about grocery preferences when they try to match people!

How free are consumers?

To be free you have to know that you can choose from more than one option without pressure, and can reject all options if they are all unattractive.

I believe that the emphasis on decision-making in most consumer behaviour textbooks has led writers to exaggerate the amount of choice that people have. In describing the consumer, Engel, Blackwell and Miniard (1995: 12) state:

> He or she is not an unthinking pawn to be manipulated at will by the commercial persuader .... Consumer behavior, as a rule, is purposeful and goal oriented. Products and services are accepted or rejected on the basis of the extent to which they are perceived as relevant to needs and lifestyle. The individual is fully capable of ignoring everything that the marketer has to say.

It may be the case that buyers have a large measure of autonomy in choices between brands and that manufacturers have limited power to influence this choice, but this does not mean that the 'consumer is sovereign' as Engel, Blackwell and Miniard suggest. This is because buyer autonomy is more restricted in other ways. In many areas technology is ahead of customer knowledge so that choice may be restricted by lack of information. Sometimes there may be little freedom at the product level; people must put petrol in the car and detergent in the washing machine, and the fact that they have a choice between near-identical brands is usually a matter of indifference. Freedom of action is also limited by habits that exclude alternatives, by limited distribution (particularly in underdeveloped economies), and by physiological dependence on products like cigarettes and alcoholic drinks. Often people have little time to spend on consumer choices.

The claim that the consumer is sovereign must be set against the evidence that people do a great number of things that they would prefer to avoid such as travelling to work on congested public transport and queueing in banks and supermarkets. In areas such as education, medicine and legal advice, the opportunity to influence that service by withdrawing custom or complaining is effectively limited by the continuing need to use the service. There are other areas where a lack of resources prevents people from doing the things they might wish to do; large houses and luxurious cars are possible for only a few. Engel, Blackwell and Miniard can sustain their view of consumer sovereignty only because they focus on the areas where suppliers must compete for the consumer's custom. These are important areas and a particular focus in consumer behaviour, but they are only part of the full description of consumption.

Exercise 1.3   Constrained actions

List goods and services that you would like to avoid but that are forced upon you by other needs. Also list fields where the supply is monopolistic. How could you influence monopolistic suppliers of products?

Has the privatization of state monopolies increased competition? This is discussed in Chapter 11.

Frustration

A number of psychological theories relate to restrictions on choice. The condition of blocked motivation – *frustration* – describes the extreme situation where no options are available. A classic study by Barker, Dembo and Lewin (1941) showed the effects of frustration on children who were shown attractive toys but who were prevented from playing with them. Eventually they were allowed to play with the toys and their behaviour was compared with a control group that had not been frustrated. The experimental group behaved much more aggressively.

Aggressive responses by consumers are most apparent when a service breaks down unexpectedly, for example, when a computer fails or the traffic stops at a time when it usually flows freely.

The early work on frustration and aggression suggested a one-to-one relationship, so that frustration always led to aggression, and aggression was always the product of frustration (Dollard *et al.*, 1939), but this is not so. Many minor frustrations lead to thoughtful behaviour designed to solve the problem. Some modes of consumption are rational responses to frustrations – replacing unreliable appliances or driving to work to avoid erratic public transport, for example. This suggests that one strategy in new product development is to look for designs that will avoid common frustrations, for example, the way staplers jam on the last staple.

Consumer frustration is involved in the topics of *consumer satisfaction and dissatisfaction* and *consumer complaining behaviour*. These are examined in Chapter 8.

Attribution

When an action is compelled by force of circumstances it is easy to say, 'I had to do it, I had no choice.' When the action is taken freely it cannot easily be disowned. People take account of the conditions that affect freedom when they allocate responsibility to themselves or to their environment. Suppose that you find yourself in a long queue at the supermarket on Friday evening. Who is to blame? You can attribute blame *internally* to yourself for going at a peak time, or *externally* to your work and other commitments that prevent you from shopping at other times, or to the inefficiency of the supermarket if some of the checkouts are unstaffed. The attribution of responsibility has its roots in the work of Heider (1944; 1958). Eiser (1986) explains how Heider saw the causation of human action:

> Heider assumes that individuals are motivated to see their social environment as predictable and hence controllable, and that they apply the same kind of logic to the prediction of social events as to the prediction of physical events; they look for the necessary and sufficient conditions for such events to occur. Such conditions may either be situational or impersonal factors, external to the person whose behaviour one is trying to predict and explain, or factors regarded as internal to the person, such as his ability or personality.

The internal or external attribution of responsibility does not apply to yourself alone. The same processes affect the way that you regard the actions of other people; you may see others as personally responsible for their actions or you may see what they do as the result of forces outside their control.

One important finding (E.E. Jones and Nisbett, 1972) is that people generally overestimate the extent to which the behaviour of other people is controlled by personal disposition while similar behaviour in themselves is ascribed to situational factors. This *actor–observer* bias was observed in a study of supermarket and post office users by East, Lomax and Willson (1991b) and is described in Chapter 9; we found that people who were delayed quite often blamed other shoppers, but they very rarely blamed themselves. This attribution of responsibility is important because it affects subsequent behaviour. If people do not see themselves as responsible when they have to wait at busy times they may be less willing to change their shopping time to a quieter period.

More generally, the idea of attribution alerts us to the fact that there are two components in any judgement. The first component is a basic fact, often presented by our environment. Such facts could be that we are waiting in a queue, that our shares have dropped on the Stock Exchange or that the price of pears is so much a kilo. The second component is the frame that we use to interpret this fact. Blame for our wait in the queue can be variously attributed, depending on the frame that we use about who is responsible. We may think that we have lost money if we compare the price of our shares with the price before the fall, or we may think that we have gained money because the shares still stand above the price we paid when they were first

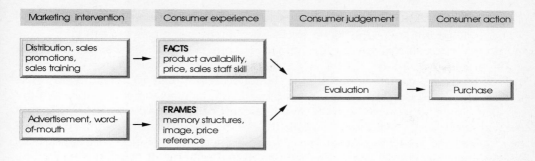

Figure 1.4 How marketing interventions affect consumers

bought. And we may think that pears are cheap or expensive depending on our assumptions about what pears should cost. The frame for interpreting facts usually resides within us, and people can therefore differ in their judgements because they use different frames. One person may see the pears as cheap because last week they cost more, while another sees them as expensive because pears are in season and the price should consequently be low. Movements in the frame of reference that people use have been related to Helson's (1964) adaptation level theory in which the judgement frame is a weighted average of past experience.

The idea of frame also lies behind *prospect theory*, discussed in Chapter 7. Some influences on consumers may affect their knowledge of facts but not the frames that they use to judge those facts, while other influences may have more impact on the frame. One of the functions of advertising is to modify the frames people use when they evaluate a product: if the ads raise the price frame, consumers may see a product as better value. Figure 1.4 indicates the way in which different forms of marketing intervention are thought to affect facts and frames. The frames are harder to change but, if ads are successful at altering them, the effects may last for some considerable time.

Social influences on purchase

Products are often bought because of other people. One theory that includes social influence is the *theory of planned behaviour* (covered in detail in Chapter 6). In this theory social influence appears as the second of three determinants of a person's intention to perform a voluntary action. The three determinants are:

1. The perceived gains and losses.
2. The beliefs about what other important persons think about the action.
3. The perceived conditions that make the action more, or less, easy to perform.

Some actions, such as a fashion purchase or safe driving (Parker and Manstead, 1996), tend to be more controlled by what others are believed to think about the action, while other actions, such as buying a replacement calculator, may be motivated more by the gains and losses of the action. Thus the theory of planned behaviour provides a means of assigning weights to the social and other determinants of action.

Another way of representing the influence of others is to describe social behaviour in the language of drama, that is, as a set of *roles*. From a cognitive standpoint, roles are sets of mutually related expectations about how you should act in relation to others and what you expect them to do in relation to you; as a customer you take account of what you think other customers and sales staff expect from you, and you expect them to behave in certain ways. From the learning theorist's standpoint, roles must be acquired and are learned when the actions of others act as reinforcers or punishers. From the standpoint of habit, roles are established patterns of behaviour elicited by familiar contexts and behaviours in others.

Exchange theory

Exchange theory extends the ideas of reinforcement, developed by Skinner and others, to the social context. Exchanges are interactions between people that, according to this theory, are maintained by reinforcement. If an exchange does not bring gain or avoid loss, it will be discontinued and replaced by a more rewarding behaviour. This means that continuing exchanges are those that bring more benefit than can be expected from alternative activities. Homans (1961), one of the exponents of exchange theory, argued that human beings *learn* to expect certain behaviours from others in response to their own actions. In the exchange, feelings such as affection and respect are extended to those who act in ways that are valued, thus reinforcing their behaviour. Similarly, people respond with dislike and blame to those who cause them distress and, by punishing the other person's behaviour in this way, may diminish its frequency. In this account the supply of goods and services for money is the commercial part of a much wider process of exchange.

One result of this process is that regular *habits of interaction* become established and people develop notions of fair exchange in which rewards are seen to be commensurate with costs. For example, those who regularly receive benefits such as pensions at the post office may tolerate delay better than those who spend money buying stamps and licences; in the first case the benefits help to compensate for the delay. In supermarkets this idea of fairness helps to explain why low-volume customers are given express checkouts despite the fact that they yield little profit to the store. Rules of exchange provide a predictable environment and become valued in their own right so that people who damage these conventions are disliked.

Some people establish better rates of exchange than others. Homans suggested that social status may assist some people to get a better deal; also relevant to the exchanges that people establish are the alternative interactions that may be available with other people. The worse their alternatives, the less power people have to strike a good bargain.

Exchange theory is particularly valuable in explaining the service encounter in consumer behaviour. Recent work using exchange theory is reviewed in Chapter 9.

Summary

Key questions for consumer behaviour come from marketing and consumer policy. In order to answer these questions we subdivide consumer behaviour into actions that are important or trivial, new or repeated, free or constrained, and individual- or group-based.

When people face difficult and involving choices, cognitive theories of decision-making are relevant to the way in which they decide. When action is repeated, learning principles apply and features of the consumer's environment may affect consumption, either by reinforcing particular actions or by acting as a stimulus so that already learned habits are elicited. To change the behaviour of consumers, the influencing agent must either alter the beliefs and values involved in a complex decision or, where the context controls behaviour, modify the consumer's environment. Traditionally, consumer behaviour texts have emphasized the cognitive approach and it is argued that more attention should be given to the habitual basis of consumption because this covers repetitive purchasing, a large part of total consumption. When behaviour is habitual, it may be controlled by use of relevant stimuli. Another effect of repetitive consumption is that people become desensitized and no longer notice unpleasant experiences.

Consumption also occurs when the consumer has little choice. This may be frustrating and people may then make efforts to overcome the constraints on their freedom of action. When people feel that they have no control, they attribute responsibility to their environment and are less likely to change their own behaviour.

An important factor affecting consumption is the influence of other people and different ways of representing this influence are described.

Further reading

Foxall, G.R. (1992b) The behavioral perspective model of purchase and consumption: From consumer theory to marketing practice, *Journal of the Academy of Marketing Science*, 20: 2, 189–98.

Beatty, S.E. and Smith, S.M. (1987) External search effort: an investigation across several product categories, *Journal of Consumer Research*, 14, June, 83–95.

Part II

Consumer patterns

Chapter 2

Loyalty, brand equity and brand extension

Introduction

Brand loyalty raises profit. Manufacturers benefit if consumers buy their brands in preference to other brands, and they benefit more if this preference is maintained for long periods. Such brand loyalty reduces the need to promote the brand and makes it harder for competitors to enter the market. The willingness of consumers to buy the brand may also allow manufacturers to charge more and thus increase their margin. But if marketers are to be effective in exploiting brand loyalty, they must understand what it is. This chapter is concerned with the nature of brand loyalty and its relationship to other variables. In Chapter 8 we return to this matter with a detailed review of the post-purchase factors that may affect loyalty and in Chapter 9 we examine store loyalty.

Loyalty is also relevant when new products are launched using the name of an established brand because this capitalizes on existing consumer buying propensities. This process of brand extension is attracting more and more research, and rightly so since large sums of money are spent on the development and launch of new products, many of which fail; thus we should be very interested in any findings that may help to reduce the failure rate. The whole chapter highlights the importance of predictable, long-term patterns of consumer response, which are then examined from a rather different standpoint in Chapter 3.

Related to brand loyalty and brand extension are three other concepts which are addressed in this chapter:

- *Brand awareness*: the recognition and recall of a brand and its differentiation from other brands in the field.

- *Brand image*: the ideas and feelings associated with a brand.

- *Brand equity* or *brand strength*: the control on purchase exerted by a brand, and, by virtue of this, the brand as an asset that can be exploited to produce revenue.

It may be argued that brand loyalty is the key factor in brand management; the growth of loyalty schemes in many countries has focused attention on the nature of loyalty and has raised some fundamental questions that are not easily answered. What is the nature and basis of loyalty, and how much does it change? In this chapter the concepts associated with loyalty are examined in turn; the aim is to answer these questions or, failing this, to show where we must make progress.

The concept of branding

Aaker (1991a: 7) defines a brand as:

> a distinguishing name and/or symbol (such as a logo, trademark or package design) intended to identify the goods or services of either one seller or a group of sellers, and to differentiate those goods or services from those of competitors.

Thus branding serves to distinguish a product from others so that it can be identified by consumers. This need to distinguish between the products of different producers was, of course, the original purpose behind cattle branding and the marking of whisky casks. Without product distinctions it is not possible to promote the specific brand except at the point of sale.

A *category*, or product field, is divided into *brands* which are in turn divided into *variants* based on flavour, formulation or other feature. Thus *Campbell's Tomato Soup* is the tomato variant of the Campbell brand of the soup category. Figure 2.1 shows these divisions. Sometimes a brand is subdivided, for example the Mondeo is a sub-brand or model in the Ford brand range, and comes in a number of specifications (variants).

Brand loyalty

What does brand loyalty mean?

There has been a lack of clear thinking about brand loyalty, which has not served us well. In everyday use loyalty has a number of meanings. In particular, a brand loyal person may:

- Feel positively disposed toward the brand – *brand attitude*.
- Buy the brand more than other brands in the category – this is a measure of proportion of category purchase which is called *preference* here.
- Continue to buy the brand over long periods of time – this longevity of purchase is called *allegiance* here.

We tend to think that these different forms of loyalty are found together, that is, that the more people like a brand, the more they will prefer it to others and the longer their allegiance will last. Though plausible, these assumptions of covariance have not been

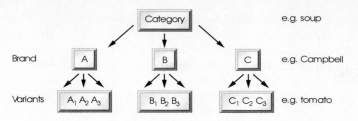

Figure 2.1 Categories, brands and variants

well tested. It is possible that there is no relationship between preference and allegiance measures; if there is a relationship it may be caused, not by brand attitude, but by another factor such as the number of brands available in the market (called *market concentration*). An early study by Farley (1964) showed that such market structure variables were associated with measures of loyalty.

Clearly, there is a need for basic research into the relationship between the different possible forms of loyalty. One reason why this has not occurred has been because researchers have focused on measures of loyalty and have not given enough attention to the concepts lying behind these measures (Jacoby and Chestnut, 1978). Also, it is difficult to measure preference and allegiance separately and this has prevented investigation of their relationship. In these circumstances researchers have used composite definitions that implicitly accept that the different forms of loyalty covary. Jacoby and Olson (1970) proposed a definition that required all three forms of loyalty to be present and this was adopted by Jacoby and Chestnut (1978). Their full definition of brand loyalty is:

1. The biased (i.e. non-random),
2. behavioural response (i.e. purchase),
3. expressed over time,
4. by some decision-making unit (e.g. household, person),
5. with respect to one or more alternative brands,
6. which is a function of psychological processes (decision-making, evaluation).

Here 3 indicates allegiance, 5 preference and 6 attitude. Like Jacoby and Chestnut, Dick and Basu (1994) argue that the idea of loyalty entails positive attitude as well as behaviour; they call repeated purchase of the same brand 'spurious loyalty' if the brand is not liked more than other brands in the category. Engel, Blackwell and Miniard (1995) also make positive feeling towards the brand a necessary part of loyalty; without such feeling the continued support for a brand is described as 'inertia'. By contrast, Tucker (1964) took a robustly behaviourist position and saw brand loyalty exclusively in terms of behaviour.

A composite definition of loyalty such as that endorsed by Jacoby and Chestnut is probably a mistake. It is difficult to operationalize, and it is likely that very few people would be classified as truly loyal when so many criteria have to be met. More importantly it puts on one side the relationship between the different basic forms of loyalty. It is quite possible for people to buy regularly a brand that they dislike, or for people to make a particular brand a small part of their portfolio yet continue to buy this brand for a long period of time. Thus people can be loyal in one respect but not in others. In these circumstances we need a number of narrowly framed measures of loyalty, with research on the relationships between these different measures. This is the approach taken here. There is no assumption that loyalty involves feeling or cognitive processes. Brand attitude may be seen as one possible determinant of loyal behaviour, but there are others, particularly distribution, market concentration and the amount of promotional activity supporting a brand.

The role of attitude

More sceptical researchers are reluctant to assume that attitudes *necessarily* play a part in loyal purchase; they note that:

■ People may like a brand but not purchase it through lack of need or opportunity. We may like brands like Porsche but most of us do not buy because we lack the wealth.

■ People may purchase consistently without any feeling for the brand; often a brand is a means to an end but is not valued in its own right. Why should people have much feeling about brands of bleach or sugar? They are concerned about results and their continued purchase of one brand may arise simply because it is accessible and they know that it works.

■ Attitude to a brand may be *caused by*, rather than be *a cause of*, purchase. This is another manifestation of the behaviourist thesis that the environment directs patterns of behaviour which then give rise to sentiments. Most of us can find examples where product availability has led eventually to liking and one example might be the way the local team (football, baseball, cricket, etc.) is often strongly supported. But causation may work the other way too; we may guess that those who supported their local team might be reluctant to change if a competitor established in the locality.

True loyalty?

The way many brands are valued as a means to an end is illustrated by the behaviour of one of my friends. He explained how he came to be a regular purchaser of Malvern mineral water. As far as he was concerned any carbonated water was as good as any other but the great advantage of Malvern was its bottle: one and a half litre, clear plastic and with the label easily peeling off, it was ideal for bottling home-made beer! He had bought it for years.

Applied to frequently purchased brands, this analysis suggests that shoppers may often buy brands that are easily available and familiar, and that, in consequence, they may sometimes come to like them. Although attitude to the brand may be caused by use of the brand, it is likely that the attitude, once established, may direct future purchasing in the category. This brand attitude may affect purchase without much conscious awareness. For routine purchases our attitude to the brand is only brought to mind when the routine is interrupted in some way. Occasionally, the regular product may fail, our preferences may be questioned or a new product may cause us to think. Then, the routine purchase may be reconsidered and conscious processing occurs – these are the rare but important times when brand allegiance may cease and alternative brands are tested.

Purchase habits also apply to brands that we routinely *do not buy*. Most of us will admit to avoiding certain brands that we dislike. Research by Hunt, Hunt and Hunt (1988) has thrown light on the way consumers hold 'grudges' against such products. Grudges are extreme forms of avoidance and usually begin with an emotionally upsetting experience as a customer. Hunt *et al.* found that grudges persist for a long time and that grudge-holders were often negative about the offending product in their conversations with others. Brand avoidance would seem to have dire consequences for a manufacturer but, despite this, it has received far less systematic study than brand loyalty.

Early work on brand preference

Research on brand loyalty began with work by Copeland (1923) on sole brand loyalty. Sole brand loyalty can be seen as an extreme form of proportional loyalty where 100 per cent of preferences go to the first brand. The majority of buyers buy more than one brand (multibrand purchase) and we therefore tend to focus on purchase of their primary brand rather than sole brand loyalty. In some early work, proportional loyalty was investigated using questionnaires, but doubts about the reliability of the data obtained in this way led Churchill (1942) to advocate the use of panels of consumers making regular reports about their household's actual purchases. The first regular panel was run by a newspaper, the Chicago *Tribune*, and G.H. Brown (1952; 1953) used data from this panel to report on the nature of brand loyalty. Brown found that brand loyalty was a reality and noted four types of purchase pattern:

1. Single (sole) brand loyalty.
2. Divided (multiple) brand loyalty.
3. Unstable loyalty (switching from brand to brand).
4. No brand loyalty.

Of these the majority of people showed single or divided loyalty.

Brown classified people on the basis of their *sequence* of brand purchases. Thus AAAAAA shows sole brand loyalty; a mix such as AABABA indicates loyalty divided between A and B; and AAABBB might be taken to indicate a permanent shift from A to B (change of allegiance) though it is clearly impossible to distinguish true switching from divided loyalty in one instance. These examples take a sequence of six purchases as the basis for analysis; some households will buy six units in a short period while others will not have completed six purchases in a year and this difference between heavy and light buyers complicates the analysis by purchase sequence. To avoid this problem Cunningham (1956) used, as a measure, the proportion of purchase devoted to the household's most popular brand over a period (*first-brand loyalty*). In a classic study which used the returns of sixty-six households in the Chicago *Tribune* panel, Cunningham confirmed the existence of multibrand loyalty and reported on a number of questions which are discussed below.

Multibrand purchase

Ehrenberg (1988) has confirmed the findings of Brown (1953) and Cunningham (1956) that most households are loyal to more than one brand; the group of brands purchased by a household are called the *brand portfolio* or *brand repertoire*. Multibrand buying may come about because:

■ Some products have *weak brand awareness*, for example, paper towels; since the brand means little to buyers of this category, they buy any brand (but they may still regularly buy the same portfolio of brands because these are the ones available to them).
■ Buyers seek *variety*, for example, in confectionery and biscuits. Also people buy different brands for *different situations*; canned beers are often acceptable at home but may be rejected in a pub.
■ A *price promotion* or *special display* may temporarily attract purchasers.
■ A preferred brand may not be *available*.
■ Purchase data are usually collected on the *household*. Members of the household may remain loyal to their personal preferences but, if these differ, the household will show multibrand loyalty.

An understanding of the factors that affect purchase in different categories is important if the right marketing decisions are to be made. Is a household's brand portfolio the result of promotion, variety seeking, an inability to find the preferred brand or because the household members have different preferences? Answers to these questions relate to policy on distribution and promotion and to the scope for introducing new brands in the product field; for example, distribution may be important in fields where variety seeking is common and purchasers are prepared to try an unfamiliar brand if it is available.

Brand loyalty is an area where self-examination is possible. Look at your own preferences for tea, toothpaste, bread, cereals, beer, etc., and ask yourself how much your brand preferences are expressed in your household purchases. The number of product categories where we would claim to have single brand loyalty may not be large; there are plenty of categories like petrol, biscuits, paper tissues, yogurt and cereals where few people would claim exclusive loyalty to one brand. Exercise 2.1 helps you to examine your purchase habits in different categories.

Exercise 2.1   How does your loyalty vary?

Answer the questions below for each category

Category	If you buy this category, do you buy only one brand? (Treat store brands as brands.)	Have you changed your main brand in this category in the last year?	What is/are your reason(s) for buying your main brand?
Tea			
Toothpaste			
Bar chocolate			
Sugar			
Biscuits			
Petrol			
Supermarkets			
Beer			
Toilet paper			
Bread			
Cereals			
Butter/Margarine			
Jeans			
Cigarettes			

Answers to the last column may confirm some of the points made so far about different reasons for purchase.

The first response column is a measure of preference and the second, a measure of allegiance. If you aggregate the 'yes' responses of a group of consumers, you can correlate the scores for the first two columns. This tests whether preference is related to allegiance across categories; if you get no correlation, the exercise indicates that there is no relationship. As with any investigation there are qualifications to be made and you might consider how sound are the measures? Are the measures 'pure' measures of preference and allegiance? Would you get the same sort of result with another selection of categories?

Loyalty proneness

Cunningham (1956) wanted to know whether the loyalty that a consumer had in one category was related to loyalty in another; he called this generalized level of loyalty, *loyalty proneness*. Cunningham found little evidence supporting loyalty proneness; among twenty-one correlations between loyalties in different categories, the highest was 0.3. However, Cunningham removed the consumers' discount purchases from the calculation of loyalty and if he had not done this, he might have shown more loyalty proneness. It seems likely that it is the attraction of a deal that may tempt many people away from their usual brand and that this *deal proneness* is likely to be generalized across categories. Those people who buy on promotion across categories will have low loyalty across categories, while those who ignore promotions will, in consequence, have higher loyalty across categories. It seems likely that deal proneness is quite common and may have the effect of *raising* loyalty proneness. (If this is confusing, remember that it is consistency of behaviour across categories that raises loyalty proneness; a consumer may be consistently high loyalty or, if deal prone, consistently low loyalty.) Some recent work has given support to this expectation. East *et al.* (1995) found correlations averaging 0.46 between loyalty measures for four grocery categories, much higher than the correlations obtained by Cunningham. If you compare the way different people responded to the first response column of Exercise 2.1, you may see some evidence of loyalty proneness.

Brand loyalty and weight of purchase

It is easy to assume that people who are proportionately more loyal to a brand will buy more of it, but whether this is so or not depends on their total purchases in the category. A person making a single purchase in the category is necessarily 100 per cent brand loyal but, with each extra purchase after the first, the buyer has an opportunity to try other brands. As a result, sole brand loyalty declines as the number of purchases of the category increases. This means that sole brand buyers are usually light buyers as noted by Ehrenberg (1988). For the same reason loyalties tend to be higher over shorter periods when few purchases have been made.

These findings suggest that we should be careful about focusing on the sole buyer. Who is more important: the consumer who buys only five units of your brand, or the consumer who buys five units of your brand and five units of other brands? Put like this we can see the importance of weight of purchase, but the issue is further complicated by the *numbers* of heavy and light buyers. As we shall see in the next chapter, light buyers are much more numerous.

Finding markers for the high brand loyal customers

Cunningham (1961) found that about 65 per cent of purchase went to the first brand across a range of grocery products. Work by Hammond and Ehrenberg (1994) indicates that the current average is about 58 per cent, so that there has been little change despite the growth in the number of brands. The average loyalty in a category conceals many different loyalty patterns. Some highly loyal consumers may regularly buy their favourite brand nearly all the time, while others divide their buying between several brands and buy their main brand less than half the time; some purchasers show brand indifference and may habitually purchase brands on discount. It would be useful if we could identify those who devote different proportions of category purchase to their favourite brand (by age, sex, working status, attitudes, etc.) because we could then target them more effectively.

The early study by Cunningham (1956) failed to reveal any demographic factors associated with the degree of brand preference, and work by Frank (1967), also in the United States, again found little association between brand loyalty and the socio-economic characteristics of consumers. Some work (e.g. G.S. Day, 1969) has shown that *older people* are more loyal, but Uncles and Ehrenberg (1990b) found little difference between the under 55 and the 55+ age groups in Britain and the United States.

Rather different results were obtained in Britain by East, Harris, Willson and Hammond (1995); they found that the more loyal purchasers of grocery items often had high incomes and spent more than the less loyal customers. Low loyalty customers were more concerned about price and it appeared that they were often less loyal because they were more attracted by discounts (as discussed before under the heading of loyalty proneness). Those with more money could afford to ignore promotions. East *et al.* found that people over 65 were slightly less loyal, but the few old people with high incomes were all highly loyal and the analysis suggested that old people have a tendency to be more loyal, but most of them are poor and their lack of money obliges them to use discounts, which reduces their loyalty.

East *et al.*'s findings have a direct relevance to the price premiums that many major brands maintain over smaller competitors and private label brands, and support the idea that reductions in these premiums will help to preserve loyalty. But heavy advertising is often funded by the price premium; if lower brand prices mean a reduction in the adspend, there is a risk that brand sales will weaken on this account.

Allegiance

So far we have treated brand loyalty as a proportion of expenditure; this is conventional for fast-moving consumer goods (fmcgs) where consumers often buy more than one brand in a category, but, for durables, industrial purchases and services, loyalty is seen more often as allegiance and is usually assessed by repeat purchase. In these fields a major emphasis has been the analysis of customer defections and their cost, and the establishment of appropriate customer retention strategies that will raise loyalty (Reichheld and Sasser, 1990; Reichheld, 1993; 1996). Reichheld (1996) claims that US corporations lose half their customers in five years and that customer retention can be very profitable because it reduces the burden of initial charges when a customer is first accepted, and because customer value tends to rise with duration of loyalty.

There is no doubting that there are set-up costs for services such as credit cards and mobile telephones and that a high level of *churn* (customers being gained and lost) raises these costs as a proportion of total costs. However, the idea that customers become more valuable the longer they are kept may not apply to those who choose to defect; such people may have a different potential spending level from those who stay. Also, if they do defect, they take their business to another provider where they will presumably spend much the same as they would have done with the company they left. This thinking suggests that the analyses of a customer's lifetime value may be questioned, but there is no doubt that the retention of profitable customers can help to build business.

Allegiance in fmcg purchase had been little studied before research conducted by East and Hammond (1996). We wanted to find out how many buyers desert a brand over a year when the overall market is stationary (that is, when those who leave the brand are counterbalanced by an equal number of new buyers). We used panel data to track the repeat purchase of the leading five grocery brands in each of nine product fields over six quarters. Those who purchased in the first quarter (Q1) were followed for the next five quarters (Q2 to Q6). For most of our brands repeat purchase was about 50 per cent in Q2; this did not mean that half the buyers had deserted the brand but that many of them had no need to buy the brand in the second quarter but might buy again in later quarters. If repeat purchase for the initial cohort of buyers stayed at 50 per cent for each successive quarter we could infer that there was no loss of allegiance but if repeat purchase fell from 50 per cent in Q2 to 25 per cent in Q6, then this would indicate that the number of loyal buyers of the brand had halved over this interval. In each quarter some buyers left and some returned, but slowly repeat purchase declined, showing that a proportion of buyers had left the brand permanently. Large amounts of data are needed for this work to smooth the fluctuations associated with sales promotions and chance irregularities. Table 2.1 shows the percentage who repeat purchased at each quarter aggregated across the nine datasets; this shows that, over an interval of a year, repeat purchasers declined by about 15 per cent. This means that when sales are stationary, a typical brand is losing *and gaining* 15 per cent of its buyers each year. This work indicates the two-edged strategy that marketers must have: they must try to retain the loyalty of existing buyers whilst also trying to recruit new buyers. We found that there was little variation between the categories studied.

Two interesting additional findings appeared in this study. We found that brand leaders showed lower erosion than other brands and it is possible that the heavier advertising of brand leaders was partly responsible for this. The second finding arose from the comparison between light and heavy buyers. It might be thought that light buyers would show more erosion – they could more easily forget the brand in the long interval between purchases. Also, light brand buyers are more often those who put the brand second or third in their portfolio. In fact, there was no detectable difference in the repeat purchase erosion between light and heavy buyers.

Table 2.1 Repeat purchase over five quarters by those buying in quarter 1. Average of top five brands in each of nine product fields

| | % Repeat-buyers in subsequent quarters: | | | | | Erosion |
	Q2	Q3	Q4	Q5	Q6	(Q2–Q6 as % Q2)
Average	55	53	51	49	47	15

Source: East and Hammond (1996).

This study shows that buyers do drop out of mature fmcg markets, but the work reveals a high level of allegiance; at the end of a year 85 per cent are still loyal and we found evidence that the erosion in loyalty fell off after the first year, which indicates that the majority of buyers stay with the brand for several years. It is easier to understand this durability of purchase patterns if the basic mechanism is seen as a habit that is rarely disturbed. Habits are manifested intermittently when the appropriate circumstances apply. Externally, there must be opportunity to buy the brand and internally a buyer must be able to recognize the brand on the shelf, or recall it to mind if it is not physically present; where there is a choice the buyer must prefer the brand to others. Actual purchase occurs through an interaction between these internal conditions and external factors (see Figure 1.4). Price changes and other short-term promotional activities are external factors, which temporarily affect sales levels, but they will have no long-term effect unless they change internal factors and this seems to be a fairly rare occurrence.

Loyalty as a brand attribute

So far we have tried to describe the different forms of brand loyalty as a characteristic of *individuals*. An alternative analysis compares the loyalty secured by brands (by virtue of the loyalty of the consumers that they attract). Market research companies report a statistic called *share of category requirements* (SCR). This is the proportion of category sales given to a brand by those who buy it at all. This is always much lower than the first-brand loyalty (1BL) measure because the SCR includes all buyers of the brand whereas the 1BL is calculated only on buyers who place the brand first. Market research companies also report market shares and repeat purchase rates. Table 2.2 shows an example of these different statistics in adjacent columns.

Table 2.2 Market shares and loyalty measures in the powdered detergent market. AGB data for the UK market, 52 weeks, 1986

Brand	Market share (%)	Share of category requirement (%)	Quarterly repeat purchase (%)	First-brand loyalty by brand (%)
Persil	30	47	75	78
Ariel	18	35	66	75
Bold	13	32	64	72
Daz	10	26	57	68
Surf	10	26	56	58
Average	**16**	**33**	**64**	**70**

Source: Data analysis by Hammond (1996).

We see from Table 2.2 that market share, share of category requirement, repeat purchase and first-brand loyalty scores are correlated; the bigger the brand the more loyal are the customers according to these measures. This is the normal pattern in brand analyses; it is unusual to observe strong niche effects in mature markets, that is, when brands with modest shares have exceptionally high loyalties. Repeat purchase is examined in greater detail in the next chapter.

Exercise 2.2   Calculation of different brand loyalty measures

Measures of brand loyalty

■ *First-brand loyalty (1BL)*. The mean of the individual percentages of expenditure devoted to the first preference brand. This is a category measure, but it can be calculated for a specific brand by selecting those cases where the brand is first preference.
■ *Share of category requirement (SCR)* is the percentage of category sales accounted for by a particular brand among those who purchased it, not just those who put it first as in 1BL.

Below are the imaginary purchases of instant coffee made by ten people. We assume that these ten people are representative and each purchase costs the same. What are the market shares of the two brands, the first-brand loyalty in the category and for each brand, and the share of category requirements for the two brand. Underneath the table we show how to work out each loyalty measure. Try to complete the calculations yourself before looking at the solutions.

Person	Maxwell House	Nescafé	Other brands	Totals
1	9	3	3	15
2	0	5	2	7
3	4	2	1	7
4	0	0	0	0
5	12	10	6	28
6	6	8	5	19
7	5	0	3	8
8	1	2	1	4
9	5	3	0	8
10	7	8	5	20
Totals	**49**	**41**	**26**	**116**

Measures

Market share: Maxwell House is $49/116 = 42\%$, Nescafé is $41/116 = 35\%$
1BL (category): $(9/15+5/7+4/7+12/28+8/19+5/8+2/4+5/8+8/20)/9 = 54\%$
1BL (Maxwell House): $(9/15+4/7+12/28+5/8+5/8)/5 = 57\%$
1BL (Nescafé): $(5/7+8/19+2/4+8/20)/4 = 51\%$
SCR (Maxwell House): $49/(15+7+28+19+8+4+8+20) = 45\%$
SCR (Nescafé): $41/(15+7+7+28+19+4+8+20) = 38\%$

You will see that 1BL is an average of individual brand:category ratios whereas SCR is the ratio of aggregate sales.

Using brand loyalty

Manufacturers want to enhance the loyalty to their brand and use this loyalty to increase profits. This has led to emphasis on a number of strategies such as brand extension (considered later), good complaint handling (Chapter 8), loyalty schemes and other techniques using database methods to 'stay close to the customer'. People who buy your brand have, by that act, indicated that they are more likely than others to buy it next time and thus are more worthy of marketing effort; this explains why airline travellers are offered frequent flyer schemes and car buyers receive information and discount offers on new models. The purpose of such schemes is to increase sales by raising preference and allegiance. One boost to such schemes was provided by claims, described above, that the cost of gaining a new customer is very much greater than the cost of retaining an existing customer (Reichheld and Sasser, 1990; Reichheld, 1993; 1996).

It is not clear whether loyalty schemes actually affect loyalty. Initially they may do so but, if the scheme is easily copied by competitors, the net result may be that most players in a market offer the same additions to their product and negate each other's influence. In the United States, those who fly a lot tend to join the frequent flyer schemes of all the airlines that they use, so that the effect of such schemes may be to raise costs and open the way for new price-competitive services. However, the new emphasis on customer retention is good for consumers if it raises product quality, aftersales service, warranty provisions and complaint handling. The effects of one loyalty scheme are reported in Chapter 4.

Postscript on loyalty

Brand loyalty has been presented here as a behavioural habit and this is consistent with the idea presented in Chapter 1 that much of our behaviour should be seen as habitual. We have other commercially important habits which may also be seen as forms of loyalty. For example, we can be loyal to stores and have habits about when we use them; this is explored further in Chapter 9. We may also show consistent habits of packsize purchase. It is attractive to see ourselves as free agents, choosing afresh each time we enter a market. In reality, we establish habits to cover much of our routine consumer behaviour and our freedom as consumers relates more to the opportunity to review our habits occasionally when there appear to be better opportunities.

Brand awareness

Brand awareness is the recognition or recall of a brand; this usually implies the differentiation of one brand from other brands by reference to one or more character-istics. In many categories the differences between brands are small, both objectively and in consumers' perceptions. This limits the influence that manufacturers can have on their customers. The buyer wants detergent, sugar, salt, cooking oil, etc., and may not care what the brand is. In some cases the branding may be so unimportant that it is ignored by the purchaser. (Do you know which brand of sugar you bought last?) Often product differences only appear in the variants (e.g. castor, granulated and Demerara sugars).

Other brand alternatives are more sharply differentiated, for example, *Snickers* from *Hershey Bars*, and *Kellogg's Corn Flakes* from Nabisco's *Shredded Wheat*. Not surprisingly, a number of studies have shown differences in consumers' perceptions of brands; Ryan and Etzel (1976) found this for toothpaste, and Tuck for detergent (reported in Ajzen and Fishbein, 1980). Consumers' ideas about brands may also differ from their ideas about the category. Mazis, Ahtola and Klippel (1975) found that the beliefs about cars *in general* omitted some specific brand beliefs about status symbolism and country of manufacture.

Manufacturers need to brand their products to make their marketing more effective but, because of the similarity between brands in many product fields, it may be difficult to establish strong brand awareness. When purchase is rare, or the product has little intrinsic interest, advertising is needed to establish awareness. Sometimes design features help to identify brands that are functionally similar to others – Perrier uses a distinctively shaped bottle, and the Swiss firm Zehnder distinguish their central heating radiators by using bright stove enamelling and unusual shapes.

When brand awareness is weak, the promotion of one brand may have the effect of promoting the whole category. Under these circumstances producers must decide whether to try to establish a strong brand awareness through advertising and product design, or to use price, sales promotions or control of distribution to secure the market. Advertising may succeed in building up the *internally* based judgement frames so that perceived value for money, brand image and brand awareness are enhanced. Sales promotion and distribution work *externally* by modifying the facts presented in the consumer's environment (see Figure 1.4). The choice of strategy depends on the type of product, the way it is bought, the actions of competitors and control of distribution.

The consequences of weak brand awareness

In Britain, one of the DIY store groups called *Do-It-All* found, some years ago, that the extra sales raised by its advertising were much the same as the extra sales they received when their competitor B & Q advertised. It seemed that the public made little differentiation between DIY stores; advertising reminded them of work that they had intended to do and they got any necessary supplies from the most convenient store. Thus the advertising of any one store had the effect of promoting the DIY retail category.

In situations such as this where brand awareness is weak, companies may decide to use sales promotions to focus buying activity on the brand, and the DIY sector in Britain now makes heavy use of price promotions and loyalty discount schemes.

Brand awareness has value to consumers as well as to suppliers. To them, brands are a variation of the product type, along with price, freshness, size, flavour, origin, colour, etc. Brands usually have consistent quality and consumers may be able to obtain particular benefits by selecting particular brands. For example, a cheese like Brie varies quite widely, and greater predictability about what you are buying may be achieved by opting for a branded product like 'Cambozola'. Thus routine buying of familiar brands can reduce risk and sometimes ensure quality or value for money.

Branding is part of the market system in which manufacturers compete against each other; because consumers can recognize and evaluate brands, they can seek out the better product and ignore substandard goods. This motivates manufacturers to improve their brands, and as a result products improve: witness the fuel economy, comfort and reliability of modern cars. It is difficult to see how these advances in car design could have occurred without competition between brands. Competition between brands is so well accepted that we may fail to see some of the hazards – for example, the promotion of cigarettes and over-refined foods. Another problem that has emerged in recent years has been the proliferation of brand variants, which has made it harder for the consumer to know what exactly he or she is buying.

Enhancing brand awareness

In Britain, the case of Hellman's mayonnaise (Channon, 1985) illustrates the way in which a clear brand awareness can pay off. In 1981 this brand was priced well above other brands of mayonnaise and had such a large share of the market that it was open to fierce competition from these other brands, particularly retailer brands. This meant that strong brand awareness was essential to hold the market and the advertising used the term 'Hellman's' rather than 'mayonnaise' to reinforce the brand name and to differentiate it from other brands of mayonnaise. The campaign was successful in making Hellman's the effective name of the category and the brand still has a large share of the market.

Becoming synonymous with the category has always been an attractive possibility for the leading brand. In Britain, 'Hoovering' means vacuum cleaning and is perhaps the best known example of this effect; another case is the way 'Fairy' has been used as a synonym for washing-up liquid in Britain.

Brand image

The minimum requirement for brand awareness is that consumers can recognize or recall the brand in relevant situations, but most of us would say that names like Ford, Mars, Levi, Rolls-Royce and Woolworth are associated in our minds with a range of meanings and feelings, which we call the brand image, and which enlarge the way in which we think of the brand.

Brand image goes beyond a brand's physical properties. The term was given currency by Gardner and Levy (1955), who believed that products have a social and psychological nature as well as a physical one and that consumers have feelings and ideas about brands that are crucial to consumer choice. The idea of brand image is also expressed by other terms such as 'the symbols by which we buy', 'brand personality' and 'brand meaning'. Another use of the term is to pick up associations that are engendered by advertising, e.g. the 'snap, crackle and pop' of the cereal *Rice Krispies* and that *Andrex* toilet paper is 'soft, strong and very long'. Different concepts of brand image have been reviewed by Dobni and Zinkhan (1990).

Exercise 2.3 Brand image

---

1. Put in order of quality the following brand names: Sansui, Ferguson, Sony, Toshiba.

2. Compare your order with that of others. In many cases you will agree. What does this suggest about brand image, advertising and pricing?

3. What in particular do you associate with Sony?

4. Does the order stay the same when a product type is inserted, e.g. CD player, amplifier?

Usually Sony tops the list in Western countries and Sansui does poorly (but not in Korea where it is a premium brand). Sony's ascendancy probably reflects product quality, innovativeness and advertising sustained over many years. However, Sony is particularly focused on electronic goods and the assurance offered by the brand name is usually less clear when it is related to electric toothbrushes or kitchen equipment.

Brand image need not sell a product; people may be well aware of gasoline brands and retailers such as Woolworths but this does not ensure that they patronize them. Similarly the wine buff may be able to quote the names of the more strongly branded wines such as Mateus Rosé, Blue Nun and Piat d'Or, but may shudder at the thought of buying these brands. Brand images, then, may be negative as well as positive. When the brand is well regarded it seems likely that purchase and loyalty are supported, and for this reason companies are jealous about their good name; the Ratner case (see the box below) shows that sales can be affected when negative perceptions are added to the brand image.

The position taken here is that improvements in brand image from advertising or other publicity *may* improve sales, but that this may not necessarily be the case. People may lack the need, time or wealth to acquire many of the brands that they admire in product fields such as cars and air travel. Fletcher (1992) estimates that consumers buy only 4 per cent of what they see advertised. Thus advertising may raise brand image without necessarily affecting purchase.

Catastrophic change of brand image

Some shifts in brand image certainly affect sales. In an unguarded moment Gerald Ratner described one of the goods sold in Ratner jewellery shops as 'total crap'. The comment was widely reported and sales in the Ratner shops declined sharply. Three years later Gerald Ratner had left, and the company was renamed Signet. The Ratner shops were changed over to the H. Samuel facia and showed up to 20 per cent gain in sales.

Brand equity

The continuity of brand loyalty and brand evaluation provides some guarantee of continuing profit, and this has led us to treat brands as an asset that should be conserved and exploited by the holding company, just as the company should make the best use of other resources such as its buildings and its sales force. Biel (1991) describes brand equity as the *value of a brand beyond the physical assets associated with its manufacture or provision* and says that it can be thought of as the additional cashflow obtained by associating the brand with the underlying product. In fact, it is rather wider than this since a well-established brand name not only makes future earnings from current products more likely, but is also a vehicle for launching new brands as brand extensions. Furthermore, companies with a strong brand name may be able to take over other companies and extend their name to the products of the acquired company. For example, a well-established hotel brand such as Marriott may be able to make more profit out of another hotel company's assets because of the strength of the Marriott name. Thus, although it is difficult to quantify brand equity, the earning potential that is locked up in human propensities towards a brand is large. Aaker (1991a) states that brand equity is based on five factors: *brand loyalty, brand awareness, perceived quality, brand associations* and *other brand assets*. In a lively and polemical contribution to this debate, Ambler (1996) argues that the brand is separate from the underlying product and that brand equity is the set of propensities towards the brand *over and above* those towards the product. This distinction has more meaning when we remember that the product that underlies the brand, and its ownership, may vary from country to country (e.g. *Crest* toothpaste is formulated somewhat differently in the United States and Britain; Safeway is owned by different companies in the United States, Britain and Australia).

Brand loyalty helps a supplier to reduce marketing costs and encourages retailers to stock; it may also lock out or weaken competitors. Leading brands are generally more profitable than lesser brands, and often maintain higher margins. The propensity to buy the well-established brand may override product deficiencies. For example, sales of the leading British toilet paper *Andrex* were not affected over a three-year period when *Kleenex Velvet* offered a technically superior product (Baker, 1993). New customers may naturally gravitate to brands that their friends and family are loyal to. Sometimes the existing customer base can be exploited further by using loyalty schemes and direct marketing.

Brand awareness may also offer prospects for further exploitation. We recognize and recall many brands that we mostly do not buy. An extension of the brand name to fields where we do buy may capitalize on brand awareness, e.g. Porsche sunglasses. Brands that have lost ground because of poor advertising support can be revived more easily if they are well known. An interesting case here is *Manger's Sugar Soap* (Broadbent, 1983); this was a familiar brand (used for cleaning walls before decorating) which had fallen increasingly into disuse until advertising re-established it. Because of the familiarity of brand names it may be costly to change them (see box, *Forsaken brand equity*).

Forsaken brand equity

Aaker (1991a) argues that managements ignore the value of their brands at their peril. He points to the name change from Datsun to Nissan which was a costly mistake; here the recognition and esteem of Nissan was found to be essentially the same as that of the old name, Datsun, in a study made five years after the change of name. Aaker estimates that the change of name cost $200 million in advertising alone and a further loss of sales; he guesses that the total cost was $500 million. In this case management threw away brand equity. In other cases, e.g. *Marathon* to *Snickers* in Britain, the change seems to have gone smoothly.

Perceived quality may raise profits because higher prices can be charged (e.g. the *Stella Artois* case, Baker, 1993). There also seems to be an asymmetry in brand extensions so that a brand with high perceived quality can be extended more easily to new products, than a low quality brand. Speed (1995) suggested that this asymmetry helped to predict success and failure with new launches in the Australian wine market.

Brand associations help to differentiate and position the brand and affect the feasibility of different potential extensions. Some brands, particularly those connoting quality, have wide application for brand extension while other names, such as *Vaseline*, have associations that restrict new applications.

Brand assets such as patents and established distribution arrangements may help to keep competitors out, and higher prices may be charged.

New brand or brand extension?

At one time manufacturers often used new names for a new product. Today new brand names are rare and, instead, existing brands are *stretched* to cover new developments. If manufacturers are already active in a market a product with a new name is described as a *flanker* brand; if they have not previously entered this field the new brand is a genuine *new product*. Brands may be stretched in two ways, either as *line extensions* within the parent category (e.g. when *Persil* first offered a clothes washing detergent in a liquid form) or as *category extensions* to product fields which are new to the brand name (e.g. when a *Persil* washing-up liquid was offered for the first time). The term *brand extension* is sometimes used generically to cover both category and line extensions but more commonly (e.g. Aaker, 1991a), it is restricted to the former. These alternatives are shown below.

New product development options for the manufacturer of *Persil*

	Established brand name	New brand name
If currently selling in the category	Line extension (liquid variant of *Persil*)	Flanker brand (*Wisk*)
If not selling in the category	Category extension (*Persil* washing-up liquid)	New product

Although category extensions claim much of our interest, it is line extensions that are most common. In the United States, Aaker (1991a) estimated that about 90 per cent of new products in the packaged goods industry were line extensions. Lines can be varied in minor ways, for example, by a change of cap or the lettering on the pack; these are not usually regarded as line extensions, but inevitably there is a degree of ambiguity about whether a variation is regarded as an extension or not. Generally, the description as a line extension is appropriate whenever the variant is intended to raise new sales or prevent major sales erosion. Line extensions are often defensive; for example Procter & Gamble introduced *Head and Shoulders Frequent* to avoid losing share to their competitors who were offering frequent use varieties of shampoo.

Brand naming practices

A brand name (together with associated pack designs and logos) is a major company asset and product naming practices are of strategic importance; because of this most companies have rules that ensure coherence and control on brand naming throughout the company. Robertson (1989) has commented on the desirable characteristics of a brand name and van Raaij and Schoonderbeek (1993) have reviewed naming practices for extensions.

Some companies use a family brand name which may cover many categories (e.g. Dunhill, Chanel, Mitsubishi). In some cases, the family brand may be followed by a sub-brand name (e.g. Heinz have used Weight Watchers as a sub-brand). Aaker (1991a) points out that 'nesting' the sub-brand name is an important way of building equity into a name which may later be used on its own. Some companies keep the brand name unique to the category (e.g. Budweiser), while others use individual names for each product in the category, a practice that is common among detergent manufacturers. The naming practice must reflect the type of product involved, its advertising support and the actions of competitors. Coca-Cola used to employ individual branding and therefore introduced their diet cola with its own name, *Tab*, but when Pepsi launched *Diet Pepsi* it was so successful that Coca-Cola had to change their policy and introduced *Diet Coke*. When *Diet Coke* was launched, *Tab* lost much of its support to the new entrant. The success of *Diet Pepsi* compared with *Tab* was because it was launched as an extension so that some of the image, recognition and buying tendencies associated with the Pepsi brand ('the halo') were transferred to the new brand. However, another reason for success may have been that *Diet Pepsi* (and *Diet Coke*) are better names because they describe the product clearly.

The model name dilemma

The launch of a new car raises problems of naming. The three components of the name Citroën BX16 TXi specify the brand name, model and model variant, and purchasers will attach some importance to each component. In 1993 when Citroen ended the BX model and introduced the redesigned and slightly larger

Xantia they discarded all the equity associated with the BX name. An alternative strategy would have introduced the new car, not as the Citroën Xantia, but as the Citroën BX Xantia and then phased out the BX name after the public had accepted the new model as a development of the BX. This procedure 'nests' the Xantia name and allows it to acquire some of the BX equity. A similar procedure could be used in the future when the Xantia eventually gives way to a new model. Precisely this policy was adopted in Australia when Daihatsu found that their rather bizarre model name, Charade, was better known than Daihatsu; when the time came to end the Daihatsu Charade they introduced the new model as the Daihatsu Charade Centro (*Sydney Morning Herald*, 7 July 1995).

Such decisions rest on managerial judgement and we saw from the earlier Datsun–Nissan change that mistakes do occur and can be costly. Some firms have kept the model name for new models, e.g. the Golf Mark II (Baker, 1993). Any decision must take account of the cost of advertising the new model.

Value the name . . .

It is unfortunate that organizations do not always appreciate the importance of a name and are too ready to change well-established descriptions. British Rail decided to rename their regional names, e.g. Southern Region became Network South-East; many commuters sensibly ignored the name change and continue to refer to Southern Region. In Manhattan, the RCA Tower became the GE Tower when General Electric took over RCA, causing confusion among hapless tourists searching with out-of-date guide books. In 1967 the BBC renamed its radio services and the Home Service became Radio 4, but even today there are still listeners who call it the Home Service.

At a more local level, name changing can cause trouble. In Richmond (Surrey, England), a famous Richmond pub called The Lass Of Richmond Hill has been renamed but residents still call it The Lass and look blank when visitors enquire about the pub by its new name.

. . . And the pack

The pack, like the brand name, signals the product and should therefore be modified with care; too much change will mean that customers fail to recognize the brand. Occasionally, the changes of words, colour and shape go too far but manufacturers are reluctant to talk about failures and so we have little documented evidence. One possible mistake occurred in Britain when British Telecom changed the colour as well as the design of its phone booths; the new designs are easily missed by a public still used to the idea that public phones come in red boxes. Affection for the old telephone boxes has ensured that many of them will remain so that BT now has more than one design of public telephone box. In 1996, after extensive research, BT unveiled a new box: the colour was red and the shape rather like the original box.

The pros and cons of an extension

Managements have to decide whether to launch new products as extensions or as new brands. Mostly they choose extensions, but sometimes their existing names may be unsuitable. For example, Toyota decided to introduce their luxury car under a new name, Lexus, perhaps because the Toyota name lacked the very high quality connotations needed. When there is a choice about whether to extend or not, the decision touches on the following issues:

1. *New brand names are not easily found.* Brand names need to:
   (a) be different from other brand names;
   (b) be easy to use and remember;
   (c) have the right associations in the originating country and in any other countries where it may be used. (The Vauxhall Nova was unsuitable for Spain because it implied that the car would not go);
   (d) not become a name that any manufacturer can use like *linoleum*. The Champagne growers have had to fight a number of legal battles to restrict the name 'Champagne' to wines from their region;
   (e) cover future extensions that may be introduced (Hotpoint refrigerators and red Bluebird cars are a bit odd);
   (f) be available. Many brand names are registered but unused by major manufacturers, e.g. McDonalds have registered many names with 'Mc' prefixes.

   The problem of finding a suitable brand name is more easily solved if names are used which are descriptive of the product, e.g. 'Overnight Delivery Success' or 'I Can't Believe It's Not Butter'; these longer names are not likely to have been registered by others, but they offer little scope for extensions. Zaichkowsky and Vipat (1993) found that respondents claimed that they were more likely to buy everyday products that were descriptively named.

2. *Brand extensions reduce launch costs.* A study of marketing practitioners by McWilliam (1993) found that cost saving was their most frequently mentioned reason for using an extension. Extensions need less advertising because they are more readily accepted by distributors as well as customers (Doyle, 1989). An established brand name capitalizes on existing consumer propensities and the new brand can often use the same market structures as the parent. D.C. Smith and Park (1992) have studied the effect of extensions on market share and advertising efficiency and conclude that extensions capture greater market share and can be advertised more efficiently than new brands. Tauber (1988) has noted that the use of an existing name helps a brand to gain shelf space in stores.

3. *New brand names may themselves be extended.* Expenditure on a new brand name is an investment. Once launched the new brand can be extended to other products and the higher launch costs of a new brand may be recouped.

4. *Parent brands can gain or lose value.* An extension increases the exposure of the brand name; this, together with any positive associations from the new extension, may add value to the brand name and improve the standing of the parent brand. The downside of this process is that failure with the new product may damage the parent brand; this may occur because the brand extension so enlarges the associations of the brand name that it loses impact and all products under that name suffer in consequence (Tauber, 1981). One case cited by Trout and Ries (1972) was the rapid diversification of 'Protein 21' by Mennen into a confusing set of alternatives; this was associated with a loss in share rather than the expected gain from the new variants.

    However the number of new extensions need not cause confusion; D.C. Smith and Park (1992) did not find that the efficiency of a new extension was reduced by the number of extensions already made. Also Dacin and Smith (1993) found that consumer confidence in new extensions was unaffected by the number of existing extensions, provided that the new entrant was compatible with its predecessors. This implies that, when a series of extensions is considered, the order of introduction of the new lines is important. Supporting this, Dawar and Anderson (1993) found that the new lines were more acceptable if they were introduced in an order that made them coherent with the products that had already been introduced.

Extensions may affect core business

In 1993 the British security firm *Group 4* extended its operations from moving money to moving prisoners. In the first week three prisoners escaped, other disasters followed and the press castigated the firm for its incompetence. *Group 4* became the butt of jokes: 'What was *Group 4* originally called? *Group 5* but one got away.' According to Stephen Moss (*Guardian*, 24 May 1993) the *Group 4* communications director said that the company had considered pulling out of its private prison contracts because of the ridicule and possible damage to the rest of its £500 million a year security business.

Sales losses by the parent of a line extension

Sometimes a new entrant enlarges a market so that the gains of the entrant are larger than the losses of other brands. Usually other brands do lose sales and these losses are of three types:

1. Existing brands lose sales to the new entrant in proportion to their market share. This is the basic effect that may be expected where brands are similar in form and function.
2. There is an extra loss of sales for a brand that is perceived to be closely similar to a new entrant. With a line extension the main similarity is likely to be the common

brand name with the result that the parent loses more sales than would be expected from market share alone – the parent is *cannibalized* by the new brand. Other extra losses by the parent and other brands will be based on similarities of formulation, packaging, pricing, positioning, targeting, distribution and physical proximity to other brands in the store.

3. Manufacturers may be denied more space in the store by the retailer so that the introduction of a new variant means that something else must be abandoned. 'Line in, line out' is the terse name for this management practice. Usually another variant of the brand suffers.

Table 2.3 Brand market shares and percentage of *Wisk* gain 20 weeks after launch (1987)

Brand	Midland market share, pre-*Wisk* launch (%)	Post-*Wisk* launch contribution to *Wisk* sales (%)
Persil	28	27
Ariel	17	22
Surf	16	8
Bold	14	12
Daz	9	11
Other brands	16	15
No previous purchase	–	5

Source: AGB.

Some data on the British detergent market are available to illustrate the way in which consumers shift support to a new brand. Table 2.3 shows how, 20 weeks after launch, the first liquid detergent on the British market, *Wisk*, was taking customers from other brands (right-hand column). Table 2.3 shows that *Wisk* (a new brand) took share from other brands roughly in relation to their market share, though *Surf*, with its value-for-money positioning, seemed to resist loss better. This shows how big brands are more at risk than small brands from volume loss to new market entrants.

This effect was further investigated in a study by Lomax *et al.* (1996). Using new data, this work confirmed that *Wisk* took share in relation to the market share of the losing brands. A second study showed the cannibalization effect of the same brand name when a concentrated version of a German detergent took disproportionately more sales from its parent. Lomax *et al.* then examined the gains of the *Ariel Liquid* detergent which followed *Wisk* onto the British market. Here there was a parent powder brand and it was anticipated that this would be cannibalized by the new liquid formulation, but this was not found. Instead the whole liquid sector enlarged at the expense of all the powders. Though unexpected, this finding is consistent with a notion of *cannibalization barriers* introduced by Buday (1989); such barriers may be based on product formulation and mean that consumers do not see the new brand as close to its parent and therefore there is less substitution. (There is a danger that, when this occurs, the new entrant will gain little benefit from the common brand name.) Another explanation for the lack of cannibalization is that the new liquid supported the *Ariel* brand by increasing the exposure of the name and effectively advertised both powder and liquid. A fourth study examined the sales of *Persil Liquid* which was launched after *Ariel*

Liquid. Again, the parent powder was unaffected and the total liquid detergent share increased. This work shows that cannibalization may be prevented, but much more research is required before we can claim to understand these processes.

There are other similarities, besides name, that can affect brand substitution. Similarity of price will have most effect in markets where prices are diverse, for example cars. Here we would expect a new entrant to the luxury car market (e.g. the Lexus) to take a larger *proportion* of Mercedes sales than of Ford sales (but, because Ford has a large share of the market, Lexus may take a larger absolute number of sales from Ford than from Mercedes).

Firms must give careful attention to the potential loss of parent brand sales when they launch a line extension; small gains in overall sales may not be justified if each variant sells less because of cannibalization. Cannibalization may be reduced by pricing, targeting and positioning the brand so that it is more similar to competitor brands and less similar to the manufacturer's existing brands. Sometimes, when cannibalization is likely, it may be wise to avoid it by using a different brand name, particularly when the existing brand has a very large share.

Exercise 2.4   The brand extension decision

■ List the pros and cons of brand extensions versus new brands.
■ How do you think that a line extension decision is affected by the market share of the parent brand?
■ What would you do to reduce loss of sales by the parent brand of a line extension?

Consumer acceptance of a category extension

When we think of brand extension the different aspects of brand equity can be condensed into two factors: *strength* and *fit*. Brand strength is the prominence of the brand in the thought and feeling of consumers which encourages purchase, while fit relates to the congruence in the properties of new brand and parent, and by implication to the acceptability of the new brand. However, the presence of good fit and brand strength do not guarantee success; effective *marketing* of an extension is also required.

Doubt has been raised about the need for the concept of brand strength or equity. Ehrenberg (1993) has argued that the meaning of equity is covered by the concept of market share, but this confines the measurement of brand value to a given market pattern and fails to recognize that a poorly exploited brand will have more potential than is indicated by its market share; also, market share does not adequately describe the scope for brand extension which helps to define brand equity.

Agreed methods of measuring brand strength are needed if this subject is to progress. One method is to offer different amounts of money to buy back a brand already purchased.

Is brand equity the same as market share?

In greater detail my argument against Ehrenberg's market share thesis has three aspects:

1. We must remember that market share is affected by marketing interventions and that any comparison between brands should start by allowing for the fact that different brands in a category have different support from distribution, price and promotion. This is discussed by Broadbent (1992). Techniques for removing the effect on share of differential price and promotion are presented by Kamakura and Russell (1993).

2. There is a problem in using market share as a proxy for brand strength when we *compare categories*. A 20 per cent share of a category used by nearly every household (e.g. bread) affects far more people than a 20 per cent share of a minority market (e.g. cat food). And what is the category? Is *Stork* 20 per cent of margarine or 7 per cent of yellow fats? Even when the penetration is the same, there are products such as chocolate and cigarettes which seem to be very attractive to those who buy them compared with other categories such as paper tissues. This means that a brand with a 20 per cent share in the bar confectionery market could have a different strength than, say, a brand of ice-cream with a 20 per cent share. Ordinarily this will not be of any consequence, but a brand extension can exhibit the difference. My guess is that confectionery brands are stronger than ice-cream brands and this helped *Mars*, and later other confectionery manufacturers, to make inroads into the ice-cream market.

3. The previous point relates to the basis of market share; purchase propensity comes from both internal and external influences. These two types of influence operate in different proportions in different categories; in some cases, purchase is strongly affected by personal preference (confectionery, cigarettes), while in other cases the external factors, such as price and availability, may be more important (sugar, paper tissues). We would expect this basis of market share, whether internal or external, to be relevant to extensions.

Fit

Fit depends on similarities between the original brand and the extension product and rests particularly on brand awareness, quality and associations. Much of the research on category extension has focused on the fit between parent and new brand. Are the associations of the parent brand appropriate for the new brand? Are the pricing, positioning and distribution of the two products compatible? A good example is the development in Britain of a dishwasher powder by *Fairy*, the brand leader for washing-up liquid. The products are both cleaning agents and the associations are similar; the parent product was positioned as 'kind to your hands' and the dishwasher powder continues this theme by offering a product that does not remove the colours from plates, i.e. 'kind to your plates'; also both products are distributed in the same way through supermarkets. In contrast Bic, well known for disposable pens and razors, was less successful when it marketed perfumes and women's tights; here there were no obvious compatibilities between the new products and the parent.

For low involvement products the similarity between parent and new brand must help since, if the new product seems plausible, it is probably accepted without much thought. Indeed the buyer may neither know nor care whether the product is new or not, and may vaguely note the brand name as some assurance of quality. By contrast there are other extensions that are not plausible because of lack of fit: supermarket groups are hesitant about putting their names on cigarettes because this would conflict with the clean and healthy image which they cultivate; *Pampers* are known for babies' nappies or diapers and, although this name might extend to baby garments, it would be inappropriate for foods.

The issue here is whether the proposed new product makes sense in association with the image of the parent. We can learn here from the attempts to create brand image using advertising. Image creation, as Jeremy Bullmore (1984) points out, is the result of a dialogue; ads do not work simply by describing a set of attributes to a passive respondent. The communication process occurs because the ideas in the ad find echo in the ideas of the receiver; attempts to communicate fail if they do not take account of the pre-existing beliefs and feelings of consumers. Similarly, an extension may fail if it invokes meanings which do not fit the expectations of consumers that are based on the parent brand.

A number of studies (Aaker and Keller, 1990; Keller and Aaker, 1992; Sunde and Brodie, 1993) have explored how people react to possible extensions that fit the core brand better, or worse, but the results are limited by the hypothetical nature of this research and the failure to find consistent results (Holden and Barwise, 1995). An alternative approach is to examine case histories of brand extensions and here Aaker (1991a, 1991b) presents some very persuasive examples of successful and unsuccessful extensions, which indicate that one key to success is the fit between parent and the extension. However, a problem with such retrospective work is the way in which examples may be chosen that support the hypothesis. Extensions have been made very successfully into fields unrelated to the parent brand by firms such as Yamaha, Mitsubishi, Virgin and Marks & Spencer, so fit is not essential.

Hartman, Price and Duncan (1990) have described a way in which people respond to possible category extensions. They agree that people will accept close extensions that are consistent with the established range of the brand. As the new product moves away from the meanings associated with the parent brand they will try to make sense of the extension in relation to the parent category. A *Pampers* baby T-shirt might belong to this class. When the extension differs further from the parent, people may dismiss the brand–category association or just fail to recognize it. Hartman, Price and Duncan suggest that consumers may make sense of large discrepancies between parent and extension when the products are high involvement, but warn that people can become more averse as well as more favourable when they have to make more effort to comprehend an association.

Supporting Hartman, Price and Duncan (1990), work by Meyers-Levy and Tybout (1989) showed that an unusual characteristic increased consumers' cognitive processing, but too many unusual features reduced it. The completely obvious may be ignored and the completely inexplicable may be rejected. Relevant here is work on the attention given to an object, which varied from completely clear to completely blurred (Berlyne and Borsa, 1968); attention was highest at an intermediate degree of blurring where ambiguity was maximal. Berlyne (1954) suggested that attention is driven by this ambiguity in meaning.

This work implies that a starting point for brand extension research is the compatibility between the two sets of meanings that the brand and extension categories already have. If the consumer processes the new brand concept, he or she will check whether the proposed extension has similarities of production, attributes, price, distribution or packaging with the parent. Unless the extension shares one or more dimension (in the consumer's mind) there is no *relatedness* and no transfer of the parent brand associations.

Problems of fit are posed by the growth of world brands like *Chanel* which embrace a wide variety of product types under one name; such names invoke quality but little detailed description. Although this gives wide scope for extensions, as Kapferer (1991) notes, there can be no precise fit.

Where the brand does have detailed associations these may be many and varied. McWilliam (1993) points out that a brand image often contains many different meanings which allow for a great variety of 'fits'; for this reason a good fit is not easily anticipated. Aaker and Keller (1990) explored the meanings associated with the fast food chain, McDonalds, and found that it was seen as: American, standardized, efficient, food-related, children-related, convenient, fun and garbage-producing. Widely different extensions can be drawn from this set of meanings and Aaker and Keller suggest that frozen fries, a theme park and a photo-lab all use some of the associations of McDonalds. At present we lack a clear procedure for identifying the most important aspects of fit that will help us to plan and evaluate extensions. McWilliam suggests that extension failures are blamed on poor fit *after* the failure; it is easy to offer rationalizations for failure, and bad fit is a more acceptable excuse than bad marketing.

Effective marketing

Barwise (1993) points out that of the three bases for effective brand extensions, fit, brand strength and effective marketing, it is the last that is often ignored.

Some quite bizarre extensions have worked because the appropriate marketing structures were available. Marks & Spencer, originally known for clothing, successfully diversified to food because they had an effective system of sourcing and distribution; Bic, known for disposable ballpoints and lighters, succeeded with their sailboard. The potential of a category extension is affected by market size, product quality, market growth, economies of scale, distribution structures and profit margin, all of which should be considered by the marketer.

Exercise 2.5   Potential extensions

Below is a list of brand names. Are extensions appropriate for these brands? Suggest any extensions which might be appropriate *and* successful. Give reasons for your suggestions.

Shell
Sony
Woolworths
Kodak
The BBC

Summary

Branding is a necessary feature of a market economy; without brands, manufacturers would find it difficult to promote their products and would lack incentive to develop new lines.

Brand loyalty is a purchase propensity that is based on internal and external factors. The internal factors cover recognition, recall and the thoughts and feelings that make up brand image. The external factors include availability, price and packaging. Consumers often divide their loyalty between several brands in a category and their resulting purchases are called a brand portfolio or repertoire.

One measure of loyalty is *preference*, the proportion of category purchase devoted to the brand. Buyers also keep their buying habits over long periods and this *allegiance* to the brand is a second form of loyalty. There is a tendency for buyers to display the same level of loyalty in different categories (*loyalty proneness*). Past work has shown little connection between demographic factors and loyalty, but one recent study indicates that the more loyal buyers are wealthier and are less attracted by discounts. Brand loyalty can be seen as a purchase habit, often supported by a positive attitude to the brand.

Most new products are launched as *line extensions* or *category extensions* and may benefit from familiarity with the established brand. A matter of great importance is to identify the most profitable extensions. Line extensions cause sales losses to existing brands when limited sales are redistributed and the parent brand may be particularly susceptible to this type of loss (called cannibalization). Category extensions work best if the parent brand is strong, the extension is similar to the parent in the minds of purchasers, and the marketing is effective.

Further reading

Cunningham, R.M. (1956) Brand loyalty – what, where, how much?, *Harvard Business Review*, 34, Jan.–Feb., 116–28.
Feldwick, P. (1996) What is brand equity anyway, and how do you measure it? *Journal of the Market Research Society*, 38, 2, 85–104.
Smith, D.C. and Park, C.W. (1992) The effects of brand extensions on market share and advertising efficiency, *Journal of Marketing Research* 29, 296–313.

Chapter 3

Stationary markets

Introduction

In order to judge how well a brand is performing we need to understand the patterns of purchase that are commonly found in markets. Such knowledge allows us to judge whether a brand is behaving in a typical manner or whether there are exceptional aspects to its sales.

Research on market patterns is done by analysis of data provided by market research companies. In particular, academic researchers use the findings of the consumer panel studies run by companies such as IRI in the United States, AGB in Britain, GfK in Germany and Nielsen throughout the world. As noted in Chapter 2, consumer panels record data by household so that the purchase pattern of single households, or a group of households, can be followed, and a long-term purchase history can be built up.

Marketing scientists have established mathematical models based on a limited set of assumptions which are very effective at mimicking the real patterns found in panel data. These models have been so successful that they now provide us with *sales norms*, which can be used to predict the performance of a brand under stationary conditions.

In this chapter the following topics are covered:

- The stability of many established markets and the reasons why they are stable.

- The value of mathematical modelling.

- Patterns that can be observed in the purchase of single brands with regard to weight of purchase and repeat buying.

- Applications of the negative binomial distribution (NBD) model.

- Patterns of purchase in the product field and inferences that can be made from these patterns about the way in which a brand's market share may change.

- Patterns of multibrand purchase, and the value of the Dirichlet model for predicting brand purchase.

The stability of established markets

Frequent purchase markets can be divided into new markets and established (or mature) markets. In this chapter we are mainly concerned with established markets; though less exciting than new markets, mature markets are larger and therefore very important. An important feature of established markets is that they usually do not change much; they tend to be *stationary*. This is not to deny that change may sometimes occur: whole product fields may decline, for example, biscuits in Britain in the 1990s; subcategories may lose share, for example, the 1980s saw a decline in the consumption of bitter beer and a rise in lager drinking in Britain; single brands may gain or lose share, for example, *Stella Artois* gained substantial share in the British lager market in the mid-1980s following a successful advertising campaign. When markets do show lasting change, this usually occurs quite slowly over a period of years. Only exceptionally do we see rapid changes that become permanent, for example, after adverse publicity about a product damages its acceptability, or when an advertising campaign is particularly successful. Markets may also change over short periods because of sales promotions, but here the gains are usually not maintained when the promotion finishes (Ehrenberg and England, 1990; Ehrenberg, Hammond and Goodhardt, 1994). Such brief gains have little impact in the longer term and the market looks quite stable when the fluctuations are averaged out over a period of months. As a result, the effects of long-term trend and short-term fluctuations are minimized when markets are analyzed over medium-length periods, typically from three months to a year, and researchers use such periods when they are exhibiting the patterns of purchase that can be found in established markets.

One reason for the relative stability of markets has been explained in Chapters 1 and 2. Individuals form stable propensities or habits of purchase which they change only under exceptional conditions. In Chapter 2 (see Table 2.1) we showed some evidence of how much change is concealed within markets that are stationary in aggregate; East and Hammond (1996) found that about 15 per cent of buyers may change brands in a year. Thus switching is not very common.

The impact of recent purchase

How does recent purchase experience affect the next purchase? In particular, is there a bias towards purchasing the same brand as last time? Learning theory, outlined in Chapter 1, suggests that the reinforcement derived from a brand purchase and consumption might raise the likelihood of repeat purchasing the last brand bought (or reduce it if the brand is unsatisfactory).

Consider two people who have both bought *Persil* and *Tide* an equal number of times over the last six months; their only difference is that last time Philip bought *Persil*, while Elizabeth bought *Tide*, e.g.

> *Philip:*   *Tide, Tide, Persil, Persil*
> *Elizabeth:*   *Persil, Tide, Persil, Tide*

Who is more likely to buy *Persil* at their next purchase? Learning theory implies that Philip is more likely to buy *Persil* next time. This is a *first-order explanation* because it takes account of the last purchase. A *zero-order explanation* takes no account of prior purchase order, and here there would be no difference between Philip and Elizabeth in terms of their likelihood of purchasing *Persil*; a zero-order finding implies that people quickly establish a habit which is unaffected by recent consumption. When the explanation is zero-order we can predict the likelihood of a future brand purchase only from the ratio of past brand purchases whereas a first-order explanation gives more weight to the last brand bought.

Since people do occasionally switch, their most recent purchase should be a better guide to their next purchase than earlier purchases. Thus it would be surprising if the most recent purchase had no extra effect at all and indeed Kuehn (1962) did find evidence in support of a first-order effect. More recently, Guadagni and Little (1983) have assumed changing propensities to purchase within a logit model[1] of brand choice. However a study by Bass *et al.* (1984) showed that the majority of purchases in most markets are zero-order. All studies have their weaknesses and Kahn, Morrison and Wright (1986) argued that, because *household* panel data were used by Bass *et al.*, the first-order behaviour of *individuals* might have been obscured; but, on balance, it seems likely that a zero-order pattern of purchase is more common in stable markets, and habit rather than reinforcement provides the best way of thinking about repetitive purchase. We conclude that people usually form stable propensities to act in particular ways, which are unaffected by minor variations in the reinforcement associated with purchase. This is not to say that reinforcement has no effect on brand choice, but rather to emphasize that this occurs exceptionally.

Exercise 3.1 Changes of allegiance

---

1. Under what circumstances do you think people might make real changes in their allegiance to a brand or product type?

2. When do you think that recent purchase has an effect on next purchase?

3. How would purchase patterns evolve if the last purchase of a brand always raised the probability of purchasing that brand next time?

When people buy familiar products they do not usually gain more knowledge about the product, so why should their frequency of purchase change? Even though you may like a product, this is no reason for raising purchase rate. In learning theory there are satiation effects that put you off products that have been too frequently experienced. It seems likely that change of purchase frequency will only occur when consumption brings new experience of the product – good or bad.

---

[1] Logit modelling explains the behaviour of different subdivisions of a sample and can therefore deal with a variety of purchasing histories.

The value of mathematical models

Stable propensities help to make purchase behaviour predictable so that, for example, repeat purchase, the distribution of heavy and light buyers of a brand, and the pattern of purchase within a brand field are all derivable from other measures using the appropriate mathematical model. Early work on these subjects was done by Ehrenberg (e.g. papers in 1959; 1969); this work was brought together in *Repeat Buying: Theory and Applications* (Ehrenberg, 1988, first published 1972) and in a more accessible form in *Essays on Understanding Buyer Behaviour* (1979) by Ehrenberg and Goodhardt. These books attacked conventional beliefs in marketing and caused a reappraisal of some of the traditional ideas about brand loyalty, brand positioning, the effects of advertising and the way in which sales grow. Work in the United States has been less polemical and has focused more on the mathematical properties of stationary market models; American researchers such as Morrison and Schmittlein (1981; 1988) are among those who have given detailed attention to the precision of models and to the modifications that might improve this precision. The model that is appropriate for the prediction of single brand purchase is the Negative Binomial Distribution (known universally as the NBD), while the more complex model used for predicting purchase in a brand field (i.e. several brands at once) is the Dirichlet.

Mathematical models help us to predict brand purchase in a product category, but can also be applied to other forms of stable repetitive behaviour. For example, Goodhardt, Ehrenberg and Collins, in *The Television Audience: Patterns of Viewing* (1975; revised 1987), have applied these methods to the study of television audiences. Another application has been to store choice, with stores being treated as brands (Kau and Ehrenberg, 1984). It is also possible to subdivide the brand and model part of a brand's purchases such as *Tide* bought at Safeway, or *Persil* in a particular packsize. Finally, groups of brands may be aggregated and treated as one brand; for some purposes all the brands in the category are treated as one.

Stationary market research does not explain *why* some people buy more than others and one brand rather than another; some critics argue that the lack of attention to motivational issues limits the application of this work, and that this is particularly so when the marketer is trying to induce change. What do you put in advertisements if people's motivations are unknown? Why do some people respond more to price cuts than others? Do those who buy more have different reasons from those who buy less? Why do people avoid some brands? When markets do expand or contract, such changes may reflect changes in motivation, income or other household circumstances. But theorists such as Ehrenberg do not claim to cover all the problems that arise in marketing and specifically exclude the qualitative aspects of motivation. What they describe is the quantitative form of stable markets; if a market is stationary, the numerical predictions from the model are usually very close to the observations derived from panel data. If the market is not stationary, the difference between the observed facts and the model prediction is often instructive and may, for example, show how the market has expanded by an increase in either new buyers or repeat buyers. Later we explain these models in a more detailed way; before that, we look at some of the patterns that the models predict that can be seen in panel data. We begin with some necessary definitions.

The purchase of the single brand

Definitions

The reader should be clear about the meaning of a number of terms and their relationship. First, we usually work with *purchase occasions* rather than sales. A purchase occasion is when a buyer buys one or more units of a brand. In most markets consumers buy one unit at a time, and sales approximately equal purchase occasions. Other important definitions are:

■ The *penetration*, b, which is the proportion of all potential buyers in a population who buy a brand at least once in a period. (Think b for *buyers*.)
■ The *purchase frequency*, w, which is the average number of purchases made *by those who purchase at least once* in a period. (Think w for purchase *weight*.)
■ The *mean population purchase* rate, m, the number of purchase occasions in the period made by an average member of the population. (Think m for *mean*.) When b is expressed as a percentage, m will be the sales per 100 buyers.

These variables are linked by the *sales equation*:

$$m = bw$$

Thus when the penetration of *Tide* over three months is 0.25 and the purchase frequency is 4, $m = 0.25 \times 4$ or 1. In words: *when a quarter of the population buy Tide, on average four times, then the average purchase occasion rate in the whole population is one.*

When people buy more than 1 unit per purchase occasion we must multiply by a correcting factor. If, for example, people on average buy 1.2 units of *Tide* per purchase occasion, then the mean population sales rate m_s will be given by:

$$m_s = 0.25 \times 4 \times 1.2$$

Similarly, average weight or price per purchase occasion can be used to get the mean weight bought or amount paid per member of the population.

Exercise 3.2   Applying the sales equation

---

1. Suppose that in a stationary market the penetration of *Sensodyne* toothpaste is 0.07 over 24 weeks. Given that *Sensodyne* is sold on 21 occasions per 100 consumers, what is the purchase frequency?

2. How many purchase occasions per 100 consumers will there be in 48 weeks?

3. If the purchase frequency for the 48 week period is 4.6, what will be the mean sales and penetration?

4. In 24 weeks 105 purchases of toothpaste of all types are made per 100 buyers. What is *Sensodyne*'s market share?

Answers

1. $21/7 = 3$.

2. In a stationary market if you double the period you will double the sales: 42 per 100.

3. $m = bw$. Therefore, $0.42 = b \times 4.6$. So $b = 0.42/4.6 = 0.09$.

4. Brand volume share is $21/105 = 20\%$ but share by value will depend on selling prices.

Do we buy at regular intervals?

One glance at the goods that we buy in the supermarket shows that we have bought all, or nearly all, the brands before. Thus we have habits about *what* we buy, but are we also habitual about *when* we buy? Purchase time habits would show up in panel data as an individual tendency to buy a brand each week or month. Habits of this sort would mean that a purchaser's probability of buying rises sharply at intervals. This pattern is found for some frequent purchases such as newspapers or cigarettes; it also applies to shopping trips for many people. Dunn, Reader and Wrigley (1983) and Kahn and Schmittlein (1989) report that households tend to be loyal to a particular day for grocery shopping, and East *et al.* (1994) found that, in Britain, the majority of supermarket users were loyal to particular times of the day. This work is considered in more detail in Chapter 9.

Despite the routine timing of many shopping trips, brands are usually bought at irregular intervals. There are several reasons for this. First we should note that most brands are bought quite infrequently, for example, a typical US household buys a coffee brand about three times a year and the category about nine times a year. The inter-purchase interval may vary because consumption may be irregular, shoppers may stockpile or run out, and they may buy any one of several brands. This makes the timing of a specific brand purchase quite variable so that it approximates to random incidence. Mathematicians describe this random incidence as a *Poisson distribution*.

However, people rarely buy a brand again immediately after purchasing it; because of this 'dead time' after purchase, the Poisson distribution does not fit so well when the period is shorter than the average category inter-purchase interval. Over the longer periods covered in panel research, the fit of the Poisson assumption is close and provides a basis for the mathematical models described later. The Poisson pattern implies some fluctuation in purchase, but the number of purchases made by a household in one period will be approximately the same as those made in an equivalent period; thus shoppers are mostly habitual about *how much* they buy.

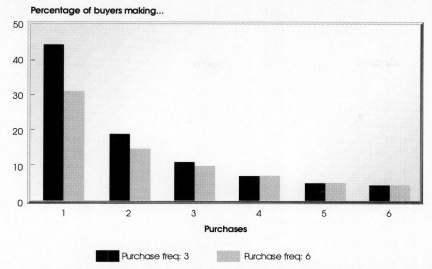

Figure 3.1 Gamma distributions of purchase for brands with purchase frequencies of 3 and 6 (penetration = 10%)

How do consumers vary in their weight of purchase?

People vary widely in how much they buy. The range of purchase frequencies in a sample of buyers has the form of a *Gamma distribution*. This is a histogram in which the largest number of buyers usually occurs for the lowest purchase frequency. Figure 3.1 shows an example of a Gamma distribution for two products with purchase frequencies of 3 and 6, both with a penetration of 10 per cent.

Few people buy heavily, but those who do so are responsible for a large proportion of a brand's sales. Table 3.1 illustrates this with purchases of *Kellogg's Corn Flakes* in the United States. In a quarter, 20 per cent of households purchase, making on average just over two purchases each. This average is based on the 55 per cent who bought once, 22 per cent who bought twice, 8 per cent who bought three times, etc. (this is a Gamma distribution). When we work out the sales from these subgroups (the bottom row) we see how important the few heavy buyers are for sales. Those who bought three or more times, 23 per cent of all purchasers, were responsible for more than 50 per cent of all sales. Just so that you understand what Table 3.1 is indicating, note the right-hand column; you see that a sample of 100 purchasers have produced 210 purchases, 2.1 per person, the purchase frequency.

Table 3.1 Quarterly sales of *Kellogg's Corn Flakes* in the United States

Penetration %	Purchase frequency	Out of 100 purchasers, the number buying:						Total
		Once	Twice	3 times	4 times	5 times	6+ times	
20	2.1	55	22	8	5	5	5	100
		Number of purchases:						
		55	44	24	20	25	42	210

Source: Ehrenberg and Goodhardt (1979).

In general a substantial proportion of purchases are made by very few heavy buyers; one rule of thumb, the *heavy half principle*, is that the lighter buying 50 per cent are responsible for about 20 per cent of all purchases while the heavy buying 50 per cent are responsible for the other 80 per cent. If you inspect Table 3.1 you will see that the lowest buying 55 per cent are responsible for about 26 per cent of purchases so this rule is supported here. Other rules are more extreme: the 80:20 rule is that 80 per cent of the brand is bought by the heaviest buying 20 per cent of consumers. Such rules are approximate and depend to some extent on the period of time used to count brand buyers; a longer period includes a higher proportion of light buyers, thus affecting the ratio of light to heavy buyers. This subject has been reviewed by Schmittlein, Cooper and Morrison (1993).

Weight of purchase among feline consumers

An interesting demonstration of how weight of consumption varies was provided by a study of 'what the cat brought home' to households in a Bedfordshire village. More than seventy domestic cats were studied and their tendency to kill and bring home sparrows, frogs, rabbits, mice, etc. was studied. One cat was responsible for 10 per cent of the total kill while, at the other end of the distribution, six cats brought back nothing in a whole year. (*Source*: Churcher and Lawton, 1987)

This breakdown of purchase shows that heavy buyers are an attractive segment in many markets and marketers may therefore try to focus their efforts upon them. For example, promotions may give progressively more attractive benefits to those who buy more. Sometimes it is possible to target the heavy buyers by adapting the distribution system. For example the 'wine warehouse', which sells by the case, may secure a larger proportion of heavy buyers. Heavy buyers have been analyzed by Hammond and Ehrenberg (1995).

Adapting to heavy and light buyers

One managerial implication of the wide variation in purchase weight is that sales effort should, in some degree, reflect the purchase weight of the buyer. Despite this, some sales staff tend to give equal weight to customers and may not even know who are heavy and who are light buyers. Thus one practical application of weight of purchase variation is to produce simple statistics and give these to those responsible for securing further orders.

How does the type of product affect purchase?

If two quite different products have the same purchase frequency and penetration, will they have the same sole brand loyalty or repeat purchase rates? Panel research shows that the answer to this question is 'Yes'. This means that the features of a brand which make it more or less popular are measured through these two quantities: purchase frequency and penetration. It turns out that repeat purchase depends mainly on purchase frequency and only slightly on penetration. A few products (e.g. cigarettes) do show somewhat higher levels of repeat purchase than would be expected from their purchase frequency, but generally the type of product or brand need not be known for the prediction of a number of important measures like repeat purchase and the proportion of sole brand buyers, provided that we know the purchase frequency and penetration. Mathematical models use purchase frequency and penetration to make these predictions.

Repeat purchase

If we compare any two adjacent sales periods, e.g. two quarters, we find that many of the buyers of a brand in quarter 1 (Q1) return in Q2, particularly the heavier buyers. Replacing the 'lapsed' buyers who do not buy in Q2 are an approximately equal number of 'new' buyers. The 'new' buyers are mostly light buyers of the brand like those that they replace and, although they did not buy in Q1, they have often bought the brand before and thus are not really new to the brand, hence the inverted commas around the first use of 'lapsed' and 'new'. At Q3 about the same proportion of Q2 buyers drop out and are replaced by others including some of those who lapsed after Q1. This intermittent pattern of purchase does not show loss of loyalty but instead reflects the fact that many people buy a brand so infrequently that they often miss quarters. The change of buyers at each quarter is explained mainly as a probability effect, though a small part of the effect is due to a change of allegiance.

This helps us to understand why repeat-purchase rates depend mainly on purchase frequency. A household that buys four times in one quarter is more likely to buy again in the next quarter than one that bought only twice in a quarter because the latter is less likely to need to buy. Because heavier buyers are more likely to repeat we find that the purchase frequency of repeat purchasers is higher (by about 20 per cent) than the rate for the whole sample.

In a stationary market the purchase rate and number of new buyers are the same as those for the lapsed buyers they replace; if this were not so the market would not be stationary. Because new purchasers tend to be light buyers we find that their purchase rate is low and usually does not rise much above 1.5 for any period. People find this ceiling on the new buyer's purchase rate odd, but if the rate were higher it would be less likely that these buyers would appear as new purchasers and more likely that they would be regular purchasers and therefore excluded from the calculation of the new buyer purchase rate. Because of this, new purchasers tend to have much the same purchase frequency in any market and over any longer period. As we noted earlier, penetration does have a small effect on repeat-purchase rates. This is illustrated in Table 3.2. Compare columns 1 and 2 and you see that a tenfold increase in purchase frequency has a substantial effect on repeat purchase, raising it from 57 per cent to 85 per cent; compare columns 1 and 3 and you see that repeat purchase moves only three points when the penetration increases tenfold. Note that it is the repeat purchase *rate* that is slightly affected by penetration. The *number* of repeat purchasers is directly affected by penetration.

Table 3.2 Repeat purchase for given purchase frequencies and penetrations

Penetration (%)	2	2	20
Purchase frequency	2	20	2
Repeat purchase (%)	57	85	60

Repeat purchase is an important diagnostic measure. If the purchase frequency for quarter 1 indicates a repeat purchase rate of 50 per cent under stationary market conditions, then deviations from this figure indicate that the market does not have the normal stationary characteristics. One application of this thinking was reported by Ehrenberg (1988: 97–8). A new brand was being heavily advertised but, despite this, sales were constant. Two explanations were possible:

1. The advertising was ineffective and the brand was creating normal repeat purchase.
2. The advertising was effective at creating new trialists, but these people were not repeating so that the brand was not gaining sales. Here analysis should show more new purchasers and less repeat purchasers than is typical for a stationary market.

Evidence that repeat purchase is normal favours the first explanation and means that the advertising should be changed. Evidence that the repeat purchase is below the normal level supports the second explanation and indicates that the brand is weak and that sales will collapse when the pool of potential trialists becomes exhausted; in this case the brand should be deleted before more money is wasted. This case is presented in Exercise 3.6.

Negative binomial distribution (NBD) theory

Negative binomial distribution (NBD) theory is a mathematical model which permits the prediction of repeat purchase and other measures from data on the penetration, purchase frequency and period.

NBD theory is based on the assumptions that total purchases of a brand are stationary, that individual purchases follow a Poisson distribution and that the long-run average purchase rates of individuals follow a Gamma distribution. These assumptions are set out by Ehrenberg (1988, ch. 4). Within these assumptions it is possible to derive an expression for the probability of making r purchases in a period, p_r. It is not necessary to follow the mathematics of the NBD but for those interested in the technicalities:

$$p_r = (1 - m/(m + k))^{-k}$$

where k is a parameter that is estimated from the purchase frequency and penetration. Expressions of the form $(1 + x)^n$ are called binomial; the equation for p_r is a negative binomial because the exponent is negative.

The calculation of the NBD requires the solution of the equation

$$1 - b = (1 + m/k)^{-k}$$

to obtain the parameter k. When purchase frequency and penetration are known, program NBD, available from the publisher, estimates k and derives a range of purchase data. When only raw data on purchase are available, or special calculations are required, the program called BUYER (Uncles, 1988) can be used.

Program NBD

This computer program accepts data on the penetration, purchase frequency and period and computes repeat purchase and new purchase rates for different periods. The Gamma distribution of persons buying once, twice, etc. is worked out for each period and the proportion of sales attributable to different rates of purchase is calculated (the negative binomial distribution). These figures are tabled on the screen and the user then has options to change the rounding and to express buyer figures as proportions, percentages or actual numbers. A copy of the screened figures can be recorded as a file for printing.

Table 3.3 shows the output for *Kellogg's Corn Flakes* using the figures shown in Table 3.1 (a quarterly penetration of 20 per cent and a purchase frequency of 2.1). Because

Table 3.3 Output from Program NBD

	1 day	1 week	4 weeks	12 weeks	24 weeks	48 weeks	1 year
Penetration (b)	0.00	0.03	0.10	**0.20**	0.28	0.36	0.36
Purchase frequency (w)	1.02	1.11	1.40	**2.10**	3.04	4.73	5.01
Repeat purchase %	2.97	16.82	40.99	**61.65**	71.61	78.88	79.60
Purchase freq of repeat buyers	1.03	1.18	1.63	**2.55**	3.67	5.60	5.91
Purchase freq of new buyers	1.01	1.09	1.24	**1.38**	1.45	1.49	1.49
Proportion							
– not buying	1.00	0.97	0.90	**0.80**	0.72	0.64	0.64
– buying once	0.00	0.03	0.07	**0.11**	0.11	0.11	0.11
twice	0.00	0.00	0.02	**0.04**	0.06	0.06	0.06
3 times	0.00	0.00	0.01	**0.02**	0.03	0.04	0.04
4 times	0.00	0.00	0.00	**0.01**	0.02	0.03	0.03
5 times	0.00	0.00	0.00	**0.01**	0.01	0.02	0.02
6 plus	0.00	0.00	0.00	**0.01**	0.04	0.10	0.10
Proportion of sales due to those buying							
once	0.97	0.82	0.52	**0.25**	0.14	0.07	0.06
twice	0.03	0.15	0.26	**0.21**	0.13	0.07	0.07
3 times	0.00	0.03	0.12	**0.15**	0.12	0.07	0.07
4 times	0.00	0.00	0.05	**0.11**	0.10	0.07	0.06
5 times	0.00	0.00	0.02	**0.08**	0.09	0.06	0.06
6 plus	0.00	0.00	0.02	**0.19**	0.43	0.66	0.69

the program does not have a quarterly column the figures were attributed to the 12 weeks column, which is highlighted. If you look down this column you see first the input penetration and purchase frequency, then the predicted repeat purchase rate of about 62 per cent; below this is the purchase frequency of repeat buyers – about 20 per cent higher than the purchase frequency of the whole group – and the purchase frequency of new buyers, about 1.4. The remainder of this column (using three places of decimals) provides the theoretical data for Table 3.4 in which empirical data from Table 3.1 are compared with the theoretical prediction. If you inspect Table 3.4, you will see that the agreement is close.

Table 3.4 Quarterly sales of cornflakes in the United States. Observed (O) and theoretical (T) values

				Out of 100 purchasers, the number buying							
Once		Twice		3 times		4 times		5 times		6+ times	
O	T	O	T	O	T	O	T	O	T	O	T
55	53	22	22	8	11	5	6	5	4	5	6
Giving sales of:											
55	53	44	44	24	33	20	24	25	20	42	36

The output of Program NBD also allows us to see how penetration and purchase frequency change when periods of different duration are used. Table 3.5 shows how the penetration and purchase frequency rise as the period of time is successively doubled. (Table 3.5 is obtained by assigning figures to incorrect time periods in Program NBD, e.g. the 12-week figures are assigned to 48 weeks so that the nominal 12- and 24-week figures are then actually 3- and 6-week.) Mean sales are given by the product of penetration and purchase frequency and, in a stationary market, these must keep step with the time period; we can see that this is so from the bottom row. This means that, when penetration is low, changes in sales are mainly related to changes in penetration, and when penetration is high, the sales changes depend more on changes in purchase frequency. When the periods are long, Table 3.5 shows that each doubling in the period produces about the same absolute penetration increase, while the purchase frequency gets close to doubling when the period is doubled.

Table 3.5 Change in purchase data over time (theoretical)

	3 weeks	6 weeks	12 weeks	24 weeks	48 weeks	96 weeks	192 weeks
Penetration (b)	0.08	0.13	0.20	0.28	0.36	0.44	0.51
Purchase frequency (w)	1.3	1.6	2.1	3.0	4.7	7.8	13.5
Mean sales (bw)	0.1	0.2	0.4	0.9	1.7	3.4	6.9

Program NBD is easy to use and is needed to answer questions in Exercises 3.3–3.6. It has one technical limitation: when the penetration is high and the purchase frequency is low the mathematical procedure for estimating k breaks down and the user must then extrapolate from results obtained with lower penetration figures.

Does the NBD give the best prediction?

Marketing scientists have tried to improve on the predictions derived from the NBD by adjustment of the mathematics. One suggestion is that NBD theory might be modified to allow for the temporary loss of buying interest following a purchase. But any gain would be marginal since the theory is already very close to panel evidence. Usually the random variation in panel data is rather larger than any differences between the predictions of competing mathematical models. In a comparison of theories, Schmittlein, Bemmaor and Morrison (1985) concluded that the NBD model was hard to beat. A further paper by Morrison and Schmittlein (1988) identified three ways in which real behaviour tended to depart from NBD assumptions, but noted that these effects tended to cancel each other out so that the NBD remained a good predictive model.

Exercise 3.3 Using Program NBD: How the period affects the data

---

1. Assume that 0.05 of the population buys an average of 1.5 *Snickers* in each 4-week period. Use Program NBD to establish the penetration, b, and the purchase frequency, w, and mean sales, m (=bw) for the given periods and fill in the table below. (If you enter the 4-week data as 1-week data, all results will be for four times the tabled period.)

	Weeks:	6	12	24	48	96	192
b:							
w:							
bw:							

    Make a plot of these variables over time and state how they change.

2. Can you compute the proportion of the population who buy no *Snickers* in four years?
3. Notice that the purchase rate for new buyers is relatively constant for longer periods. See whether it remains so for different b and w input data.

Exercise 3.4 Collecting panel data for comparison with NBD predictions

---

NBD predictions can be tested against panel data gathered by the class. You, and others, must keep a diary and record when you engage in a consumer activity such as phoning your friends or drinking beer. Table 3.6 records the data from 224 students for one day together with the distribution that is predicted from the NBD model; you can see that the fit is close.

Table 3.6 Number of students making 1, 2, 3, etc. telephone calls in a day

Number calling:	Once	Twice	3 times	4 times	5 times	6+ times
Observed:	75	30	8	0	0	1
Predicted:	75	28	8	2	0	0

Note: b = 0.51; w = 1.46.

Exercise 3.5   Exploring the relationships

---

1. Use the *Snickers* data from Exercise 3.3 to work out the ratio of the purchase frequency of repeat buyers to the general purchase frequency (both given by Program NBD). Try this for other data inputs. You will find that it is consistently about 1.2.

2. What proportion of all *Snickers* purchases are made by people buying more often than once a month? How might you promote the product to such people?

3. Treat all cigarettes as one brand. Suppose that the penetration is 0.33 and the purchase frequency is 5 for the whole population per week. The NBD calculation shows that 79 per cent should repeat purchase, but panel research gives a much higher figure. The market is stationary. How would you explain this discrepancy? What is the real population here?

The point to note here is that the penetration of cigarette purchasing *among cigarette smokers* is near 100 per cent in a week so that 33 per cent penetration in the whole population is an artificial figure and produces discrepancies if used for the calculation.

Exercise 3.6   Marketing analyses

---

1. Brand R was launched 18 months ago. With continuing advertising support it has maintained a penetration of 4 per cent and a purchase frequency of 1.4 per quarter, but is scarcely viable. Panel research shows a repeat purchase rate of 21 per cent. Should you stop the advertising? Withdraw the brand? Maintain both? To answer this you need to calculate, using Program NBD, the theoretical repeat purchase and see whether it agrees with the observed figure. Also see the earlier section on repeat purchase.

2. The consumption of soup rises in the winter and falls in the summer. Find out whether all those who buy soup reduce their consumption in the summer or whether there are two groups: those who buy it all the year with much the same frequency, and those who buy it only in the winter. Panel data show that those who buy soup in the summer show a penetration of 32 per cent and a purchase frequency of 5 over 12 weeks. When these people are followed into the higher consumption winter period, panel data show that their quarterly repeat purchase is 79 per cent. What do you conclude? You need to calculate, using Program NBD, whether this repeat purchase is the norm for a stationary market. If it is then you have two separate groups: the all-year stationary buyers and seasonal buyers who only enter the market in the winter. For more information see Wellan and Ehrenberg (1990).

3. In January, 5 per cent of the population bought brand C on 4.4 occasions. In February, C was promoted and 8 per cent of the population bought it. Panel data show that 79 per cent of January buyers bought again in February. How did the promotion affect repeat purchase and new purchase respectively? Fill in the rest of the table given below. Start with the February total which you get from the ratio of the penetrations, 5 per cent and 8 per cent; if you get 100 purchasers when the penetration is 5 per cent how many will you get when it is 8 per cent? Next, calculate the repeat purchasers expected from the NBD model. The remaining figures can be inferred by subtraction from the totals.

For every 100 buyers in January the buyers in February will be		
	Expected from NBD model	Observed from panel data
Repeat purchasers		79
New purchasers		
Totals	100	

Patterns of purchase in the whole category

We now address the following questions:

- How do penetrations and purchase frequencies vary in a product category?
- What changes do we see in penetration or purchase frequency when market share changes?
- Can we predict the buying frequency and penetration of a new entrant to the market when it achieves a given market share?
- When people buy more than one brand, what pattern of cross-purchase is found?
- Does the evidence favour a 'niche' or a 'me-too' strategy in product positioning?
- Is television watching like brand purchasing?
- How can multibrand purchase patterns be modelled mathematically?

Purchase frequencies and penetrations in a product field

Table 3.7 presents data on the US instant coffee market in 1981, ordered by average sales. You can see that penetration and purchase frequency are related. This table is typical of what is found in most packeted goods markets and it deserves careful scrutiny. We see that although the purchase frequencies rise with increase in penetration, they *do not increase much*. If you compare *Maxim* with *Folgers*, which has three times the sales, you can see that the higher sales level is derived mainly from the higher penetration.

Table 3.7 Penetrations, purchase frequencies and mean sales (%) in the US instant coffee market. MRCA panel data over 48 weeks, 1981

	Penetration (b) %	Purchase frequency (w)	Mean sales (bw) %
Maxwell House	24	3.6	86
Sanka	21	3.2	69
Taster's Choice	22	2.8	62
High Point	22	2.6	57
Folgers	18	2.7	49
Nescafé	13	2.9	38
Brim	9	2.0	18
Maxim	6	2.6	16
Mean	**17**	**2.8**	**48**

On reflection, the low variation in purchase frequency is not so surprising. If the purchase frequency of *Folgers* is much larger than *Maxim*, it is either because *Folgers* people drink more coffee or because a higher proportion of their brand portfolio is *Folgers*, in other words, they are more loyal. It seems unlikely that the brand of coffee that a person drinks has much impact on total consumption. We do not expect everyone to drink the same amount, but it would be odd if the people who drink *Folgers* consume, on average, much more or less than those who drink *Maxim*. Indeed, often people will drink both brands and therefore necessarily have the same category consumption. In fact, for each brand, the average category purchase is close to nine units a year. The other possible explanation was that those who buy brands with a high market share are more loyal and make the brand a higher proportion of their portfolio; a buyer could make all their purchases *Folgers* instead of less than a third. In practice, there is a small tendency to be more loyal to the bigger brands; brand leaders in particular tend to be more exclusively bought and we see that *Maxwell House* is bought on 3.6 occasions in the year, distinctly higher than the average purchase frequency.

The relationship between penetration and purchase frequency occurs for stable markets and may not apply during the turbulence of a sales promotion. Motes and Woodside (1984) found gains in both penetration and purchase frequency during a sales campaign. But once sales have stabilized after a market intervention, any change in market share will show up mainly as a change in the penetration variable. However, this conclusion assumes relatively low penetrations and the picture changes when we assess sales over long periods of time when penetration is near its maximum; we return to this matter shortly.

Double jeopardy

The relationship between penetration and purchase frequency in a product field fits the pattern known as *double jeopardy* (Ehrenberg, Goodhardt and Barwise, 1990). Double jeopardy was described by the sociologist McPhee (1963: 133–40) who credits the original idea to the broadcaster Jack Landis; McPhee noted how less popular radio presenters suffer in two ways: fewer people have heard of them and, among those who have heard of them, they are less appreciated. Applied to brands, double jeopardy implies the pattern seen in Table 3.7: that less popular brands are not only bought by fewer people (lower penetration) but are also bought less often (lower frequency) by those who do buy them.

Ehrenberg, Goodhardt and Barwise show that double jeopardy is a ubiquitous phenomenon, occurring in such fields as the consumption of TV programmes, consumer durables, industrial goods and newspapers. McPhee's explanation for double jeopardy took account of differential awareness. People who are aware of less popular presenters are usually also aware of more popular presenters and thus are more likely to 'split their vote' compared with those who have only heard of the more popular broadcasters. Applying McPhee's account to brands, the less popular brand is bought by fewer people, many of whom will also buy more popular brands and will thus have to divide their purchases more, while those buying more popular brands are more likely to buy only such brands. Ehrenberg, Goodhardt and Barwise point out that the challenge for the less popular brand is not only to equal the quality of its better known competitor, but also to make itself more widely accepted.

Attempts to raise purchase frequency

There are some situations where increased consumption of a brand might be expected to come from more frequent use by existing buyers rather than by adoption by new buyers. One such situation arose in the case of Hellman's mayonnaise when it was new to the British market. The manufacturers found that the British used Hellman's mayonnaise on little else but salads, a habit which had been learned from earlier experience with salad cream (this vinegary concoction, beloved by the British, looks rather like mayonnaise). The advertising for Hellman's was therefore designed to expand the number of uses of the product.

The case report (Channon, 1985) shows that, following the advertising, 40 per cent of users were trying the product in the new ways suggested in the campaign, and claimed to be doing this more than buyers of competitive products. This suggests that there was some gain in purchase frequency relative to other brands but exact figures are not reported. However, there was also a substantial gain in penetration which accounted for much of the increase in sales. Although this case provides some evidence of gain in purchase frequency, it also underlines the importance of making a penetration gain if a brand is to increase its share.

What changes when market share changes?

Table 3.7 is useful in showing the way in which penetration and purchase frequency may be expected to change. Major changes over short periods of time are rare, but if *Brim* were to treble its sales, it is unlikely, looking at Table 3.7, that it could do so by getting all existing buyers to use three times as much. The closeness of brand purchase frequencies in the category means that sales have to grow mainly by increases in penetration and this means that, if *Brim* trebled its sales, it would have a purchase pattern similar to that of *Folgers* with most of the sales gain coming from an increase in penetration. Sometimes a gain in frequency may be possible by persuading consumers to find new uses for a product, for example, by pouring bleach down drains to disinfect them, or by eating cereals at tea-time, but this is a new use of the *category* which is likely to raise the purchase frequencies of all brands in that category.

This analysis can be applied to *Curly Wurly*, a chocolate-coated toffee liked by children in Britain. In 1982, advertising substantially increased purchase over four months and the new level then remained approximately constant for the rest of the year (Channon, 1985: 168). From the published data it appears that among 7–11-year-old children the two-monthly penetration shifted by an average of 60 per cent while the purchase frequency increased by a mere 6 per cent. Among adult purchasers the main gain was also in penetration. Thus this case showed that sales gains arose mainly from penetration gains, in line with the double jeopardy pattern.

The relative constancy of purchase frequency is also important to those who are hoping to break into a market with a new brand. With enough advertising money and a sound product they may occasionally achieve high market share but what they cannot expect is a sales pattern that is radically different from that achieved by established brands. If they succeed with the new brand the double jeopardy pattern defines the form of their success in terms of penetration and purchase frequency. Supporting this, Wellan and Ehrenberg (1988) found that, after rapidly established market leadership on the British market, a new soap called *Shield* registered a purchase frequency appropriate to its new position, i.e. slightly more than its competitors. This evidence gives little comfort to those who want their brand to be a niche product which is bought heavily by only a small proportion of category buyers; such patterns are rare and marketing plans that assume such outcomes are unlikely to be fulfilled. The limits that market patterns place on marketing objectives are discussed by Ehrenberg and Uncles (1996).

Treasure (1975) has pointed out that when sales figures are aggregated over long periods, changes in purchase level appear to be based more on changes in purchase frequency and less on penetration. Over short periods an infrequent buyer tends to be a non-buyer in the reference period and is therefore registered as a penetration gain when he/she buys in a later period. Over longer periods the infrequent buyer is more likely to purchase in the reference period and therefore any gains in purchase in later periods will be recorded as purchase frequency gains. Treasure's observation does not change the fact that, over typical periods, any major shift in sales pattern is normally within the double jeopardy frame. What we should note is that light buyers are involved in sales change whatever the period taken and that the sales gains among light buyers show as a penetration or frequency gain, depending on the period of assessment.

We have already seen that brands have many light buyers and few heavy buyers; because of their numbers, light buyers *in aggregate* may offer more scope for sales gain than the heavy buyers. However, when purchasers of a brand are considered *individually* it is clear that most time should be spent on the few heavy buyers whose loss could be very damaging. Thus techniques like advertising that access many people may be most relevant to light buyers, while the more resource-intensive methods of relationship marketing are probably better focused on the heavier buyer.

Exactly how the new sales are distributed when a brand gains share is not fully understood. For example, new purchasers could show the same frequency profile as existing purchasers or they might show a lower average purchase rate with the old buyers increasing their frequency a little. The Wellan and Ehrenberg (1988) evidence suggests that new buyers have much the same frequency distribution as old buyers; this might also be inferred from the East and Hammond (1996) study, which showed that the erosion of repeat-purchase loyalty (and the gain in new purchasers) is not related to weight of purchase.

Patterns of multibrand purchase

As we saw in Chapter 2, most buyers buy more than one brand in the category. In the US instant coffee market, the average share of category requirement is 30 per cent; in the British gasoline market it is 20 per cent. In the cereal market, where people seek variety, the SCR is even lower. Table 3.8 presents data on 'other brand buying' by buyers of specified brands of cereal in the United States and the United Kingdom which shows the low SCR, particularly in the United States where there are more cereal brands available. Ehrenberg remarks that 'your buyers are the buyers of other brands who occasionally buy you'. (However, remember that the SCR includes any buyer of the brand and, if we just look at those who buy the brand in preference to others, the first-brand loyalty is much higher than the SCR.)

Table 3.8 Cereal brand purchases in a year by those buying a specified brand

	Specified brand	Other brands
Nabisco Shredded Wheat (USA)	4	37
Nabisco Shredded Wheat (UK)	7	33
Kellogg's Corn Flakes (USA)	5	29
Kellogg's Corn Flakes (UK)	10	23

In Chapter 2 a number of reasons for multibrand buying were presented. Some of these reasons imply that people see certain brands as substitutable and therefore they buy them interchangeably. If most buyers see brands X and Y as substitutable in this way, we would see this effect in aggregate data on cross-purchase. Such cross-purchasing of brands would create purchase subsets or *market partitioning*. Ehrenberg and Goodhardt (1979) demonstrate that this effect does occur, e.g. in children's cereals, where those who buy one sweetened cereal are more likely to buy another sweetened cereal rather than an unsweetened brand. What do we find in most grocery markets? The evidence shows that usually the frequency of purchasing of other brands is directly proportional to the penetration of those other brands. Ehrenberg (1988) calls this the *duplication of purchase law*. This law is a logical consequence of the fact that there is little market partitioning; if people do not collectively cluster their other brand purchase around special similarities between brands, then the aggregate effect of their other brand purchasing must reflect the way in which purchasers generally distribute themselves, i.e. penetration levels.

Some people find this puzzling because they know from their own behaviour that they do substitute a limited number of brands in a category. But although many of us will have our own personally preferred groupings of brands there may be little agreement between us. One person may buy *Colgate* and *Crest*, another *Crest* and *Macleans*, a third *Macleans* and a retailer's own label. When these diverse combinations are put together, the different individual preferences will average out so that, usually, there is little evidence of market partitioning at an aggregate level. When a partitioning does occur it can usually be connected with distinct product features such as price, product form (e.g. liquid/powdered detergent, leaded/unleaded petrol) or common brand name, rather than with the less tangible claims of the brand that may be identified in advertising. M. Collins (1971) has reviewed this issue in a succinct paper.

Table 3.9 shows how buyers of one brand of toothpaste also bought other brands. The brands are arranged in market share order. The second row from the bottom shows the average cross-purchase, i.e. the mean percentage of people buying the brand in addition to another brand, and we see that the brand leader *Colgate*, with an average of 34 per cent, is bought by buyers of other brands rather more than the rest. But this cross-purchase is in line with its penetration (bottom row) and fits the relationship between cross-purchase and penetration shown by other brands. To show the correspondence between the bottom two rows the penetration is multiplied by a constant, in this case 1.5. The constant (known as the duplication constant, D) varies from market to market.

Table 3.9 Cross-purchase in the British toothpaste market

% buyers of:	Market share	Colgate GRF	Aquafresh	Who also bought Crest	Macleans Fresh	Mentadent	Colgate gel
Colgate GRF	18	–	19	18	20	12	32
Aquafresh	9	30	–	26	28	14	23
Crest	8	32	28	–	23	17	24
Macleans Fresh	8	31	27	20	–	12	21
Mentadent	7	28	21	22	18	–	20
Colgate gel	7	53	24	23	23	15	–
Average duplication (all brands)		**34**	**24**	**21**	**23**	**15**	**22**
1.5 × penetration		**36**	**22**	**21**	**24**	**15**	**21**

Source: AGB (1985).

Table 3.9 also shows a higher level of cross-purchase between *Colgate GRF* and *Colgate gel*, i.e. the buyers of one version tend to buy the other version more than would be expected from their penetrations. This effect is common where two products with the same brand name compete in the same field. This helps to illustrate how cannibalization of parent sales occurs when a line extension is launched (see Chapter 2); the new brand is more likely to take sales from the parent.

The implications for positioning

In marketing, much importance has been given to positioning. A brand's positioning is the set of beliefs about it that the manufacturer and advertising agency seek to establish in the minds of potential purchasers: it is an *intended brand image*. For example *Stella Artois* is sold in Britain as 'reassuringly expensive', a strapline implying high quality. One consequence of the cross-purchase evidence is that new brands do not need to have some unique formulation to succeed, a finding which has worried those who value brand positioning. But if cross-purchase between brands depends largely upon penetrations with exceptions relating only to price, formulation or brand name, we must conclude that the product positioning exercise may be overvalued. Consumers do not usually appear to group fmcg brands on the basis of image features, and positioning, with its implication that each brand occupies a distinct niche, is poorly supported; when advertising does succeed (as in the case of *Stella Artois*) it may be because the product has high awareness as a result of the advertising and not because it is seen as subtly different from other brands in its category. Indeed, many successful brands may do well because they are perceived as typical of other brands in the category rather than as different from those other brands. Thus Ehrenberg recommends that manufacturers focus on the strategy which is often called 'me-too' – copying the formulation and appearance of existing successful brands and thereby trading on established purchase habits. This is a strategy much used by retailers when they design private label brands.

Despite this analysis, the niche approach is well established in marketing thinking and the evidence that there is little market partitioning surprises brand managers and those responsible for new product development, who give careful attention to the positioning of their brands. They are clearly right to do so when there are real differences between brands, e.g. in the confectionery market. What is more at issue is whether minor differences, in fields such as washing-up liquid, can have much effect on sales.

Niche markets

There is one defence of niche branding that should be mentioned. It may be agreed that we each have a preferred group of brands as individual buyers and that personal preferences tend to cancel out in the aggregate. However specific population segments could have markedly different patterns of preference which are obscured in the overall average. To test for this it is necessary to compare the consumers who buy different brands to see whether they differ in terms of demography or beliefs. One study has compared the demographic profiles of brand buyers in different categories (Hammond, Ehrenberg and Goodhardt, 1996); this work showed very little difference between the buyers of different brands, except in the case of cereals where certain brands were bought only when there were children in the household. Given this evidence, the realistic assumption is that there is little difference between the buyers of any two brands in a packaged goods category; this is not so surprising when we remember that buyers of one brand may often be buyers of the other brand.

The close association between 'other brand' purchase rates and penetration will fail when brands lack a common distribution structure; the availability of brands obviously affects choice alternatives. Thus local variation in distribution will produce local variation in other brand purchases. Those who prefer John Smith's beer may sometimes find themselves drinking Tetley's as an alternative in Yorkshire because this brand is abundant there; in Surrey the second choice could have been Courage. Uncles and Ehrenberg (1990) have shown this effect with stores; in the United States the cross-purchase between Safeway and Lucky is higher than the prediction from the penetrations because these chains tend to have stores in the same areas.

Watching television

Television viewing has been shown to have similarities to brand purchase in studies by Goodhardt, Ehrenberg and Collins (1987). When the programme is a serial, repeat viewing is like repeat purchase and we can ask how much programme loyalty exists, as measured by repeat viewing. The evidence shows that there is loyalty, particularly for the serial with a very high rating; in Britain about 55 per cent of those watching a serial will repeat view in the following week, but this figure is derived from several different loyalties. Some people watch more than others (i.e. are loyal to the medium) and this raises their chance of being a viewer; some people are channel-loyal so that serials on favourite channels have a better repeat-viewing chance; and some people watch more at particular times of the day so that time-loyalty may enhance repeat viewing. These three loyalties ensure that people who have been watching a serial are quite likely to be tuned to the same channel at the same time of the week *after the serial has ended*. The difference between this end-of-serial viewing and the repeat viewing when the serial is running indicates the true loyalty to the programme. This analysis has similarities to other ways of partitioning loyalty, for example, to the way in which loyalty to a car is divided between brand, model and specification.

Goodhardt, Ehrenberg and Collins (1987) do find some programme partitioning, for example, those who watch one sports programme are more likely to watch other sports programmes, but they also note that people watch a wide variety of programmes so that a relatively unpartitioned duplication of viewing occurs. This means that terrestrial TV is a *broadcast*, not a *narrowcast*, medium and this makes it difficult to target specific social groups accurately using the main television channels. This is surprising to many programme planners who think that a specialist programme is watched by a specialist audience; they have 'programme positioning' assumptions similar to the niche positioning assumptions of some marketers. Developments in media may lead to changes in the patterns of viewing; satellite and cable channels dedicated to sport or music have had some success and this may be partly because channel and programme content loyalties are here combined.

The opportunity to watch (or record) a serial is restricted to the time when it is transmitted and this makes TV viewing slightly different from purchase which is less time constrained. This difference is allowed for in the mathematical theory used to predict viewing rates.

The Dirichlet model

The Dirichlet theory was foreshadowed in work by Chatfield and Goodhardt (1975) and treated more fully by Bass, Jeuland and Wright (1976); it was later presented in a comprehensive form by Goodhardt, Ehrenberg and Chatfield (1984). The Dirichlet is a mathematical model which predicts the likelihood of purchase for *all* the brands in a product field. The assumptions are similar to those for the single brand NBD model but, in addition, it is assumed that the market has no partitioning. The model does not apply if there is appreciable evidence of brand clustering on any other basis than penetration.

Inputs to a Dirichlet analysis are:

■ The penetration for the product type, B, that is, the proportion of households that buy the category at all in a given period.

■ The purchase frequency for the product type, W, that is, the average number of purchases made by households that buy the product at all in a given period.

■ The number of brands and the market shares of individual brands (or individual b and w values for each brand).

Two programs work on Dirichlet assumptions. BUYER (Uncles, 1988) is a computer program for Dirichlet predictions which accepts aggregate measures or alternatively raw data from which these measures can be computed; it is not user-friendly. Another program, DIRPRED, is used commercially.

The output of BUYER can give predictions of penetration, purchase frequency, sole buyers, sole buyer purchase frequency, proportions of buyers at different frequencies and sales distributions for single brands or the whole field. This output therefore illustrates the theoretical market position of a brand in relation to other brands and is useful for evaluating actual brand performance. Table 3.10 shows the real data for US instant coffee together with the Dirichlet norms. In most cases the fit is close but we see some small discrepancies. In particular, brand leaders tend to exceed the Dirichlet norms for purchase frequency and sole brand buying. We also note that the purchase frequency of *Brim* is below the norm; this figure was corroborated for that year by other research but did not happen in later years; it could have occurred as a result of a larger than usual number of sales promotions which raised the proportion of one-off purchasers and therefore reduced the purchase frequency.

Table 3.10 Observed and predicted purchase frequencies and sole brand buyers in the US instant coffee market. MRCA panel data over 48 weeks, 1981

	Purchase frequency (w)		% buyers who are 100% loyal	
	Observed	*Dirichlet*	*Observed*	*Dirichlet*
Maxwell House	3.6	3.2	20	18
Sanka	3.3	3.0	20	17
Taster's Choice	2.8	2.9	24	16
High Point	2.6	2.9	18	16
Folgers	2.7	2.9	13	15
Nescafé	2.9	2.8	15	14
Brim	2.0	2.6	17	13
Maxim	2.6	2.6	11	13
Mean	**2.8**	**2.9**	**17**	**15**

Applications of models in marketing

Ehrenberg and Uncles (1996) point out that mathematical models provide norms against which real markets can be assessed. One management implication of such norms is to define the realistic options that are open to those who want to improve the share of their brand or who want to launch a new brand on the market. Models also provide norms for cross-purchase in an unpartitioned market and illustrate the long-run propensity to buy a repertoire of brands. When markets are partitioned (e.g. powdered and liquid detergent), we can see the extent to which this partitioning affects cross-purchase. In some cases the market analysis, coupled with Dirichlet norms, may help to show how much of a market is accessible to competition; for example, if a new environmentally friendly detergent is being contemplated, is the competition all detergents, or all detergents that make environmental claims?

My own view is that a major value of this work lies in management education; an understanding of stationary markets helps managers to read their own brand statistics and to understand the ways in which change may, or may not, be brought about. With regard to change, I think that Ehrenberg and Uncles (1996) are somewhat pessimistic about the scope for marketing intervention; they treat the stationary market as normal and argue that it is rare to find growth or exclusive loyalty. One may agree with this but still be less pessimistic. Often marketers cancel out each other's actions but sometimes they may do a bit better than their competitors by careful analysis of the possibilities or by using an exceptionally creative campaign. Thus, sometimes marketing effort is rewarded by growth, and when this occurs the new sales levels fit the model norms. We saw this with *Curly Wurly* and it implies that the Dirichlet is no straitjacket. Also stationary market research has generally been confirmatory in approach, showing the fit between data and models, rather than testing for exceptions. When exceptions have been found they have not been zealously pursued, though it is information on such exceptions that may help us to see how to 'buck the market'. Finally, we should note that stationary market analysis ignores long-term trends which do occur and which can be important to profits.

Summary

Over periods of three months to a year the sales of most established brands are approximately stationary: short-term fluctuations are averaged out and longer-term trends are too long-term to have much effect. The steady state of such markets arises because most buyers in a category maintain their propensities to buy the same group of brands for long periods of time.

The penetration and purchase frequency of a brand are key statistics. These measures encode most of the buying patterns of the brand so that there is no need to know anything more about the brand in order to predict other sales characteristics. This makes mathematical modelling possible.

Brands have few heavy buyers but these are responsible for much of the sales; the heaviest half of buyers typically make 80 per cent of the purchases.

When the brands in a category are compared, it is found that variation in sales is mostly accounted for by the variation in penetration (over shorter periods). Purchase frequency rises only slightly as penetration rises and this pattern fits the rule of double jeopardy.

The NBD and Dirichlet models will predict the distributions of sales in a stationary market and rest on assumptions that purchase incidence is Poisson, purchase rates in a population of buyers are Gamma, and that (in the case of the Dirichlet) there is no market partitioning. The predictions from such models usually fit the data derived from panel research; where the fit is poor, the model provides benchmark norms for interpreting the exceptional behaviour of the market.

Analysis of panel data shows that sales gains tend to come from the large number of light buyers rather than the small number of heavy buyers, which makes it unlikely that market success will occur because of intensive purchase by few people.

Analysis of cross-purchase suggests that there is little market partitioning; the absence of substitution patterns between specific brands raises problems for those who believe the brand positioning claims made for fmcg brands.

Further reading

There is a very useful working paper by Ehrenberg, A.S.C. and Uncles, M.D. (1996) *Dirichlet-Type Markets: A Review*, South Bank University Business School.

The phenomenon of double jeopardy is well explained by Ehrenberg, A.S.C., Goodhardt, G.J. and Barwise, T.P. (1990) Double jeopardy revisited, *Journal of Marketing*, 54, July, 82–91.

A clearly written but technical account of the NBD is by Morrison, D. and Schmittlein, D.C. (1988) Generalizing the NBD model for customer purchases: What are the implications and is it worth the effort?, *Journal of Business and Economic Statistics*, 6: 2, 145–66.

Chapter 4

Consumer response to price and sales promotions

In this chapter you will find:

- Evidence on shoppers' knowledge of prices and the way price references are used to form judgements about a product.

- Reports of how brand price elasticities can be measured and evidence from research on these elasticities.

- Descriptions of the sales impact and duration of effect of price discounts, and evidence of the way they combine with other sales promotion methods.

- Evidence on the differential impact of price promotions on different loyalty segments.

- A report on the effects of a long-term loyalty scheme.

- A discussion of 'small brand advantage'.

Price

In traditional economics prices have been treated simply as costs; the recognition that a price serves to inform the consumer about the good is of more recent origin. In free markets, consumers judge whether a product is good value or not, and if so, whether they should buy it or not. Often there is little direct information on the quality of the product, and price is one of the indicators used to assess quality and hence value for money. Usually higher price signals better quality,[1] and the gain in perceived quality reduces the deterrent effect of price.

The deterrent effect of price is not a simple function of its magnitude, but depends upon whether the price is judged to be high or low for that particular product. As we noted in Chapter 1, judgements have two components: one is the piece of information

---

[1] But not always. When there is a glut of fruit or vegetables, the price is often low and the quality high.

such as price; the second component is a frame of reference against which the information is evaluated. Thus whether a given price is seen as high or low depends upon the frame used by the consumer. Such frames of reference affect our judgement about whether a price is fair, good value, etc. (Gabor, 1977; 1988).

Knowledge of price

No judgement is possible if shoppers take no heed of price and here the evidence is mixed. An early study by Gabor and Granger (1961) found that 82 per cent of Nottingham housewives could state a price for products that they had bought in the previous week, and of these at least 70 per cent were correct. It should be noted that this study was conducted when manufacturers could enforce prices and there was little price variability between stores or over time. In the United States there was no price control and price recall figures were lower; in 1974, *Progressive Grocer* reported that customers knew the price (to within 5 per cent) for only 20 per cent of the sixty highly advertised and competitive supermarket brands chosen for study. Ten years earlier, *Progressive Grocer* had found a greater knowledge of price, and Gabor points out that the high inflation in 1974 could have affected recall; another explanation for the decline in price knowledge could have been the increase over the ten years in the total number of brands available to shoppers. The *Progressive Grocer* studies did not require the respondents to have purchased the brands and this also helps to explain the shoppers' lack of price knowledge.

Riley-Smith (1984) found that 40 per cent of British shoppers did not look at prices. More recently, Dickson and Sawyer (1990) found that less than half of US shoppers could give the correct price for the item that they had just put into their shopping trolley; this finding was corroborated by Boutillier, Boutillier and Neslin (1994) for coffee, but not for soda, where 71 per cent could recall the exact price they paid. This indicates that we need to study a number of categories to measure shoppers' knowledge of prices. If recall of price has fallen, this change could be related to more promotions, more brands and greater affluence (making price less important to consumers than before). McGoldrick and Marks (1987) discuss some of the retail changes that could affect shoppers' knowledge of prices.

This evidence suggests that price is of no consequence to many purchasers but this simplifies the issue. Although people may take prices on trust on many occasions, they may at other times check on how much they are paying and react against suppliers who are seen to overcharge. In addition, the price of a limited number of goods may be used as a key to the overall value for money offered by a store.

Exercise 4.1 Your price knowledge

Keep the scanner record of your last purchases in a supermarket. Without looking at the prices get someone else to test you on your knowledge of the prices you paid. Score your responses according to whether they are exactly right, within 10 per cent, or outside this range. Compare your results with others.

■   Is there any evidence that frequently bought items are better remembered?
■   Are students likely to remember prices better?
■   Do members of a class of students differ in their accuracy and if so, why is this found?

Price ranges

Stoetzel (1954) suggested that consumers have an *acceptable price range* with *upper* and *lower limits*; when the price is beyond the upper limit the product is seen as too expensive by the buyer, either because it offers more than they want or because, at this price, it is not seen as good value for money; when the price is too low, the buyer may suspect the quality of the good and so avoid it. Thus to be considered for purchase the product must fall within the acceptable price range.

Raju (1977) found that the evaluation of three brands of stereo receiver accelerated and then decelerated with price, indicating a mid-range where the acceptability was highest. Rao and Monroe (1988) noted that those with little product knowledge have to rely on cues that are extrinsic to the product and these cues include price. Rao and Sieben (1992) reviewed the work on the prices that are acceptable to people with different knowledge of the product field. They argue that those with little product knowledge will have lower limits, essentially because they are unaware of product qualities that are worth paying for, a finding supported in their study. They also pointed out that those with little product knowledge would make more use of price as a quality indicator than those with medium knowledge. Somewhat tenuously they argue that very knowledgeable consumers will take account of price in markets where there is a strong price–quality relationship so that, in such markets, it is the most and the least knowledgeable that take most account of price when making a judgement. They found support for this effect using women's blazers as the product, but this may be a special case.

Although research using cars, microwave ovens and women's blazers indicates support for the idea of an acceptable price range, it is unlikely that fmcgs will show a lower limit because, in such markets, the brand authenticates the product so that its quality is not in question. If there is a lower limit, we would expect to find occasions where a rise in price *increases* sales as the price passes above the lower limit, but there is little evidence available of such an effect. Gabor (1977) cites cases where people prefer the higher priced brand of ink or car wax, but points out that in these situations the price of the brand is overshadowed by the cost of the fountain pen or car; such cases give no support to the existence of a lower price limit for most products. Doubts are increased when we look at the way in which the lower limit is measured; Gabor's question is:

Which is the lowest price at which you would still buy – I mean the price below which you would not trust the quality?

This question is biased and leads the respondent; a more neutral way of measuring any lower price cutoff is obviously possible – with such a measure there may be no discernible lower limit. There are also cases where individual brands clearly breach any category-based upper limit – consider the success of Dualit toasters (see box below).

Out of range?

Marketers would normally price a brand within the range set by existing products in the field but there are exceptions. In Britain, toasters are sold in a range of about £12–£30 and a toaster priced at £100 seems 'out of range'. But the Dualit toasters are priced at £100 or more and seem to have secured a share of the market. Designed for caterers, the Dualit products are solidly built in chrome and black and possess the minimum of gadgetry. The success of this brand in the retail market probably comes in part from their uncompromising style, which makes a statement about the owner. Such products indicate a person who is serious about their food and their kitchen. Clearly the Dualit has succeeded despite the price range assumptions that people may have.

Reference prices

A *reference price* (Monroe, 1979) is the figure that a would-be purchaser expects to pay; this reference price would fall within the acceptable price range, if there is one. There appears to be an area of price insensitivity around the reference price (Kalyanaram and Little, 1994). Whether they are accurate or not, reference prices act as frames for judging actual prices. When a product is cheaper than expected it is more likely to be purchased, and vice versa. Techniques for setting appropriate prices may survey consumers' reference prices and use the results to infer the proportion of potential purchasers that would buy at different prices. (There are a number of pricing techniques that are not discussed here; the reader is referred to Morgan, 1987.)

There are some problems with the reference price concept because a number of reference prices are possible. People may compare against the price they would *like* to pay, the price they *usually* pay or the price they regard as *fair* (Klein and Oglethorpe, 1987). Gabor (1977) claimed that the reference price could be treated as the price paid last time, while Jacobson and Obermiller (1990) point out that often the response to current offerings may be referenced against the price that consumers expect to pay *later*. Winer (1988) proposed eight different possible definitions of price reference.

The price–quality relationship

In marketing a *price–quality relationship* has been accepted for some time; it has been assumed that better quality goods tend to be more highly priced, so that people may

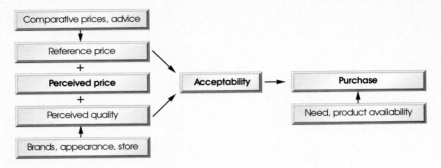

Figure 4.1 Price, acceptability and purchase

infer quality from price. We note first that, if they occur, such inferences may be mistaken; Hjorth-Anderson (1984) found little relationship between price and *objective* quality (derived from the product assessments in *Consumer Reports*, the publication of the American Consumer Association). An analysis of US studies by Tellis and Wernerfelt (1987) found a mean correlation between price and product quality of 0.27; this relationship was statistically significant, but the effect is small. The strength of the relationship is affected by the range of prices in the category and appears to be stronger for consumer durables. At the subjective level, Etgar and Malhotra (1981) showed evidence that price was unimportant to consumers as an indicator of quality for some products, and Sproles (1986) found evidence of a price–quality relationship for only 50 per cent of the categories studied. Zeithaml (1988) reviewed nearly ninety studies and found mixed support for a relationship between price and subjectively assessed quality. It seems that the inference of quality from price is rather less ubiquitous than has been supposed.

Quality perceptions depend on a number of factors in addition to price, such as the appearance of the product, the reports of others, the brand and the store which sells the product. High ticket items in upmarket stores may have their quality authenticated by the store context. By contrast, luxury goods may seem out of place in downmarket stores, and this may partly explain the reluctance of fashion manufacturers to distribute their products through discount shops. Shapiro (1973) looked at the effect of price, brand and store on a range of merchandise and concluded that all three had an influence on the perception of quality. Wheatley and Chiu (1977) found that darker carpet colours were associated with more quality; Pederson (1977) found that the colour of bread had more effect on quality perception than nutrition labelling or price, even though the colour was often produced by colouring agents. The quality of many products, such as vegetables, can usually be estimated by sight and touch, but other products, such as electronic goods, cannot easily be judged by their appearance which makes inference from price more likely.

From this review we see that price can influence acceptability either because of quality inferences or because of reference prices; this gives us the model shown in Figure 4.1. Notice that, as price rises, the acceptability of the product is raised by the price–quality relationship but reduced by the comparison against reference prices. Normally we expect the reference price effect to be stronger since otherwise sales would rise with increase in price.

The effect of initial selling price

Two pricing strategies for launching products are commonly identified. *Penetration* pricing keeps the initial price low, purchasers are gained more rapidly and competitors are discouraged, while *skimming* takes advantage of any monopoly position at launch to charge high prices and make more initial profit. When the product is relatively unfamiliar to purchasers the launch price helps to determine the reference price and may also affect the judgement of quality; a product launched at a high price may be seen as more valuable so that later, when the price is reduced, it is bought more heavily. Supporting this, a shop-based experiment by Doob *et al.* (1969) found that there were more total sales when the initial selling price was high than when it was low.

Such evidence does not mean that high initial selling prices are always to be preferred; the choice depends upon a number of marketing considerations, as noted above, and these may favour penetration pricing.

Variation in reference prices

Urbany, Bearden and Weilbaker (1988) have shown that the reference prices cited by respondents will change with experience; when people were given information about real prices they found that there was a movement of the reference price towards the real prices. An implication of this finding is that people differ in their reference prices for the same product, depending upon their experience. We would also expect that reference prices will vary somewhat for different brands in a category. Often the brand leader is more highly priced than the average; a higher reference price for the leader may come about through obvious public endorsement, advertising support or superior specification.

Price sensitivity

When sales are much affected by price changes we describe the consumer (and the product) as price-sensitive. Price sensitivity may vary between consumers, over time and between countries. Assael (1994) argues that the 1970s and 1980s saw a rise in price-consciousness among US consumers, which he relates to inflation and recession. Work at Kingston University (reported more fully in Chapter 9) showed a rise in the importance of price among British grocery buyers when recession effects were strong in 1994; parallel work by Debra Perkins at Purdue University (unpublished) indicated a similar effect in the United States in 1992 when recession effects were strongest. Changes in price awareness and sensitivity are also revealed in a detailed study of a city where supermarket provision doubled over a period of a month with accompanying price competition and heavy price-oriented advertising (Seiders and Costley, 1994). There was a 50 per cent shift in patronage in the city, with price quoted as a particularly important reason for change; consumer perceptions of the price levels of the different supermarket groups were very accurate. Compared with other shopping areas where there was less intense competition, price was more heavily cited as a reason for store use.

Research on brand price elasticity

Price elasticities are the ratio of sales change to price change; thus if sales go up 20 per cent when the price is cut by 10 per cent (a negative change), the price elasticity would be -2. Price elasticities tend to be non-linear and to increase disproportionately with larger discounts. One way of understanding this is to think of a $1 product and to cut the price by successive 10 cent amounts. The first cut is a 10 per cent discount, but the next cut is on 90 cents, making it an 11 per cent cut on this base, the next 10 cent cut on a base of 80 cents is a 12.5 per cent discount, and so on. As the implicit base falls the proportionate effect of the discount increases.

Researchers have tended to treat brand elasticities as relatively permanent and this may not be justified. We saw above how consumer price sensitivity could change with economic conditions, which implies an increase in elasticity (i.e. a larger negative number). A variety of other market factors may also affect a specific brand elasticity, such as the relationship between the brand's price and the prices of other brands in the category. If the price elasticity of a brand changes as a result of changes in market conditions, we must conclude that elasticity is not so much a property of the brand (constant over time and market context) but a property of the market.

Brand price elasticities have been measured in three ways: first, by comparing sales of discounted brands in stores with those at normal price; second, by using field experiments in which consumers are offered goods at regular intervals and the price is manipulated; and third, by statistical analysis of brand sales at the different prices that apply over a period of time. We consider these different methods below.

Store-level research

Studies using store data allow us to look at sales before and after the introduction of a discount. An attraction of this method is that the price change clearly occurs before any sales response so that any sales change can be treated as an effect of the price change with some confidence. A review of IRI findings by Fulgoni (1987) revealed a mean elasticity of about -2, but showed that the effect of a discount could be multiplied several times if either ad feature or product display were used with the discount; this research is considered in greater detail in the next section on sales promotions.

A number of studies have looked at sales after the promotion has finished and price has been restored to the pre-promotion level. If sales do not return to their previous level, there is a residual gain or loss which should be included in the elasticity calculation. The most comprehensive study on this issue (Ehrenberg, Hammond and

Goodhardt, 1994) found no net change, but other research has indicated a drop in purchase after prices return to the pre-deal level (Shoemaker and Shoaf, 1977; Helsen and Schmittlein, 1992), though effects seem quite small.

A further problem with store studies is that extra sales may come either from other brands and category expansion, or from the sales of the target brand in other stores where it is not discounted. When large stores and shopping malls advertise cuts they may increase local traffic at the expense of other outlets (Bucklin and Lattin, 1992). From the retailer's standpoint such gains are worthwhile, but the manufacturer secures no benefit from the displacement of sales from one store to another.

Field experiments
Ehrenberg and England (1990) investigated price elasticity using a field experimental method. Staff made fortnightly home visits to housewives and offered a limited selection of cereal, confectionery, soup, tea and biscuit brands for sale at prices that were a little below those in local supermarkets. After two visits, the prices of some brands were raised or lowered. The order of price changes was altered for different subgroups so that any effects based on price sequence could be detected.

Ehrenberg and England (1990) found that the response to price changes was immediate and was unaffected by the order of earlier changes, in other words, it was zero order. Price increases had slightly less percentage impact on sales than decreases, a result that is consistent with the usual shape of the demand curve. The mean elasticity obtained by Ehrenberg and England (weighted by brand size) was −2.6. Large brands had lower elasticities, so the unweighted mean was rather greater. There was little variation in price elasticity when categories or brands were compared, and Ehrenberg and England argue that the uniformity of their results stems from the uniformity of market conditions established by the experiment; the authors suggest that the response to a price change relates to the market context and in particular to the price relationships between competing brands. This means that we should look to differences in market conditions to explain differences in price elasticity between brands or categories. Supporting this, Ehrenberg (1986) showed that price sensitivity was much greater when the competitive brands in the experiment were very similar, and Castleberry, England and Ehrenberg (1989) found that price sensitivity was amplified when a price change produced price parity with a reference brand.

It is possible that Ehrenberg and England's field experimental method creates more homogeneous brand purchase groups than those found in the natural setting, which might account for the small differences between the observed elasticities. In normal markets we would expect price-sensitive consumers to gravitate towards cheaper or good value brands, while premium brands would be bought by people for whom price was not a priority. This leads us to expect that some brands will show more price elasticity than others under normal conditions because they are bought by more price-sensitive people. The field experimental design could encourage participants to buy brands that they would normally avoid, with the result that all the brands in a field experiment have rather similar buyer groups and hence tend towards a common elasticity.

Regression estimation

This technique creates a plot of sales by price from measures taken over a period of time and finds the slope of the line that fits the scatter of points best. In this procedure brand prices are related to the average price paid in the category, so that it is relative price rather than actual price that is used for the estimation.

Roberts (1980) found an average brand elasticity of -1.7. A meta-review by Tellis (1988) took account of 367 elasticities, drawn from 42 diverse studies; Tellis showed that a number of market factors were related to elasticity and that the mean elasticity across all the studies was -1.8. Tellis found more dispersion of price elasticities than Ehrenberg and England, a result that is to be expected from the wide range of market conditions under which the elasticities were estimated. Similarly, Telser (1962), Roberts (1980) and Broadbent (1989), using regression methods, have all reported a wider spread of elasticities than Ehrenberg and England.

Some concerns about brand price elasticities derived by regression are raised by Hamilton, East and Kalafatis (1997). In this study, elasticities were estimated on the top five brands in 100 categories (i.e. 500 brands) using three years' data from the AGB Superpanel. A major puzzle revealed by this study was that lower elasticities were obtained when the estimation had low reliability. The average elasticity (when it was negative) was -1.9 but this rose to -2.5 when estimates with an R^2 of less than 0.2 were excluded. Low reliability of the regression process should increase the spread of estimates, but should not affect the mean elasticity obtained. A surprisingly large 19 per cent of elasticities were positive, and here again the exclusion of weak estimates raised the average elasticity of the remainder from 1.0 to 2.3.

One explanation for the association between estimation reliability and elasticity is associated with the use of relative price. Brands will show a large change in relative price when they are discounted and small changes in relative price when competitors cut their prices. But consumers who do not buy a competitor brand are unlikely to show a response when it cuts its price; they will continue to see, and buy, their usual brand at its usual price, even though its relative price has changed. This thinking implies that brand A's discount often has little effect on brand B's sales – a fact confirmed by Totten and Block (1987). Small movements of relative price, usually caused by the discounts of competitor brands, will result in poor estimation (because this is related to size of movement) and will show a low elasticity because consumers are less responsive to price changes in other brands; this provides a possible explanation for the findings of Hamilton, East and Kalafatis.

The impact on competitors

In the economy as a whole, one brand's gain is at the expense of other potential purchases or savings. In some fields like toilet paper, petrol and detergent the total consumption of the category is relatively fixed and therefore any gain is likely to be at the expense of other brands in the category. The consumption of other products such as confectionery, canned tuna and biscuits is more flexible and promotional gains need not be at the expense of competitors in the same product field. The impact on competitors has been studied by Totten and Block (1987) who state:

> the actual data, however, show that competitive brands seldom have major sales declines during the promotional periods of other brands. On the contrary, sometimes competitive brands enjoy sales increases.

An important consequence of the evidence that competitor sales volume is often little affected by another brand's promotion is that sales volume is preferable to market share as a measure of promotion effect. Even though its sales do not change, the market share for brand A falls when a competitor has a successful promotion that draws purchases from outside the category; this makes sales volume a more reliable indicator of how a brand is performing.

When elasticities are established from store-level data, or from field experiments, the basis of the calculation is a change in the actual price of the focal brand, not in the relative price caused by changes in competitor prices. Because of this, our analysis suggests that store-level calculations and quasi-experimental results should give higher elasticities than regression estimates. In general this is what we find, and industry sources report that regression estimates are generally lower than calculations based on discounts when both are done for the same brand.

A further problem associated with regression estimates is the effect of a brand sales trend. Sometimes, on a rising trend, managers may raise prices to avoid out-of-stock and to make more profit. On a falling trend they may cut prices to stem the sales loss. Such actions could produce sales/price points that indicate a less negative or even a positive elasticity.

The management value of an estimated price elasticity for a single brand seems limited. This is because of doubts about the estimation process and because the elasticity may change under different market conditions. Large numbers of estimates, along with other methods, do have value for comparing market features to see how these relate to elasticity. In the Hamilton, East and Kalafatis (1997) study, for example, there was weak evidence that advertising weight and brand leadership were associated with lower price sensitivity, but we do not yet have a clear idea of how all these different market factors work together. Some market effects are fairly predictable; for example, we may see more sales effect when a leading brand discounts to parity with the store brand than when the store brand is discounted by the same amount.

Gijsbrechts (1993) has reviewed a range of findings on price and promotion effects, some of which are covered in the next section.

Sales promotions

Introduction

Promotions can take many forms, but there is limited research on the effects of the different types of promotion. One recent study compared the effect of free samples, coupons and cashback offers on subsequent purchase (McGuiness, Brennan and Gendall, 1995). Using three product types this research indicated that free samples were about twice as effective as coupons, and the cashback offer was very effective in the one product field where it was applied.

Despite the great variety of schemes the majority of promotional activity focuses on discounts (often called 'deals' in the United States). Trade deals are discounts to the retailer who may, or may not, pass on the saving in cost to the customer. In the United States, the 'pass through' averages about 70 per cent. The consumer offer is a direct discount on price, extra product, a quantity offer (e.g. 'buy two – get one free'), coupon discount or bundled goods (e.g. a toothbrush with the toothpaste). These price-related promotions are often associated with special displays and local advertising. Most consumer sales promotions are short-life and offer immediate benefits, but there is growing emphasis on *loyalty schemes* where benefit accumulates and product use may have to reach some minimum level before the benefit can be realized, e.g. *Airmiles* in Britain and *FlyBuys* in Australia.

In recent years the value of discounting has been questioned more actively. Advertising agencies dislike it since it may take part of the ad budget; supplying companies have to carry the costs of administration and pack changes, and these expenses add to the cost of the price reductions applied to the brand. On top of this, a successful promotion may bring retaliation from competitors, which damages later profits. Procter & Gamble have calculated that promotions take 25 per cent of salesperson time, 30 per cent of brand management time, and that, in the food industry, trade promotion alone adds 2.5 per cent to retail prices. These findings have led Procter & Gamble to review their discounting policy and to use more *every day low pricing (EDLP)*. In aggregate, the effects of sales promotions seem to cancel out, leaving a cost that has to be added to the price of goods. Would we not all be better off (except the sales promotion agencies) if discounting in mature markets was limited?

To a company, the value of a sales promotion depends upon the extra sales generated and the cost of running the promotion. Whether or not sales promotions lose their prominence depends in part upon evidence about their effects on profit; this evidence has been much improved by the scanner measurement of store sales and there is now a substantial body of research on this subject, which is considered below. In Chapter 10 the relative benefits of investments in sales promotions and media advertising are considered.

Much of our evidence on sales promotions comes from the United States where marketing practices are rather different from those applying in Europe. In the United States we find:

- More lines are normally offered on deal.
- Discounts are usually larger.
- Promotion periods are usually a week, shorter than in Europe, and they are often driven by short-life coupons. In other countries coupons are less popular.

The promotional bump

The effect on sales of a discount has two aspects: the first is the increase in sales during the period of the promotion – sometimes called the *promotional bump*, and the second is any change after the promotion has finished – the *carryover effect*.

The promotional bump may be measured as an increment in absolute volume, but more commonly it is reported as a percentage change. Percentage measures are useful in assessing the return on a promotion when the discount is the main cost but where the promotion involves large initial costs (e.g. on repackaging) a percentage may be misleading. Cotton and Babb (1978) found wide variation in the sales effects of promotions ranging from gains of about 20 per cent to 400 per cent. Garrick (1986a) similarly found that seven instances of a promotion plus ad feature produced increases ranging from 43 per cent to 600 per cent.

The combined effect of discount, display and ad features

Although sales promotions often combine display, ad feature and discount it is useful to see the separate effects of these different components. IRI (1989) have circulated an analysis of these effects based on their 1988 data on sales in 2,400 grocery stores in sixty-six markets in the United States. The data are normalized on a price-cut of 15 per cent. The main findings are shown in Figure 4.2. This shows that the price-cut on its own increases sales by 35 per cent (an elasticity of −2.3); when the discount is coupled with an ad feature the effect is 173 per cent, i.e. 138 per cent more than the price-cut on its own, and when the price-cut is paired with an in-store display the sales gain is 279 per cent, 244 per cent more than the sales gain alone. Of particular interest is what happens when price-cut, ad feature and display are combined; the sales effects could simply add together, i.e.

$$35\% + 138\% + 244\% = 417\%$$

Figure 4.2 shows that there is a gain of 128 per cent above the 417 per cent which suggests that the three components of promotion act synergistically. Totten's (1986) study also found that ad feature and display interacted to produce a greater effect and that this phenomenon was amplified when the line was also discounted.

Unfortunately this sort of evidence can be ambiguous. It appears that the different combinations of promotions occur in different stores for different products and at different times; like is not necessarily compared with like. It could be that the stores that feature the threefold promotion of discount, display and ad feature take more trouble with each component (Totten (1986) notes this possibility); if so, the extra effect may be due not to synergy, but to the fact that the promotions were better managed when all three elements were combined. The possibility that unmeasured variables may be responsible for an effect is always present when the data are derived from non-experimental designs. The true experimental design randomizes the influence of variables that are not under investigation.

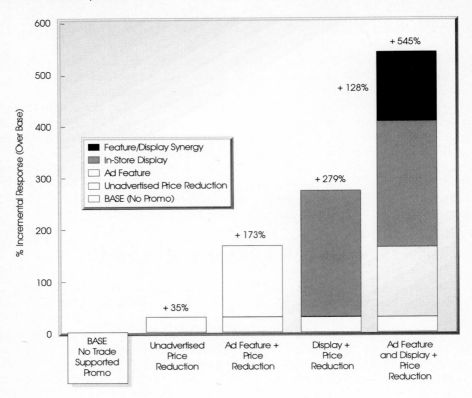

Figure 4.2 Response to promotions

Other work has confirmed the strong effect of the other (non-price) marketing mix variables in price promotions. Bemmaor and Mouchoux (1991) found that elasticities increased from 20 per cent to 180 per cent when the deal was advertised. Inman, McAlister and Hoyer (1990) also found that sales were much amplified by in-store display.

The IRI data were also split into different categories and showed that the combined effect of discount, ad feature and display varied widely across brands; for example sales were multiplied ten times in the case of toilet tissue but only twice in the case of sanitary protection. This might be because some products are inherently more suited to display, or that factors such as price relativity or frequency of purchase were relevant.

Elements in the promotional mix do not always interact positively. Totten and Block (1987) found that for many groceries the sales response to a *small* discount was negligible when the brand was also supported by displays. This can be explained by reference to Figure 4.3. The lower curve shows the relationship between sales and price and here discounts always increase sales; the higher curve shows the relationship between sales and price when there is additional display. Between $3.20 and $3.35 the

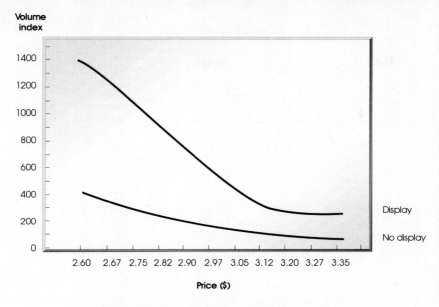

Figure 4.3 The price/promotion response model

curve flattens showing that *small* discounts in this price range bring no extra sales and are thus a waste of money. This effect probably arises because displays are associated with discounts in customers' experience and thus signal good value, even when they are not. Retailers will not normally make display space available unless the goods are discounted, but this evidence suggests that, where there is a choice, it is better to offer substantial discounts with a display, or none at all.

Carryover effects

What happens after the sales promotion has finished? Consider the possibilities (which are illustrated in Figure 4.4):

■ Some consumers may buy and consume a discounted brand more with no effect on later consumption.
■ Some buyers may switch brands or maintain a raised consumption after trying a brand on promotion. Rothschild and Gaidis (1981) suggested that this effect was implied by learning theory but it is contrary to the idea that most consumption is habitual.
■ Some regular consumers may accelerate purchase and stockpile a brand on deal; as a result they will buy less later. Though plausible, this requires more planning than is usually found among consumers of frequently purchased goods.

Figure 4.4 Three possible carryover outcomes

The availability of scanner data has made research on carryover effect more feasible and the *overall* picture shows little carryover effect. The effect on sales of a discount occurs immediately when the discount is introduced and this usually reverts back to the pre-discount level when it ends. Cotton and Babb (1978) did find higher post-promotion purchase rates for some dairy products, but the effect was small. Shoemaker and Shoaf (1977) found a drop in the repurchase rate after a promotion, suggesting some stockpiling, a finding replicated by Helsen and Schmittlein (1992). McAlister (1986) found no stockpiling in instant coffee promotions, and there was no evidence of carryover effects in the Ehrenberg and England (1990) field experiments. Totten and Block (1987) found little evidence of post-promotion sales change. They illustrate this with the sales of Pepsi Cola (Figure 4.5), which continue in the non-promotion periods as though the promotions had not occurred. Totten and Block did find some evidence of stockpiling among heavy users when promotions were rare. (When the promotions are frequent, which is common for grocery products in the United States, there is no need to stockpile.)

The most comprehensive study in this area, cited earlier, is by Ehrenberg, Hammond and Goodhardt (1994), who used panel data from Britain, Germany, America and Japan on twenty-five established grocery products. The researchers identified 175 sales peaks of 25 per cent or more for different brands in these product fields and compared sales levels before and after these episodes. The procedure excluded cases where the sales pattern was irregular either before or after the peak.

The overall outcome of this study was a sales increase of 1 per cent, which is effectively no effect. A check was made by measuring the repeat buying rates for the 8-week period after the peak; the average was 43 per cent – almost the same as the 44 per cent inferred from NBD theory (see Chapter 3), which showed that buying was stationary in the post-promotion period. Differences between countries were small and there was no evidence that categories showed a consistent movement when data were available on the same category from more than one country.

In sum, these studies show little evidence of carryover effect, though some heavy buyers may stockpile in markets where discounts are rare, and this could be important in Europe where discounts are less common than the United States. A lack of carryover effect is quite difficult to explain. How is it that a spike of extra sales, often several times the normal level, does not disturb the base-level sales? One explanation offered

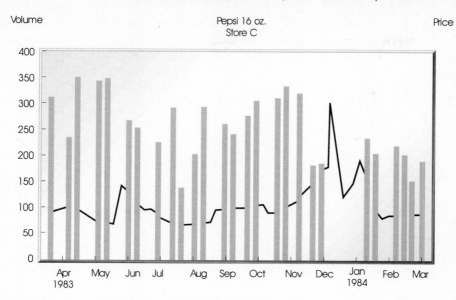

Figure 4.5 Sales of Pepsi Cola show no relationship between promotional sales and base-rate sales (from the *Marketing Fact Book* Scanner Data Base, Information Resources Inc.)

by Ehrenberg *et al.* is that deals touch only a minority of the brand's customer base; many regular buyers would not see a promotion and their behaviour could not be affected. A second explanation offered by Ehrenberg *et al.* is that the extra purchasers attracted by the deal were nearly always people who had bought the brand in the past (see Table 4.1); thus a promotion does not *introduce* new buyers to the brand. Those who respond to promotions are past and current buyers who are already familiar with the brand characteristics.

Table 4.1 Percentage of those buying on promotion who had bought the brand before

| Product | Bought promoted brand in previous | | | |
	6 months %	1 year %	2 years %	$2\frac{1}{2}$ years %
Ground coffee (Germany)	78	83	91	95
Detergent (US)	76	76	88	93
Yogurt (US)	71	78	90	91
Ketchup (US)	52	68	88	91
Detergent (Germany)	61	90	98	na
Soup (US)	75	90	91	na
Carbonated drinks (Germany)	70	79	90	na
Instant coffee (US)	70	80	90	na
Crackers (US)	55	65	78	na
Average	**68**	**79**	**89**	**93**

Source: Ehrenberg, Hammond and Goodhardt (1994).

It appears that those who buy a brand on promotion tend to have lower proportionate loyalty and purchase a wider portfolio of brands in the category. In an investigation of tuna purchase, McAlister and Totten (1985) segmented purchasers into five groups on the basis of loyalty. Table 4.2 shows these five groups and their purchases of brand A when it was not promoted, and when it was promoted and sales rose 136 per cent; the third column shows the distribution of the *incremental volume* to the different segments.

Table 4.2 The purchase of brand A tuna by different loyalty segments

	Not promoted %	Promoted (+ 136%) %	Incremental volume %
Less than 80% loyal to any brand	43	66	83
80–99% loyal to another brand	2	3	3
80–99% loyal to brand A	21	14	8
100% loyal to brand A	31	15	4
New to category buyers	3	3	2

Source: McAlister and Totten (1985).

We can see from these figures that 83 per cent of the incremental volume produced by the promotion comes from those who are less than 80 per cent loyal to any brand – called *discount switchers* by the authors of the study; only a few sales come from those who are loyal to other brands, new buyers of the product type or from increased purchases by existing loyal buyers. Since the discount switchers buy more on deal they have less influence on base-rate sales; thus deal-to-deal buying helps to explain the fact that base-rate sales do not seem to be affected by promotions (see Figure 4.5). So, according to the discount switcher theory, promotions mainly service a group of price-sensitive consumers who are not brand loyal.

This example shows the value of using loyalty measures to divide up the consumer base. McAlister and Totten use a high first-brand loyalty criterion (80 per cent purchases) to distinguish a switcher from a loyal purchaser; this compares with first brand loyalty averages of about 60 per cent in grocery categories. The 80 per cent definition means that over 50 per cent of the population are classified as switchers; this makes their share of incremental sales rather less impressive.

There are some unresolved issues in this account: the United States tuna market may be exceptionally volatile and evidence from other categories is required; we need to know also whether the switchers do buy from a wider portfolio than most consumers or simply buy any discounted brand. Finally, it must be remembered that American promotions are so frequent that consumers can adopt a strategy of buying only on promotion (more canned tuna is bought on deal than at regular prices); rather different effects might be found in other markets.

A thoughtful paper by Neslin and Stone (1996) compares seven different explanations for the lack of post-promotion effect; they suggest that many people are insensitive to the stock of purchases already made so that household inventory has little effect on purchase decisions. As a result the effect of deal purchases is spread over a long period of time and produces no post-promotion dip. The effect of discount sales is to reduce base-level sales; without promotions the base rate would rise. The relative merit of everyday low pricing over a 'Hi–Lo' promotional strategy depends upon how people would behave without promotions, but we have limited knowledge of purchasing behaviour under such conditions.

Long-term effects of promotions

A concern in advertising agencies is that there may be some long-term effects of promotions that are not revealed in the shorter-term studies testing for carryover effect. Broadbent (1989) and Ogilvy (1987) are among those who have suggested that the heavy use of sales promotions will degrade brand equity; this may occur because frequent discounts lower reference prices so that consumers refuse to buy at normal prices. Alternatively, customers may see the lower price on discount as evidence of poorer quality.

Davis, Inman and McAlister (1992) found that the evaluation of brands did not decline after a three-month sales promotion period. Totten and Block (1987) looked beyond the immediate post-promotion period to see whether there are any longer-term effects on base-level sales, but found no evidence with three products. Studies by Guadagni and Little (1983) and Lattin and Bucklin (1989) suggest that discounts have a small effect on reference prices and therefore could affect future sales. Thus, on balance, the evidence suggests that frequent sales promotions *might* erode long-term customer support; certainly, short-term promotions do *not* enhance brand equity, whereas this may sometimes be achieved with media advertising.

The effects of loyalty schemes

This review has concentrated on the effects of short-term discounts on established brands. Rather different effects might be obtained in long-term loyalty schemes where the duration of the promotion may develop a purchase habit. A loyalty scheme raises two sorts of question: What are the residual effects if it is discontinued? And what are the effects when it is running? There is little published evidence on carryover effects with long-term promotions, but some ideas come from the response to long out-of-stock periods which are the opposite of incentives to buy. When *Perrier* was removed from American stores for five months it lost a large proportion of share. There may be special considerations here – a mineral water has little to distinguish it from others – and the competitors took maximum advantage of the absence of *Perrier* from the shelves. If a long stockout loses customers, it seems likely that a long loyalty scheme may gain or help to keep customers so that, on its withdrawal, sales would fall back over a period of time.

Perrier

One case where loyalty was permanently changed occurred when *Perrier* water was withdrawn from the shelves for five months when traces of benzene were found in it in 1990. Although it had come to symbolize sparkling mineral water, in the glass it was indistinguishable from other waters. Aaker (1991a) suggests that, in the United States, customers came to realize that *Perrier* was no better than many other brands, and that many customers transferred their loyalty or simply stopped asking for *Perrier* by name when it was not available. In America, share fell from 50 per cent before the withdrawal to less than 20 per cent after its return in late 1990.

The second question concerns the effects of a loyalty scheme when it is running; here it seems likely that its impact is often nullified by competitive action. For example, all major US airlines offer frequent flyer schemes and those who fly a lot tend to join the schemes of the airlines that they use; the result is that there is then no pressure on frequent flyers to choose a particular airline. The consequence of this is that airlines have to give away flights and price up their product to take account of this; in so doing they expose themselves to price competition by those who do not use giveaways. But schemes evolve to take account of competitors. British Airways, for example, gives points on its frequent flyer scheme in relation to competition, not distance covered.

It does seem likely that there are some cases where firms appear to have gained an advantage through a loyalty scheme and it is interesting to see how this may come about. There are three possible effects which may operate together:

- The proportionate loyalty (preference) may rise. Here we would expect to see first-brand loyalty increase as customers substitute the promoted brand for other brands in the category.
- The long-term loyalty (allegiance) to the brand may be increased. The brand will lose a lower than average proportion of buyers compared with other brands in the category.
- The brand will recruit proportionately more buyers than other brands in the category. The net gain in buyers from allegiance and recruitment will show as an increase in penetration.

A study at Kingston University allows us to report on these effects. Two surveys of supermarket use in England and Wales were conducted on the same group of respondents in March 1994 and November 1995. Those who answered both question-naires (541 respondents) were compared and we report on those who declared themselves to be primarily loyal to either of the two leading supermarkets, Sainsbury and Tesco. In the interval between the surveys, Tesco had wrested supremacy from Sainsbury in terms of market share. Tesco had achieved this through three main initiatives: more new store openings and takeovers, the introduction of a new range of tertiary brands to compete with the discounters, and the introduction of a loyalty card scheme. Sainsbury opened fewer new stores, did not offer tertiary brands until after our second study, and flirted with loyalty cards but then abandoned the idea (only to take it up again in 1996). Only one other store group, Safeway, introduced a loyalty card, so that Tesco was relatively unchallenged by competitors in this respect.

From the respondents' returns it was possible to calculate an approximate first-store loyalty; Table 4.3 shows that Tesco did marginally increase their first-store loyalty but this was no more than that found for the whole market and we conclude from this that Tesco's initiatives had a limited effect on the proportionate loyalty of their total customer base. However, there could be differences in the numbers of primary patrons recruited and lost by Tesco compared with Sainsbury.

Table 4.3 First-store loyalties

	March 1994	*November 1995*
Sainsbury	80	81
Tesco	78	81
All	75	78

To explore this we looked at those who were gained, those who remained loyal, and those who were lost as primary patrons of Sainsbury and Tesco. Over this period 35 per cent of patrons to all stores changed their primary loyalty. Table 4.4 shows that against the 1994 patronage Sainsbury lost 36 per cent and gained 17 per cent while Tesco lost only 16 per cent and gained 48 per cent. Sainsbury, therefore, lost ground because it failed to recruit, whereas Tesco gained ground because it retained customers better and had above-average recruitment. These changes raised Tesco's penetration and market share.

Table 4.4 Percentage of patrons gained and lost over 21 months, 1994–5, by Sainsbury and Tesco

Customers	*Sainsbury*	*Tesco*
Gained	17	48
Lost	36	16

It is possible to gain good customers and lose poor customers, so, as a further check, we computed the mean first-store loyalty, main trip supermarket expenditure and mean frequency of shopping for those who stayed loyal, and those who were gained and lost by the stores. (For those who had left Sainsbury and Tesco, these calculations were based on their shopping at their new store.) Table 4.5 shows that those who were recruited by Sainsbury had slightly lower first-store loyalty, mean spending and trips per week than those who were loyal or those that were lost, whereas Tesco's new customers appeared as profitable as their loyal customers or those who had left. Thus Sainsbury did slightly worse in respect of the quality of customers gained and lost.

Table 4.5 Expenditure data on customers of Sainsbury and Tesco

Customers	Sainsbury			Tesco		
	First-store loyalty (%)	Main trip spend (£)	Mean trip freq. per week	First-store loyalty (%)	Main trip spend (£)	Mean trip freq. per week
Loyal	83	58	1.8	82	51	1.7
Gained	73	50	1.6	79	60	1.8
Lost	81	64	1.8	80	60	1.7

Finally, we examined the attitude of Sainsbury and Tesco customers to their store. We asked which store respondents would use if they were all equally accessible – in effect which was the best store – and then we measured the proportions indicating that their usual store was the best. Table 4.6 shows that, despite the growth in size of Tesco, Sainsbury remained ahead in the estimation of its customers.

Table 4.6 Percentage believing that their usual store was the best

Customers of:	March 1994	November 1995
Sainsbury	75	66
Tesco	66	57

It is not possible to apportion credit for Tesco's gains to the different innovations of the company. There was some evidence that the loyalty cards were attractive – those who joined Tesco were much more likely to have a card than those who left.

Small brand advantage

McAlister (1985) found that lower penetration brands benefit proportionately more from price promotions. High-penetration brands have less headroom for growth so that promotions cannot produce spectacular *percentage* increases. Another reason why large brands are less responsive may be that large brands are bought by less price-sensitive customers than small brands. Further, Shoemaker and Tibrewala (1985) found that regular purchasers claimed to redeem coupons whatever their value, whereas non-users stated that they were more likely to use a coupon with a high value. Regular purchasers erode profit when they buy on discount rather than the full price. The bigger the brand the larger the number of regular purchasers who act in this way to reduce profit. Totten (1986) confirmed that small brands fare proportionately better than large brands in promotions in a study of 116 categories using IRI data, and 'small brand advantage' has become widely accepted in marketing. But the supporting evidence is in terms of percentage increases; small brand advantage should be demonstrated after taking account of the set-up costs of the promotion, with profit being used as the criterion of success.

Although small brands may benefit proportionately more from sales promotions than large brands the reverse is true for media advertising where there are economies of scale for large brands. Advertising often works by supporting existing purchase and the larger the existing sales, the larger the support. In addition, small brands are likely to have weaker brand awareness than big brands so that the sales effect of media advertising may leak from the advertised brand to the whole product class. This makes media advertising an unattractive method for supporting most small brands.

As the discount increases, there are more sales, but margins get smaller. This means that there is an optimum value for discounts, which may be calculated if the fixed costs of the promotion, the price elasticity and the profit margin are known. Exercise 4.2 is designed to illustrate the decision on discount level.

Exercise 4.2   Optimal discounts

Plus is a canned soft drink selling at $1 for a four-pack. The margin is 50 cents and the elasticity is -4.

1. Assuming no additional fixed costs or competitor retaliation, would a discount of $12\frac{1}{2}$ per cent make money?

2. What is the optimal discount? The profit is given by the number sold multiplied by the margin, i.e. profit $= (100 + 4d)(50 - d)$ where d is the discount as a percentage. If you multiply this out, differentiate, equate the differential to zero (slope is zero at highest point), you can calculate the optimum discount.

3. Is the promotion still profitable if sales over the period of the promotion are $1 million and fixed costs for the promotion are $40,000, ignoring competitor response?

4. If competitor retaliation reduces subsequent profits by $20,000, is the promotion still worthwhile?

Answers

1. For every 100 sales at normal price there will be $100 + 4 \times 12.5$ sales at the 12.5 per cent discount, i.e. 150 sales, and the profit will be $0.375 \times 150 = \$56.25$ instead of $0.5 \times 100 = \$50$. Therefore, the discount is more profitable than the usual price, assuming no other costs.

2. Multiplying out, profit $= 5000 + 100d - 4d^2$. Differentiating, slope $= 100 - 8d$. Therefore, equating slope to zero, d $= 12.5$ per cent. In words, the optimal discount is 12.5 per cent.

3. On a million sales the profit is $0.375 \times 1,000,000 = \$375,000$ and without the discount the profit on the reduced sales would be $333,333. The profit advantage is $41,667, reduced to $1,667 after taking account of fixed costs.

4. If competitor retaliation costs a further $20,000 the exercise would be loss making.

Summary

A large proportion of purchasers are unaware of the actual price of the goods that they buy. Price, when perceived, may act as a cue to quality along with other cues. The price of a product deters purchase more strongly when it is above the *reference price*. Reference prices differ between brands and individuals.

Research on price elasticity has shown that different methods of measurement produce different results; in particular, the price elasticities determined by regression are lower than those obtained by other methods. Often elasticities determined by regression are positive and tend to be smaller when the estimation is less robust. Elasticities are affected by market conditions such as the prices of competitor brands and store displays.

Sales promotions mostly involve temporary reductions in the unit cost of a product. The expenditure on such promotions has recently been examined more critically since promotions take management time and involve set-up costs which may not be recouped by extra sales of the product.

The sales gains from discounts are large when they are combined with special displays and/or local advertising. The extra sales occur mainly over the period of the promotion; there appears to be little carryover of sales effect into the post-promotion period. One reason for this is that most of the discount purchasers have bought the brand at some time before so that promotions rarely introduce the brand to a new purchaser. A second reason is that the promotion is missed by most of the people who buy a brand, who will therefore continue to buy normally. Promotions are used more heavily by low-loyalty purchasers, who switch more easily to a brand on discount.

It has been argued that discounts affect brand equity either through the mechanism of the price–quality relationship, or because they reduce the reference price. The evidence for this effect is limited.

Extra sales gained by one brand are not always at the expense of other brands, so managers should look at volume as well as share effects when deciding on promotional strategy.

The long-term loyalty scheme could raise preference (proportionate loyalty) and may also increase the retention and/or recruitment of buyers. One study of store patronage indicated that gains were achieved mainly by increased retention and recruitment.

Sales promotions have value in shifting stock and they are particularly useful to small brands which show higher proportionate gains from promotions (and poorer gains from media advertising).

Further reading

On pricing, see Rao, A.R. and Monroe, K.B. (1988) The moderating effect of prior knowledge on cue utilization in product evaluations, *Journal of Consumer Research*, 15, September, 253–63.

On promotions, see Blattberg, R.C., Briesch, R. and Fox, E.J. (1995) Empirical generalizations
and conflicting findings for sales promotions, *Marketing Science*, 14, 3, Part 2 of 2, G122–G132.
See also Gijsbrechts, E. (1993) Prices and pricing research in consumer marketing: some recent
developments, *International Journal of Research in Marketing*, 10, 115–51.

Part III

Reasons for purchase

Chapter 5

Attitudes, beliefs, intentions and behaviour

Introduction

This chapter is concerned with the nature and measurement of attitudes, beliefs and intentions, and their relationship with behaviour. This has a clear relevance to marketing – we need to predict sales and to understand why people buy if we are to create products in the right quantity and direct them to consumers who want to buy them. In addition, if we know the bases of their behaviour, we may be able to influence consumers by using mass communications that are focused on the beliefs and attitudes most related to their behaviour.

The investigation of consumers' reasons for action is a province of market research. Despite this, there is a gap between the methods of market researchers and the material reported here. Market researchers elicit information from respondents that has direct relevance to consumption, but their work often lacks any theoretical rationale. The main purpose in this chapter and Chapter 6, is to give a wider theoretical framework so that we can explain why people act in the ways that they do when they have a relatively free choice. In this way we shall establish a more general understanding and provide a better basis for market research methods.

Attitude research and behaviour prediction has applications well beyond the field of marketing. I have tried in this and the following chapters to provide the information and methods that are needed by someone who wants to use these methods for investigation. For this reason the topic is covered in considerable detail.

In this chapter you will find:

- A focus on the definition and measurement of attitude.

- An explanation of attitude in terms of expected values; this is a 'bundle' account of attitude.

- An account of how the parts of the bundle are elicited and used in a questionnaire.

- Alternative approaches to attitude and belief measurement.

- A review of evidence on causal priority: Does attitude cause behaviour or behaviour cause attitude? Or is there some middle way in this dialogue between cognitivists and behaviourists?

- A review of evidence showing that attitudes formed through experience are more strongly predictive of future behaviour than attitudes formed in other ways.

- A history of the prediction of behaviour from attitudes.

- A description of intention measurement and the relationship between intention and behaviour.

Definitions and measurements

We start with *attitudes*. Attitudes are what we feel about a *concept* which may be a brand, a category, a person, an ideology or any other entity about which we can think and to which we can attach feeling. Attitudes are thus about the evaluation that we give to a specific concept; they are not like mood, which is a generalized state of feeling with no clear focus, and they are not thought structures with no feelings attached.

An important class of attitudes are those about *actions*, including those commercially relevant behaviours such as buying, renting, using, eating, betting, stealing, etc. We focus on attitudes to actions because, as we shall see, it is these attitudes that relate most to actual behaviour. Thus it is the attitude to *playing* the National Lottery or *buying* a mobile phone that we are most concerned with. The attitude to the object (the National Lottery or mobile phones), though interesting, is less directly related to an action than the attitude to that action.

We know about a person's attitude from observation of his or her behaviour and from what he or she says. Thus attitude may be inferred from actions or measured using a systematic questioning procedure. For example, our attitude to playing the National Lottery can be measured using the question:

For me, playing the National Lottery is:

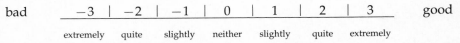

Usually we use more than one scale to reduce error and to cover those situations where people have mixed feelings about an action. Often people are ambivalent when an action carries quite different short-term and long-term implications; for example, many smokers would say that 'giving up cigarettes tomorrow' is *both* unpleasant and good, and for this reason we would use both unpleasant–pleasant and bad–good scales to measure their attitude. In this case these two scales catch the ambivalence that most smokers have towards quitting cigarettes.

The concept can be seen as a set of *beliefs*. When the concept is an action, the beliefs largely concern the concomitants and outcomes of the action. If I play the National Lottery I shall be able to dream of untold wealth, be excited at the draw and probably be disappointed at the outcome. 'Giving up cigarettes tomorrow' carries the promise of living longer, avoiding unpleasant diseases and suffering from considerable tension. The main concept breaks down into these beliefs; and just as we evaluate the main concept, so we can also evaluate each of the beliefs, positively or negatively.

Some outcomes are definitely associated with the main concept, while others are less certainly connected. Some people will not suffer from unpleasant diseases if they continue to smoke and others will experience little or no tension if they give up cigarettes. These uncertainties may be reflected in attitudes to giving up. Thus we need two scales when we measure beliefs: one to measure the perceived likelihood that the outcome belief is associated with the main concept, and a second to measure the evaluation of the outcome if it is experienced. For example:

If I play the National Lottery I will win:

unlikely	-3	-2	-1	0	1	2	3	likely
	extremely	quite	slightly	neither	slightly	quite	extremely	

Winning the National Lottery is:

bad	-3	-2	-1	0	1	2	3	good
	extremely	quite	slightly	neither	slightly	quite	extremely	

We usually denote the likelihood measure as b (for belief) and the evaluation measure as e. The full outcome measure is an expected value and is expressed as the product of b and e; with bipolar scales this will be positive if the respondent values winning (as most of us would) and thinks that winning is likely, but negative if winning is seen as unlikely.

The expected-value theory of attitude

Most of the alternatives from which we choose are *multi-attribute*. Do I go to Wales or Luxor for my holiday? To choose between them I have to take account of weather, cost, travelling effort, food, opportunities for recreation, the charms of meeting Welsh and Egyptian people, and more. Consumers do not have objective measures of the association between these different outcomes with the main concept but, as described above, they do have perceived likelihoods (also known as expectancies or subjective probabilities) and evaluations. The attitude to an alternative is given by the sum of these expected-value products, i.e.

$$A = b_1 e_1 + b_2 e_2 + b_3 e_3 + \ldots b_i e_i$$

or

$$A = \Sigma b_i e_i$$

When a person has a choice between several options we expect him or her to take the one with the largest expected value. Edwards (1954) described this model as the subjective expected utility (SEU) model of decision. This way of thinking about decisions accommodates Haley's (1968) idea that, to a buyer, a product is a bundle of expected gains and losses.

We can generalize this thinking to attitudes about other concepts than behaviour. Here there are no behavioural outcomes, but there are *attributes*. Thus the National Lottery (as opposed to playing the National Lottery) has the attributes of attracting particular social groups, helping charities, being entertaining and creating problems because of the amount of money spent on it by people who can ill-afford to gamble. As before, these attributes have an evaluation, and a likelihood of being attached to the main concept; thus the $A = \Sigma b_i e_i$ relationship applies to any attitude. Rosenberg (1956) pioneered this approach to attitude theory and Fishbein (1963) tested the relationship between A and $\Sigma b_i e_i$ using the beliefs and attitudes of fifty subjects. If A is related to $\Sigma b_i e_i$, then subjects with high scores on one measure will have high scores on the other; similarly, low scores on one will be matched by low scores on the other measure. By correlating respondents' scores on the two measures, we can see the extent to which A is related to $\Sigma b_i e_i$. Sum scores were calculated for each respondent by aggregating the *be* products to produce $\Sigma b_i e_i$. Fishbein also asked direct questions to measure the overall, or *global*, attitude. The correlation between the sum score and the global measure was 0.80, which gave strong support to the idea that global attitudes are based on the sum of the expected values of the attributes.

The semantic differential

Fishbein adopted the seven-point scales developed by Osgood, Suci and Tannenbaum (1957) for their work on the semantic differential, a technique for measuring meanings. Osgood *et al.* used scales with verbal markers at the extremes, for example:

$$bad -3\_|\_-2\_|\_-1\_|\_0\_|\_1\_|\_2\_|\_3 \; good$$

$$slow -3\_|\_-2\_|\_-1\_|\_0\_|\_1\_|\_2\_|\_3 \; fast$$

$$unpleasant -3\_|\_-2\_|\_-1\_|\_0\_|\_1\_|\_2\_|\_3 \; pleasant$$

(Scales may show additional verbal referents such as 'extremely', 'quite', 'slightly', to aid response.)

Any two concepts measured in this way are deemed to have the same meaning if they score at the same point on each scale; thus difference of meaning between concepts is indicated by the discrepancies between scale measures. Osgood *et al.* found that the responses obtained from a large number of scales could be reduced to three basic dimensions of meaning: *evaluation, potency* and *activity*. Evaluation accounts for most variance in the definition of meaning and corresponds with its everyday meaning; it is measured by scales using referents such as good–bad, favourable–unfavourable, and pleasant–unpleasant.

Fishbein's expected-value treatment of attitude has been supported in a large number of published studies and can usually be verified in students' practical work (see the correlations between $\Sigma b_i e_i$ and A in Table 6.2). Fishbein's correlation of 0.8 is higher than most of the correlations obtained for this relationship which are typically in the range 0.4–0.6.

Fishbein's treatment of attitude assumes a process of compensation: that the unspoilt beaches of Wales can offset the bad weather there, and that the archaeological interest of Luxor can be set against the extra time and cost of getting there. At best compensation is likely to be partial. Just taking account of the main outcome of one alternative requires some thought, and when several alternatives are present the assessment is obviously more complicated. As we noted in Chapter 1, extended thought before choice is a rarity, but we probably consider more attributes when important decisions are taken, particularly when circumstances extend the decision-making period. Another way of looking at measured attitudes is to see them as a summary of past reinforcement effects; from this standpoint the attitude could be predictive even when respondents did not bring attributes to mind.

Exercise 5.1   The expected-value matrix

Use the computer program ATALYS to exhibit the features of the expected-value model for a multi-attribute action. This program applies the expected-value theory of attitude and shows how the global attitude may be changed by altering the belief components.

ATALYS records an expected-value matrix from the data that you give, which can be printed and used in class discussion. What are the limitations of this sort of rational analysis of decision-making?

For example: can people easily combine the positive and negative consequences of an experience to make one score? Do they think differently about immediate results and long-term consequences? How many factors do individuals take account of when making a decision on restaurants as described in ATALYS?

Modal salient beliefs

Fishbein's theory of attitude is about what *individuals* think and feel, but it has to be tested on groups of people and each member of the group may have a somewhat different basis for their attitude. To take account of this, some studies have asked each person about the attributes that they, individually, thought were important, for example, Budd (1986) on cigarette use and Elliott and Jobber (1990) on company use of market research; this raises the measured relationship between global and sum measures, but it would be laborious to use individually salient beliefs as a standard procedure (and it would be of little use in marketing). Fortunately on many issues there is substantial agreement between people on the factors that are important, even though the value which different individuals attach to these factors may differ. This degree of agreement between people justifies the use of the same questionnaire for all respondents; even so, the procedure obviously introduces a degree of error because people have to answer some questions about outcomes that are not salient for them.

To establish the commonly held beliefs about a concept it is necessary to perform an *elicitation*. This is a series of questions about the positive and negative associations of the concept which are put to members of the target group. The beliefs that come easily to mind are recorded and those that occur frequently in a group (called *modal salient beliefs*) are used for the questionnaire. The process of getting these salient beliefs is low pressure. Fishbein and Ajzen[1] (1975) argue that non-salient beliefs which have to be dredged up from the recesses of the mind are unlikely to have much effect on behaviour though, opposed to this view, Belson (1988) has noted that the percentage of people offering any particular idea is far smaller than the percentage that either believes the idea or regards it as important.

After similar responses have been grouped together the list of modal salient beliefs is usually quite short. Complex issues, such as getting married or using oral contraceptives, may have a dozen or more salient items; simpler issues, such as buying chocolate, may have rather fewer. Exercise 5.2 illustrates how to elicit salient beliefs. This exercise anticipates developments explained in Chapter 6 so that the elicitation covers not only the gains and losses of a prospective action, but also the influence of other people and the personal and environmental factors that make the action easier or more difficult to perform.

Exercise 5.2   Eliciting salient beliefs

(N.B. This procedure also covers the elicitation of salient referents and control factors which are explained in Chapter 6.)

1.   *Define the action clearly*, for example 'buying *Snickers*', 'buying wine at Safeway', 'giving blood when the blood transfusion service comes to the campus'.

2.   *Define clearly the target group*, for example, you might be particularly interested in children buying *Snickers*, or women wine buyers.

3.   *Elicit salient beliefs.* In a sample of people from the target group, ask each person questions about the advantages and disadvantages of the defined action. After each response prompt with: 'anything else?' but do not press hard for ideas. Record the responses for each person. A typical encounter might be:

    Q.   'Can you tell me what you think are the advantages of buying wine at Safeway?'
    A.   'It's cheap.'
    Q.   'Anything else?'
    A.   'There's a good choice.'
    Q.   'Anything else?'
    A.   'Not really.'
    Q.   'Can you tell me what are the disadvantages of buying wine at Safeway?'
    A.   'It's difficult to buy cases.'
    Q.   'Anything else?'
    A.   'No.'

[1] 'Ajzen' is pronounced 'Eye-zen'.

Q. 'Is there anything else that you think of about buying wine at Safeway?'
A. 'No.'

4. *The negative action.* Certain actions may have different salient beliefs associated with *not* doing the action. For example 'not having children' and 'not taking drugs' may be seen as actions with their own rationale, and are not just the opposites to having children and taking drugs. When this is likely it is wise to elicit salient beliefs to the negative action. This is because the propensity to act is measured on a bipolar scale ranging from taking the action to not taking the action; since both of these alternatives are investigated the salient beliefs about both should appear in the questionnaire.

5. *Salient referents* (refer to Chapter 6). Ask each respondent in the sample whether there are people or groups who think that the respondent should do the defined action. Repeat with 'should not'. Ask if there are other people or organizations that come to mind when they think of the action. Use the prompt 'Anyone else?', but do not press for responses.

6. *Control factors* (refer to Chapter 6). Ask each respondent about their abilities and opportunities that make the action easier or harder to perform. Again, prompt with 'Anything else?'.

7. *Refine the list of beliefs.* Combine similar beliefs. Compile a list of modal salient beliefs using the ones most frequently mentioned. The decision to include a belief depends on the frequency with which it is mentioned and the time and money available to support the research. When the questionnaire is intended to be used *both before and after* exposure to advertising or the product, it is important to include beliefs that may become salient as a result of this exposure.

8. You can use the computer program, NEWACT, to make up a questionnaire according to the methods of *planned behaviour theory* which is explained in Chapter 6.

Other methods for measuring beliefs

So far we have emphasized beliefs that are associated with evaluations because these are likely to be connected with behaviour. But many of our belief systems are not directly connected with feeling or behaviour but instead provide us with a framework for making sense of the world around us. Barwise and Ehrenberg (1985) call such beliefs *descriptive* and compare them with *evaluative* beliefs.

Evaluative and descriptive beliefs

This distinction was examined empirically by Barwise and Ehrenberg (1985), who studied beliefs about cereals and detergent. The beliefs that were broadly evaluative such as 'good value for money' were closely associated with brand usage. More descriptive measures such as 'stays crispy in milk' differentiated brands such as *Weetabix* and *Kellogg's Corn Flakes* irrespective of usage and thus provided a framework for describing cereals which was independent of behaviour.

Rossiter (1987) takes issue with Barwise and Ehrenberg over a number of aspects of their 1985 paper. One of Rossiter's concerns is about the classification of descriptive and evaluative beliefs *post facto*, after they have been found to relate differently to behaviour. Barwise and Ehrenberg (1987) responded by pointing out that most people can see the difference between attributes that describe the product such as 'stays crispy in milk' and attributes that describe the user's evaluative response such as 'fun to eat'. Quite a number of the characteristics of brands such as the colour and shape of the pack have little value to consumers but are important in describing and differentiating products.

Barwise and Ehrenberg used data collected by a method established by British Market Research Bureau Ltd (BMRB) in the preparation of the Advertising Planning Index (API). As can be seen from the box, this method lacks refinement and essentially measures the likelihood that a brand possesses an attribute; the value of the attribute is not measured.

The BMRB method for measuring brand attributes

The British Market Research Bureau Ltd (BMRB) used a standard method for measuring attitudes to products for the preparation of the Advertising Planning Index (API). In this procedure each respondent is shown a list of the 5–10 leading brands in a product field. The interviewer then asks, for each of 10–15 attributes, which brands have the attribute. Respondents are also asked about their frequency of brand use.

This procedure lacks a theoretical rationale. The questions used may relate to use, purchase or neither. If purchase is to be predicted, it is the attributes related to purchase that are most relevant, not any brand characteristic or recalled advertising slogan. Often commercial research neglects the more negative aspects of products e.g. 'bad teeth' and 'spots' from eating confectionery, and the unpleasant smell of pet food. These factors may be very important in any explanation of why some consumers exclude themselves from certain markets.

The BMRB method is a crude measure of the *likelihood* that an attribute is possessed by a brand. Respondents have to use some implicit probability above which the brand is credited with the attribute. A scale could be used that would avoid this yes/no choice. The *evaluation* of attributes like 'lots of food value' is not measured in the BMRB research; such values are assumed, even though different attributes may have different values, and several people may differ in their evaluation of a single attribute. For example, while most people will value 'lots of food value' positively, others will see it negatively if they are trying to lose weight. But even when people agree that something is good, there remains the matter of degree: how good is it? These problems reduce the value of research on brand attributes using the BMRB method.

Repertory grid analysis

One of the problems about the BMRB method is the way in which attributes are selected. A procedure is required which will elicit the beliefs which people use to interpret their environment. A technique called repertory grid analysis does this. It was first applied in marketing by Frost and Braine (1967).

Repertory grid analysis comes from a field of psychological research called *personal construct theory* which was developed by Kelly (1955). Kelly saw human beings as actively concerned to make sense of their environment by using frames of reference called *constructs*. In a marketing context we would begin with a number of brands from the same category. The constructs are elicited by taking the brands in threes and asking a respondent to state one way in which two of the three are similar and different from the third. The relationship which differentiates the two brands from the third is the construct. This procedure is repeated with different triads of brands and new constructs are added to the list. This is a lengthy process, even with one respondent, and it is speeded up by using a computer program for presenting the alternatives and recording the constructs. Constructs may also be elicited by taking pairs of brands and asking for the differences; this might be a more parsimonious approach if brand differentiation was the main concern. Exercise 5.3 is intended to apply the thinking behind construct analysis.

Exercise 5.3   Constructs

Go to a local supermarket which stocks wine. Look at the way in which the wine is grouped on the shelves by colour, sweetness, origin, strength, price, etc. Try to determine which constructs are used to organize the display and whether there is some hierarchy of constructs embodied in the layout. How would you decide whether the display fitted the way people think about wine? Are there any other considerations that you would have if you were in charge of a wine display?

This exercise reveals the constructs that are implicit in the thinking of supermarket managers and their customers. To present an intelligible display it is necessary to reflect such constructs, otherwise customers will be confused, unable to find what they want and will go elsewhere. It is important to distinguish this descriptive order from the reasons that people might have for buying, say, Australian Shiraz or New Zealand Chardonnay which might be revealed by an evaluatively oriented study.

A feature of construct analysis, which is illustrated in Exercise 5.3, is that the procedure shows how people think rather than how they feel about alternatives, i.e. it is descriptive rather than evaluative. This bias is acceptable if the method is used to identify the way brands are perceived, but the lack of evaluation in the method means that it is unsuitable for predicting behaviour.

One problem about Kelly's approach is that it is a method for exploring the thinking of single individuals. In consumer behaviour we need to know how groups of people will behave and therefore the constructs of a sample of people have to be expressed in some aggregate form. This procedure introduces some distortion; as with Ajzen and Fishbein's method for producing modal salient beliefs, some constructs will be irrelevant to some people.

A further point about construct analysis is that it leaves out features that the brands have in common. Only differences are elicited but commonalities between all brands could be important. For example, apples are not too juicy, and this makes apples a rather more convenient fruit for a lunchbox than, for example, peaches. The lack of juiciness of apples would not be elicited by the method of triads.

Although the constructs that we use may not bear directly on our behaviour they do so in a less direct way. The way we think about products, and link them to different situations, makes them relevant or not to certain forms of consumption. For example, people may differentiate bread into white, brown, French, wholemeal, granary and dense organic wholemeal. These types may be linked in different ways to health, taste, convenience and ecological values in the thinking of respondents, and their choice of bread is likely to relate to their own self-definition in relation to these different values. Such connections may be explored as *means–end chains* using a technique called laddering (see for example Grunert and Grunert, 1995).

Attitude and behaviour

Reasons for action

When alternatives are well differentiated and the choice is free we expect people to predict and to explain their preferences by referring to features of the alternatives that they like and dislike. This leads us to treat this sort of consumption as rational within the limits imposed by knowledge, habit, effort, etc. People can make an informed choice between brands of confectionery or fax machines, and they can decide carefully between holiday options. They may also make more basic choices such as whether to cut out confectionery from their diet, whether to take a holiday at all, and whether or not to have a fax machine.

This rational treatment of consumption will fail when choice is not free, when the outcomes of choice are so trivial that people do not think about them (e.g. some brand choice), or when the choice is so new to people that they lack relevant knowledge. Rationality is favoured when the choice is repetitive because it can then evolve by a selection process; people do not continue with unsatisfactory products when they think that there are better alternatives available. Choices made without experience may be reasoned but, none the less, may be ill-made because of poor knowledge.

Behaviourism and cognitivism

This account makes thought the precursor of action, but the traditional behaviourist rejects the idea that thought and feeling are the initiators of action and explains action only by reference to the circumstances that applied to previous performances of the action. When an action has been rewarded, the propensity to repeat the action is strengthened. If past action has been negatively reinforced, then the potential to repeat the action is diminished. This approach was endorsed by B.F. Skinner (1938; 1953), whose work was introduced in Chapter 1. To a behaviourist, thought and feeling are *effects but not causes*; like ripples on the surface of a pond, they indicate the fish's movements but do not move the fish. If this account is correct, we can use attitude data only as an indicator of behaviour, to *predict* but not to *explain*.

Such narrow behaviourism is usually rejected today. One reason is that it is difficult to describe action without taking account of the thought and feeling that lie behind it; words become insults or praise only through an understanding of the motives of the person uttering them. The behaviourist position is not subtle enough to deal with this complexity of human behaviour. Opposed to behaviourism is the view that thought and feeling can produce change in action directly. This is *cognitivism*; in its strongest form, experience is interpreted and used to change attitudes and knowledge, which then control behaviour. From a cognitivist perspective, behaviour may be modified by communication, which changes attitudes and knowledge, and this process may help to explain how some advertising and word-of-mouth communications affect consumer choices.

Examples

Some support for the cognitivist position can be found in the way new information seems to change behaviour. For example, reductions in the consumption of tobacco followed the publication of the US Surgeon-General's reports on the risks associated with smoking. Perhaps one of the most remarkable effects of information was in Japan in the early 1950s. In one year the birthrate fell from the usual 18 or 19 per 1,000 to 11 per 1,000; this was caused by a widely held belief that children born in this year would be ill-fated. More recently we have seen Europe-wide reductions in beef eating, following concern about the transmission of BSE ('mad cow disease') to human beings. There is no doubt that people do respond to information of this sort by adjusting their behaviour.

There are also examples where behaviour precedes attitude. Clare and Kiser (1951) asked parents of completed families about the number and sex of the children that they would like if they were to start again. There was a strong tendency for parents to prefer both the size and the sexual composition of the family that they had already. At the time of the study there were no ways of controlling the sex of offspring, so the preference for the same sexual composition can be explained only as a product of experience. In many other cases the priority between attitude and behaviour may be in doubt. The preferred number of children is a case in point. In the last example the parents might have had two children because they wanted two; or, having had two children, they might have come to prefer this number. Such alternative explanations complicate many consumer, social and economic problems.

Karl Marx argued that it was not man's ideology that determined his system of social relations but his social relations that determined his ideology. This is the sociological equivalent of the primacy of behaviour over attitude and it was the basis for Marx's claim that he had turned the philosopher Hegel, who espoused the primacy of ideas, on his head. But in later work Marx placed less emphasis on such social determinism; it was difficult for him to invoke a revolutionary ideology in support of change when all ideologies, *including Marxism*, were the product of social forces.

Many economists avoid explanations where mass attitude change has causal primacy; most prefer to find an environmental basis for economic changes in the tradition of the behaviourists. But economists do use some attitude measures to predict economic change; leading indicators of industrial growth are often based on what industrialists expect (though these expectations of industrialists may themselves be based on perceptions of the economic environment). Consumer confidence partly reflects trends, but may also cause them (see, for example, the review by Pickering, Greatorex and Laycock, 1983). Curtin (1984) gave similar precedence to collective thinking when he argued that growth in the economy was stimulated by consumer willingness to incur debt; this suggests that the economy may be 'talked up' by national figures, who bring about growth by inspiring confidence that it will happen. No doubt this process is much helped when the credibility of predictions is enhanced by objective indicators of likely growth.

Evidence on frequently purchased goods

A study by Bird and Ehrenberg (1966) indicated that, with frequently purchased brands, it was usage that preceded intention to buy. Bird and Ehrenberg found that two-thirds of those who have used the brand at some time express an intention to buy it. A declining brand has a long tail of past users whereas a rising brand has few users, past or current. Because intentions depend on past usage, the much larger group of past users for a fading brand creates a 'tail effect', enlarging the number of stated intentions. The Bird and Ehrenberg analysis shows that there is a causal process from usage to stated intention, and the authors found no evidence for the reverse process that intention leads to purchase in a subsidiary analysis in the study.

Some other studies also suggest that brand attitudes follow the purchase of fmcgs. Barnard, Barwise and Ehrenberg (1986) found that the percentage of people stating that a brand had an attribute was constant, but that only about half those people who credited a brand with an attribute on one occasion did so again on a second occasion. This stochastic pattern was similar to the irregularity of purchase. Some understanding of how brand attributions fluctuate comes from a further analysis by Barnard (1987) who found that people were more likely to associate positive attributes with a brand if they were currently using it; it seems that a large part of the variation in brand attributions is associated with usage and that attitudes follow purchase in fmcg markets. Consistent with this, Sandell (1981) examined the relationships between brand attitudes and purchase using panel data and found that attitudes were aligned with purchase immediately after buying, but then, over time, reverted to the pre-purchase pattern.

Beyond fmcg

In fields other than fmcg, the cognitivist account is better supported by the evidence. For example, Pickering (1984) found that purchase expectations for consumer durables were often followed by later purchase; in this field it is harder to argue that experience forms attitude since the opportunity to try the durable is not available to all prospective purchasers.

Systematic research into the causal order between attitude and action has related measures of the one to later measures of the other in a cross-lagged correlation. A panel is used so that changes in the attitudes and actions of the same people can be tracked. Eagly and Chaiken (1993) noted four studies of this form which generally favoured the A→B (attitude causing behaviour) process. For example, Kahle and Berman (1979) found that in two cases 'voting for Carter' and 'voting for Ford' (as Presidential candidates) the attitude change preceded any change in behaviour; on two other applications, drinking and religious observance, Kahle and Berman found ambiguous results, but these still favoured the primacy of attitude.

A number of other studies illustrate the attitude–behaviour relationship in different fields. Korgaonkar, Lund and Price (1985) found that attitude caused store choice, but that the reverse effect was insignificant. My own data, reported more fully in Chapter 9, showed a contrary effect. I found that store choice was heavily influenced by store location and that the store most used came to be seen as the best store in the majority of cases. Liking may direct store choice in some cases, but shoppers following this pattern seem to be in the minority. Newcomb (1984) found that attitude predicted sexual behaviour in women rather better than the reverse. Marsh and Matheson (1983) looked at smoking attitudes and subsequent behaviour. Those who saw large benefits for themselves if they stopped smoking (attitude) were more likely to stop; however, most smokers believed (wrongly) that either they did not smoke enough to do themselves damage or that they had already smoked so much that the damage was irreversible and in both these cases cessation was less common.

Other research has looked at the relationship between liking other people and associating with them. There is little doubt that we seek out those we like and avoid those we dislike, but Homans (1961) also noted that those who are brought together by force of circumstances tend in most cases to come to like each other. Horst and Jarlais (1984) examined such effects among students; changes took place slowly, many taking more than a month, and the authors argued that the attitude and behaviour changes overlapped and that this ruled out any simple 'A→B' or 'B→A' accounts.

One problem with such attitude–behaviour research is that it is usually conducted by social psychologists who have more interest in the sort of high involvement problems most likely to show the A→B rather than the B→A direction of causation. Thus there may be selection effects in the choice of research and its publication, since few researchers set out to show that thought and feeling are products of experience.

The competition between cognitive and behavioural explanations permeates the social sciences; each side can claim some support and it is realistic to assume that causal priority, when it can be detected, will depend upon the person, action and context. But this review also indicates that it may be mistaken to assume any simple causal primacy. Thought and feeling seem interwoven with behaviour so that any change in one component is likely to affect the other components of the system.

Experience, information and attitudes

The relationship between attitude and behaviour is important because we want to know how to intervene to change action. A key question is:

> Are there differences in the subsequent behaviour between those who have changed their attitude as a result of indirect experience (e.g. communication, including advertising) and those who have changed their attitude as a result of direct experience?

A study by Smith and Swinyard (1983) found that attitudes were changed much more by trial than by advertising, and that subsequent purchase was better predicted by attitudes derived from trial. However, it is difficult to make a fair comparison between trial and advertising communication. In this case trial involved taste which cannot be conveyed adequately in an advertisement, and some ads are better than others, which makes the generalized comparison of trial and advertisement impossible without many examples of each.

Fazio and Zanna (1981) find that evidence generally supports the view that direct experience of an object leads to more strongly learned associations between attitude and behaviour, that is, the association of attitude with action is more predictable and consistent when the attitude has been formed through direct experience. Regan and Fazio (1977) and Fazio and Zanna (1978) provide supporting studies. Fazio (1986) explains this effect as a result of the greater strength or *accessibility* of attitudes that have been learned through experience. What people do is constrained by what they can call to mind and, in this way, attitude accessibility affects action. Attitude strength or accessibility is indicated by speed of response, confidence in the evaluative judgement and attitude stability. An interesting aspect of this work is that attitudes can also be strengthened by repetition; when this is done behaviour is more consistently related to attitude (Powell and Fazio, 1984). This suggests that communications that create internal rehearsal of attitude in relation to behaviour may be effective at increasing the production of the behaviour.

The evidence that attitudes learned by direct experience have stronger association with behaviour may have other bases than attitude accessibility. Fazio and Zanna (1981) have suggested that indirect experience provides less information and is therefore less well anchored and more likely to be changed when the attitude object is actually confronted and more information becomes available. In many situations one might expect that behavioural trial would be a powerful stabilizer of attitude because of the amount of relevant information that could be imparted through such experience. In other situations, where the item is intangible, long-term or complex (e.g. an investment advice service), it may be difficult to test the product behaviourally and information through news, advice and advertising may be the only feasible method of promotion.

Fazio's research is reviewed by Fazio (1990), and by Eagly and Chaiken (1993: 193–201). For Fazio an attitude is *an association in memory between a given object and one's evaluation of that object.* Two objects may both be given the same evaluation on questioning, but if the association is more strongly formed in one case, then, in this case, the attitude is more likely to affect behaviour. Furthermore, the presentation of the attitude object will automatically activate the attitude and, with this activation, raise the likelihood of behaviour. However, work by Bargh *et al.* (1992) has shown that even weakly established attitudes can be primed by attitude objects, and this raises doubts about whether attitude activation and its subsequent effects are related to strength of association between attitude object and evaluation. It seems likely that the idea of attitude strength may have to be modified; Fazio has concerned himself mainly with the strength of linkage between attitude object and evaluation, but another dimension of strength is the complexity of cognitive–affective structure, that is, the *number* of linkages between a concept and other concepts and values. This is considered again in Chapter 6.

When attitudes fail to predict action

In the earlier discussion about the direction of causation between attitude and action, the possibility that there was little or no relationship between the two was ignored. However, when Wicker (1969) reviewed the matter, he concluded that:

> It is considerably more likely that attitudes will be unrelated or only slightly related to overt behaviors than that attitudes will be closely related to actions.

Wicker's pessimistic conclusion was based on forty-seven studies and cast doubt on the competence of social psychologists to predict behaviour from measures of attitude. Following Allport (1935), attitude is usually seen as 'a preparation or readiness for response', and thus should be a predictor of behaviour, except when freedom of action is restricted. The inability to show reliable relationships between attitude and action indicated a deficiency in either measurement or theory; in the event the problem has now been resolved by developments of both theory and measurement.

Often quoted in this context is the study by LaPiere (1934). LaPiere accompanied a Chinese couple on a tour of America and observed that hotel proprietors were generally courteous and nearly always provided the accommodation requested. Later, in response to a letter from LaPiere, many of these proprietors indicated that they would be reluctant to have Chinese guests. Another example of apparent attitude–behaviour inconsistency was provided by Vroom (1964), who found little overall correlation between the evaluation of 'one's job' and measures of job performance (median of 15 studies, r = 0.14).

'Other variables'

Different researchers adopted different positions in the face of the evidence that there was little relationship between attitude and action. Abelson (1972) took the extreme position and accepted that attitudes could not be used to predict behaviour. Others were concerned about the selection of studies made by Wicker; there were omissions from Wicker's review and, in particular, he left out a number of surveys where significant correlations were obtained. Surveys (as compared with laboratory experiments) tend to be concerned with more important issues such as voting. Another group of researchers (e.g. Schuman and Johnson, 1976) took the approach called 'other variables' by Fishbein and Ajzen (1975), and emphasized the control on behaviour exerted by the social and physical environment. Factors mentioned under the 'other variables' heading are personal abilities (or the lack of them), social constraints and uncertainties about the outcomes of action. These factors can pre-empt action and swamp the volition of individuals so that they cannot express their preferred mode of action; this might apply in organizational settings and could help to explain Vroom's findings. This also helps to explain the discrepancy between the hoteliers' overt behaviour and their response to LaPiere's enquiries; as Campbell (1963) pointed out, norms of good manners may stop hoteliers from expressing negative behaviour. From this standpoint there is no real inconsistency between what the hoteliers stated in response to LaPiere's letter and their behaviour. It would have been inconsistent if they had stated that they would turn away a Chinese couple under particular conditions and had not done so when these conditions occurred, but such precise predictions were not tested.

Discrepancies between attitude and behaviour may also arise when the *measures are taken at different times*. People may change their attitudes and intentions over time in response to new information so that a measure of attitude at one time may fail to predict action taken at a later time. For example, the attitude to voting for a political party may be affected by political events and a measure of voting attitude taken close to an election has more predictive value than one taken years before. However, although this effect of time lapse seems common sense, a study by Randall and Wolff (1994) found no evidence that the length of the interval was related to the correlation between intention and behaviour.

The compatibility of measures

Some of the earlier problems of behaviour prediction arose from an unsatisfactory conceptualization of attitude called the three component model (Rosenberg and Hovland, 1960; see Figure 5.1). In this approach attitude is seen as a disposition that is expressed by evaluative, cognitive and behavioural responses. A positive attitude to cheese is measured by statements about liking cheese, statements about the valued properties of cheese and by actions such as purchasing and eating cheese. Thus, in the three component model, the attitude concept *includes* evidence of relevant behaviour. With this definition there *has to be* some correlation between the attitude to cheese and its purchase, but it is better if we can ask whether the liking for cheese is associated with purchase when each is measured independently. There are occasions where we might not expect to find an association between liking cheese and buying it, for example, when a purchaser, who dislikes it, buys it for someone else in the family.

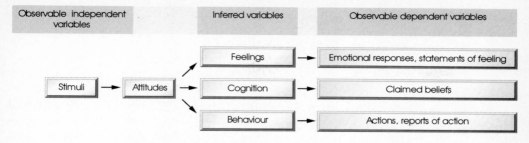

Figure 5.1 The three component model of attitude

This issue was clarified by Fishbein and Ajzen (1975), and Ajzen and Fishbein (1977). First, their theory rejects the three component model and treats attitude as an evaluative concept only, not as an aggregation of evaluations, cognitions and behavioural dispositions. They then introduce the idea of corresponding measures of attitude and behaviour which are now described as *compatible* (Ajzen, 1988), to avoid confusion with other meanings of 'corresponding'. They argue that the attitude to an object is not necessarily related to the attitude to behaviour towards that object. This further explains the relationship between liking and behaviour. People who dislike cheese may still buy it as an ingredient in cooking. People who like cheese may not buy it because it is not part of their diet plan. In both cases, if the question had been about their *attitude to buying cheese*, the attitude measure would have related to purchase propensity. We should not expect high correlations between attitudes to objects and actions towards those objects. On the other hand, an attitude *to a behaviour*, such as buying cheese, should be consistent with that behaviour. This is because the attitude to *buying* cheese is based on salient beliefs that can include its use in cooking and its relevance to diets.

Essentially, Ajzen and Fishbein (1977) argued that the attitude which had been used to predict behaviour was often incorrectly chosen. In their review of research, Fishbein and Ajzen (1975: 360) concluded that 'many of the studies that have been viewed as testing the relation between attitude and behavior are actually of little relevance to that question'. Where there is an incompatibility between the action and the attitude measures we cannot expect much correlation. The degree of compatibility between measures, and the resulting correlations, is illustrated by an unpublished study on 270 women by Jaccard, King and Pomazal (1975, reported by Ajzen and Fishbein, 1977). In this work three attitudes and a behaviour were measured:

1. Attitude to birth control.
2. Attitude to the birth control pill.
3. Attitude to using the birth control pill.
4. Use of the birth control pill.

The correlations were:

$$
\begin{array}{ll}
1{:}4 & 0.16 \\
2{:}4 & 0.34 \\
3{:}4 & 0.65
\end{array}
$$

We see here that there is a high correlation between the attitude to using the pill and actual use, but the correlation drops away as the concepts of attitude and action become less compatible. This effect is readily explicable if we think of the motivations of different women; for example, a woman might be very positive about the pill, but neither use it nor be positive in her attitude to using it if she wants to become pregnant. Similar results were obtained in another study of the correlations between attitudes to 'religion', 'church' and 'attending church this Sunday' and actual church attendance.

One form of incompatibility occurs when we expect attitudes that embrace a set of circumstances to predict a single behaviour (Fishbein and Ajzen, 1974; Ajzen and Fishbein, 1977). For example, a measure of a person's attitude to the environment might give a rather low prediction of their bottle recycling behaviour because specific factors may affect the decision to recycle bottles. If, however, a multiple-act measure of environmental behaviour is constructed which also includes use of recycled paper, refusal to buy overpackaged products, recycling of metals and newsprint, donations to environmental groups, refusal to buy tropical hardwoods, boycotting the products of environmentally suspect firms, taunting women in fur coats, etc., we would expect this measure to have a stronger correlation with the attitude to the environment. This is because the specific factors affecting each action tend to be different and to cancel each other out in the combined measure leaving the common theme of helping the environment. Consistent with this, Weigel and Newman (1976) found that the attitude to environmental preservation correlated better with a multiple-act measure of environmentally concerned behaviour than with single measures. A consequence of this thinking is that attitudes to generalized actions like smoking may have limited relevance to the more specific action of giving up cigarettes, an argument conveyed in a report to the Federal Trade Commission by Fishbein (1977). The attitude to giving up cigarettes covers a range of personal concerns about tension, loss of concentration and the likelihood of relapse not found in the attitude to smoking. For this reason plenty of smokers are negative about smoking, but not positive about giving up cigarettes. Another grouping of behaviours occurs when people set themselves *goals* such as weight loss. Because weight loss depends on a number of behaviours, it is best predicted using a composite of attitudes to those behaviours.

In consumer research the compatibility principle means that attitudes to the *purchase, hiring,* etc. of the product must be measured if it is these actions that we are concerned to predict. This simple lesson about using compatible measures has not been well learned. Usually attitudes to the brand are studied rather than attitudes to purchasing the brand. Often there is substantial overlap between the attitude to the product and the attitude to buying the product but, as Ajzen and Fishbein show (1980, ch. 13), this is not always so. It is also important to study the attitude to *using, eating,* etc. since repeat purchase rests heavily on a satisfactory experience with the product.

The notion of compatibility has given us a major methodological advance in attitude research. The earlier work in marketing, health education and social science had frequently involved measurement of an incompatible attitude, and this was the case for many of the studies reviewed by Wicker. The more compatible the attitude and behaviour measures, the higher their correlation. The rules of compatibility can be illustrated with an example. Consider your attitudes to:

- Wine
- White wine
- Buying white wine
- Buying white wine from Safeway
- Buying white wine from Safeway this weekend
- You buying white wine from Safeway this weekend

Which one of these attitudes is going to correlate best with your likelihood of buying white wine from Safeway this weekend? It is not hard to recognize that the last attitude is likely to capture more of the factors behind this action. Ajzen and Fishbein (1977) summarize the aspects of compatibility under five headings: Target, Action, Context, Time (remember: TACT), and the personal nature of some action.

- The *target* is the focus or object of the action; in the example it is white wine.
- The *action* is buying.
- The *context* is Safeway.
- The *time* is the weekend.
- The *personal aspect* is ensured by using terms like 'for me' and 'I' in measures.

Exercise 5.4   Compatibility test

This exercise uses swimming as the central concept, but other examples might be chosen, e.g. reading a broadsheet newspaper each day, calling parents on the telephone.

Circle the numbers that are closest to your feelings

Swimming is:

bad	-3	-2	-1	0	1	2	3	good
	extremely	quite	slightly	neither	slightly	quite	extremely	

Swimming in my local swimming pool is:

bad	-3	-2	-1	0	1	2	3	good
	extremely	quite	slightly	neither	slightly	quite	extremely	

For me, going swimming in my local swimming pool over the next month is:

bad	-3	-2	-1	0	1	2	3	good
	extremely	quite	slightly	neither	slightly	quite	extremely	

I will go swimming in my local swimming pool over the next month:

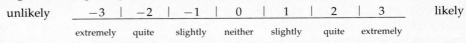

| unlikely | −3 | | −2 | | −1 | | 0 | | 1 | | 2 | | 3 | | likely |

extremely   quite   slightly   neither   slightly   quite   extremely

In an exercise like this we cannot measure behaviour, so a measure of intention, the last scale, is used as a proxy. The scores of students in a class can be entered on a data file and the correlations between the last intention measure and each of the other measures calculated. You should find that the more compatible a concept with the intention measure, the higher the correlation and the smaller the discrepancy in the measures.

Ajzen and Fishbein (1977) used these five criteria to check on the compatibility of attitude and action measures for 142 attitude–behaviour relations reported in 109 investigations. They sorted the data into three groups:

1. Those with low compatibility between the measures.
2. Those with partial compatibility.
3. Those with high compatibility (this group was subdivided because some measures were not clearly specified).

Table 5.1 shows their findings. The correlation between compatibility and the magnitude of the attitude–behaviour relation in Table 5.1 was 0.83. Retrospective analyses such as this may carry some benefit from hindsight, but Ajzen and Fishbein's evidence on compatibility has been supported in subsequent studies.

Table 5.1 Analysis of attitude–behaviour studies

Compatibility	Significance of attitude–behaviour relationship		
	Nil	Low (<0.4)	High (>0.4)
Low	26	1	0
Partial	20	47	4
High – questionable measures	0	9	9
High – appropriate measures	0	0	26

Source: Ajzen and Fishbein (1977).

Are messages more effective if they are compatible with the desired behaviour?

The foregoing work suggests that a message that is exactly specified so that it is compatible with desired behaviour will be more effective at producing this behaviour than one that is less precisely focused; this is because such a message will provide arguments that are more closely related to the desired behaviour. One study relevant to this by McArdle, is summarized in Ajzen and Fishbein (1980).

McArdle, a medical practitioner, tried to persuade alcoholics to join an alcoholic treatment unit (ATU) using three experimental conditions and a control. In a *traditional fear appeal* the dire consequences of continued drinking were spelled out. In a second *negative* condition these same consequences were related to not signing for the ATU; in the third *positive* condition these consequences were presented as costs avoided by signing for the ATU. In the *control* condition there was no appeal. In all conditions the alcoholics were invited 'to sign up for the ATU now'. The focal interest here is whether the second and third conditions were more effective at moving the alcoholics towards the desired behaviour of signing for the ATU.

Table 5.2 Percentage of alcoholics signing for the alcoholic treatment unit

Appeal	Initially unwilling %	Initially willing %
Traditional	5	50
Negative	30	100
Positive	20	95
Control	14	82

Table 5.2 shows the percentages who subsequently signed up among those who were initially willing or unwilling to take this action. Signing was significantly lower in the traditional fear appeal group – lower even than the control condition. Analysis of beliefs showed that those in the traditional fear group had accepted the message in the form presented as a set of consequences of *continued drinking*; they had elaborated on this message by producing counter-arguments and had failed to make inferences to the action of *signing up for the ATU*. The other two experimental groups had received a message which bore directly on the consequences of signing or not signing for the ATU; in these conditions many accepted and changed relevant beliefs and increased their signing for the ATU to a level above the control condition.

McArdle's data have a parallel in consumer advertising that concentrates on the product rather than the purchase. For example, the ads for personal computers that concentrate on the technical specifications of new machines do little to explain to less technically minded people why they should buy a new model. For such people, advertising should concentrate on the benefits that would be perceived as a result of purchase, for example, the speed of loading and saving programs.

Purchase intentions

Attitudes predict behaviour and also begin to explain it by providing one basis for the action. Intentions only predict behaviour since no reason is supplied for taking the action by an intention statement. In marketing, prediction may sometimes be all that is needed. Purchase behaviour may be predicted either from stated intention or from a person's estimate of their purchase probability.

Work on purchase prediction goes back to research by Katona (1947) and Ferber (1954) who investigated consumers' 'purchase plans'. Much of the work is on established markets but Infosino (1986) found that purchase likelihood could forecast new product sales, though Tauber (1975) found that only the first purchase of a new product was predicted; any repeat purchases were presumably decided by reference to the initial purchase experience. Although intention discriminates between those likely and unlikely to purchase, it is of limited value in forecasting total purchase potential because of the effect of other economic factors (Pickering, 1984).

Measures of intention have been well tested in the field of consumer durable purchase. Pickering and Isherwood (1974) used a scale to measure intention and found that 61 per cent of those who said they were 100 per cent likely to purchase actually did so; this compares with the 5 per cent of respondents who made a purchase even though they had expressed *no intention* to purchase the durable in the next 12 months. These findings were close to those obtained by Gabor and Granger (1972) from a Nottingham sample.

Since intention-to-buy measurements can discriminate quite well between prospective buyers and non-buyers it is possible to compare prospective purchasers and non-purchasers in the same way that users and non-users are compared. This suggests that market research may be used to predict which consumers will buy before they have actually done so, and then find out why they are going to buy. Such research could be used for refining products before launch.

The Juster Scale

This is an eleven-point scale with verbal descriptions and probabilities associated with each number:

10	Certain, practically certain	(99 in 100)
9	Almost sure	(9 in 10)
8	Very probable	(8 in 10)
7	Probable	(7 in 10)
6	Good possibility	(6 in 10)
5	Fairly good possibility	(5 in 10)
4	Fair possibility	(4 in 10)
3	Some possibility	(3 in 10)
2	Slight possibility	(2 in 10)
1	Very slight possibility	(1 in 10)
0	No chance, almost no chance	(1 in 100)

There are two reasons for discrepancies between predicted and actual purchase (Bemmaor, 1995): first, the true probability of purchase may be inaccurately measured by the scale point checked, and second, people may change their intention or be unable to fulfil it. The first type of discrepancy is reduced by improved scaling. Juster (1966) used an eleven-point, verbally referenced scale to measure intention, and asked respondents to estimate their likelihood of purchase (see box). In a review of intention measurement Day *et al.* (1991) argued that the best results are obtained using the Juster Scale. Day *et al.* found that the Scale was particularly effective for anticipating car purchase and that frequent purchases were predicted more accurately than infrequent purchases. There was also a tendency to predict more purchases than were actually made.

Intention measures are also used in the planned behaviour research reported in the next chapter. In this field the seven-point semantic differential scale has been used and there has been the same comparison between intention and probability estimates that has been made for consumer purchase prediction. Intuitively, the estimate seems likely to be more accurate because it may take account of conditions that may frustrate an intention. For example, people may intend to give up cigarettes but be more realistic if asked to estimate the likelihood that they will give up. Sheppard, Hartwick and Warshaw (1988) reviewed a large number of attitude–behaviour studies but found only marginal superiority for estimates over true intention measures.

With durables, the great majority of people express no purchase intention, so that even a small percentage of buyers in this group yields a large fraction of the total number of buyers. Pickering and Isherwood found that 55 per cent of all buyers came from the group expressing no intention to buy. This compares with findings by Theil and Kosobud (1968) in the United States that 70 per cent of purchasers were in this category, and by Gabor and Granger (1972) in Britain that 65 per cent of purchases came from those stating a zero purchase probability.

The extent to which people fulfil their intentions has been reviewed by McQuarrie (1988), who assembled data from thirteen studies. McQuarrie noted that those who intended to purchase did so, on average, 42 per cent of the time, whereas those not intending to purchase did so 88 per cent of the time; this asymmetry is probably related to the fact that it is easier not to do something than to do it: effort is usually required for a positive action while inertia favours inaction in most cases. People may also change their minds and therefore not do as they have previously indicated. East (1993) studied the application for shares in three British government privatizations and found that of the 94 persons intending to apply, 63 did; 136 respondents intended not to apply and of these 135 did not do so. Respondents who intended to apply, but then did not do so, were asked for the reasons for their change. Their reasons were equally divided between change of mind (e.g. because the investment looked less advantageous) and inertia explanations (forgot, could not be bothered). Pickering (1975) investigated the failure to purchase consumer durables when a respondent had previously stated an intention to do so. He found that respondents had usually changed their minds because of unforeseen circumstances (e.g. lack of money, or because the current durable was lasting better than expected).

Summary

Attitudes are an evaluative response towards a concept. The concept is a cluster of attribute beliefs, each with attaching value. Thus the attitude to the concept should relate to the aggregate value of the attribute beliefs. Generally, this view of attitude has been upheld by research and it fits the idea that the purchase of a product can be seen as the acquisition of a bundle of expected costs and rewards.

Investigations have focused on the causal relationship between attitude and behaviour. Some studies indicate that attitude change follows behaviour change and this effect seems more marked for fmcg purchases. The reverse sequence is more often found for more involved behaviours. However attitudes that have been learned through direct experience predict future behaviour better than attitudes established by indirect experience such as communication.

In many studies the correlation between attitude and behaviour measures has been weak. There are two reasons for such weak relationships. The first is the 'other variables' explanation, that behaviour is dependent on other factors than attitude; in particular, conditions that make behaviour involuntary or put it under normative control may diminish the causal role of attitudes. The second reason is that the measures of attitude and behaviour may not be compatible, that is, these measures may not refer to the same action, target, context and time. A mismatch here means that the wrong attitude is being used to predict behaviour.

The closest prediction of behaviour is provided by measures of intention.

Further reading

Ajzen, I. and Fishbein, M. (1980) *Understanding Attitudes and Predicting Social Behavior*, Englewood Cliffs, NJ, Prentice Hall, Chapters 1, 2, 4 and 12 and Appendix A.

Eagly, A.H. and Chaiken, S. (1993) *The Psychology of Attitudes*, Orlando, FL, Harcourt, Brace, Jovanovich, Chapter 4.

LaPiere, R.T. (1934) Attitudes vs. actions, *Social Forces*, 13, 230–7.

Chapter 6

Predicting and explaining action

Introduction

One objective of marketing, advertising and applied social science is to influence behaviour. In order to do this, researchers try to understand the bases of action from a theoretical standpoint and to develop appropriate measures for these bases. The evidence reported in Chapter 5 shows that there is often a close association between beliefs, attitude, intention and behaviour when these variables are appropriately measured. In this chapter these variables are now related more precisely within the *theory of planned behaviour* (Ajzen, 1985; 1988; 1991). This theory is itself an extension of the *theory of reasoned action* (Ajzen and Fishbein, 1980). A detailed explanation will follow, but the reader will be helped by the following sketch of the theoretical development in this field.

■ Fishbein's (1963) *expected-value theory of attitude*, together with the idea of *compatibility* (Ajzen and Fishbein, 1977), explained in the last chapter, relate attitudes to behaviour, but 'other variables' may prevent people from engaging in the behaviour that is consistent with their attitude.
■ The *theory of reasoned action* (Ajzen and Fishbein, 1980) makes attitude to the behaviour a determinant of intention and introduces a second determinant, called *subjective norm*, which is the internalized influence of people who are important to a respondent. The subjective norm can be seen as a measure of one type of 'other variable'.
■ The theory of planned behaviour (Ajzen, 1985; 1988; 1991) introduces a further determinant of intention called *perceived behavioural control*.

The theory of planned behaviour has been widely used, but its application is held back by uncertainties about the design of questionnaires and the analysis of results. The program NEWACT, on disk with this book, assists questionnaire design. Students can often use planned behaviour in their dissertation research and, in this chapter, I have included much of the measurement detail required for this type of practical work.

This chapter contains:

- An account of the origins and development of the theory of planned behaviour, evidence in support of the theory and illustrations of its application.

- Details of how to measure concepts in the theory.

- An account of the different sorts of explanation offered by the theory, and the inferences possible from this type of research.

- Discussion of some of the outstanding problems associated with this theory.

The theory of reasoned action

The theory of planned behaviour and its forerunner, the theory of reasoned action, fit the actions of a 'reconstructed economic man'. Traditional economic man was knowledgeable, selfish and optimizing. By comparison, 'reasoned action person' has limited knowledge of the outcomes of action and takes account of only those outcomes that can be brought easily to mind. Second, actions are done partly in response to the normative influence of other people and groups. Third, people have limited power to realize their preferences; for this reason it is their *intentions* rather than their actions that are predicted in the theory. Often action will follow intention, but circumstances may intervene to obstruct or change intention so that later actions may not conform to earlier plans.

Figure 6.1 illustrates this theory. The theory incorporates the attitude theory developed by Fishbein, which was explained in Chapter 5; that is, the attitude to an action (a *global variable*) is derived from the sum of the action's expected outcomes (a *sum variable*). A similar treatment applies to the influence of referents; a sum variable accumulates the influence of the different referents and this is equated with a global variable, subjective norm, which measures the overall propensity to act as other persons (who are important to you) think you should act. The relative strength of attitude and subjective norm in determining a given action is given by the weights w_1 and w_2. Since

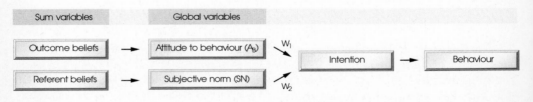

Figure 6.1 The theory of reasoned action

these strengths vary from action to action, w_1 and w_2 are established empirically, using regression or structural equation analysis such as LISREL (Jöreskog and Sörbom, 1989).

This theory gives a place to altruism – action done out of a sense of social obligation rather than for personal benefit. For example, some forms of life assurance only pay out on death and therefore do not offer personal benefit to a person paying the premium on his or her own life. Despite this, people may willingly take out such insurance to cover close relatives in the event of their unexpected death. One explanation for such behaviour is that it is controlled by the subjective norm, i.e. instigated by the desire to act as others think you should act. Sometimes, socially worthy acts bring internally generated feelings of self-respect or pride, while failure to act in this way may invoke feelings of shame or self-reproach. Subjective norm is therefore internally controlled; it does *not* operate through external social reinforcement such as the overt congratulations or hostility of others. The different referents involved in the subjective norm may be friends, parents, doctors, political parties, religious organizations, etc. The subjective norm (usually abbreviated to SN) is 'subjective' because it is what *the agent* thinks, and a 'norm' because it is the agent's understanding of what others think he or she *should* do.

The development of reasoned action theory

The theory of reasoned action was given this name by Ajzen and Fishbein (1980) in a restatement of their work in which they applied it to practical concerns such as health, consumer behaviour and voting; the authors had already presented much of the theory in earlier publications (e.g. Ajzen and Fishbein, 1969; Ajzen, 1971; Ajzen and Fishbein, 1972). The most complete account of the work appeared in *Belief, Attitude, Intention and Behavior* (Fishbein and Ajzen, 1975). Before 1980 the theory was known as the *Fishbein–Ajzen behavioural intentions model* or as the *extended model*; i.e. an extension of Fishbein's (1963) expected-value theory of attitude which forms part of reasoned action theory.

In the early 1970s Fishbein's work was in vogue among British practitioners of consumer research such as Sampson, Tuck and Cowling and the 1971 ESOMAR Seminar in Madrid was devoted to the Fishbein model (Fishbein, 1972). The theory was not always well tested in early applications; inappropriate measures for some of the components were used and there was some disappointment with the results. In commercial practice the theory gave way to other methods, and particularly to conjoint analysis which was more obviously tailored to the selection and design of products. Meanwhile, those with less numerical inclination made increasing use of qualitative research. The result of these new directions was research without theory, and the understanding of consumer behaviour has probably been held back as a result.

In the United States, the theory of reasoned action has been much used in academic consumer research, but there have been disagreements between the authors and those seeking to apply it. Some of these disagreements appear in: Bass and Talarzyk (1972); Cohen, Fishbein and Ahtola (1972); Sheth and Talarzyk (1972); Sheth (1972); Songer-Nocks (1976a, 1976b); Fishbein (1976) and Fishbein and Ajzen (1976a, 1976b). These controversies show that the theory is quite complicated in application and this may have deterred its use.

The principle of sufficiency

In the theory of reasoned action, evaluation is carried on beliefs and therefore all change in attitude and behaviour must come about through the acquisition of new beliefs or the modification of existing beliefs. In other words, belief changes are a *sufficient* explanation for 'downstream' changes in attitude, subjective norm, intention and behaviour. Ajzen and Fishbein (1980) assert that variables *external* to the theory such as past experience, personality, age, sex and other social classifications are associated with behaviour only because these factors are related to relevant beliefs, and hence to A_B or SN. They state:

> Although we do not deny that 'external' variables of this kind may sometimes be related to behavior, from our point of view they can affect behavior only indirectly. That is, external variables will be related to behavior only if they are related to one or more of the variables specified by our theory. (Ajzen and Fishbein, 1980: 82)

Thus beliefs and the other components of reasoned action theory mediate the effect of external variables. This uncompromising cognitivism has been tested in a number of studies by including external variables in the regression analysis to see whether these significantly improve the prediction of intention compared with A_B and SN alone. Often demographic variables have little effect; for example, Marsh and Matheson (1983) found no direct effects of age or sex on intention in a study on smoking cessation; i.e. any effects of age or sex occurred through differences in A_B and SN. Similarly, Loken (1983) found no direct effect of external variables on television watching.

However this *principle of sufficiency* is a difficult position to maintain; in particular, it is usually found that past experience has a direct effect on intention and sometimes on behaviour (Bagozzi and Kimmel, 1995). In the Marsh and Matheson (1983) study the previous experience of attempting to stop smoking had a direct effect on intention and a small direct effect on later attempts to stop smoking. Similar direct effects of past behaviour on both intention and subsequent behaviour have been found by Bentler and Speckart (1979; 1981), Fredricks and Dossett (1983) and Bagozzi (1981).

These studies were not always a fair test of sufficiency. Ryan (1982) pointed out that in some cases the relevance to the theory of reasoned action was low because inappropriate measures were used. But, allowing for this, it seems clear that past experience often has an effect that is not mediated by the concepts of reasoned action theory. Some direct connection between past experience and behaviour may be produced by unconscious learning which is activated in relevant contexts. Bentler and Speckart (1979) and Fredricks and Dossett (1983), following Triandis (1977), take the view that past behaviour establishes a *habit* which may affect later behaviour without altering components of reasoned action theory. However, most habits can be rationally justified and it seems a mistake to equate habit with behavioural continuities that have no consciously expressed basis.

The theory of planned behaviour

The direct effect of past experience on intention and later behaviour has led to a search for other variables, which may be included alongside A_B and SN. Such factors must have a substantial effect on intention; modification to the theory of reasoned action is only worthwhile if adequately defined measures can be shown to work quite strongly across a range of actions. There have been two particular variables proposed as additions to the theory: *moral norm* and *perceived behavioural control*.

Moral norm

If our behaviour is affected by salient persons and groups then it must also be affected by our own personal values. For this reason Ajzen and Fishbein (1969) included personal normative beliefs, or moral norm, in an early version of their theory but this variable was often highly correlated with intention so that these two measures were effectively equivalent. It appeared that the moral norm measure picked up both the A_B and SN effects and therefore failed as a separate measure of the personal normative factor (Ajzen and Fishbein, 1980: 247). When moral issues are strongly involved in the behaviour under investigation, and operate against other factors, moral norm has often raised the prediction of intention (e.g. Beck and Ajzen, 1990; Parker, Manstead and Stradling, 1995), but the effects are usually small and this measure is not widely used.

Perceived behavioural control

Perceived behavioural control was introduced by Ajzen (1985; 1988; 1991) in the theory of *planned behaviour*. Figure 6.2 shows the general form of the theory and Figure 6.3 gives an example. In this theory, perceived behavioural control (PC) is a determinant of intention together with A_B and SN. PC is measured as a person's self-perceived ability to take some action if he or she wants to take that action. This is much the same as the measure of *confidence* that one can act, which was used by Marsh and Matheson (1983) in a study which, in some degree, anticipated the theory of planned behaviour. 'Being able to do something if you want to' is a measure of freedom, and this revision of reasoned action theory therefore quantifies the degree to which an action is voluntary. Ajzen and Madden (1986) point out that there is often an overlap between past experience and PC because past experience reveals the situational opportunities and the personal abilities upon which PC is based; thus the inclusion of PC in a predictive theory will reduce the residual explanation derived from past experience.

Evaluating the theory of planned behaviour

The theory of planned behaviour (Figures 6.2 and 6.3) contains a direct connection between PC and *behaviour* which applies when people have limited control over their

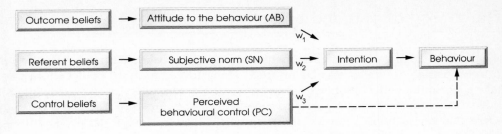

Figure 6.2 Theory of planned behaviour

actions. For example, a man may intend to give up cigarettes, but temptations in the environment and his own weakness may undermine resolve. PC indicates the extent to which such a person can manage his environment and his temperament, and thus helps to quantify this risk to his intended action. In support of this, a study of weight control by Schifter and Ajzen (1985) found that actual weight loss was better predicted when PC was used with intention. Ajzen (1991) found that PC contributed to the prediction of *behaviour* in 11 out of 17 studies reviewed. Madden, Ellen and Ajzen (1992) found that the PC measure improved on the prediction of behaviour (from intention alone) in those cases in which people had limited volitional control.

PC is a clear predictor of *intention*. In three attitude–behaviour studies, Ajzen and Madden (1986) showed that the inclusion of PC raised the prediction of intention substantially. Ajzen (1991) found that PC added significantly to the prediction of intention in all of the 19 studies reviewed; SN emerged as the weakest of the three predictors of intention, being significant in only 9 of the 19 instances. East (1993) found a significant gain in the prediction of intention from adding PC in 3 studies. In their review of 10 studies, Madden, Ellen and Ajzen (1992) showed that, in most cases, the addition of a measure of PC to the model substantially improved the prediction of intention.

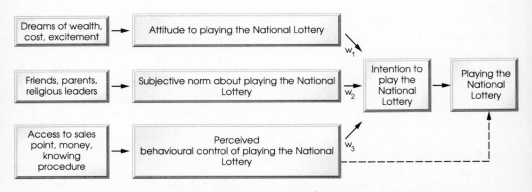

Figure 6.3 Theory of planned behaviour applied to playing the National Lottery

From one point of view the inclusion of PC in the determination of intention lacks logical support. If, for example, someone was only 50 per cent sure that they could do something, then all likelihoods and hence payoffs should be halved, thus taking this uncertainty into account. However, this reasoning treats human cognitive processing as a logical process when it might better be described as the outcome of associative mechanisms (Chapter 7). The ultimate test is empirical and, on this basis, PC has earned its place; in practice there is little relationship between PC and either A_B or SN.

The role of perceived behavioural control in determining behaviour has also been shown in a number of studies based on the work of Bandura (1977). Bandura used the term 'self-efficacy' to mean much the same as perceived behavioural control; he states that 'perceived self-efficacy is concerned with judgements of how well one can execute a course of action required to deal with prospective situations'. Condiotte and Lichtenstein (1981) found that people with low self-efficacy scores showed higher relapse back to smoking, supporting the Sutton, Marsh and Matheson (1987) finding that confidence was a major predictor of success (see box below); they also found that smokers were able to predict their areas of vulnerability where relapse would occur, suggesting that PC might be changed by training in these weak areas. Another study by McIntyre, Lichtenstein and Mermelstein (1983) found that self-efficacy scores were raised by training in smoking cessation skills (but the effect disappeared after a year).

An application to giving up cigarettes

In 1978 the Joint Committee on Research into Smoking recommended that a new study should be undertaken on attitudes towards smoking in the United Kingdom. One stimulus to this work was a 1977 report on attitudes and smoking behaviour prepared by Fishbein for the US Federal Trade Commission; this recommended a shift of focus from 'attitudes to smoking' to 'attitudes to giving up cigarettes'. The new study was conducted by the Office of Population Censuses and Surveys. *Smoking Attitudes and Behaviour*, the report by Alan Marsh and Jil Matheson, was published in 1983. The research used the attitude and PC (but not the subjective norm) measures of planned behaviour theory and is one of the most substantial tests ever given to a theory in social psychology.

A feature of the Marsh and Matheson research was the care that was taken to measure the different attitudes to the principal options of stopping and continuing to smoke. This is like a comparison of attitudes to the different brands in a category. The researchers predicted behaviour on the basis of the *difference* between the expected values of these two options. It is this difference that shows the personal gain or loss of taking one option rather than the other. An example clarifies the point. Most smokers accepted that smoking caused lung cancer (73 per cent) and heart disease (59 per cent), but the study showed that most of these people believed either that they did not smoke enough to do any damage, or that any damage was already done and was irreversible; for such people, cessation held no promise of reduced risk. The only smokers who saw a benefit from stopping were the minority who believed *both* that they had an enhanced risk *and* that cessation would diminish this risk. The researchers predicted that these people would make more attempts to stop and this was confirmed when smokers were followed up six months later. This evidence therefore supports a causal process from attitude to action.

A LISREL analysis of the data by Sutton, Marsh and Matheson (1987) showed that *intention* was predicted by attitude, confidence and a measure of past behaviour (previous attempts to stop); this shows that the model was not sufficient in this case and past behaviour added substantially to the prediction of future action. *Actual attempts* to stop smoking were predicted mainly by intention and slightly by previous attempts (see Figure 6.4). Attempts may not succeed; to explore the basis of *success*, Marsh and Matheson investigated those who had given up for a period of time and found that success was closely related to confidence.

This research explained intention and action by reference to beliefs and supports a strategy of trying to persuade smokers to stop by changing relevant beliefs. The study showed where to place emphasis in health education in order to get people to try to quit, for example, by explaining that the risk from cigarettes is related to the number smoked, that there is no threshold at which health hazards begin, and that there are health benefits for nearly all people who stop smoking. The study also showed that eventual success in quitting was strongly dependent on confidence and that health education should therefore emphasize 'how to stop' methods which would build this confidence.

Applications of planned behaviour theory

There has been a large number of planned behaviour studies in recent years; in most of these studies the performance of the theory was compared with the theory of reasoned action. Planned behaviour theory generally gives better predictions than reasoned action theory which it has now largely displaced. Recent applications have been to:

- Physical activities, exercise (Ajzen and Driver, 1992; Courneya, 1995; Godin, Valois and Lepage, 1993; Harrison and Liska, 1994; Kimiecik, 1992; Norman and Smith, 1995).
- Condom use, safe sex (Boldero, Moore and Rosenthal, 1992; Chan and Fishbein, 1993; Dewit and Teunis, 1994; Kashima, Gallois and McCamish, 1993; Morrison, Gillmore and Baker, 1995; White, Terry and Hogg, 1994).
- Health self-examinations (McCaul *et al.*, 1993).
- Addictions (Morojele and Stephenson, 1992).
- Quitting cigarette smoking (Devries and Backbier, 1994; Godin, Valois and Lepage, 1993).
- Blood donation (Giles and Cairns, 1995).
- Problem drinking (Schlegel, Davernas and Zanna, 1992).
- Controlling infant sugar intake (Beale and Manstead, 1991).
- Food choice (Dennison and Shepherd, 1995; Raats, Shepherd and Sparks, 1995).
- Engaging in collective action (Kelly and Breinlinger, 1995).
- Recycling (Boldero, 1995; Taylor and Todd, 1995).
- Internet use (Klobas, 1995).
- Risky driving (Parker, Manstead and Stradling, 1995; Parker *et al.*, 1992).
- Accident avoidance behaviour (Richard *et al.*, 1994; Rutter, Quine and Chesham, 1995).
- Why entrepreneurs seek equity funding (Desroches and Chebat, 1995).
- Buying gifts (Netemeyer, Andrews and Durvasula, 1993; Sahni, 1994).
- Application for shares (East, 1993).
- Complaining (East, 1996).

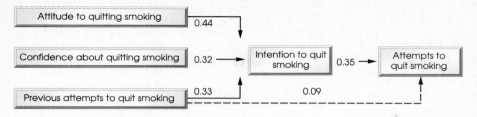

Figure 6.4 Coefficients relating attitude, confidence and previous attempts to intention and later attempts to stop smoking (Sutton *et al.*, 1987)

Measurements, explanations and applications

Measurement of variables

Outcome beliefs
In attitude–behaviour theories the belief–attitude link, i.e.

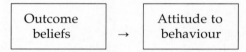

is the expected-value model of attitude, which was explained in Chapter 5. To cover both expectation and value each outcome belief is measured on two scales, e.g.

If I play the National Lottery next week I will spend a lot:

unlikely	-3	-2	-1	0	1	2	3	likely
	extremely	quite	slightly	neither	slightly	quite	extremely	

Spending a lot is:

bad	-3	-2	-1	0	1	2	3	good
	extremely	quite	slightly	neither	slightly	quite	extremely	

The expected value for *spending a lot on the National Lottery* is the product of the two measures, and the sum of the products for all the salient outcomes of playing the National Lottery, i.e. $\Sigma b_i e_i$, defines A_B.

Referent beliefs
A similar measurement procedure applies to the referent beliefs, e.g.

My friends think I should play the National Lottery next week:

unlikely	-3	-2	-1	0	1	2	3	likely
	extremely	quite	slightly	neither	slightly	quite	extremely	

I want to do what my friends think I should do:

unlikely	−3	−2	−1	0	1	2	3	likely
	extremely	quite	slightly	neither	slightly	quite	extremely	

Here the first measure assesses *normative belief (n)* and the second *motivation to comply (m)*. The two measures are multiplied together to give the effect of this referent and the sum of the products for all the referents, i.e. $\Sigma n_i m_i$, defines SN.

Control beliefs

The same procedure is used to measure control beliefs, the two components are the probability that some factor facilitates the action (p) and access to this control factor (c), e.g.

I can play the National Lottery more easily if I understand the system:

unlikely	−3	−2	−1	0	1	2	3	likely
	extremely	quite	slightly	neither	slightly	quite	extremely	

I understand the system for playing the National Lottery:

unlikely	−3	−2	−1	0	1	2	3	likely
	extremely	quite	slightly	neither	slightly	quite	extremely	

The sum of products, $\Sigma c_i p_i$, defines PC.

Before these scales can be set up it is necessary to establish the relevant salient beliefs using the procedure described in Exercise 5.2. Once these salient beliefs have been obtained it is convenient to use the computer program NEWACT which asks for each belief and composes a draft of the questionnaire.

Global variables

Intention is measured as a statement of intent or as an estimate of behaviour, e.g.

I intend to play the National Lottery next week:

unlikely	−3	−2	−1	0	1	2	3	likely
	extremely	quite	slightly	neither	slightly	quite	extremely	

I will play the National Lottery next week:

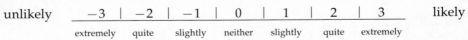

unlikely	−3	−2	−1	0	1	2	3	likely
	extremely	quite	slightly	neither	slightly	quite	extremely	

Attitude is measured using two or more scales, e.g.

For me, playing the National Lottery next week is:

bad	-3	-2	-1	0	1	2	3	good
	extremely	quite	slightly	neither	slightly	quite	extremely	

unpleasant	-3	-2	-1	0	1	2	3	pleasant
	extremely	quite	slightly	neither	slightly	quite	extremely	

boring	-3	-2	-1	0	1	2	3	exciting
	extremely	quite	slightly	neither	slightly	quite	extremely	

Subjective norm is usually measured with the format:

Most people who are important to me think that I should play the National Lottery next week:

unlikely	-3	-2	-1	0	1	2	3	likely
	extremely	quite	slightly	neither	slightly	quite	extremely	

Perceived behavioural control may be measured using the scale:

For me, playing the National Lottery next week is:

difficult	-3	-2	-1	0	1	2	3	easy
	extremely	quite	slightly	neither	slightly	quite	extremely	

Explanation of behaviour using the theory of planned behaviour

Level 1: Behaviour
The whole theory provides an explanation of behaviour by identifying factors that underlie action, but the immediate precursors of behaviour in planned behaviour theory are intention and perceived behavioural control. This, then, is the first level of explanation and it has been tested by (among others) Madden, Ellen and Ajzen (1992). Usually, perceived behavioural control is the weaker factor and may have no direct impact on behaviour. As noted above, PC directly affects behaviour when people try to achieve a goal over which they have limited control such as giving up cigarettes or losing weight, and it is interesting to see how the activities of behaviour therapists relate to this process. Much of behaviour therapy is designed to change and manage the environment so that contextual cues and reinforcement are benign and do not precipitate an undesired behaviour. They train clients to anticipate difficult conditions and to have the appropriate role behaviour at hand for situations that cannot be avoided. For example, obese people are advised never to buy any prepared foods that can be eaten without delay, and smokers are rehearsed through the behaviour of declining a cigarette. Such therapy may be seen as raising actual control (and, as a result, raising perceived behavioural control).

There are other cases where people have little control and they solve the problem by deciding not to do the action. East (1993) noted that this applied to buying shares in utility privatizations. This means that it is only in those decisions where people have little control, but for outcome and normative reasons they want to do the action, that PC is a direct determinant of behaviour.

This level of explanation is also concerned with the strength of the connection between intention and behaviour. Fishbein (1966) compared the link between intention and behaviour in a study of sexual activity among students. The study showed that men were less successful than women in realizing their sexual intentions. In the cultural climate prevailing at the time of the study, women in the United States had more control than men: a woman could more easily persuade a man to become her lover, and she could refuse unwanted offers; men found it harder to persuade women and therefore had less freedom of action.

Level 2: Intention

The next level of explanation is the relative importance of A_B, SN and PC in predicting intention; the priority varies from application to application. For example, Jaccard and Davidson (1972) found that among college women the use of the contraceptive pill was associated more with A_B than with SN; this probably reflects the importance of avoiding pregnancy for this group. Davidson and Jaccard (1975) found that married women with children placed somewhat more emphasis on the normative component.

A number of applications of planned behaviour theory have related to consumer matters. East (1993) found that applications for shares in privatizations were influenced by A_B, SN and PC but the weights differed across the three cases studied (which probably reflected the rather different conditions of the three privatizations). What was of interest, though, was the difference between these results and what might have been expected if the application for shares was a business proposition determined largely by outcomes. In that event the application for shares would have been dominated by A_B; this was not found, showing the importance of normative and control factors in fields that are supposedly decided on rational criteria. In East's study, access to finance was a major determinant of intention, and Sahni (1994) has suggested that, in purchase decisions, perceived behavioural control will often be determined by financial resources. Sahni found that a financial control measure helped to determine expenditure intentions.

In a study of complaining, East (1996) showed that the intention to complain was more widely based than has generally been supposed. Much of the work that has explored the motivation to complain has examined dissatisfaction with the product and the likelihood of redress – essentially factors covered by A_B. Researchers have not used questionnaires that cover *all* the potential factors that might affect complaining. The study used two conditions, and in neither case was A_B the strongest determinant of intention to seek redress. This study is reported more fully in Chapter 9.

Level 3: Specific factor explanations

The third level of explanation relates specific outcome, referent and control factors either to global variables or to intention. In the theory, specific factors relate to intention through the appropriate global variable, but it is not always clear which global variable a factor belongs to when an investigation is being conducted. Referent beliefs are usually most associated with SN, but other factors may act as either A_B or PC determinants, or as both. For example, embarrassment about complaining might be seen as an outcome or as a control factor. East (1996) found that embarrassment acted primarily as a control factor obstructing complaining, rather than as a cost if complaint was made. Level 3 explanations help us to choose intervention strategies. If a firm wants to encourage customers to express their grievances, the key factors affecting complaining must be addressed. For example, if many people lack confidence about complaining it is best to provide a clear procedure and encouragement to use it.

Because a factor may work through more than one global variable there is a danger that it is 'double-counted', but Fishbein and Ajzen (1975: 304–7) point out that a piece of information such as the effectiveness of a drug may lead to two separate effects: when a doctor prescribes a drug, the medicine may be taken because the doctor is a referent *and* because inferences are made about the strongly beneficial effects of the medicine. Under some circumstances the same piece of information may result in attitude changes that oppose the normative changes. For example, a man who drinks a lot may be *less* inclined to use a drug when a doctor has convinced him of its potency, for fear of amplifying the effect of alcohol. Generally, there is a degree of separation between the paths of the model and Fishbein and Ajzen (1981) claim that usually A_B and SN correlate with intention more strongly than they correlate with each other. Trafimow and Fishbein (1995) show evidence that people do distinguish between outcome and normative beliefs.

Double-counting is not a problem when the correlation between specific factors and intention is reported. Examples of dominant factors affecting the intention are:

For complaining:

- being confident about complaining,
- getting a replacement,
- what friends think you should do,
- standing up for one's rights.

For applying for shares:

- what relatives and friends think you should do,
- access to funds,
- the effort of making the application,
- making a profit or a secure investment.

Exercise 6.1   Analyzing why people complain

The software available in association with this text carries a set of files covering a study of *complaining*.

The questionnaire COM.TXT was used. You can print it out and work out which items measure intention, A_B, SN, PC, past experience, the different beliefs and their evaluations, etc.

The COM.DAT data were gathered from a number of respondents. Look at this on the screen; each line is the data for one respondent. The first three digits are the number assigned to the respondent; the next digit specifies one of two scenarios used at the head of the questionnaire; the other numbers are the ones checked by the respondent in the order in which the items appear on the questionnaire.

COM.SPS is a mainframe SPSSX program for analyzing the data. If you are unfamiliar with SPSS, you should still be able to work out what each line is concerned with. For instance, you will see that products are produced from pairs of measures and then aggregated to produce the sum measures, SUMEV, SUMREFS and SUMCBS.

COM.LST is the output from the SPSS analysis. Inspect this and work out (for discussion in seminar):

■ Is complaining most related to A_B, SN or PC?

■ Does the addition of the past experience measure (PE) raise the prediction of intention?

■ Do A_B, SN and PC correlate with their supposed determinants, i.e. SUMEV, SUMREFS and SUMCBS?

■ Which specific factors correlate most with the intention?

■ Which specific factors might be used in advertising designed to promote complaining?

■ What are the shortcomings of this study and analysis?

Using evidence from planned behaviour research

It is easy to overstate the application of any explanative theory. Even when we have good evidence about how a state of affairs came about, it may not be easy to apply it. When the findings are used to influence others, the influence attempt may not succeed. Beliefs may resist change, any change may not be large enough to affect behaviour, and other belief changes may be induced which have an opposite effect on behaviour. Fishbein and Ajzen (1981) have stated that studies of the existing basis for action give no more than an indication of where best to place emphasis in an influence attempt: 'it is impossible to tell in advance the exact extent to which . . . a given item of information will influence a person's attitude or subjective norm'.

Despite these concerns, planned behaviour research offers an advance on qualitative research methods. Planned behaviour gives an order of importance to the ideas gleaned from elicitations and may be used in decisions on product development, positioning and advertising themes. Usually, ads can say little in the time available and evidence on what principally drives purchasers to buy a category is very useful for positioning a brand. Research may also show that suppliers and consumers have rather different views about what the important features of a product are.

Dynamic tests of the theory

Most attitude–behaviour studies are designed to predict intention and behaviour and the results are open to different explanations. In some studies, when behaviour is concurrent with the study, the factors that predict behaviour may be caused by behaviour rather than the reverse. For example, Morojele and Stephenson (1992) found increases in personal control as patients recovered from addictions. Such findings leave open the question of what happens first; patients might be expected to gain a sense of personal control *as a result of recovery*.

It is better to observe beliefs and attitudes, and then predict from these measures which persons will change. This was done by Marsh and Matheson (1983) when they predicted who would stop smoking; by Desroches and Chebat (1995), who predicted which entrepreneurs would make stock issues; and by Kimiecik (1992), who predicted physical activity among employees. In these studies, beliefs, intentions, etc. occur before action and therefore are more likely to be the cause of behaviour.

A more stringent test, and one that is more relevant to influence, is to use an experimental design and *change* those beliefs that planned behaviour research identifies as the keys to behaviour, and then observe whether the 'downstream' effects of these changes fit the theory. If they do, we have evidence supporting the linear causal sequence from beliefs through global variables to intention and behaviour.

There are a number of studies which are relevant to this *dynamic test* of the theory. Ajzen (1971) has argued that the weightings of the global variables are an indicator of where to pitch an influence attempt and Ajzen and Fishbein (1972) showed that it was possible to devise messages that affected either the normative or the attitudinal component. Lutz (1977; 1978) conducted a study in which belief change was manipulated; the flow of changes fitted reasoned action theory quite well but there was not much transmission from $\Sigma b_i e_i$ to A_B. Ryan (1982) also found that the $\Sigma b_i e_i \rightarrow A_B$ connection was weak. Beale and Manstead (1991) used an experimental comparison to examine the effect of health advice on giving sugar to infants and found that the intervention modified the attitudes of mothers, but the effect on intention, though in the expected direction, was not significant. Only in one case is there evidence of strong effects. McArdle (1972) found a strong $\Sigma b_i e_i \rightarrow A_B$ connection (correlations of 0.63 and 0.77 in relevant conditions) and an impact on behaviour. McArdle used ten reasons in face-to-face persuasion to persuade alcoholics to join a treatment unit and thus targeted many more beliefs than other studies.

Weak findings do not refute the theory, but neither do they give confidence in its utility. It is possible that small effects occur because it takes time for people to take account of new evidence and adjust their attitudes and intentions. Lutz (1977), following Rosenberg (1968), suggested that there may be thresholds for change; such 'stepped' changes might be assisted by messages drawing conclusions along the pathway of the attitude–behaviour model. Some evidence of delay in processing is found in Marsh and Matheson's (1983) research on smoking cessation. Their data suggested that slow, belief-based changes were at work and it took some time for these to harden into a resolve to stop smoking. Devries and Backbier (1994) also found evidence of stages in the quitting of cigarettes.

Identifying factors

Table 6.1 helps us to see which likelihoods and which evaluations are most closely connected with the use of oral contraceptives. The connections may be because people who have these beliefs tend to become users, or because users learn to have these beliefs, or the relationship may arise though some common cause such as family subculture. Such data are far from conclusive about what makes people likely to use the pill. But, in the absence of stronger evidence, we have to exercise judgement in assessing data like those in Table 6.1.

Table 6.1 Mean beliefs and outcome evaluations for college women who intend, and do not intend, to use the birth control pill (scales −3 to +3)

| Using birth control pills . . . | Outcome | | | |
| | Likelihood | | Evaluation | |
	Intend	Not intend	Intend	Not intend
Leads to major side-effects	−0.4	1.2*	−2.5	−2.5
Leads to minor side-effects	1.4	1.3	−1.1	−1.8
Produces birth defects	−2.4	−0.4*	−2.5	−2.5
Is unreliable	−2.3	−1.1*	−2.5	−2.0
Is the best method available	2.0	0.9*	2.7	2.1
Would avoid pregnancy	2.4	1.1*	2.8	2.2
Would affect my sexual morals	−1.9	−0.4*	−1.4	−1.6
Is immoral	−2.7	−0.7*	−1.8	−1.8
Would give me guilt feelings	−2.3	0.1*	−2.4	−2.4
Is expensive	−0.9	−0.8	−1.1	−1.6
Is convenient	2.6	1.8	2.7	1.7*
Allows me to control the size of my family	2.7	2.2	2.7	1.8*
Allows me to regulate the interval between pregnancies	2.7	2.2	2.7	1.9
Allows me to regulate my menstrual cycle	2.4	0.8*	2.1	1.4
Would increase my sexual pleasure	0.5	−0.1	2.2	1.1*

* Significant difference (p < 0.05) between intenders and non-intenders.
Source: Ajzen and Fishbein (1980: 146)

An expected value can change either because the subjective likelihood alters or because the evaluation of the outcome changes. Usually the evaluations are more stable and vary less than the belief probabilities. We see in Table 6.1 that there are only three significant differences of evaluation between intenders and non-intenders, whereas there are nine significant differences of belief likelihood. In other words users and non-users often have the same values, but differ in their beliefs about how an action relates to these values. One explanation for this is that the evaluations rest on another set of beliefs and this complexity gives stability to the attribute evaluation.

Some factors are more changeable than others. Some likelihoods and evaluations may be *strongly anchored* and therefore difficult to influence. For example, the value of regulating the size of one's family partly depends upon how many children you have already, which is not a perception that can be changed by information. *Differences between intenders and non-intenders provide an indicator of changeability.* Table 6.1 shows that the convenience of the oral contraceptive is accepted by both intenders and non-intenders so that the scope for change seems limited in this respect. On the other hand, the efficacy of the method could be emphasized to non-intenders, who accept this less than intenders.

Another indicator is *headroom*, i.e. how much a measure can change in the required direction before it reaches the top or bottom of the scale. Table 6.1 shows that there is little headroom for changing non-intenders' beliefs about regulating their family size and the interval between pregnancies, but the likelihood of guilt feelings among non-intenders might be changed.

Finally, the data in Table 6.1 should be checked to see whether some beliefs are *at odds with established knowledge*, for example, fears about birth defects may be unsubstantiated.

Student studies

For some years I have been conducting attitude–behaviour studies at Kingston University with the help of students. Initial work was done as student exercises using the theory of reasoned action. The numbers of respondents used are mostly small and the work should be seen as exploratory, but it does give an idea of the applications of attitude–behaviour theory and suggests a number of possible lines of research. Table 6.2 summarizes the applications based on reasoned action theory.

Table 6.2 Summary data from student studies using the theory of reasoned action

| Topic | Sample size | Adj. R^2 | β weights predicting intention | | Correlations | |
			A_B	SN	$\Sigma b_i e_i$ and A_B	$\Sigma n_i m_i$ and SN
Buying a *Mars Bar* this week	21	0.51	0.77	0.15	0.51	0.23
Buying *Mars Bars*	32	0.37	0.45	0.30	0.38	0.49
Taking regular exercise	20	0.50	0.83	0.42	0.74	0.50
Taking exercise next week	30	0.79	−0.09	0.95	0.60	0.57
Giving blood	20	0.13	0.12	0.39	0.46	0.71
Giving blood	28	0.18	0.48	0.02	0.27	0.45
Watching Breakfast TV						
–naive	30	0.30	0.24	0.39	0.40	–
–experienced	30	0.47	0.60	0.27	0.47	–
–after service started	40	0.49	0.62	0.17	0.52	–
Working in the library	22	0.21	0.53	−0.02	0.24	–
Having a building society account	21	0.49	0.56	0.23	0.59	0.80
Getting married in the next five years	75	0.57	0.63	0.22	0.36	0.78
Drinking alcohol at lunchtime	29	0.24	0.56	0.05	0.57	−0.17
Going to McDonalds	29	0.25	0.46	0.15	0.50	0.53
Buying a computer for the first time	26	0.33	0.08	0.58	0.42	0.69
Watching *Neighbours* on TV	29	0.44	0.42	0.37	0.63	0.44
Means		**0.39**	**0.45**	**0.29**	**0.48**	**0.50**

Prediction of intention

The adjusted R^2 figures in Table 6.2 show the degree to which variance in intention is predicted by A_B and SN; the mean adjusted R^2 was 0.39, showing quite a good fit for the model. The beta weights show the relative importance of A_B and SN in predicting intention. The correlations between A_B and $\Sigma b_i e_i$, and SN and $\Sigma n_i m_i$, test Fishbein's (1963) attitude theory; the averages of 0.48 and 0.50 respectively are typical of what is generally found. Some other points from this work were:

Blood donation

Giving blood gave poor R^2 results on both occasions that it was studied, which suggests that other factors are at work, such as PC, and Giles and Cairns (1995) have now reported that PC has a strong effect on the intention to give blood.

Watching Breakfast TV

In an unpublished study, East, Whittaker and Swift (1984) investigated the beliefs about watching Breakfast TV nine months before the service started. They conducted the research on a naive group, who were given no information about the programmes they might see, and on a second group who were shown details of American and Australian Breakfast TV services and who were informed about the nature of the service that they could anticipate in Britain. The intentions of the naive group were based on SN, while the intentions of the experienced group were most related to A_B. This was to be expected since the information given to the experienced group was related to attitude and not to subjective norm factors.

Later, a further group of viewers of Breakfast TV were examined after the service had started; data from this group showed a pattern very similar to the experienced group and this indicated that the experience of new products could be simulated effectively by such experiments.

Key beliefs

Some of the specific factors most associated with intention in the student studies were unexpected.

- One surprise was the dominant reason given for taking exercise; among students, exercise was taken mainly for the social contacts that it brought, not for health and fitness as might be supposed by health educators.
- Drinking alcohol at lunchtime was controlled by perceived consequences such as expense and difficulty in working later, not by deference to social referents such as lecturing staff.
- One *Mars Bar* study also indicated some interesting reasons for consumption. Men were attracted to eating *Mars Bars* by their good value and because they satisfied hunger; women gave taste as a reason for eating/not eating *Mars Bars* and they were worried about bad teeth. Table 6.3 shows these findings.

Table 6.3 Expected-value of outcome correlated with intention to buy *Mars Bars*

Factor	Men	Women
Get good value	0.9*	0.2
Feel less hungry	0.8*	0.2
Enjoy the taste	0.6	0.7*
Suffer bad teeth	0.4	0.7*
Get spots	−0.4	0.4
Put on weight	0.5	0.4

* Significant at $p < 0.05$.

■ For both men and women students, the intention to marry in the next five years was influenced more by A_B than by SN, and there was a marked similarity between the views of men and women about early marriage. The only differences were that women thought that they would have less money and reduced career prospects if they married in the next five years, beliefs that were probably well founded.

Exercise 6.2   Research by the student group

1. Select an action of mutual interest. The action must be individual and voluntary, e.g. watching a popular TV programme, using second class post, carrying an organ donor card, buying a second-hand car, going to the dentist regularly, reading a newspaper every day or playing the National Lottery. Make sure that the action is appropriately specified in terms of target, action, context and time. Avoid actions that are done by very few people or nearly everyone because these are likely to be involuntary.

2. Choose the target group. This is often other students because they are accessible, but this will limit the generalizability of findings.

3. From a sample of the target group elicit the salient outcome, referent and control beliefs about the action. Each member of the student group should gather one or two sets of salient beliefs which are then reduced to an agreed list. The elicitation procedure is described in Exercise 5.2.

4. Use the program NEWACT to create a planned behaviour questionnaire. The program asks for:
   (a) the title of the questionnaire,
   (b) the intention,
   (c) the outcomes,
   (d) the referents,
   (e) the control factors.

The program sets up the different scales for each item and works out the form of some of the items by parsing your input. The best way to get used to this program, and to the questionnaires it produces, is to try using it on your own. Mistakes and poor grammar need to be rectified by wordprocessing the questionnaire file that is produced. Age, sex and occupation items are added automatically, but may be deleted if not required. The program creates second measures for some variables and these may be deleted to shorten the questionnaire. Often the phraseology for control items is clumsy and needs adjustment. I find that the questionnaire will usually cover two sides of paper when printed in two-column landscape format. Do not forget to put 'PTO' in the bottom right-hand corner of the first side. The questionnaire looks better if scale referents such as 'extremely', 'quite' and 'slightly' are italicized. These referents are positioned correctly for normal proportional fonts.

5. Print copies of the questionnaire. Each member of the class must get these completed by members of the target group. A demonstration of the theory is usually obtained from about forty respondents but more improves the reliability of results.

6. To analyze the data using SPSS, edit an existing analysis program such as COM.SPS which is on the diskette (see Exercise 6.1). NEWACT numbers the scales 1–7, or 7–1, but when the data are processed it may be appropriate to recode to a scale of -3 to $+3$. The product of -3 and -3 is quite different from the product of 1 and 1 and the scaling chosen affects the correlations with other variables (Bagozzi, 1984). Ajzen (1991) now recommends *optimal scaling*, i.e. adding a constant to each scale to produce the highest correlation between the sum and global variables. This procedure gives some benefit to random effects and I prefer to restrict the choice to -3 to $+3$ and 1 to 7. To do this, test the correlation between the sum and global variables using the 1 to 7 and -3 to $+3$ alternatives for each of the two scales used in the construction of product variables (i.e. four combinations) and use the combination giving the highest correlation in each sum group. Usually evaluation is bipolar and motivation to comply is unipolar, but there is no theoretical basis which allows us to anticipate which scalings are optimal. A detailed treatment of optimal scaling appears in East (1993).

7. Examine your analysis and answer the following questions:
    (a) Is the action most related to A_B, SN or PC?
    (b) Do A_B, SN and PC correlate with the corresponding sum measures?
    (c) Which specific factors correlate most with intention?
    (d) Which specific factors might be used in advertising, if any?
    (e) What are the shortcomings of this study and analysis?

8. Write a brief report of the work.

Some outstanding problems in planned behaviour theory

The theory of planned behaviour has been very successful in explaining and predicting a wide range of behaviour, but a number of problems have emerged. Here we consider the following questions:

- How is salience best established?
- Why are the correlations between sum and global variables low?
- How different are deliberate and spontaneous forms of behaviour?
- Are there explanations for the effects of past experience that occur outside the variables of the theory?
- How does past experience affect A_B, SN and PC?

How is salience best established?

The methods for eliciting salient beliefs and referents are *ad hoc* and the use of modal salient beliefs inevitably means that some respondents have to answer questions that may not be salient for them. However, any vagueness in the measurement counts against the theory in empirical test; if the theory works using these methods, the problems cannot be too great.

Differences in salience within a group have been illustrated by Kristiansen (1987) who showed that users and non-users of cigarettes have different salient beliefs. Similarly Petkova, Ajzen and Driver (1995) found that the salient beliefs of those who were pro-choice on abortion differed from those who described themselves as pro-life. Generally, users have more salient beliefs than non-users and this complicates any comparison between them.

One recent approach has been to link salience with accessibility (discussed in Chapter 5). Ajzen, Nichols and Driver (1995) measured accessibility by latency of response and found that those beliefs that were more quickly elicited were more accessible and gave higher correlations with global variables.

From a practical standpoint it is necessary to set some criterion of exclusion when choosing salient beliefs in planned behaviour research. Non-salient items waste time and take space in the questionnaire, and they weaken correlations with global variables, but exclusion from the questionnaire is usually done on the basis of the frequency of elicitation of beliefs and this may not be a full test of salience. Non-salient beliefs may also be excluded at the analysis stage; this procedure is open to the charge of capitalizing on chance but any such effect seems slight and I would recommend the practice. A study of playing the National Lottery included outcomes on becoming dependent on gambling, having social problems as a result of major winnings and being disappointed at losing; these items were generated in the elicitation, but none of them was significantly related to either A_B or intention and, when they were excluded, the correlation between $\Sigma b_i e_i$ and A_B rose.

Why are the correlations between sum and global variables low?

Ajzen (1991) has noted that the correlations between sum and global variables (typically about 0.5) are modest, given that one is meant to determine the other. A number of reasons have been given for this. One of these is that individuals have fewer salient beliefs than the modal salient belief list and this is why correlations tend to rise when the weakest beliefs are deleted from the analysis. If the sum variable is calculated only on *personally salient beliefs* the correlations rise (Elliott, Jobber and Sharp, 1995), but these expedients do not make much difference and, in any case, are not practicable in most research. East (1993) has suggested that even the personal salient belief list is too long as a set of causes of intention and action, and that people might, in practice, base decisions on one or two beliefs only.

Another proposal (Ajzen and Driver, 1992) is that global variables such as A_B are composites of two or more different variables; this implies that better correlations will be obtained if the global variable is subdivided and matched to appropriate subsets of beliefs. Ajzen and Driver distinguished between the more affective consequences of some actions, such as a sense of relaxation after exercise, and the instrumental consequences, such as being healthier. East (1993) saw much the same division, but related it to short- and long-term consequences of the action. Ajzen and Driver (1992) showed some increase in correlation when concepts were subdivided along these lines, but the procedure complicates the theory. There is also a divide in the PC concept between opportunity and ability, that is, the control vested by the environment and the control vested by personal abilities. Because we need to appraise both the external and the internal domains of control, there is a real possibility that PC is poorly measured by the usual instruments.

More radical redefinitions of concepts have been proposed for the elements of reasoned action theory (Burnkrant and Page, 1988; Miniard and Cohen, 1979; 1981; 1983; Oliver and Bearden, 1985; Shimp and Kavas, 1984). These proposals are based on empirical analysis, but there is a danger that what works for one behaviour may not work for other behaviours. The theory is a set of ideas that makes conceptual sense and this coherence should not be abandoned unless consistent results are obtained across a wide field.

Deliberate and spontaneous action

In an interesting review, Fazio (1990) divides the prediction of behaviour into two fields, one largely guided by the work of Fishbein and Ajzen where deliberate processes of decision-making are modelled, and the second guided by Fazio (1986) and his followers whose work has been introduced in Chapter 5. Fazio describes behaviour that is spontaneously produced when relevant attitudes are activated. Fazio's model is reproduced in Figure 6.5.

In Fazio's account, attitudes are automatically activated by observation of the attitude object. The attitude then guides perception, and the individual becomes aware of related parts of the environment. The definition of the event then occurs as these perceptions are related to a normative understanding of the situation, and, out of this definition of the event, behaviour may follow.

Not all objects activate attitudes. Fazio argues that this occurs only when the object and its evaluation have been well established in memory, usually through direct behavioural experience. Thus spontaneous production of behaviour is restricted to familiar contexts, leaving planned behaviour to explain the more unusual situations. However this rather cosy division of the field has been disrupted by evidence from Bargh *et al.* (1992), reported in Chapter 5, that a wide range of objects can elicit attitudes. This casts doubt on automatic activation as a distinguishing criterion between deliberate and automatic control of behaviour.

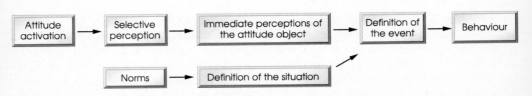

Figure 6.5 Fazio's (1986) diagram of the attitude–behaviour process

My own view is that often both types of explanation may apply to the same phenomena. The planned behaviour account may cover fairly automatic and habitual behaviour because people, in retrospect, have reasons for such behaviour which can be summoned up when making responses to a questionnaire. Fazio (1990) has shown that priming objects can alter responses in studies of deliberate behaviour, and Baldwin and Holmes (1987) have shown systematically different accounts when different social referents were visualized before response. These studies show the effect of automatic processes when people are making considered responses.

The role of experience in predicting intention

Past experience helps to form A_B, SN and PC and is therefore strongly predictive of intention. Although A_B, SN and PC predict intention quite well, the addition of past experience to the regression analysis usually raises the adjusted R^2 significantly, and this suggests that A_B, SN and PC capture only part of the effect of experience. Thus there is a need to explain this excess effect of past experience on intention and four types of explanation can be offered:

1. A measure of experience may act as a supplementary measure of A_B, SN and PC where these measures are deficient. A measure is deficient when it captures only a part of the variable that it is designed to measure; deficiency is reduced by the use of multiple scales and we can therefore test this hypothesis by examining the effect of past experience before and after improvements in the outcome, referent and control measures. A reduction in the R^2 gain when past experience is added to the model indicates that past experience is a supplementary measure for A_B, SN and PC.

    The global measures can be improved by including sum variables as well as global variables in the regressions predicting intention. An average of results from eleven studies showed a slight drop in the R^2 gain from 0.08 to 0.06, when the A_B, SN and PC measures were doubled in this way and past experience was added to the model. Thus measurement error plays a minor part in the improvement in the prediction of intention when past experience is added to the model.

2. The excess effect of past experience may indicate that a further variable, akin to A_B, SN or PC, is missing from the theory. The usual candidate here is moral norm, but gains from this source tend to be small (see, for example, Parker, Manstead and Stradling, 1995).

3. The effect may indicate unconscious learning, which is not reflected in A_B, SN or PC measures; such learning could still affect intention which seems less complex than the global variables. Fazio (1986; 1990) shows that attitudes learned through experience are more accessible and this suggests that the connections between global variables and both intention and behaviour will be stronger among more experienced people.

4. It may be possible to enlarge the theory so that more is explained by its constructs. The leading contenders here are Bagozzi and Warshaw (1990) and Bagozzi (1992);

see also Bagozzi and Kimmel (1995). These theories are more complex than the theory of planned behaviour and any gain must be balanced against a loss of parsimony.

The development of A_B, SN and PC

As experience increases, people become more informed and the cognitive–affective basis for future action is changed. This is a situation that is particularly pertinent to consumer behaviour. Consumers are naive when they enter markets that are new to them and they become more experienced as they repeat purchase. Sometimes, with truly novel products, we are all placed in the naive segment until experience with the product raises knowledge. From the standpoint of planned behaviour, the growth in experience is expressed as changes in the belief basis of A_B, SN and PC. When these changes are positive, intention will be enhanced; if the experience is negative, intentions will be reduced and further trial curtailed. Thus, under the voluntary conditions that attach to most consumer behaviour, we would expect to find that those who are highly experienced have stronger intentions – it was their stronger intentions that led to the behaviour that made them experienced.

When intention changes there should be corresponding modifications of A_B, SN and PC. This can occur when the beliefs underlying the global variables become more numerous and more strongly linked to the behaviour. If experience elaborates the belief basis of planned behaviour constructs we may ask whether it has the same effect on A_B, SN and PC, and East (1992) has suggested that the progression from novice to expert consumer is a movement from behaviour based mainly on SN to actions based more on A_B and PC. This proposal is founded on the idea that, in the absence of detailed knowledge, people have to make decisions on the basis of simple ideas or heuristic processes, and 'what others think I should do' will be better known or more easily guessed than the benefits and opportunities related to an unfamiliar prospect. Consumers who are better informed may derive their knowledge from the mass media and from the advice of others, but often such knowledge is based on direct experience. Thus those who have experience of an action will, in consequence, know more about the benefits and costs, and the control factors affecting that action, and will therefore be able to call on such information when making a decision.

East (1992) found three minor studies that supported the view that experience shifts the basis of choice from subjective norm to the attitude factor. He reports two unpublished studies done in the context of the theory of reasoned action. In one case the *first-time* purchase of a computer was found to be heavily based on subjective norm; the study lacked a comparison with experienced computer purchasers but it would be surprising if a product with so many outcomes was purchased on a normative basis by knowledgeable consumers. The second study was by East, Whittaker and Swift (1984), cited earlier – here the prospective viewing decisions of two groups of people were examined before Breakfast TV was introduced into Britain. In one group (novice) there was no explanation of the service to come, and SN was the stronger determinant of intention. In the second group (experienced), details and examples of Breakfast TV from the United States and Australia were provided. Viewing intentions were better predicted in the second group and the stronger determinant here was A_B. A third study by Knox and de Chernatony (1994) found that non-users of mineral water were much more influenced by subjective norm than users. Relationships between experience and variables of the theory of planned behaviour are not usually reported in studies, but Beale and Manstead (1991) did find a positive correlation between experience and PC.

East (1992) tested his proposal using two studies of application for shares in UK government privatizations; several privatizations had occurred before these studies were undertaken so that people could vary in their knowledge of privatization as well as share-dealing. East compared those who were experienced in this type of share purchase with the novices, but the results were equivocal and it seemed that a larger number of studies was required to provide an effective test of the hypothesis. Ten additional studies have now been accumulated and two (related) effects are predicted:

1. A measure of past experience will correlate more strongly with A_B and PC than with SN.
2. When the measure of past experience is added to the regression analysis predicting intention, the reduction in the β weights in respect of PC and A_B will be greater in magnitude than the corresponding reduction in the β weights for SN. This should occur because SN is relatively unaffected by experience.

Table 6.4 shows the correlations with past experience in the ten studies. In nine out of ten cases the correlation of past experience with A_B was greater than that with SN; similarly in nine out of ten cases the correlation with PC was greater than the correlation with SN. This supports the first prediction.

The second prediction was also supported. This work does suggest that experts make less use of SN than A_B and PC when making decisions and has an obvious relevance to marketing. It suggests that products need to be advertised in different ways, depending on the expertise of the target group. Social reference emphasis should only occur when the targeted purchasers are novices, and, as products mature, there should be increasing emphasis on those factors affecting A_B and PC.

Table 6.4 Correlations with past experience

Behaviour	Attitude	Subjective norm	Perceived behavioural control
Applying for shares in BT	0.34	0.25	0.31
Redress-seeking 1	0.43	0.08	0.26
Redress-seeking 2	0.20	0.21	0.37
Going to the theatre	0.41	0.35	0.38
Complaining in restaurant	0.36	0.03	0.41
Starting a pension	0.31	0.24	0.43
Playing the National Lottery 1	0.66	0.41	0.16
Redress-seeking 3	0.24	0.16	0.54
Redress-seeking 4	0.05	0.03	0.17
Playing the National Lottery 2	0.56	0.27	0.38
Mean (unweighted)	**0.36**	**0.20**	**0.34**

Overview of planned behaviour theory

The development of the theory of planned behaviour has been a success story. Social psychologists have emerged from the dark days of 1969 when Wicker claimed that there was little or no connection between attitude and behaviour. We now have a predictive and explanative model which works effectively. There are, however, some worries and I have tried to show these here.

It is also worth looking at the theory as a whole, as a set of ideas with a coherent form. One aspect of this is whether the theory describes any recognizable components of our thinking. My own judgement is that much of the appeal of the theory is that the global variables are recognizable aspects of our consciousness, and the distinction between propensities driven by returns from the environment (A_B) and those driven internally (SN) makes intuitive sense. Similarly, we do take account of what is possible in different circumstances and this makes PC a recognizable factor in choice.

The sum variables in the theory have a less clear basis in our consciousness. We do not enact the cognitive arithmetic involved in the sum measures, but this is not claimed by the authors of reasoned action and planned behaviour; they suggest that the arithmetic summarizes the effects of the different beliefs but this then raises the question: what are the mechanisms that connect beliefs and global variables? We may have developed our attitudes and subjective norms from a series of learning experiences in which beliefs become more strongly linked; alternatively we may just 'see' relationships and modify attitudes in the light of rational appraisal. Ajzen and Fishbein (1980) tend to take the second path:

> Generally speaking the theory is based on the assumption that human beings are quite rational and make systematic use of the information available to them. ... We argue that people consider the implications of their actions before they decide to engage or not engage in a given behavior.

In the review of this work it was apparent that we need more experimental research on the dynamic effects of new information on components of the model. Some work on the impact of information has been conducted, but the earlier review shows that changes do not seem to 'cascade' through the components of the model in a smooth and predictable fashion. One reason for this may be that new information must be repeated to strengthen its position in memory and thereby overcome the established memory structures; this emphasizes a learning process and relates to Fazio's work.

Finally, there is a need to use the theory more effectively in marketing. It may be used to study the activities of marketers – why they opt for or against particular practices (e.g. Elliott, Jobber and Sharp, 1995), and it applies to a host of consumer practices. The theory is of limited use in explaining the preference for one brand over another. This is partly because the model is more easily applied to doing or not doing A, rather than choosing A versus choosing B; also the trivial differences between many brands mean that such choices are not easily investigated by a theory that focuses on reasons rather than habits. However, the discretionary purchase of product types and subcategory choices that are distinctive – holidays to particular destinations, for example – are appropriate applications.

Market researchers make extensive use of qualitative research; planned behaviour starts with elicitation, a qualitative procedure, but then goes further and attaches relative importance to the different factors elicited. Researchers also use techniques like multi-dimensional scaling for positioning, and conjoint analysis for deciding what benefits to put in a product. Planned behaviour research is not a substitute for these techniques, but it has some virtues that they lack. In particular, the elicitation process is comprehensive so that factors controlling behaviour – particularly normative and control factors – are not missed out as they may be with the other techniques. Also, compared with conjoint analysis, planned behaviour research places less burden on the respondent and does not ask questions about attribute combinations that may make little sense.

Summary

The relationships between beliefs, attitudes, intentions and behaviour have been explained by two theories: the theory of reasoned action (Ajzen and Fishbein, 1980) and the theory of planned behaviour (Ajzen, 1985; 1988; 1991). In the theory of reasoned action it is the intention to act that is predicted (by attitude to the action and subjective norm); intention relates to actual behaviour but is partly controlled by contingencies outside the power of an agent. The theory of planned behaviour focuses more on behaviour and uses perceived behavioural control as an additional predictor of intention and, separately, of behaviour since a judgement of personal control covers some of the actual control over behaviour.

The theories give different levels of explanation of behaviour. At a practical level, the theories help to identify the limited number of specific factors that most relate to behaviour.

Most research in planned behaviour has tested the model in a static framework. A limited number of studies have examined the effects of changes in specific beliefs. The results are patchy; effects are usually in the direction predicted, but are usually weak.

There are residual problems about the selection of salient items for the questionnaire, the rather low correlations between sum and global variables, and the demarcation between deliberate and spontaneous action.

Measures of past behaviour give additional prediction of intention and behaviour to that derived from attitude to the behaviour (A_B), subjective norm (SN) and perceived behavioural control (PC). This 'excess' prediction is not fully explained as a deficiency in the measurement of global variables or as the omission of moral norm from studies; more automatic learning processes may produce the effect. Some work is reported which indicates that more experienced people base their decisions more on A_B and PC than SN.

Further reading

Madden, T.J., Ellen, P.S. and Ajzen, I. (1992) A comparison of the theory of planned behavior and the theory of reasoned action, *Personality and Social Psychology Bulletin*, 18: 1, 3–9.

Ajzen, I. (1991) The theory of planned behavior. In Locke, E.A. (ed.) *Organizational Behavior and Human Decision Processes*, 50, 179–211.

Part IV

Mechanisms in choice and consumption

Chapter 7

Information processing and judgement

Introduction

The theory of planned behaviour presents decision-making as an ordered, logical process, but this does not really describe how people think. People do not assign likelihoods and evaluations, multiply them and sum the products to form their attitudes. Planned behaviour theory works *as if* people figure out their interests in this way, but no claim is made that they actually do this. Similarly, NBD theory assumes that people's actions can be treated in some respects as if they were random, but its authors do not assert that people actually work like dice.

From this standpoint, planned behaviour theory is concerned with the outcomes of information processing, not its mechanisms. This leaves a gap in our explanation of human behaviour. If people do not do the cognitive operations implied in planned behaviour theory, what do they do? It is important that the mechanisms involved in human inference are recognized because it is these that may be commandeered by successful advertising. Though the content of advertising may be chosen in part by reference to rational ideas like those found in planned behaviour theory, its effect will depend on whether it activates relevant mechanisms.

Despite the great sophistication of human beings we have limited attention and comprehension; we economize on thought by using habits of mind which often guide us well but sometimes lead us astray. When we do reason out our problems, our analysis is often flawed. The information processing that we use has to serve a variety of purposes, and some of these may be better served than others; we should not assume that the mechanisms that underpin our actions are ideal. The processes of decision-making are revealed by research and this chapter focuses on some of the work that has been done in this field.

In this chapter you will find:

- A description of processes involved in recognition and judgement.

- Evidence on the way in which objective evidence of value and probability is processed and changed to utility and subjective probability, and the relevance of these processes to decision-making.

■ A review of the way in which post-decisional evaluations and other behaviour are affected by the decision, and the role of information and arousal in this process.

■ A description of rules that might explain how decisions are made, and an alternative approach that focuses on the way in which attention is controlled over the decision sequence.

Mechanisms and meaning

Recognition

Advertisements have to compete for attention; similarly brands on a supermarket shelf need the shopper's attention and some level of recognition if they are to be bought. The recognition may be minimal, perhaps just a sense of familiarity that takes no detailed account of the brand. But, whatever their form, the processes which draw attention and lead to recognition are important if we are to understand consumer responses to frequently purchased goods.

Recognition has also become important in a quite different sphere, in artificial intelligence, where it is a prerequisite for more discriminating exchanges between a computer and its environment. Reading characters, understanding speech, differentiating voices and labelling different aspects of the environment all involve recognition, that is, the identification of one stimulus from all those that are possible. The comparison with computers helps to show what is involved in human recognition. Interestingly, computers used to perform poorly in recognition tasks compared with human beings and more recent improvements in computer recognition have needed the much increased computing power now available. This relative weakness of computers seems to lie partly in their centralized design in which memory and processing occupy discrete areas, so that the procedure for identifying a stimulus requires that large amounts of information are swapped between these two locations.

The brain is constructed on a different principle with memory and processing functions distributed throughout its structure. In the brain we find an enormous number of neurones, each of which may have as many as 2,000 synaptic connections with other neurones – this structure is effectively the program. The recognition problem ('is it X, Y, Z, etc.?') can be represented as message-transfer down alternative pathways in the brain, which eventually activate a structure that matches the form of the incoming signal; these pathways occur as interconnections between neurones which have been built up from past learning.

Another difference between computers and brain operation is the extent to which processing takes place in parallel rather than series. Until recently computers have had little capacity to engage in different functions at the same time whereas this is normal in human information processing, although we may be aware of only a part of the processing. One stimulus has many aspects and can activate multiple pathways in the brain so that we can deal simultaneously with a range of questions generated by the same stimulus. For example: Is it a cat? What colour is it? Is it friendly? Parallel processing also implies integrating structures which keep the answers to these questions in one domain; in due course we know that we are doing just one action when we stroke a friendly black cat, but this does not mean that these processes are integrated from the start.

Psychologists describe thinking and recognition as a chain of internal responses, each stimulating the next. The alternative pathways are represented as alternative internal response chains. The speed of recognition depends on the extent that one internal response path is clearly dominant over the others. This means that ambiguous stimuli, and stimuli that are novel, changeable, surprising, incongruous, complex or indistinct tend to be recognized more slowly; our control mechanisms seem to take account of this and we give more attention to such ambiguous aspects of the environment. Human beings have a need to resolve the response competition or conceptual conflict (Berlyne, 1954) created by such ambiguous stimuli so that attention is sustained while the conflict remains. By resolving the conflict and identifying the stimulus, a person makes his or her environment easier to predict and manage.

Response competition

This is demonstrated in the Stroop test. You are asked to call out the colour that is written on the overhead the moment that it is revealed. The first display is RED written with a red colour; the second display shows RED written in a blue colour and this gives a longer response delay than the first condition. In the second case two competing responses are aroused: to say 'red' and to say 'blue'. The competition delays the production of the correct response.

Arousal is high when people are over-stimulated or *when they are under-stimulated* (or bored). People prefer low levels of arousal and are therefore guided to intermediate degrees of stimulation. Conceptual conflicts may be welcome when people are inactive because under these conditions more stimulation reduces arousal; at other times unusual stimuli may raise arousal (Berlyne, 1965; Berlyne and McDonnell, 1965) and when this occurs the stimuli may be disliked. This explains why Harrison (1968) and Saegert and Jellison (1970) found that the objects that were more investigated were often liked less. Although the stimuli that create response competition are generally not much liked, they are given disproportionate attention time. This creates a problem for mass communications since the stimulus that secures attention is often less attractive because it creates response competition. But people may appreciate such attention-drawing stimuli more when they receive them under low stimulation conditions; this may aid advertising in media such as television which are often received under low arousal conditions. By contrast, billboards at complicated traffic intersections should keep the message simple and avoid adding to arousal.

Mere exposure

Response competition has been used to explain an interesting phenomenon first reported by Zajonc[1] (1968). Zajonc observed that repeated exposure to a new stimulus made people like it more. This effect of *mere exposure* was so called because a change in the observer's evaluation occurs without any of the associations that are required in classical and operant conditioning (discussed in Chapter 1).

Zajonc observed this effect in both laboratory and field experiments, using nonsense words, Chinese-like characters and photographs of men's faces as the initially unfamiliar stimuli. For example, in Zajonc and Rajecki's (1969) field experiment, nonsense words like NANSOMA were printed like advertisements in campus news-papers. Later, the researchers asked large numbers of students to rate the words on evaluative scales and there was unequivocal evidence that the frequency of exposure correlated positively with the evaluative rating. Zajonc found that each doubling of exposures produced about the same increase in liking. Zajonc's explanation for this was that the unfamiliar words created response competition in the minds of readers, which was reduced by repeated exposure. Because response competition is generally disagreeable, a reduction in competition is liked and should produce a more positive evaluation. Harrison (1968) measured response competition as the time delay before any response to the stimulus and found, supporting Zajonc's explanation, that the delay was reduced as the number of exposures increased. Lee (1994) offers another ingenious explanation: that repeated exposure facilitates recognition, and that, because the stimuli that we recognize more easily tend to be those that we like, we assume that we like the stimulus more because we recognize it easily.

The mere exposure research draws attention to the importance of choosing the right name for brands, logos, packaging and ad designs, i.e. those that will acquire a positive evaluation at typical levels of exposure among purchasers. This suggests that prospective brand names should be 'soak-tested' (compared after heavy repetition). Some stimuli are disliked *more* on repeated exposure, so testing of this sort is wise.

Mere exposure has been related to the low involvement response to advertising. Batra and Ray (1983) have conducted a number of studies that simulate the rushed, noisy and irrelevant conditions under which most advertising is received. They found that increased awareness of the brand seemed to lead by a direct path to increased disposition to purchase, and that attitude change followed later. Batra and Ray suggest that the attitude change was a delayed effect arising from mere exposure and that repetitive advertising works partly by reducing response competition and partly by keeping brands in memory. However, the relevance of mere exposure effects to advertising has been questioned. Bornstein (1989) has reviewed this research and notes that it typically occurs for short exposures of the order of a second; Rossiter and Percy (1997) point out that this limits the relevance of mere exposure to advertising where exposures are rather longer.

---

[1] Zajonc is pronounced Zionse.

The response to thought and feeling stimuli

We tend to think that recognition is a necessary precursor to any evaluation of a stimulus. If you cannot name the concept, how can you have any affective response to it? This order of response has been put in question by work done by Zajonc (1980) and by Zajonc and Markus (1982).

Zajonc has assembled evidence showing that thought and feeling are initially processed independently. The processing is assumed to follow an internal stimulus–response pattern. According to Zajonc, the feeling aspect of thinking is processed faster than the knowledge component and the processing mechanisms are different. Much of the processing of feeling occurs below the level of awareness. Zajonc argues that people react to two classes of stimulus, preferenda (feeling) and discriminanda (cognition), and he points to the survival value attaching to a fast response to dangerous stimuli: it is better to jump without thought than to recognize that it is a car that is hitting you.

Zajonc presents a number of experimental findings. For example, Kunst-Wilson and Zajonc (1980) found that preference judgements were made marginally more quickly than recognition judgements, despite the fact that conventional thinking suggests that recognition is needed before any judgement of preference.

Another study was more startling still. Marcel (1976) used an instrument called a tachistoscope to present words or blank space with equal likelihood. Words were either short or long, and either pleasant or unpleasant. If the subjects thought they saw a word they were asked to judge its length against comparison words and to say whether the word was 'good' or 'bad'. A good word might be 'food' while a bad word might be 'evil'. The duration of exposure was reduced until the subjects were guessing the presence of words at chance level and could not therefore have been recognizing anything; at this duration Marcel found that word-length judgements (also cognitive) were at chance level too. However, at this point, the subjects were still scoring at above chance on their evaluative judgements of words when these were present, thus indicating that the feeling response was generated faster than the recognition response, and could occur without it.

Zajonc's ideas have not gone unchallenged; Anand, Holbrook and Stephens (1988) and Anand and Sternthal (1991) have argued that affective judgements can rest on cognitive processes without recognition occurring. They propose that recognition is only one part of cognitive processing and that other cognitive responses may underpin evaluative response. Vanhuele (1994) gives a brief review of this work.

Fast recognition judgements of the sort studied by Zajonc are quite different from the choices typically faced by consumers, but these studies do show the sort of mechanism that may underlie consciously experienced thought and feeling.

Schemata

Ideas have form. Schemata are these forms and they are the key to recognition, recall and inference. According to Crocker, Fiske and Taylor (1984: 197) a schema is:

Figure 7.1 Bartlett's battleaxe

an abstract or generic knowledge structure, stored in memory, that specifies the defining features and relevant attributes of some stimulus domain, and the interrelationships among those attributes. . . . They help us to structure, organize and interpret new information; they facilitate encoding, storage and retrieval of relevant information; they can affect the time it takes to process information. . . . Schemas also serve interpretive or inferential functions. For example they may fill in data that are missing or unavailable in a stimulus configuration.

The notion of the schema was implicit in Bartlett's (1932) work on remembering; Bartlett wrote of the 'effort after meaning' and showed how unusual structures that fell short of representing any object were interpreted by reference to more familiar ideas. Figure 7.1 shows an object that may be recognized as an axe, turf cutter, anchor or key; it is not quite like any of these but we use such related schemata to make sense of the object. The term 'schema' covers notions like cognitive category, stereotype (assumptions about persons or groups), relations such as 'is the cousin of' and behaviour sequences (also called 'scripts'). In their most abstract form, schemata may cover relationships like logical validity and causality, or hierarchy, transitivity and symmetry (described by De Soto and Albrecht, 1957).

Miller (1959) noted how information was more readily remembered if it came in 'chunks' and schemata provide an explanation of why this is so; the chunk has 'shape' and can be recognized by reference to a schema with the same 'shape'.

New information, if accepted, usually modifies how we think about a concept; usually we revise our judgement by incorporating the new information alongside existing information. For instance, new information on the reliability of a brand of computer may be added to our knowledge of the brand and cause us to update our 'value for money' assessment. But sometimes the new information may alter our views so that a concept is interpreted by reference to a different schema. For example, some new computing assemblies are effectively communications systems and we may classify these differently from PCs. Occasionally we may try to get consumers to look at a product by reference to a different schema, i.e. to reposition the product. For example, we may be used to regarding plain black chocolate as a snack but it might also be presented as a culinary ingredient in chocolate mousse. Such category shifting advertising may be a high-risk strategy compared to normal advertising because there is less likelihood that the more substantial change will be accepted.

Some amusing examples of category shifting come from the work of an Australian activist group which tried to counter the advertising of the tobacco and drink companies. The group was called the Billboard Utilizing Graffitists Against Unhealthy Promotion (BUGA UP) and they specialized in 'refacing' the posters of their adversaries, particularly the ads for cigarettes. When a cigarette company offered a car as a prize, their poster was given the caption 'From the people who put the "car" in carcinogen'. The adjustments to the posters, and the speeches in court when members of the group were prosecuted, gave entertainment to the people of New South Wales who much appreciated the sight of multinational companies being humbled.

Many of BUGA UP's more successful enterprises were legitimate. One BUGA UP activity occurred when a tobacco company sponsored work at the Sydney Opera House; well-dressed members of the group distributed leaflets at the entrance which expressed regret at the unsavoury association between tobacco and the arts. Another BUGA UP enterprise sabotaged a Marlboro 'Man of the Year' competition in Australia. BUGA UP proposed their own candidate; their choice was a man disabled by smoking, confined to a wheelchair, and smoking through the hole in his throat provided by a tracheotomy operation. The man himself was a willing accomplice and starred in a poster which was printed and sold in large numbers. The idea of the strong heroic figure that Marlboro had tried to cultivate was ridiculed; in its place were put the schemata of disease and disability, which are more accurately related to smoking cigarettes. Marlboro eventually awarded the prize in private; it had acquired a negative news value. A further 'anti-promotion' was to counteract the free distribution of cigarettes in shopping malls. To most people a gift is a kindness and the giver is regarded as well meaning. To oppose such promotions, BUGA UP distributed free pieces of apple and arranged for children to parade around the mall with banners saying DANGER – DRUG PUSHERS AT WORK. This apparently transformed the perception of the tobacco companies' representatives from benign kindliness to malign self-interest. Tobacco companies have a squalid history of refusal to admit to the hazards of their products; they *are* licensed drug sellers and an important part of their public relations is to counteract such facts by sponsoring orchestras, sport and research. BUGA UP's achievement was to reassert the drug-seller schema as the one by which the tobacco company's actions were judged.

Heuristics

The term 'heuristic' was used by Kahneman and Tversky (1972; 1973) and Tversky and Kahneman (1974) to cover inexact or rule-of-thumb processes which may be used unconsciously in thinking. Kahneman and Tversky thought that ideas that were more readily accessed (were more 'available') tended to be given a greater probability or weight by people. Heuristics facilitate information processing, but they may also lead people to make errors of inference. Kahneman and Tversky argue that people do not appear to follow the calculus of chance or the statistical theory of prediction when making decisions. Instead, they rely on a limited number of heuristics which sometimes yield reasonable judgements and sometimes lead to severe and systematic errors. The term 'available' has some similarity of meaning to Fazio's term 'accessible' but the two research fields have not been much linked.

Exercise 7.1 Availability effects

In Britain, approximately 600,000 people die each year from all causes. How many people die prematurely each year from the following causes? Enter the figures that you think apply:

Smoking
Road accidents
Industrial diseases
Industrial accidents
Asbestos
Nuclear industry

Markus and Zajonc (1985) provide a nice example of the way in which heuristic reasoning may support the prestige of the medical profession quite unjustifiably. They point out that the 'no treatment' control condition is necessarily absent in most medical supervision of illness. People may get better without treatment but, when treatment has been given, there is a tendency to assume that it has helped recovery. This may be seen as an example of the availability heuristic at work. When therapy has been given it is more cognitively available as a cause of recovery than ideas about the natural processes counteracting disease that occur within the body. As a result people may judge that therapy is more effective than it is.

The judgement of risk is notoriously erratic. Much of the reason for this may lie in the poor information about actual risks in the media, but judgement may also be distorted by the action of heuristics. Lichtenstein *et al.* (1978) have suggested that some risks are exaggerated by people because they hear about them more often in the media. Those who completed Exercise 7.1 are likely to have overestimated the risk of death from road accidents, asbestos and nuclear emissions and underestimated the effect of smoking, which kills with little publicity. The approximate answers are given below.

Approximate annual numbers of deaths in Britain by cause:

All causes	600,000
Smoking	100,000
Road accidents	4,000
Industrial diseases	7,000
Industrial accidents	500
Asbestos	20
Nuclear industry	20

Other popular examples of risk misjudgement might be the reluctance of Americans to come to Europe in 1986 following the US attack on Libya. Americans were fearful of reprisals, but the risk was clearly small and they might have been safer than at home, where murder is rather more common. Exaggerated fears are also seen when oral contraceptive scares have caused women to abandon the pill even when the identified risk was very small in absolute terms; in April 1996, a 10 per cent increase in legal abortions in Britain was attributed to earlier announcements that a number of contraceptive pills should be phased out because of small associated risks. People seem to have difficulty in taking account of background risk and may focus instead on large percentage increases. For example, women may be shocked to hear that those over 35 who smoke and take the contraceptive pill have eighteen times the risk of pulmonary embolism compared with those who do neither of these actions; but embolisms are very rare in the 35–45-year-old range and hazards that affect many more people present far more risk, e.g. smoking. In these cases the 'eighteen times' fact seems to be more available and to dominate in judgement; a more responsible way of handling the data would be to report the personal increment in risk for smoking pill users in general, for example that one in a million might die as a result.

The idea that availability may affect the likelihood attached to an event has a number of general implications that deserve attention. A particular worry is that it shifts intervention from preventive practice to remedial response. Good management anticipates problems and stops them from happening, and preventive medicine stops diseases before they occur. As a result they have no visible outcome. By contrast, crisis management and remedial medicine have immediateness and impact because of the manifest problems that they address. Do such practices get too much attention and detract from the effort that should be put into pro-active control where good practice ensures that there is no tangible outcome?

Availability will operate in favour of the visible, well-defined happening and against intangibles and events avoided. This suggests that people may:

- Give too much support to the status quo; what is happening is available, but what could happen is harder to imagine.
- Draw too easily on hindsight to support a case.
- Not see the value of pro-active campaigns such as anti-racist policies in schools.
- Find it easier to sell products if they are goods rather than intangible services.

Another heuristic mechanism is representativeness. This is the tendency to judge likelihood on the basis of similarity between the case in hand and assumptions about the class to which the case belongs. For example, a person may be seen as a barrister, because of features of dress and delivery of speech. In this case the judgement draws on the stereotype of a barrister, but such a judgement takes no account of the low number of barristers in society, which makes it unlikely that the person belongs to this group.

Heuristics are relevant to the content of persuasive messages; these must draw on the more easily accessed ideas so that the message is more readily understood and its claims are given high likelihood. When the subject is obscure a more familiar analogy may help in the presentation.

Exercise 7.2   Who was to blame?

Solve the following problem:

A cab was involved in a hit-and-run accident at night. Two cab companies, the Green and the Blue, operate in the city. You are given the following data:

■ In the city 85 per cent of the cabs are Green and 15 per cent are Blue.
■ A witness identified the cab as a Blue cab. The court tested his ability to identify cabs under appropriate visibility conditions. When presented with a sample of cabs (half of which were Blue and half of which were Green) the witness made correct identifications in 80 per cent of the cases.

Question:

What is the probability that the cab involved in the accident was Blue rather than Green? Decide on your answer before reading on.

Source: Abridged from Tversky and Kahneman (1980).

What is your judgement in Exercise 7.2? Tversky and Kahneman put this problem to several hundred subjects; the median response was 80 per cent. Thus subjects tended to take note of the witness's skill in recognizing cabs and ignored the market shares of the two cab companies. Clearly, if there had been no Blue cabs, the witness could not have been right so the proportion of Blue cabs is relevant. For the correct answer we want the ratio of probabilities: *correct identification as Blue* to *total identification as Blue*. The chance that the cab was Blue (0.15) and was recognized correctly (0.8) is 0.15 × 0.8, and the chance that the cab was Green (0.85) and was recognized wrongly as Blue (0.2) is 0.85 × 0.2. The required ratio of correct identification to total identifications is therefore:

$$\frac{0.15 \times 0.8}{0.15 \times 0.8 + 0.85 \times 0.2} = 0.41$$

Bias in judgements often occurs because people use heuristic reasoning when problems are hard to understand. Happenings, cause and effect, etc. are discontinuities and are more available than continuing states; this means that more weight is given to the witness test than the market shares of the cab companies. Tversky and Kahneman's work is laden with examples like this; for most readers the problems point to one sort of solution, which then turns out to be false. In particular, people give disproportionate weight to the causal data and neglect background frequency data that may be equally informative. Another example helps here:

Which of the following events is more probable:

(a) that a girl has blue eyes if her mother has blue eyes;
(b) that the mother has blue eyes, if her daughter has blue eyes;
(c) that the two events are equally probable.

The correct answer is (c) but among those who did not choose this answer, three times as many people preferred (a) to (b). The mother to daughter inheritance is causal, unlike the daughter to mother relationship.

It appears that we use a mechanism that directs attention to the more active aspects of our situation; we are tuned to change and intervention. By contrast, data dealing with the unchanging background appear to be pallid and uninteresting. This mechanism probably serves a useful purpose in general by drawing attention to aspects of the environment that require response, but it can cause mistakes in particular cases.

The availability of causal data has a particular relevance to marketing. Marketing interventions are attempts to cause changes under circumstances that are often relatively unchanging; in particular, the brand market share and the system of distribution do not change much in the medium term. These market conditions limit the effects of an intervention like advertising, but may get less attention than they deserve because of their constancy. It also seems quite likely that work which focuses on market stasis (much of Chapter 3) may be harder for people to accept and attach importance to.

Tversky and Kahneman's work is now attracting more critical comment and the reader is particularly referred to Gigerenzer (1991).

Processing value and probability

Value

Objective value, expressed in money or other units, and objective probability, measured or given, are processed by human beings to produce internal evaluations (or utility) and subjective probability. The internal representations do not bear an exact correspondence with the objective forms.

There is some sense in this. To most people, two *Snickers* are not twice as attractive as one. The relationship between value and utility has a long history going back to Bernoulli (1738), who described how the utility value curve flattens as value increases, and marginal utility therefore diminishes as value rises. This can be seen in Figure 7.2.

One obvious interest of this sort of effect to economists is the justification that it gives for exchanges. The marginal utility of additional supplies of a good to person A who already possesses a lot of that good is low, and this disposes A to make exchanges with person B, who is short of this good but well supplied with another good that A needs. In such circumstances both A and B can gain utility. Another aspect of the non-linear relationship between utility and value is that it gives sense to redistribution of wealth through political action; the poor person's gain in utility is greater than the loss of utility incurred by the rich loser.

The relationship between value and utility can be shown through exchanges, but it is most clearly indicated by the preferences expressed by individuals about different betting choices. Bernoulli gave the example of a pauper who, finding a lottery ticket offering an equal chance of winning 20,000 ducats or getting nothing, might quite

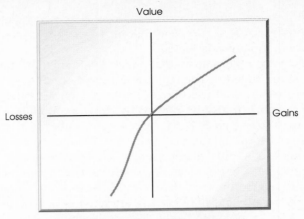

Figure 7.2 The value–utility relationship

reasonably ensure a gain by exchanging his ticket for a guaranteed 9,000 ducats; such options have now been examined more systematically.

Exercise 7.3 Positive and negative choices

---

1. Which do you prefer?
   (a) £9,000 for certain, or
   (b) £10,000 with a probability of 0.9; otherwise nothing.

2. Which do you prefer?
   (c) Losing £9,000 for certain, or
   (d) Losing £10,000 with a probability of 0.9; otherwise nothing.

In Exercise 7.3 people generally prefer (a) to (b). The concavity of the value–utility relationship for gains explains why people are risk-averse for positive utilities. What about the avoidance of losses? In Exercise 7.3 most respondents prefer (d) to (c). Below zero, utility falls somewhat more steeply in relation to value and then curves back toward the X-axis, as shown in Figure 7.2. This produces a risk *preference* for losses; a 0.9 chance of losing £10,000 has a smaller negative value than a certain loss of £9,000 (try marking in hypothetical utilities for £9,000 and 0.9 × £10,000 on Figure 7.2; you will find that the second is above the first, i.e. less negative and therefore preferred).

Probability

Exercise 7.4 The Allais paradox

Allais (1953) asked one group of subjects to choose between the two options:

(a) $4,000 with a probability of 0.8; otherwise nothing.
(b) $3,000 for certain.

Which do you prefer?

Another group were asked to choose between:

(c) $4,000 with a probability of 0.2; otherwise nothing.
(d) $3,000 with a probability of 0.25; otherwise nothing.

Which do you prefer?

Faced with the choices in Exercise 7.4, 80 per cent of subjects preferred option (b) to (a) but 65 per cent preferred option (c) to (d). This is paradoxical because the ratio of the values and the ratio of the probabilities is the same in each choice pair, yet the preference order reverses for most subjects. One explanation for this is that probability is weighted as it is converted to subjective probability. Figure 7.3 shows the proposed form of subjective probability in relation to objective probability. Kahneman and Tversky (1979) suggest that the weighting diminishes the subjective likelihood of high probabilities so that B is preferred to A. In the choice between (c) and (d), (c) is the

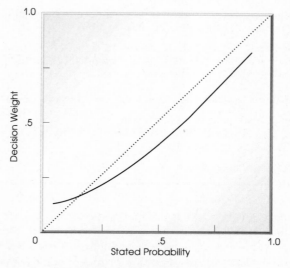

Figure 7.3 The probability relationship

better risk on average outcome, and Figure 7.3 shows that any weighting differences of the subjective probabilities favours the lower probability, so (c) is preferred.

No mathematical expression has been given for the probability weighting function, but the enhancement of subjective probability below objective probabilities of 0.15 could help to explain why people take out insurance and take high-odds gambles. Above about 0.15 the weighting depresses subjective probability so that risks are subjectively perceived as rather lower, for example, a 1 in 2 risk is nearer to 1 in 3 subjectively.

Prospect theory

Kahneman and Tversky (1979; 1984) and Tversky and Kahneman (1986) incorporated the subjective conversion of value and probability in prospect theory and proposed that the utility of a prospect (a potential choice) is established in two stages. In the first framing and editing stage, the choices are restructured by turning them into outcomes based on some reference point in the mind of the decision-maker and complex choices may be simplified (edited); thus a person may see the price of a car not as £7,000, but as £2,000 more than he or she expected to pay, and the cost of extra features may be incorporated into this figure. This stage is followed by an evaluation stage in which each alternative is given a value based on the framed utility and subjective probability weight, and the best is selected.

Exercise 7.5　Life and death

An unusual disease is expected to kill 600 people and two interventions are proposed. Which do you prefer on the basis of the following information:

- If programme A is adopted, 200 people will be saved.
- If programme B is adopted, there is a 1 in 3 probability that 600 people will be saved and a 2 in 3 probability that no people will be saved.

When you have decided, consider how you would react to this alternative formulation:

- If programme C is adopted, 400 people will die.
- If programme D is adopted, there is a 1 in 3 probability that no one will die and a 2 in 3 probability that 600 people will die.

Source: Tversky and Kahneman (1981: 453).

The reference point concept used in prospect theory is familiar in psychology. Thibaut and Kelley (1959) used the term 'comparison level', while Helson (1964) used 'adaptation level'. The way in which a problem is presented has an impact on the preferred solution because the presentation primes specific frames, making them more available for later judgements. Although the second formulation in Exercise 7.5 is the same as the first (A = C, B = D), 72 per cent preferred programme A to B and 78 per cent preferred programme D to C. By framing the problem in terms of the gains (i.e. lives saved) it is possible to steer preference to the risk-averse option A in the first choice. In the second choice the framing in terms of losses (lives lost) makes people risk-prone, and steers them to option D. Using the appropriate frame is clearly a lesson for anyone in the field of persuasive communication.

Thaler (1985) suggests some interesting *mental accounting* implications of framing when presenting gains and losses. Framing suggests that both gains and losses have more impact when presented separately. This means that losses are best presented in aggregate to minimize their impact and gains are best presented singly to maximize their effect. Another application of framing is to present costs as an increment to another large expenditure, the cost of carpeting a house that has just been bought, for example, or warranty extensions on a new car. In these circumstances the extra cost is experienced as a small decrement in utility because it is framed on the flattened part of the utility curve. In general, people assess costs in proportional terms and will take more trouble to save $5 off a $20 item than $5 off a $100 item. Heath, Chatterjee and France (1995) compare absolute and percentage discounts; when attention is drawn to large percentage discounts their effect is enhanced. When the percentage discount is small it is best to present it as an absolute cost reduction.

Thaler (1987) also discusses what is called the *endowment* effect. People feel more loss of utility when they lose an object that they own than increase in utility when they acquire the object. This is explained in relation to the steepness of the utility curve below the origin compared with the less steep rise in the curve above the origin.

Prospect theory has provided a major stimulus to those economists who are keen to question the basis of their subject. It shows that judgements are affected by the salience of particular ideas and raises the question of whether suboptimal judgements will be repeated under everyday conditions. According to some economists, such errors tend to disappear either because bad outcomes redirect behaviour, or because the more accurate people in a market benefit most and drive it towards optimality. Tversky and Kahneman (1986), and Thaler (1987) contest this and point to examples where judgemental bias persists over time.

'Mutual-Fund Pros Panicked in Peso Crisis While Small Investors Stood Their Ground'

Among share-trading professionals the folklore is to stay in a rising market and sell when it turns. Framing suggests that people might do the opposite; in particular, once they see that the market has fallen, and that they have made a loss by reference to recent prices, they may resist selling because now they are risk-prone. This headline suggests that ordinary investors follow the framing hypothesis, and the professionals have learned to reverse it.

Source: Wall Street Journal, 13 January 1995, headline.

Problems with prospect theory

The possibility of using framing in persuasive communication has seized the imagination of researchers but the potential may be reduced when the theory is more widely evaluated. Van der Plight and van Schie (1990) gathered evidence on risk-aversion and risk-proneness among European populations and confirmed Kahneman and Tversky's findings, but the effects were less strong. Leclerc, Schmitt and Dubé (1995) find that people making decisions under risk were often risk-averse about time loss when, according to prospect theory, they should be risk-prone.

In principle, prospect theory has application to bargaining, advertising and the stabilization of commodity and share markets where risk-proneness on loss may prevent mass selling in some crises (see box, '*Mutual-Fund Pros Panicked . . .*'). In practice, the deficiencies in the evidence supporting prospect theory limit its scope. Prospect theory has not been much demonstrated in field conditions. One problem is that, outside an experiment, reference points differ between people and may change over time; it is not easy, therefore, to establish the reference points that will affect a decision under natural circumstances. The studies of subjective probability and utility are done using rather artificial and often hypothetical examples. There is no check that the gains and losses presented in the problems are accepted without additional assumptions by the respondents. There is also concern about using 'majority verdicts' for each problem; we need to know more about the minority who do not follow the rest. In prospect theory, the weighting of probabilities gives rise to *subcertainty*; that is, the subjective probabilities of A and not-A add up to less than unity for much of the range and this is intuitively odd.

Dissonance theory

Leon Festinger (1957; 1964) introduced the theory of cognitive dissonance; his ideas were tested extensively in the 1960s and 1970s and this led to modifications in both the form of the theory and in its predictions. Over this period competitive theories rose and fell, and it is not my purpose to spend too long on the more abstract arguments that were generated. The reader is referred to Rajecki (1982, ch. 6), Eiser (1986, ch. 4) or to the more comprehensive review by Eagly and Chaiken (1993, chs 10 and 11) for careful accounts of the issues.

Festinger's original statement described a condition of arousal, called cognitive dissonance, that occurred in people when their beliefs did not 'fit together'; this condition led them to change their thought, feeling or action in such a way that the fit was improved. The lack of precision of the term 'fit' led to attempts to clarify the definition and Brehm and Cohen (1962) suggested that dissonance was felt when people committed themselves to an action which was inconsistent with their other behaviour or beliefs, or which later turned out to have undesirable consequences that might have been foreseen. Another way of putting this point is to say that dissonance is aroused when there is *insufficient justification* for an action. This version of the theory makes it relevant to consumer behaviour since it implies that people may experience dissonance when they commit themselves to a high involvement purchase, particularly when they are uncertain about the benefits. If purchase does give rise to dissonance, it will induce changes that bolster the purchase choice, for example, attitude change in favour of the brand selected, recommendation of the brand to others, and an interest in any information that justifies the purchase. Such effects imply that people making a difficult choice will be most receptive to information *after* purchase; this shifts interest from before to after purchase, and suggests that ads may have most impact on the reputation of a brand in the post-purchase period.

A study of post-purchase re-evaluation was made by Brehm (1956), who offered undergraduate women a choice between durables which they had either valued at much the same level (high dissonance, since it is hard to justify preference for any one durable in these circumstances) or which they had valued quite differently (low dissonance). Brehm's hypothesis was that, after they had made their choice, the women in the high dissonance condition would up-value their chosen alternative and down-value the product that they had rejected, and that they would do this more than the women in the low dissonance condition. Brehm's findings supported his hypothesis.

More generally the evidence was mixed and was open to alternative explanation. I conducted a study similar to Brehm's and, like him, I obtained a re-evaluation effect (East, 1973). But this re-evaluation change only occurred just after the choice. When the alternatives were rated later, along with other objects, the re-evaluation effect disappeared. It seemed likely that re-evaluation in this case was a communication emphasis and arose from attempts to make a more definite statement about the choice that had just been made. A person who has just chosen A and rejected B makes this clear by rating the chosen alternative above the rejected one.

Another failure of the theory concerned the information that was sought after a choice. According to the theory, there should have been preference for facts that justified the choice, but Sears (1968) found that people were generally open to any evidence relevant to their choice, whether it was positive or *negative*. Facts about the malfunctions of a recently purchased product may raise dissonance but they are also useful, and people do not seem to discriminate much against such information.

Some of the research on dissonance theory was conducted with an experimental design called 'forced compliance' in which subjects were persuaded to do something they were opposed to. The classic study in this mould was done by Festinger and Carlsmith (1959). They persuaded the student subjects, who had just completed a boring task, to lie about it to a new subject. They were asked to tell the new subject (actually an accomplice of the experimenters) that the task was interesting; for this they were paid 1 dollar in one condition, and 20 dollars in the other. The researchers argued that 20 dollars was sufficient justification for lying and would cause little dissonance, whereas the 1 dollar payment was insufficient. This meant that the researchers predicted that the less the payment the more the dissonance and, supporting this, they were able to show that there was more attitude change in the low payment condition; those paid 1 dollar tended to see the task as less boring than 20 dollar subjects and this shift of attitude had the effect of diminishing the lie.

Some of the studies in the forced compliance design failed to show most effect under the low payment condition but instead showed an incentive effect, i.e. the more the payment, the more the attitude change. These exceptions could have occurred because other factors varied with the incentive. Researchers such as Linder, Cooper and Jones (1967) and B.E. Collins *et al.* (1970) showed evidence that the degree of commitment and freedom of choice were relevant to whether or not dissonance was aroused, and such factors are related to the level of incentive.

However, most of the variation of results at different incentive levels was explained by Nuttin (1975), who argued that previous researchers had failed to show which condition was most arousing. Instead, they had made assumptions that were never tested in the experiment. Nuttin suggested that the highest arousal could sometimes occur with no reward, sometimes with low reward and sometimes with high reward and that this explained why the experimental findings had become so unpredictable. In a series of experiments, Nuttin was able to corroborate this argument and show that high dissonance could not always be expected under low reward.

Self-perception

The main counter-theory to dissonance has been a form of attribution theory (discussed in Chapter 1) which was proposed by Bem (1967); he called it self-perception theory. Bem argued that our attitudes are verbal reports based on observation of our own behaviour. Just as we infer the attitude of another person by noting what they do and say, so also, according to Bem, do we infer our own attitudes from observations of our own behaviour: 'I must like it because I did it.' Bem was able to point to a seminal study by Schachter and Singer (1962) where the experimenters used a drug to induce arousal and the subjects, who were ignorant of the effects of the drug, reported widely different emotions from anger to euphoria, depending on the cues presented by the experimenter; here the subjects' descriptions of their state could be seen as inferences from their situation.

Following this argument, Bem reasoned that people who were given details of the experience of subjects in a dissonance experiment would be able to predict their responses. When Bem 'ghosted' people through the Festinger and Carlsmith experiment and got them to rate the boring task as they thought the subjects in the original study would have rated it, he was able to confirm that their ratings corresponded with those obtained in the conditions of the original experiment. Bem reasoned that if observers could do this it was reasonable to propose that the original subjects acted in the same way, observing their own behaviour and then inferring their attitude to the task from their self-observation. For Bem, the implicit reasoning of the 1 dollar group was 'I said it was interesting and since I did this for only one dollar it probably wasn't that boring', whereas the 20 dollar subject might be saying 'for 20 dollars who wouldn't say that a boring task was interesting?' A consequence of this argument is that arousal, whether or not it occurs, may be unnecessary for attitude change.

There is evidence that arousal does occur in dissonance studies. Gerard (1967) conducted a study on choice in which arousal was measured by capillary blood flow using a device called a photoplethysmograph. When a person is aroused his or her capillaries constrict and the amount of blood in the tissue diminishes; the photoplethysmograph measures light reflected back by the tissues, and the light increases when there is less blood present. Gerard measured arousal at the point of decision and found that more subjects were aroused in the high dissonance condition.

But there remains the possibility that the arousal is unrelated to any dissonance reduction effects. This issue was resolved by a clever experiment designed by Cooper, Zanna and Taves (1978). In their study they used drugs to modify arousal under three conditions: (1) amphetamine (a stimulant) raised arousal; (2) phenobarbital (a tranquillizer) reduced arousal; (3) the subjects received a placebo (milk powder) which had no effect. All subjects were told that they were being given the placebo so that they did not attribute their physiological state to drugs. The subjects were then put through a forced compliance procedure in which they wrote an essay favouring a free pardon for Nixon (something which students were generally against). After this they were asked to give their ratings in favour of a pardon for ex-President Nixon on a 31-point rating scale. The results are shown below in Table 7.1.

Table 7.1 Average ratings of subjects in favour of a pardon for ex-President Nixon under different conditions (31-point scale; higher scores favour pardon)

No drug, no essay control sample	Tranquillizer	Subjects given Placebo	Stimulant
7.9	8.6	14.7	20.2

Source: Cooper, Zanna and Taves (1978).

This evidence shows that arousal is necessary for change in attitude; when it was eliminated by the tranquillizer there was no appreciable effect. Under normal circumstances (with the placebo) there was an attitude shift and this was increased when arousal was increased by the amphetamine. In this study the inferences that the subjects could make were held constant by telling them all that they had the same placebo. What about the reverse situation when subjects are aroused by dissonance but are led to attribute their arousal to a drug? Do they show dissonance reduction shifts of attitude under these conditions?

This had been explored in an earlier study by Zanna and Cooper (1974). In this experiment subjects were told that the purpose of the research was to investigate drug action. All subjects actually received a placebo, but one group was told that it was a tranquillizer, one that it was a placebo and one that it was a stimulant. Dissonance was aroused by requiring the subjects to write an essay against their beliefs, this time in favour of banning inflammatory speakers from the campus, which was generally opposed by American students. After the essays the students' ratings were obtained (see Table 7.2).

This time most effect occurred when subjects thought that they had been given a tranquillizer; presumably the dissonance arousal was all the more evident when subjects expected to feel sedated and it thus produced more attitude change. By contrast those subjects who attributed their arousal to a stimulant showed virtually no dissonance reduction effect. Thus, although they were aroused, there was no effect and this shows that a change of attitude requires both arousal and that the arousal must be related to the attitude object by the subject. Eagly and Chaiken (1993) review this area and note supporting studies.

Table 7.2 Ratings in favour of a ban on inflammatory speakers on the campus (31-point scale; higher ratings favour ban)

No drug, no essay control sample	Subjects believed they had been given		
	Tranquillizer	Placebo	Stimulant
2.3	13.4	9.1	3.4

Source: Zanna and Cooper (1974).

This stream of research has a number of applications to consumer behaviour. In the first instance it defines the limits of dissonance effects in respect of a purchase. Effects will only occur when the purchaser is aroused and attributes that arousal to making the purchase. This effectively excludes minor purchases which are unlikely to create arousal. When a purchaser is confident about purchase there should be no dissonance, but it should occur when the purchase is hard to justify and this may arise for a variety of reasons: the purchaser may feel that the brand is too expensive, may worry about quality or after-sales service, and may have doubts about the appropriateness of the brand, etc. Such arousal will activate post-purchase behaviour but, as noted, there is little evidence that people are selective and that they pick information and activities that will justify their purchase. It should also be noted that there are other forms of arousal engendered by purchase. Some people are elated by a new possession and could be receptive to information because of this non-dissonance arousal. Such post-purchase satisfaction is probably much more common than dissonance (see Chapter 9).

Dissonance research helps us to understand how to produce effective persuasion. It suggests that we must create a *relevant* disturbance in the recipient, using the issues on which change is sought. Very often the poster or commercial will create a disturbance by using ideas that are extraneous to the issue. When this occurs it is unlikely that any attitude or behaviour change will be focused on the object of the advertisement. I can illustrate agreement between arousal and message with one health education poster produced for the Health Education Council (England and Wales) which was designed to deter pregnant women from smoking. The poster showed a naked, substantially pregnant woman who was smoking. The nakedness made the pregnancy manifest; the poster was shocking to many people, a response that was amplified by the incongruous smoking. The poster carried a series of points about the risks to the foetus if a woman smoked during pregnancy. The campaign using this poster was associated with a major change in admitted smoking by pregnant women.

Researching the sequence of decision-making

Self-awareness in thinking

Our focus now shifts to those moment-by-moment events which go on inside us when we make a choice. You may think that introspection will reveal the processes used in judgement and decision-making, but this is doubtful. Nisbett and Wilson (1977) and Evans (1980) have presented evidence showing that the subject's reports of his or her own strategy in solving problems cannot be relied upon. We may know our beliefs and feelings, but not how we came to think and feel them (earlier in this chapter we saw that heuristic processes can affect judgements without our being aware of the process). However, this issue has drawn counter-arguments; Smith and Miller (1978), for example, claim that Nisbett and Wilson rely too much on a simple distinction between content and process in thought, and that people can have privileged access to some of the processes that they use. This literature has been reviewed by P.A. White (1988).

The questionable reliability of introspection has raised considerable doubt about the value of consumer investigations that rely on the subject's reports of his or her own thinking processes; one conclusion from this is that we should prefer observations of behaviour to introspective reports. These problems are discussed in relation to consumer behaviour by Rip (1980) and by Wright and Rip (1980).

Decision rules

Nisbett and Wilson's work shows that objective studies are required to establish how people process information when they choose between products. Much of the research on these choice processes has been designed to establish a decision rule which will explain which alternative people choose under given conditions. Investigations have been conducted to see whether the full compensatory multi-attribute model works best or whether predictions are improved by abandoning compensation and assuming that the decision is reached by evaluating alternatives in a more limited way. For example, by ignoring attributes below a threshold value (conjunctive), by choosing the alternative with the most attributes above an arbitrary threshold (disjunctive), or by processing first by reference to the most important attribute and then moving to the next most important attribute only in the event of a tie (lexicographic). Tversky (1972) proposed a variation of the lexicographic procedure in a rule called 'elimination by aspects' (EBA). Here attributes are weighted; the most important is considered first and all alternatives that fall below the threshold for this attribute are eliminated. Attention then shifts to the next most important attribute and this process continues until one alternative remains. A problem with this method is that it implies a large amount of processing when there are many alternatives.

This type of research always produces a 'winner' since, of necessity, one model is going to give better results than the others in any contest but, undermining such research, is the way in which the winner varies from study to study. One reason for the variety of findings lies in the sensitivity of the decision process to environmental factors. Some of these factors arise from the method of investigation itself; methods such as real time reports (protocols) and eye movement studies are likely to affect the subject. Svenson (1974), not surprisingly, found that booklets on each brand induced processing by brand rather than by attribute. Park (1976) found that the decision process was affected by product complexity and familiarity, and van Raaij (1977) found effects from distraction, information availability and time pressure.

In the face of this chaotic range of effects, Bettman (1977), Bettman and Zins (1977) and Bettman and Park (1980) suggested that people construct a tailor-made decision procedure when faced with a particular choice, using fragments of different decision rules. This requires a general rule that explains how the fragments are put together and the reader may feel some doubt about this whole approach; it is not as though people have rules in their minds when they choose.

Russo and Leclerc (1994) describe a change of emphasis in this field from one in which decisions are seen as *comprehensive, planned, optimizing* processes, to one that treats them as *constructed, adaptive and simplifying*. Thus there has been a shift from assumptions of rational response to the recognition that environmental stimulus and heuristic mechanisms probably control choice, and the new approach emphasizes observation of the moment-by-moment detail of decision-making. Even so, I find the current approach continues to use the language of the rational agent. Payne, Bettman and Johnson (1993) refer to 'heuristic decision *strategies*', and 'a desire to make accurate decisions and to minimise cognitive effort which is adapted to the situation'. These and other comments imply a level of conscious control which I suspect is rarely achieved. I think that the processes in decision-making are more automatic than this language would imply and that awareness is mainly concerned with the outcome of such automatic activity. One fairly automatic process is the allocation of time to the different alternatives in a decision; such an attention mechanism is likely to affect the decision made and this is addressed below.

The attention mechanism in choice

This subsection reviews research on the time spent on the different alternatives before choice and proposes two mechanisms that together could account for the findings.

A central problem for decision researchers who seek to study our thought is the lack of any behaviour that can be observed. To discover how people learn to use a computer we can observe their actions; these actions may be corroborated by subjective reports but, generally, actions speak louder than words. In decision-making, the observable action is often restricted to the overt choice; however, when the alternatives are physically present, it is possible to observe the direction of gaze and to infer from

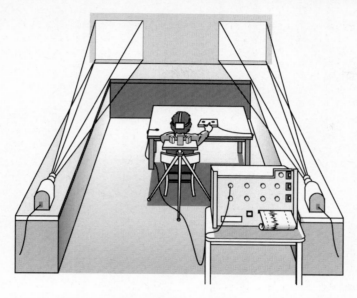

Figure 7.4 Gerard's set-up for recording attention to alternatives

this which alternative a subject is thinking about. Gerard (1967) first used this method of investigation; he employed two projectors to show the alternatives, a light source, a mirror on the back of the subject's head, two photocells and a multi-channel recorder to log the direction of gaze of the subject. Figure 7.4 shows a diagram of this apparatus.

My own work in this area began with a small study of option choice among students (East, 1972). On their course the students could choose two optional subjects out of five, and talks were arranged on each subject so that the students could form some idea about the issues covered by each alternative. Each student was asked to put the options in order of preference before and after the talks and was asked to state which talks had been attended. A rational analysis of the choice suggests that the talks on the options ranked second and third would be the most important to attend. Often the student would be sure about his or her first preference and doubt would centre on whether to do one or other of the next two. Was this reflected in the attendance? Student attendance at the talks is shown in Table 7.3. Since they sometimes changed their preference, the attendance is shown with respect to the preference order both before and after attendance at the talks. We see that the students attended the talk on their first preference most; this was followed by the attendance at the talk on their third preference, then the second, fourth and fifth.

Figure 7.5 Subject choosing between alternatives displayed on viewers

Table 7.3 Numbers of students at option talks

Preference order	Before talks	After talks
1	26	31
2	19	25
3	21	26
4	17	16
5	11	15

Source: East (1972).

These results suggest two effects. The high attendance at talks on the third option seems to reflect the strategic requirement to sort out the choice between the options ranked second and third, but the findings also show that the evaluation of an option has a direct effect on attendance.

Following this study, an apparatus was designed to measure the durations of time spent on alternatives before a decision is made. The apparatus used slide viewers connected with a hidden time measurement. As in the earlier study by Gerard (1967), the choice was made between French Impressionist paintings. The subjects were led to believe that they would get a poster of the picture that they chose. Control of the viewers was left entirely in the hands of the subjects so that the time spent on the different alternatives was unconstrained. Figure 7.5 shows a subject seated at the viewer assembly.

Two experiments were conducted (East, 1973). The first presented subjects with two alternatives and the second with three, and both experiments had two levels of choice difficulty: high, between alternatives that had previously been rated equally by the subject, and low, between alternatives that had been rated unequally.

This sort of study allows subjects to change their order of preference and several of those in the high choice difficulty condition did so. These subjects were asked at what stage they changed their minds and the attention data were reallocated to the contemporaneous preference order. With or without this correction, the results showed that the subjects spent more time looking at the alternatives that they liked more, i.e. that the ratio of attention times was a function of the ratio of the evaluations (see Table 7.4). This indicates that attention is driven by evaluation, a simple mechanism that may not be consciously apprehended. (When I have asked students, they do not seem to know whether they look most at the alternative they will choose or the one that they will reject; thus the attention mechanism seems to operate without awareness.)

Choice difficulty raised the time taken to decide, a finding that has been consistently found. Contrary to assumptions often made in psychology, more alternatives under high choice difficulty did not raise the decision time. This may indicate that simpler mechanisms come into play when decisions become too elaborate or difficult.

Table 7.4 Mean durations of attention (in seconds) to the alternatives in choice experiments

Choice difficulty	Order of preference	Two alternatives	Three alternatives
	1	46	25
High	2	37	23
	3	–	21
Totals:		**83**	**69**
	1	24	24
Low	2	18	16
	3	–	9
Totals:		**42**	**49**

Source: East (1973).

Gerard (1967) had earlier found that more time was given to the alternative that was *not* chosen, and he explained this as an attempt to come to terms with not having this alternative. My results were directly contrary. There is no obvious explanation for this difference in findings, but Gerard, who reported only one study on a two alternative choice, used a complicated apparatus for recording attention and it is possible that measurements were attributed to the wrong channels, thus reversing the results. A study by Russo and Leclerc (1994) supports the East (1973) finding. These researchers used video equipment in a simulation supermarket situation and measured the number of eye fixations on alternatives (rather than duration of time spent) at different phases in the decision sequence. They found that in the longest phase the number of fixations clearly favoured the alternative later chosen. Right at the end of this phase, with the decision, there was a tendency for the ratio of fixations to reverse and favour the rejected alternative but this result did not reach significance; this is of interest because Gerard also found a reversal in the focus of attention after choice.

Russo and Leclerc note that one of the requirements of decision research is to establish stopping rules that define when investigation finishes and the decision is made. Following Payne, Bettman and Johnson (1993), they see decision-making as an adaptive process in which immediate behaviour is controlled by past behaviour and the current context. Their stopping rule is presented in terms of the purposes of the decision-maker, and not as the product of decision-making mechanisms.

I offer an alternative stopping rule which rests on mechanisms rather than purpose. I see investigation (and thinking) as energized by obstructed motivation. In a decision, the obstruction to choosing alternative A is largely set by the attractiveness of other alternatives and therefore the energy to investigate will be greater when there is more inclination to choose other options. This energy from obstructed motivation is used up by investigation and this often clarifies the attractions of the alternatives; when the energy is gone, or largely gone, an individual makes the overt decision. Thus, stopping occurs when energy for investigation is exhausted. This approach connects with other, more familiar, ways of thinking; obstructed motivation is frustration, and frustration is known to power attempts to find solutions.

A further mechanism is required to explain the division of attention between the alternatives. The evidence supports a simple controlling process with the evaluation of alternatives guiding attention. In natural settings people have to allocate time to parts of their environment and good adaptation requires that they attend to objects offering the most potential gain. Their evaluations of the objects around them provide one indicator of potential gain. (They also need to avoid loss so decision-makers are also likely to attend to noxious features of their environment, but these were not present in the experiments described here.)

If evaluation guides attention it means that second and third preferences will get proportionately less attention and their worthwhile attributes will be less likely to be discovered. This mechanism therefore carries a bias in favour of existing preferences, but it is an efficient way of allocating the scarce resource of time since it ensures that little time is wasted on low-rated prospects. This attention mechanism will confirm our existing preferences when new observation supports what is already known. However if investigation of the first preference leads to negative findings so that it is downrated, more time will be allocated to lesser alternatives.

It is quite difficult to see how to use the attention mechanism to persuade people to change their minds. One possible strategy is to bury information about the less attractive alternative within a message on the preferred alternative. In this way it is more likely to receive attention. The attention mechanism also suggests that negative information about a first preference is more likely to get attention than positive information about a second preference. This indicates that knocking copy may work best against a brand leader.

Summary

This chapter is about the mechanisms involved in recognizing, thinking, evaluating, judging, investigating and deciding.

Recognition is performed well by human beings and involves some match between external patterns and internal representations, or schemata. When there are alternative schemata, or competing internal responses, recognition is delayed. Stimuli creating response competition draw attention but are less liked; liking usually grows with more exposures.

The evaluative response to stimuli is often faster than the cognitive response and these responses, in the initial stages, seem to involve relatively independent processing.

Recognition, recall and inference are affected by the way information fits schemata. These schemata range from familiar concepts like product types to abstract relationships such as causality. Influence may cause people to revise their thinking within a schema or, less commonly, to relocate their ideas in a different schema.

In making judgements people use simplifying processes called heuristics. They make more use of information if it is more discrete, eventful, vivid or recent, and this more *available* information is given higher probability. Heuristic processes affect judgement of risk and cause people to neglect information that is less available, even though it may be relevant.

We convert the objective forms of value and probability into internal forms of utility and subjective probability. The utility function is concave to the X-axis as value increases in magnitude. There is evidence that objective probabilities of less than 0.15 tend to be overestimated and that objective probabilities above about 0.15 are underestimated. These effects are incorporated into prospect theory. The value conversion helps to explain some common responses to risks, in particular that most people are risk-averse for gains and risk-seeking for losses.

The search for decision rules has produced much variety and little order. A rather different way of understanding decision-making is to find out what drives investigation during the pre-decision period, and evidence is presented on mechanisms that explain the direction of attention and the duration of decision-making.

Further reading

Kahneman, D. and Tversky, A. (1984) Choices, values and frames, *American Psychologist*, 39: 4, 341–50.

Thaler, R. (1985) Mental accounting and consumer choice, *Marketing Science*, 4, Summer, 199–214.
Zajonc, R.B. (1980) Feeling and thinking: Preferences need no inferences, *American Psychologist*, 35, 151–75.

Chapter 8

Satisfaction, quality and complaining

Introduction

Over the past two decades there has been a steady development of research on the post-purchase phase of consumption (described by Day and Perkins, 1992). This has two related aspects: consumer satisfaction and dissatisfaction (CSD), and consumer complaining behaviour (CCB). Satisfaction often depends on the quality of goods and services and, therefore, CSD research is closely associated with the measurement of quality. In the United States, Hunt and Day set up the first conference on consumer satisfaction in 1976 and work in this field grew rapidly: Perkins (1993) noted over 3,000 references in this field. In Europe, CSD and CCB have received rather less emphasis than in the United States and, starting with the work of Grönroos (1978), the emphasis has fallen on the perception of quality, particularly with regard to services. Service quality has been researched in the United States by Parasuraman and his colleagues, but their work has been questioned in a number of ways. In marketing, the raising of product quality is spurred on by evidence that high quality products are more profitable: they yield better margins, are more easily sold and extended, and command higher loyalty.

In this chapter you will find:

- A review of factors that have raised the importance of CSD and CCB.

- An analysis of the product as part-service, part-physical good.

- An explanation of the *confirmation* and *disconfirmation* models of consumer satisfaction.

- An account of the development and criticism of the *SERVQUAL* model.

- An analysis of consumer responses to satisfaction and dissatisfaction.

- Research on complaining.

- Reports of how consumers respond to service delay and advice to management based on this work.

- Management lessons for raising satisfaction with products.

Influences on quality

Research on quality has been influenced by some important changes in industry, in particular:

- The concept of 100 per cent reliability, which was promoted by NASA as an essential part of any successful space programme, and which caught the public imagination in the 1960s.
- The dramatic impact of Japanese goods on US and European markets. With their high quality and reliability Japanese products chastened Western manufacturers and gave consumers new expectations.
- Completely new developments in technology. Though not without quality control problems themselves, computer chips and robotics have assisted in the manufacture of reliable, high performance products.
- Services, or the service components of a product, have become a larger fraction of industrial activity, and services are harder to standardize and therefore more likely to cause dissatisfaction than physical products. In 1978, Grönroos put the service sector at about 50 per cent in advanced economies; in 1984, it accounted for 66 per cent of US GNP and 58 per cent of European GNP (Grönroos, 1990); Bateson (1989) reports a rising trend in service provision, and Koepp (1987) estimated that 85 per cent of all new jobs created since 1982 in the United States are in the service sector. Schugan (1994) judged that in 1995, 67 per cent of all production and 77 per cent of all jobs in the United States were in non-goods industries. From this evidence it appears that services have grown as a proportion of the economy in advanced countries, and this makes service quality a more important issue.

Research on quality and satisfaction is powered by the search for competitive advantage, and has been stimulated by two research traditions in particular:

- The Boston Consulting Group's Profit Impact on Marketing Strategy (PIMS) programme of research (Buzzell and Gale, 1987) showed that quality was profitable; next to being big, it was good to be high quality because your margins could be larger, and often you became bigger as a result.
- It costs less to retain existing customers than to gain new ones (Fornell and Wernerfelt, 1988; Reichheld, 1993; 1996; Reichheld and Sasser, 1990). One way of achieving this is to raise quality relative to competitors so that customers are more satisfied.

Accompanying the improvement in the quality of goods and services has been a quiet revolution in management practice. The Total Quality Management (TQM) concept has become widely accepted and is supported by specifications of high quality management practice. In Europe, the ISO 9000 code sets TQM targets. A firm that reorganizes its practices in accordance with ISO 9000 may still not deliver quality, but the code does ensure that the firm is structured in a way that facilitates a high quality product. Such a well-organized firm will be checking on consumer satisfaction, materials, equipment and procedures, and will be planning ahead and testing new product concepts; a high quality firm will also be training employees and ensuring that critical aspects of service are precisely defined. When these managerial functions are fully addressed, quality is likely to follow. To a consumer such as myself, who can remember the inadequate goods and service of past decades, the change has been impressive and has resulted in a genuine improvement in the quality of life.

Over this period there has been an increased awareness that the market-place is the ultimate test of a product offering. Designers may try enhancements to a product but only those product features that are appreciated by consumers will help the product to survive. This realization has focused attention on the consumer's satisfaction with products. This is now a substantial field of enquiry and in this chapter we review the main ideas in CSD, perceived quality measurement and CCB. Attention is then focused on a perennial feature of service delivery – delay – and some managerial lessons are drawn from research.

Quality in all things

Heidi Fleiss, accused of running an expensive call-girl circuit for the elite of Hollywood, rebutted criticism from Madam Alex, the previous leader of the circuit, who claimed that she had stolen her clients. 'In this business', Heidi Fleiss is reputed to have said, 'no one steals clients. There is just better service.'

Source: Abridged from *The Guardian*, 11 August 1993.

Goods and services

Economists divide national production into goods and services (or non-goods). In marketing, the treatment is rather different and it is recognized that most commercial exchanges involve both a physical product and a service with the ratio varying from product to product. For example, when we go to a restaurant we buy physical products, the food and drink, but we also benefit from the environment of the restaurant and its staffing so that eating a meal in one restaurant could be a quite different experience from eating the same food in another restaurant. The service component can be subdivided – Rust and Oliver (1994) describe it as having three parts. The physical context is the *service environment*: the cleanliness and seating, the flock wallpaper in Indian restaurants, the ornamentation in Thai restaurants and the line and desk in some US restaurants at which patrons obediently wait on entry. The operational features of the restaurant are the *service product*: taking the order, cooking and serving the food, and billing the customer. In addition, the personnel perform their functions with more or less style and expertise when they take the order and present the food; this is *service delivery*. Figure 8.1 illustrates these divisions. Services vary in the ratio of these components; restaurants usually offer more service than supermarkets but perhaps less than many professional services such as dentistry and legal advice, where the one-

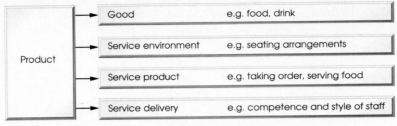

Figure 8.1 Components of the service product

to-one contact between professional and client raises the emphasis on the service component.

The Bonfire of the Vanities

A good example of the different features of the service product is found in Tom Wolfe's book, *The Bonfire of the Vanities*. The hero, Sherman McCoy, is a million dollar a year Ivy League bond trader who, threatened with prosecution for a criminal driving offence, consults his legal adviser. The lawyer's service environment is impeccable and service delivery is fine, but his expertise is suited to a moneyed clientele that rarely has problems such as hit-and-run driving. His lawyer cannot offer a service product and redirects him to a downmarket lawyer in an unpleasant office where the service delivery is indifferent but the service product – handling the hit-and-run offence – is very much better.

Services exist in time

Services are *transitory*; service products are consumed as they are made available and cannot be stockpiled like physical products. If an airline seat or a hotel bedroom is left vacant, revenue is lost. When there is little demand, personnel can sometimes be switched to consolidation activities such as stock checking and cleaning, but the transient, perishable aspects of services affect their marketing and are relevant to their quality. One obvious consequence of the fact that every service happens in real time is that there is more possibility for getting it wrong. Because services are intangible they cannot be stockpiled and quality checked like goods. As a result, every service production failure is experienced by the customer. Furthermore, the interactive nature of service delivery limits standardization so that any service encounter is likely to differ (and may need to differ) from others. This means that the service component of product quality is harder to ensure and, as industrial activity has shifted more to services, there has been a corresponding increase in the need to monitor service quality.

Points of dissatisfaction

The greater fallibility of service means that it is this, rather than the physical product, that usually generates most complaint. In a study conducted by Technical Assistance Research Programs (TARP, 1979) only the third of the five main targets of complaint was specifically concerned with the physical product:

Problem	Households reporting problem %
Unsatisfactory repair or service	36
Store did not have advertised product for sale	25
Unsatisfactory product quality	22
Long wait for delivery	10
Failure to receive delivery	10
All other problems	77

Consumer satisfaction

The confirmation model

Early thinking about satisfaction treated it as meeting consumer expectations. This is the *confirmation model* of consumer satisfaction and Oliver (1989) described the successful outcome as *contentment*; we are contented when a refrigerator continues to keep food cold. Though Oliver did not develop the idea, this low arousal state is matched by *discontent* when negative expectations are met; this applies to the routine use of inadequate services such as congested roads, late buses and slow checkouts, and to the continued use of unsatisfactory goods such as dripping taps and lumpy mattresses. In these situations poor satisfaction may be ignored because of habituation; for example, the glass base plate of my refrigerator was cracked and, although I was aware of the defect, I did nothing about it and it remained like that for three years until my attention was drawn to it rather more forcibly. People put up with many troubles of this sort because they have become used to them and no longer notice that there is a problem. The confirmation model relates, therefore, to habitual usage. Consumer contentment and discontent are not normally overtly expressed and only become manifest when people are questioned, or when other factors raise the salience of a product's performance; others may comment on the dripping tap, for example, or an ad for beds may make people think of their own bedtime discomfort.

The toleration of product deficiencies is explained by adaptation theory (Helson, 1964). This theory makes perception relative to some standard which may change over time in response to experience. As long as positive and negative deviations from expectation are small, they will be accommodated as normal experience and will have little effect on the reference standard; but large deviations will affect the adaptation level. In Oliver's (1981) view, expectations provide the adapted level used for evaluating related experience.

Exercise 8.1   Lurking dissatisfactions

The reader is reminded of Exercise 1.2, which concerns habits. This exercise is similar. Think of everyday products that you use: refrigerators, dental floss, car mirrors. Are these satisfactory? If you look at these products with a more critical eye, there are often weaknesses that could be corrected. Does your refrigerator ice up too easily and contain plastic shelving which cracks? Do you use dental floss in one of those containers that fall apart when you pull the floss out? And does your car use three mirrors and still leave blind spots?

Often solutions could have been invented years before; what was missing was the idea, rather than the technology. And people may not have had the ideas because habituation stopped them from recognizing a problem.

See if you can think of products that we take for granted but which could be better?

If consumers have little awareness of the shortcomings of everyday products, they will feel little pressure to change their behaviour and this can be a matter of concern. Our tendency to adjust to our environment may be to our disadvantage. When inadequate products are frequently experienced, any improvement would be frequently experienced too, and it is a pity if habituation leads to an absence of effort to improve the product. Although people may not notice continuing product weakness, they may well notice and appreciate the change when the product is improved because this change may surprise them. Research has moved away from the confirmation model which is shown as a diagram in Figure 8.2, but we return to it later for the study of service delay.

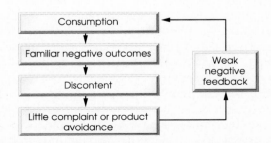

Figure 8.2 The confirmation model applied to an unsatisfactory product

The disconfirmation model

Most research has been focused on the high arousal condition where the product disconfirms expectation, either by exceeding it and giving satisfaction, or by falling short of expectation and causing dissatisfaction. This comparative definition has gradually evolved. Cardozo's (1965) laboratory work is often cited as the first empirical treatment of disconfirmed expectation and Howard and Sheth (1969) were among the first to recognize that people use standards of assessment in judging products. For them satisfaction was 'the buyer's cognitive state of being adequately or inadequately rewarded for the sacrifice he has undergone'.

This essentially cognitive account has now been modified. In more recent treatments the (dis)satisfaction is described as a jag of arousal that modifies the continuing attitude to the product. Satisfaction is:

> the summary psychological state resulting when the emotion surrounding disconfirmed expectations is coupled with the consumer's prior feelings about the consumption experience. Moreover, the surprise or excitement of this evaluation is thought to be of finite duration, so that satisfaction soon decays into (but nevertheless greatly affects) one's overall attitude toward purchasing products. (Oliver, 1981)

In the disconfirmation model the consumer is surprised by product features that are better or worse than expected. This model is often described as though the expectations are held in mind prior to the experience and then compared with the delivered product; often this sequence is reversed and an experience, pleasant or unpleasant, forces us to bring to mind what is appropriate in the circumstances – which we call our expectation. In the disconfirmation model, the magnitude of surprise is related to the size of the discrepancy between expectation and experience. A second determinant of (dis)satisfaction is the importance or value of the product, which may be measured by expectation; clearly, we expect more satisfaction from a car than from a minor consumer durable such as an electric heater. A third factor affecting satisfaction is the perception of the performance of the product; if you have high expectations and the performance is high, there is no disconfirmation, but you are more satisfied than when the performance is expected to be low, and is low; this may be seen as the satisfaction effect from the confirmation model which remains present when disconfirmation is added.

These three determinants of dissatisfaction create a quite cumbersome model and there is variation in the emphasis placed on the different determinants. Researchers have generally been most interested in the disconfirmation variable. Some researchers (e.g. Oliver, 1980; 1981; Swan and Trawick, 1981) have emphasized expectations separately from disconfirmation, while others (e.g. LaTour and Peat, 1979; Churchill and Surprenant, 1982; Tse and Wilton, 1988) have given attention to perceptions. Figure 8.3 illustrates these ideas when the product is unsatisfactory.

A series of studies (e.g. Oliver, 1980; Swan and Trawick, 1980) found that satisfaction is influenced mainly by disconfirmation. Rather at odds with this, Churchill and Surprenant (1982) found that satisfaction with a durable good, a video disc player, was determined solely by the product performance and any disconfirmations had no

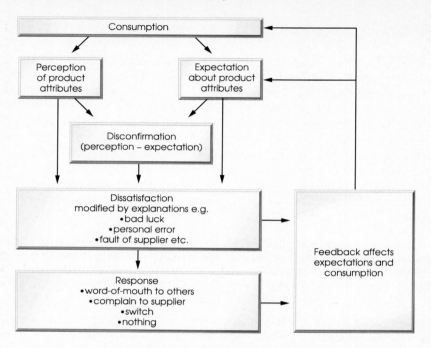

Figure 8.3 The disconfirmation model applied to an unsatisfactory product

residual impact on satisfaction. This result may have occurred because the product was unfamiliar so that respondents had few expectations about it; alternatively, the result may reflect the fact that durables have to last for a long period of time, which differentiates them from some everyday consumables and services, which are used more briefly. Dissatisfaction with a service might occupy most of the time over which the service is consumed and this might not be true for durables.

Some initial work indicated that satisfactions were additive, suggesting one basic form. Westbrook (1980) examined the way in which shop customers combine satisfactions with store performance and found that an overall measure of retail satisfaction correlated well with a simple addition of the satisfactions and dissatisfactions that customers experienced with regard to different aspects of store service. Later work (Westbrook and Oliver, 1991) showed that consumers subdivided CSD into three components; they separate negative emotion from positive satisfaction, and further divide positive satisfaction into a part related to surprise and a part based on interest. If this evidence is confirmed it suggests that the measurement of CSD requires questionnaire items that address the different components. Similarly, the design of products may need to take into account these different ways of reacting to them if they are to give full satisfaction.

Although it seems clear that an unexpectedly negative experience with a product will discourage loyalty and promote negative comment, an unexpected positive experience may not have exactly converse effects. Researchers have claimed that loyalty is raised by increased liking for the product, but there are grounds for questioning whether positive disconfirmation always leads to increased loyalty. Surprise is activating, whether negative or positive, and it thus seems quite likely that those who are unexpectedly pleased with a product may also be more open to change. This is an important issue since suppliers are being encouraged to surprise their clients with good service. The result could be that they become restless and explore competitor offerings, but there is little evidence on any responses to positive disconfirmation as Hunt (1991) notes. Most customer retention research (e.g. Reichheld, 1996) has focused on the elimination of dissatisfactions rather than the creation of positive surprises.

The disconfirmation model has much in common with other conditions such as frustration, shock, inequity and dissonance, in which experience causes a spike of arousal. Although dissonance has been recognized as one form of disconfirmation by consumer satisfaction theorists, there has been limited attention to the findings from the dissonance literature that are relevant to how and when dissonance changes attitude. In the section on dissonance in Chapter 7, we saw that human beings have only one physiological condition of arousal, which is interpreted as one of a number of states depending upon the conditions that are perceived to have caused it (Schachter and Singer, 1962); this suggests that evidence on the handling of dissonance arousal could be relevant to other forms of arousal such as consumer satisfaction responses. In particular, the Zanna and Cooper (1974) study seems relevant and suggests that the meanings that people attach to their CSD experience will affect the direction of any attitude change.

These considerations focus attention on the way in which surprises are interpreted and consumer satisfaction models therefore incorporate a stage in which the meaning attached to product experience is decoded. When the experience is negative, the explanation that the respondent gives for the outcome may influence whether he or she complains, changes brands or does nothing; these different responses are discussed in detail later.

Exercise 8.2   Good and bad surprises

The apparently fresh Brie is acrid, the new vacuum cleaner blocks, the car ventilation makes peculiar noises, or the waiter in an expensive restaurant is unhelpful. Here the dissatisfactions arise because our prior expectations were for a better experience. Conversely, we may be pleasantly surprised and satisfied when expectations are surpassed, e.g. when the roads are unusually clear, the cuisine nouvelle arrives in substantial portions, the train arrives on time or students get their work in well before the deadline.

Think back to the last time you were surprised by your experience as a consumer. Did the surprise make you satisfied, dissatisfied or neither? How would you explain what happened? Who was responsible? If you have the opportunity, will you try to repeat the experience?

Slow to mature

I had an experience which illustrates some of the issues in consumer dissatisfaction. I use a particular home brew beer kit; on one occasion the beer had a peculiar flavour, which I thought might have been due to the new, extra-sedimentary yeast that had been provided. I wrote to the manufacturers and provided a sample of some of my beer. There was no response. After a further prompt, I received a rather dismissive reply and some samples of the old yeast. On balance, I blamed myself for not sterilizing the fermenting equipment properly and continued to use the same beer kit with occasionally unsatisfactory results. Some years later I noticed that the extra-sedimentary yeast had been abandoned and I wrote again, innocently inquiring why this was so. I received vouchers for £15. I wrote again explaining that I had not complained in my previous letter, but I would now like to do so, and reported my difficulties with the product. I received vouchers for £30. I still use the beer kit.

In this real illustration, the product was defective, it was difficult to recognize this, and I misattributed blame to myself. The manufacturer handled the matter badly at first and, if they had listened to complaints when first made, they might have rectified their mistake much earlier. Now the manufacturer has instituted a proper complaint handling service, but the scale of compensation is quite large and may encourage false claims.

Customer satisfaction has value in its own right, and the world is a better place when products please consumers. But CSD has instrumental value too because it influences consumer behaviour and this may affect profits. Satisfied consumers may commend products to others, buy them more exclusively, repeat purchase and try line extensions. A dissatisfied consumer may comment unfavourably about the product to other potential customers, may complain to the seller or manufacturer and may switch brands. Thus, although the satisfaction of consumers may be regarded as an intrinsically worthwhile aim that consumer policy should endorse, there are further benefits from satisfied consumers which must be considered.

Perceived product quality

The disconfirmation model focuses on an *episode*, a happening in the life of the consumer. In practice, consumption is often a series of events, and one failure by a supplier may not result in dissatisfaction if properly handled. Swan, Powers and Hansen (1995) illustrate how this occurs in an industrial context. Over a period of time, satisfaction rests on an aggregate of performances which may be measured by customer attitude rather than by the customer response to particular episodes. The attitude measuring approach is the one that has been used for the measurement of perceived quality.

SERVQUAL

Discussion of the nature of perceived product quality can become very obscure, as Holbrook (1994) demonstrates; since obscurity is not our purpose, we shall focus on the main points. SERVQUAL is a service quality measuring instrument designed to cover all services with one set of questions. SERVQUAL was developed by Parasuraman, Zeithaml and Berry (1985; 1988) and draws on ideas proposed by Grönroos (1984). SERVQUAL measures customers' expectations of what firms should provide in the industry being studied and their perceptions of how a given service provider performs against these criteria. The 1988 version of the instrument contained twenty-two questions covering such specific service facilities as up-to-date equipment, visually appealing premises and polite employees. Later Parasuraman, Berry and Zeithaml (1991) modified the instrument slightly; they changed two items and altered the wordings of some others; the negative scoring on some items was removed and the wording of the expectation measures was changed so that respondents were asked what an 'excellent service would provide', rather than what 'firms in the industry should provide'. With the previous phraseology most responses clustered at the top of the scale so that it was difficult to separate the more important from the less important aspects of service provision. The box below shows the items in the 1991 scale applied to telephone companies.

SERVQUAL expectation components and classification

Tangibles

1. Excellent telephone companies will have modern-looking equipment.
2. The physical facilities at excellent telephone companies will be visually appealing.
3. Employees of excellent telephone companies will be neat-appearing.
4. Materials associated with the service (such as pamphlets or statements) will be visually appealing in an excellent telephone company.

Reliability

5. When excellent telephone companies promise to do something by a certain time, they will do so.
6. When customers have a problem, excellent telephone companies will show a sincere interest in solving it.
7. Excellent telephone companies will perform the service right first time.
8. Excellent telephone companies will provide their services at the time they promise to do so.
9. Excellent telephone companies will keep error-free records.

Responsiveness

10. Employees of excellent telephone companies will tell customers exactly when services will be performed.

---

11. Employees of excellent telephone companies give prompt service to customers.
12. Employees of excellent telephone companies will always be willing to help customers.
13. Employees of excellent telephone companies will never be too busy to respond to customer requests.

Assurance
14. The behaviour of employees of excellent telephone companies will instil confidence in customers.
15. Customers of excellent telephone companies will feel safe in their transactions.
16. Employees of excellent telephone companies will be consistently courteous with customers.
17. Employees of excellent telephone companies will have the knowledge to answer customer questions.

Empathy
18. Excellent telephone companies will give customers individual attention.
19. Excellent telephone companies will have operating hours convenient to all their customers.
20. Excellent telephone companies will have employees who give customers personal attention.
21. Excellent telephone companies will have the customers' best interests at heart.
22. The employees of excellent telephone companies will understand the specific needs of their customers.

Source: Parasuraman, Berry and Zeithaml (1991).

The initial analysis of the twenty-two items showed that they could be reduced to ten dimensions, and later work (Parasuraman, Zeithaml and Berry, 1988) reduced this list to five: tangibles, reliability, responsiveness, assurance (knowledge and courtesy of employees and their ability to inspire trust and confidence) and empathy (caring and individual attention to customers). The five-factor structure has not been well supported, and Cronin and Taylor (1992) found only one general factor.

The idea that SERVQUAL will apply to a variety of services without much modification has been contested. The instrument allows for variation in the importance of different measures, but Carman (1990) found that some functions require additional measures for adequate explanation; in retail settings, Koelemeijer (1992) found poor generalizability and Finn and Lamb (1991) also found that the SERVQUAL instrument was not appropriate in the retail context. It is easy to argue that some of the items are inappropriate for certain services, e.g. religious services having modern-looking equipment, neat appearance in academic settings or the providers of sexual services keeping error-free records. Thus, customization of the instrument seems required for application to different settings and, although Parasuraman, Zeithaml and Berry (1994) accept this, the changes may need to be substantial, which weakens the idea of a general instrument. Dabholkar, Thorpe and Rentz (1996) have now developed a scale for retail service quality measurement that draws on SERVQUAL and additional qualitative research. This scale gave a much better fit with other measures of retail satisfaction.

The computation of quality judgement from the questionnaire responses has also raised problems. SERVQUAL uses the difference score (gap) between expectation and perception (see box below, item 1) so that a positive score occurs only when perceptions exceed expectations. Expectations tend to be uniformly high and show little variance. Although the aggregate of the gaps correlates reasonably well with an overall measure of quality (Parasuraman, Berry and Zeithaml, 1991; Babacus and Boller, 1992; Cronin and Taylor, 1992), the low variance of the expectations measure makes it insensitive and difference scores usually give a worse explanation of overall quality judgements than perception-only scores. For this reason, Cronin and Taylor (1992) recommended that the measure is restricted to performance perceptions (which they call SERVPERF). Although Parasuraman, Zeithaml and Berry (1994) concede that a perceptions-only measure may give better predictions, they continue to see diagnostic and conceptual value in a separate measure of expectations.

Brown, Churchill and Peter (1993) have shown that the use of difference measures raises methodological problems, and there has been some examination of alternatives. Babacus and Boller (1992), like Carman (1990), suggested that the discrepancy between expectation and perceived performance could be measured in a single combined item (see box below, item 2) as has been proposed in research on consumer satisfaction (Oliver and Bearden, 1985; Swan and Trawick, 1981). In yet another measurement approach, DeSarbo *et al.* (1994) used items covering the ten dimensions in a conjoint procedure.

Exchanges between Parasuraman, Zeithaml and Berry (1994), Cronin and Taylor (1994) and Teas (1994) do not appear to take the debate much further. In a review of SERVQUAL's history, A.M. Smith (1995) concludes that few of the original claims remain undisputed. The aim of generic measurement of service quality is attractive because it may assist managements to deliver a better product, but this goal may be unobtainable because of variation in the nature of services and because of lack of agreement about concepts and measures.

Alternative scales

1.   SERVQUAL expectation and perception scales:

Firms in XYZ's field should have modern-looking equipment
   Strongly disagree __1__|__2__|__3__|__4__|__5__|__6__|__7__ *Strongly agree*

Firm XYZ has modern-looking equipment
   Strongly disagree __1__|__2__|__3__|__4__|__5__|__6__|__7__ *Strongly agree*

2.   Combined item:

XYZ's modern-looking equipment
   Greatly falls __1__|__2__|__3__|__4__|__5__|__6__|__7__ *Greatly exceeds*
   short of   *my expectations*
   my expectations

The nature of expectations

In SERVQUAL the expectation measures are normative, i.e. they establish what facilities the respondents think an excellent firm *should* have; they are not expectations describing what will normally be found. This distinction between normative and descriptive expectations has been noted by Swan and Trawick (1980), among others, with regard to the measurement of CSD. These meanings of 'expect' are quite different; it is quite possible to think that a firm *should* have a facility but not to expect that it *does* have it. Under such circumstances a customer will be surprised if the firm does, in fact, have the facility. We see here a difference that is particularly evident when customers have less control over their use of services. When service use is fully discretionary, for example, when you choose a restaurant, you will usually select one that presents food in the way that you think that it should be presented and, unless the restaurant lets you down, normative and descriptive expectations will often coincide. This is likely to be less true when you are trying out a restaurant for the first time and you have less knowledge of the likely service.

Woodruff, Cadotte and Jenkins (1983) argued that a normative measure was more appropriate for CSD, and Tse and Wilton (1988) found evidence that consumer satisfaction was based on both forms of expectation.

Evidence on the effect of different sorts of expectation is found in Yi's (1990) review of CSD. Bloemer and Poiesz (1989) discuss alternative expectations that consumers may have and Liljander (1994), in an interesting comparison of quality and CSD approaches, considers other expectation standards than those discussed here. Other differences between CSD and quality concepts are examined by Patterson and Johnson (1993).

Particular respondents may agree that a service should have particular features, but may not personally attach much importance to them. For example, we might expect certain standards of plumbing in a hotel, but still tolerate quite happily some of the more eccentric pipework of a French family hotel. Other problems arise if respondents try to take account of the competing expectations of the different stakeholders with whom service providers deal. An example is provided by Taylor (1996), who points to a number of deficiencies in business education in the United States and points out that delivery to students is partly a function of the need to deliver in other relationships. Consumers may take such matters into account; for example, students may see staff attention to research either as a diversion of effort away from teaching or as necessary groundwork if staff are to provide expert advice.

Responses to consumer satisfaction and dissatisfaction

A number of studies have indicated that products are frequently regarded as unsatisfactory by consumers, although the figures vary by product type and country. Examples of dissatisfaction levels are given by Andreasen (1988), who quoted a figure of 15–25 per cent in the United States; and Stø and Glefjell (1990), who found similar figures for a range of goods and services in Norway. More divergent results are found for some products: Moore, Maxwell and Barron (1996) found that 83 per cent of retail customers were not even fairly satisfied in Glasgow, and Benterud and Stø (1993) found that 34 per cent of those using a TV shopping channel in Norway were not satisfied.

Hirschman (1970) suggested that perceived product failure led to two types of response which he described succinctly as *exit* and *voice*. Exit is switching to other products or suppliers, or simply boycotting the product; voice, or complaining, has a number of forms: negative word-of-mouth (grousing to other consumers), redress-seeking from suppliers and occasionally formal complaints through legal or trade authorities. Conversely, Hirschman noted that satisfactory products led to loyalty and positive word-of-mouth. An interesting extension of Hirschman's outcomes by Huefner and Hunt (1994) details vandalism, theft, disruption and other activities that aggrieved customers sometimes engage in. Also Blodgett, Granbois and Walters (1993) have suggested that when a complaint is made, the character of complaint handling will determine further loyalty and word-of-mouth behaviour.

Work by Oliver (1980), Oliver and Swan (1989) and Fornell (1992) indicates that, although repurchase intentions are much reduced by dissatisfaction, many consumers are reluctant to change. For example, Feinberg *et al.* (1990) found that repurchase intentions for different goods in the United States were still 47–84 per cent after an unsatisfactory warranty repair; this compared with 90+ per cent repurchase intention when the repair was satisfactory. There is, of course, some doubt about whether repurchase intentions are an adequate guide to actual behaviour in this context; we saw in Chapter 5 that inertia operates against change, and it seems likely that many of those who say that they intend to change their loyalty may fail to do so. We must also recognize that often it is not feasible to change patronage; sometimes the product is satisfactory in many other respects and there may be substantial switching costs.

Attribution

The exceptional performance of a product, positive or negative, can be interpreted in a variety of ways by consumers; Burns and Perkins (1996) cover a wide range of possible responses to such situations. The consumer's interpretation of the product's performance then affects how he or she responds. Consumers may commend the product and stay loyal if their experience is positive and they attribute this to good performance by the supplier, or they may voice complaints and switch suppliers if a poor performance is seen as the fault of the supplier. In other circumstances dissatisfied consumers may not blame the supplier; the attribution they make may be affected by other conditions, and the *availability of explanations* and *causal inferences* have been studied in particular.

Availability
As we saw in Chapter 7, the ease of recall, or *availability*, helps to determine what expectations are used as frames of reference. Vivid, distinct ideas are more easily

brought to mind and are judged more probable. Folkes (1988) gives an interesting example of how this can work. She asked people who were approaching the escalators to their apartment in a six-storey building how often the escalators broke down. The escalators only went to the fourth floor so that those who lived on the fifth and sixth floors always had to climb the stairs for the last part of their ascent. These people, who always had to use the stairs for part of their journey, estimated that the escalators broke down *less* often than the rest for whom an escalator failure was more distinctive in its effect. The distinctiveness of a product failure raises its availability and the perceived likelihood that it will occur again, and this will raise dissatisfaction. The supplier should, therefore, try to make failures less distinctive; for example, if customers are occupied in some way when service quality is reduced, they may form a less distinct memory of the poor performance.

Worse-than-expected outcomes have more impact than better-than-expected out-comes (DeSarbo *et al.*, 1994). This difference could be an endowment effect explained in prospect theory (Chapter 7).

Causal inferences

Weiner (1980; 1990) has examined the explanations given for success and failure and has suggested three causal dimensions that are relevant to the consumer response: stability, locus of causality and controllability.

Stability is shown when the cause can be consistently attributed to a particular person or feature of the environment; locus of causality relates to whether the purchaser or the supplier is seen to be at fault, and controllability reflects the ability of an agent to intervene and change outcomes. From the consumer's standpoint, an unstable negative event is less threat; e.g. an out-of-stock may be seen as exceptional (unstable) and unlikely to be repeated. It is, therefore, better for a seller if the cause of their failure is seen as unstable by the customer. By contrast, it is best to have stability in product success since this encourages continued usage. Folkes (1984) suggests that when conditions are perceived to be stable a consumer will prefer to have a refund for a product failure since a replacement carries the same risk as the original, but, if the failure is seen as unstable, consumers will be more willing to accept a replacement.

Weiner's other dimensions also affect consumer response after product failure. For example, with respect to locus of causation, persons may blame themselves and therefore expect no redress when they purchase a poor product; but if they see the failure as the responsibility of the manufacturer, they may then expect replacement or refund and an apology. If people feel that they have no control over their outcomes they may feel anger towards those who they think do have control. Sydney airport, for example, is notoriously overstretched so that delays on landing are common and passengers waiting in the skies above Sydney can do little but feel irritation towards the planners who have bungled the airport development.

Complaining

Factors affecting complaining behaviour

Despite evidence that dissatisfaction with products is very common, the available evidence shows that people are often reluctant to complain. The most common response to unsatisfactory products is to do nothing. Andreasen (1988) and Stø and Glefjell (1990) found that 60 per cent of dissatisfied consumers did nothing; Benterud and Stø (1993) found that 95 per cent of those dissatisfied with their TV shopping did not complain.

Dissatisfaction is likely to be a necessary condition for complaining, but it is not a sufficient reason; evidence on negative word-of-mouth suggests that this occurs in a minority of cases of dissatisfaction. Day and Ash (1979) report that about a third of those who are dissatisfied with goods comment about the product to family and friends. Day (1984) and Singh and Howell (1985) have noted that complaining is affected by how people explain product failure, their expectation of redress, the likely time-cost and the effort involved. There is evidence that the *degree* of dissatisfaction has a modest relationship with the likelihood of complaint (Day, 1984; Oliver, 1981; 1987; Malafi *et al.*, 1993; Singh and Howell, 1985). Oliver (1981) reports a correlation of about 0.4 between dissatisfaction and complaining.

Letters of complaint

Although a grievance is usually required to make a complaint, some of us scarcely need it. Complaining also has its entertaining aspects which I commend to the reader. Two examples of teasing the great and the good follow. Sadly, the responses were rather bureaucratic.

Sir Bryan Nicholson
Chairman, Post Office

Dear Sir Bryan,

Recently I paid money into an account by first class post and bills by second class post. The second class post was so fast that the cheques paying the bills were presented before the money entered my account and I incurred a charge from the bank for going into overdraft.

People like myself rely on the second class post being second class and cannot afford capricious improvements in service. Could you ensure that your staff maintain the slowness of second class mail so that a reliable product is offered to the public?

Yours sincerely,

Robert East

The Pope
The Vatican

Dear Holiness,

Does the fluctuating date for Easter vex you as much as it does me? Is there any religious necessity for Easter Sunday to be on the first Sunday after the date of the first full moon that occurs on or after March 21st? I would like to suggest that, as the principal leader of the Christian religions, you open discussions with other leaders of the Christian faith about fixing Easter on a particular date.

The benefits would be considerable. People would know the date of Easter and would not have to inspect their diaries. Academic terms could be fixed and not change each year and holiday arrangements would be simplified. If Easter were fixed late rather than early many people might benefit from taking holidays when the weather is better.

It would be good to see the Catholic Church take a lead on this matter; it would show people that the Church was not beholden to tradition and was willing to change when there was benefit to people.

Yours sincerely,

Robert East

Research on complaining has tended to focus on single factors, but why seek singular explanations when we can ask people about all the reasons they might have for complaining in one instrument? Applying Ajzen's theory of planned behaviour, three types of influence may be identified:

1. *Expected outcomes* – gains and losses, including opportunity costs, that follow complaining.
2. *Normative influences* – what people think reference persons or groups think they should do.
3. *Control factors* – that make it more or less easy to register a complaint.

Expected outcomes
Hirschman (1970) suggested that complaining was related to expected returns and opportunity costs and these expected outcomes have received most attention from researchers. Positive outcomes may include replacement, apology and better goods or service in the future, while negative outcomes may include lost opportunities, wasted time and embarrassment. The perceived likelihood of success in obtaining redress has been found to be associated with complaining in a number of studies (Day and Landon, 1976; Granbois, Summers and Frazier, 1977; Richins, 1983; 1987; and Singh, 1990). Richins (1985) has also found evidence that the importance of the product affects the likelihood of complaining. The potential approval or disapproval expressed by others may also be an expected outcome. For example, people may avoid criticizing restaurant service if they think that this will upset their companions.

Normative influences

Consumers may also be influenced by what they believe others think they should do, even when these other people can never be aware of the respondent's behaviour. Normative influences on redress-seeking have not been studied systematically though Richins (1981) has noted instances where consumers felt that they 'ought' to complain.

Control factors

These are knowledge, skills, time and other resources that can make complaining easier or harder. Examples are the ease of access to key personnel, an understanding of the workings of the organization causing dissatisfaction and confidence about complaining. Control factors help us to distinguish between those who complain and those who do not. Two studies (Caplovitz, 1967; and Warland, Herrman and Willits, 1975) found that non-complainers seemed powerless and had less knowledge of the means of redress; and Grønhaug (1977) found that there were more complaints to a Norwegian consumer protection agency from citizens who lived closer to it. Grønhaug and Zaltman (1981) also recognized the importance of resources such as time, money and confidence; this study is cited by Yi (1990) as an important pointer to differences between complainers and non-complainers. A matter of concern is that vulnerable consumers (the old, ill and disadvantaged) complain less than others (Andreasen and Manning, 1990), and this is likely to be related to the reduced control that such consumers have.

A study of factors influencing the intention to complain

East (1996) tried to capture *all* the individual factors that are positively and negatively associated with the intention to complain in a specific context; the study used Ajzen's theory of planned behaviour to frame questions on the factors associated with seeking redress when goods fail.

To focus the answers of respondents, two scenarios were used. The first was:

> Please imagine that you have bought a pair of leather shoes for £40 from a local shop. You use them about half the time and six weeks after you bought them you notice that the stitching is going on one of the shoes. This questionnaire is about how you feel about taking the shoes back to the shop where you bought them.

The second scenario was identical except for an additional sentence (in bold) inserted after the second sentence:

> **You recall that when you were in the shoe shop another customer was complaining to the manager about some shoes and eventually left without any compensation.**

The questionnaire items were based on taking the shoes back to the shop and covered the standard variables of planned behaviour theory. The elicited outcome beliefs were 'getting a refund or new pair of shoes', 'standing up for my rights', 'having an argument with shop staff', 'being embarrassed', 'wasting time'. The salient referents were 'family' and 'friends'. The control beliefs were 'keeping the receipt' and 'being confident about complaining'.

The second scenario was intended to reduce the likelihood of complaining but respondents seemed to resist the implied threat to their consumer rights and were slightly more likely to complain.

Under Scenario 1, the intention to seek redress was strongly associated with *confidence about complaining, refund or replacement of the product, the normative influence of friends* and the need to *stand up for one's rights*. Under Scenario 2, *confidence* and *standing up for one's rights* again figured strongly.

A second study was undertaken in which the scenario was modified and the shoes now failed after four months instead of six weeks and complaining was shown to have a time-cost. Both changes were designed to reduce the tendency to complain and this was observed with 30 per cent stating that they were extremely likely to complain compared with 48 per cent in the first study. Under these circumstances the strongest correlates of complaining remained *getting a refund or replacement, standing up for one's rights* and *confidence about complaining*, thus showing no change in reasons for complaint as the strength of intention changed. It is interesting that cost/benefit reasons do not dominate: standing up for rights is associated with normative and control dimensions, and confidence in complaining is control related.

This study examines complaint to a retailer about one type of product. Further evidence is required about different product failures, complaints to other agencies, and the effect of using letters and telephone rather than face-to-face confrontation.

The benefits of receiving complaints

Fornell and Wernerfelt (1987) argued that, within cost limits, it is profitable to gather and evaluate the complaints from dissatisfied customers, and some companies, particularly in the United States, put toll-free telephone numbers on the packaging for this purpose. One reason for this is that an effective response to the aggrieved customer by the company may reduce negative comment to other potential customers which could damage sales. A second reason is evidence that, in some contexts, those who complain are more likely to repeat purchase (TARP, 1979; Gilly and Gelb, 1982); however, in other cases those who complain are more likely to exit, for example Solnick and Hemenway (1992) found that those who complained about health provision were much more likely to leave than those who did not complain. Better repatronage after complaint may occur because people intended to repatronize and wanted to benefit from changes induced by their complaining, or it may occur because the complaint-handling resolved the customer's dissatisfaction. It is likely that good complaint-handling raises loyalty and this is now seen as very important since the cost of attracting new customers is claimed to be much greater than the cost of retaining old customers. Estimates of this cost ratio vary with the application: Reichheld and Sasser (1990) claimed six times for credit cards and Fornell and Wernerfelt (1988) claimed three times for Volvo cars. A third reason for receiving complaints is for market research, that is, to gather information about products so that product weaknesses can be corrected. Often a fourth reason for running a complaint service is to gather further sales.

Despite the good reasons for a positive approach to complaints, this may still be the exception rather than the rule. In 1984, Fornell and Westbrook found that complaint-handling departments were neglected by management and that the neglect was greater if the proportion of negative consumer communications was larger. As usual, the causation in this relationship is unclear, but it could indicate a counter-productive managerial response: that the more the message indicates a problem, the more the messenger is despised. This raises the question of statutory support for complaint-handling; when far-sighted companies already facilitate complaining there may be scope for pressure on the remaining companies to provide a service that is positive about receiving complaints. It seems likely that legal enhancement of the rights of the complainer will raise the proportion of dissatisfied customers who do complain, and that this could benefit both consumers and suppliers; there could even be a beneficial effect to the economy if more complaints focused management attention on product deficiencies. Regulations should take account of consumer motivations that affect complaining. For example, if my findings (East, 1996) are substantiated, regulations should emphasize consumer rights and require clear procedures that will make consumers confident about pursuing a complaint.

Companies' complaints handling

Yi (1990) reviews work in this field. Evidence from a number of studies indicates that the handling of complaints affects consumer satisfaction and repurchase intentions. Monetary reimbursement and speed of response both raised satisfaction and repurchase intentions (Gilly and Gelb, 1982).

Not surprisingly, suppliers and customers often differ in their perception of a complaint. The customer more often sees the complaint as legitimate and wants redress, while the manager wants to satisfy the consumer, even if the complaint seems dubious (Resnik and Harmon, 1983).

The consumer's response to delay

Delay in the delivery of service is a perennial feature of retailing and other services; indeed it is an inherent liability of a product that is produced and received in an interval of time. Consumers wait for counter service in banks and post offices, for train tickets in booking offices, and at the checkout in supermarkets; they also wait for public transport and get held up in traffic jams; they may have to wait to talk to someone on the telephone, and for professional advice. For the individual, delay is frustrating, and for the economy it is wasteful because people waiting in line are neither producing nor consuming. Pruyn and Smidts (1993) argue that increased production means that people need more time to consume products and time has become more valuable. Pruyn and Smidts found that checkout delay was the most irritating feature of shopping

for Dutch shoppers and that respondents to a survey waited, on average, over half an hour per day for different services and appointments.

In Britain, 70 per cent of respondents in a Consumers' Association *Which?* report (February 1990) on supermarkets mentioned 'a lot of staffed checkouts' as desirable, placing it fourth in importance compared with other store features, and another report on post offices (*Which?*, September 1989) put cutting queueing time at the top of service improvements suggested by respondents even though the research recorded an average wait of only $3\frac{1}{2}$ minutes in post offices. Bitner, Booms and Tetreault (1990) noted that delay was a major feature of incidents causing dissatisfaction. Chebat and Filiatrault (1993) and East, Lomax and Willson (1991a) found that dislike of delay was related to its expected frequency and duration.

Organizations that create delay by poor design of services do so at their peril. Waiting is a punishment that may become associated with the whole service experience and a number of studies have shown that the longer the wait the lower the evaluation of the whole service (Clemmer and Schneider, 1987; Katz, Larson and Larson, 1991; Taylor, 1994; Tom and Lucey, 1995; Feinberg, Widdows and Steidle, 1996). Organizations may not notice the irritation that delay causes because of perceptual differences between the service provider and the customer; Feinberg and Smith (1989) found that when the customer at the checkout thought the average delay was 5.6 minutes the staff perception was 3.2 and the actual time was 4.7 minutes.

It is likely that people are less bothered by delay when it is expected (Maister, 1985). Supporting this, an experiment on bank queues by Clemmer and Schneider (1987) in the United States showed that the more unexpected the delay the more it was disliked. This suggests that we can identify two types of dissatisfaction with delay: a low involvement discontent when the delay is predicted, and a high involvement

disconfirmation effect. As delays become more common and impose a more frequent time-cost they also become more predictable. Thus frequency may have offsetting effects on customer toleration of delay: they dislike the greater time-cost but find it easier to put up with expected delays, and this may be why Taylor (1994) did not find that common delays were associated with significantly more irritation.

Maister (1985) proposed that people tolerate a wait better if they have a *reason for the delay*. The provision of delay information is now standard among transport operators such as airlines, and London Underground provides display boards reporting the wait before train arrivals; such information seems to be much appreciated despite the fact that it does nothing to reduce the waiting time. Another useful innovation is queue position information when waiting on the telephone. Maister also notes that people are less irritated by delay if they can *fill their time* in some way; one example here is the way in which Disneyland entertains its queues; another is the provision of mirrors in places where people have to wait, e.g. at elevators. Taylor (1995) used two groups in an experiment to test the effect of filling waiting time; both groups were delayed by 10 minutes but only one was allowed activities to offset the delay. In this study the evaluation of the service was reduced by delay, but this reduction was less when waiting time was filled. In fact, some of those who were delayed did not even realize that they had been held up and most of these people were in the filled waiting time condition. Taylor's work also suggested that the more *control* the service provider was thought to have over the delay, the more negative was the perception of the delayed service; this is consistent with Weiner's (1980; 1990) suggestion that people become more irritated when they believe that the service provider has control of the situation.

Other studies on queues have used experiments to examine the effect of changing factors in the waiting context; for example Milgram, Liberty and Toledo (1986) found that customers saw intrusions into a queue as a *breach of social norms*, and reacted accordingly. Schmitt, Dubé and Leclerc (1992) explored customer reactions to intrusions into queues by those with different social roles; they found that people objected to intrusions by other customers more than they did to intrusions by retail personnel, which were not contrary to the norms. The person next in line seemed to have a special obligation to respond to intrusions.

Studies by Dubé-Rioux, Schmitt and Leclerc (1989) and Dubé, Schmitt and Leclerc (1991) showed that when delay occurred at the *beginning or end of a process* – in this case a meal – it was evaluated more negatively than mid-process delays. It was better to take the order and then impose the delay, than to wait before taking the order. However it is not always clear when a service starts and finishes; for example, delays to air travel occur when going to the airport, at check-in, passport control, the departure lounge, before take-off, before landing, at baggage reclaim and again at passport control; people may think of this sequence as a number of services or just one, and the way they regard it may affect how they tolerate delay at different points.

A study by East, Lomax and Willson (1991) showed that 31 per cent did not mind waiting at the checkout in supermarkets. In banks and post offices this figure rose to 50 per cent and in building societies 57 per cent. A cynic might see this as evidence of British stoicism and Maister has noted drily that, when the British see a queue, they join it. Anecdotal support for the British reverence for the queue comes from a 1989 newspaper report of two pensioners who, after deciding to rob a bank, waited in line before drawing a gun and demanding money from the teller. However, anecdote is no substitute for systematic evidence and studies in Britain (East *et al.*, 1992a) and in the United States by Perkins (unpublished) permitted a cross-national comparison of the attitude to waiting. In Britain 52 per cent, and in the United States 63 per cent, either did not mind, or minded a little, when delayed at the checkout. Superficially, it would appear that the Americans tolerate delay better than the British. However the dislike of delay was related to *how much people expected to be delayed*; the US respondents expected delays to be shorter and this probably explains their greater tolerance. We can therefore explain findings on toleration of delay without resort to national stereotypes (though national differences probably do occur). In the East, Lomax and Willson (1991) study it was clear that people expected to be delayed more in supermarkets than in other outlets, and this may explain why they were less tolerant of waiting in supermarkets than in banks, building societies and post offices.

The finding that dislike of queueing is related to the expected waste of time also fits an exchange theory account of social interaction. Homans (1961) argues that human beings learn to expect certain behaviours from others in response to their own actions so that patterns of exchange become established. In this exchange, liking and general appreciation are accorded to those people and organizations that act in ways that are rewarding, while dislike, abuse and blame are given to those who create costs.

Homans suggests that ideas of equity are involved in the process of exchange, that is, that people expect their costs to be commensurate with their rewards in an exchange.

This would imply that those receiving benefits in an exchange would be more tolerant of delay than those incurring costs. This fitted East, Lomax and Willson's (1991) data on post office use. Table 8.1 shows the findings subdivided by age. In each age range, those spending money in the Post Office, buying stamps or licences, were less tolerant of delay than those receiving benefits such as pensions or allowances.

Homans and others have pointed out that the attraction of an exchange is dependent upon what the alternative is. Older people, who often have fewer activities to occupy their time, could find a service queue more tolerable than younger people with family and work pressures. We see support for this in Table 8.1 since the older respondents are more tolerant of delay, whatever the nature of their transaction.

Table 8.1 Percentage who dislike waiting by type of Post Office transaction and age

	Those buying stamps, licences or paying bills %	Those receiving pensions, allowances or benefits %
Under 65 years old	61	49
65 or more	50	18

Note: Chi square tests: Under 65, p < 0.04; 65 or more, p < 0.001.
Source: East, Lomax and Willson (1991).

Perception of responsibility for delay

Although exchange theory helps us to understand the dislike of queueing it does not account for the way people may explain a delay. Of particular interest is the way people explain who is responsible when they have to wait for service, since customers who see a service provider as clearly responsible are likely to be more irritated by the delay (Weiner, 1980).

In the study by East, Lomax and Willson (1991) respondents were asked who they held responsible when they were delayed in the supermarket. Table 8.2 shows that more of the people who disliked waiting blamed management for their delay. The investigations of delay in post offices, building societies and banks gave very similar results. Taylor (1994) also found that those who blamed management were more angry about the wait. Surveys of this sort do not tell us what is cause and what is effect, or whether the relationship is reciprocal; people may dislike waiting all the more because they see management (which has more control than other parties) as responsible, or, disliking delay, they may look for a satisfactory object of blame and management fulfils this best. Folkes, Koletsky and Graham (1987) found that customers became more angry and expressed more resistance to repurchase when they saw that a delay was avoidable by management.

We see from Table 8.2 that few people are self-blaming; although they too are customers they are much more likely to blame *other* customers than themselves. This is consistent with the *actor–observer bias* (E.E. Jones and Nisbett, 1972), that an actor tends to see others as the cause of their behaviour while the actor sees the same behaviour in himself as caused by the situation (e.g. circumstances or other people).

Table 8.2 Those held responsible for delay in the supermarket

	No one	Self	Other customers	Checkout staff	Management	Total
Don't mind waiting %	35	2	33	5	25	**134**
Dislike waiting %	18	2	18	4	59	**297**

Source: East, Lomax and Willson (1991).

Delay management

This research on the response to delay helps us to understand how to manage this service problem better. There are three approaches:

1. operations management,
2. influencing demand,
3. perception management.

Where feasible, managements should try first to avoid delays by *increasing service supply*; this is the approach of operations management. For example, supermarket managements could count shoppers entering the store and open checkouts in advance of the calculated demand, and they could use their fastest checkout operators at peak times.

The second approach uses *regulation and incentives* to draw demand away from busy periods and towards quiet periods. A reservation system is used for many services and differential pricing may also shift demand, e.g. Monday is often a cheap day at the cinema in Britain. In supermarkets, East *et al.* (1994) judged that the scope for promoting the off-peak periods was limited, but real (see Chapter 9).

Know the customer

There is a tendency for suppliers to treat variations in customer demand as a given and not something that can be influenced or adjusted to. When a service is available for a period such as 3.00–5.00 pm there may be a tendency for people to go at 3.00 pm and just before 5.00 pm. This was the experience of a veterinary surgeon whom I know. The response should be to encourage attendance at 4.00 pm.

The third approach is to try to ensure that the customer *sees the delay in a way that does least damage*. When delay occurs it helps to take Maister's (1985) advice and supply information. Providing diversion for the queue is also recommended by Maister, as well as by Katz, Larson and Larson (1991), but it is easy to offend customers with mindless music on the telephone and inappropriate advertising on screens. Tom and Lucey (1995) suggest free samples and literature at the checkout in supermarkets, and this could work well because the activity is then under the control of the customer; one problem about standardized ways of filling time is that this implies that the delay is normal (stable) and management is only interested in alleviating the discomfort of waiting, not in eliminating it.

Exercise 8.3   Dealing with service delay

The plane was due to take off for London from Newark at 8.00 pm. At 8.05 the pilot reported that 'maintenance was still on board' and that they hoped to take off shortly. At 8.20 he reported again that maintenance was still working and that he expected to be clear soon. He reported again at 8.35 and then at 8.45 when he explained that the problem was minor but that they were having problems resolving it. At 9.00 he said that they expected to resolve the problem soon and that the stewards were distributing comment forms so that customers could register their feelings. A few minutes later the problem was resolved and the plane cleared for take-off. After take-off the pilot announced that the airline was offering one free alcoholic drink per passenger in compensation for the delay. About an hour after take-off the comment forms were collected. What is your assessment of this procedure?

Not surprisingly, managements receive much of the blame for delay, but often the cause is accidental or brought about by other service providers on whom management had relied. This suggests that management needs to distinguish between the cause of the delay and responsibility for its consequences. Staff should clearly accept responsibility to *remedy a problem*, but it will help if they can explain that they did not create the problem since the evidence (e.g. Taylor, 1994) shows that the service is liked less if blame is attributed to the service provider. For example, the cause of an air traffic delay may be that a service company has failed to deliver airline food on time, that a mechanical fault has been revealed by standard checks before take-off, that bad weather has delayed the plane's arrival, or that airport congestion is worse than normal. In all these cases it is possible to see the delay as caused by the carrier or as 'just one of those things'; timely announcements may help to deflect blame.

Sometimes there is choice about *when* the delay occurs. If some delay is anticipated in a service it is best to start the service (registering the patient, taking the order) and then impose the delay because mid-process delay is resented less (according to Dubé-Rioux, Schmitt and Leclerc, 1989; 1991).

When queues have a visible form they can often be organized as either *multiple line* or as *single line*. The single line can also be 'snaked' which reduces its apparent length. One alternative that is sometimes possible is the *queueing ticket* system which is used at delicatessen counters in supermarkets. Queueing tickets allow people to conduct other business while they wait; in banks, for example, they can sit down and read instead of standing in line. The relative attraction of these three systems was tested by East *et al.* (1992b) in their investigation of bank and building society use (see Table 8.3).

Table 8.3 'If there are queues, would you rather have . . .'

	Banks %	Building societies %	Mean %
. . . separate queues at each counter?	15	12	14
. . . a single queueing system?	78	81	79
. . . queueing tickets?	7	7	7

Source: East, Lomax and Willson (1992b).

The single line queueing system is much preferred despite the fact that this system introduces further delay as customers make their way to a vacant counter. The advantages of single line systems are twofold: delays are approximately equal and therefore fair, and they are more predictable since excessive delays with one counter will not affect waiting time much when there are several counters in use. The multiple line system seems particularly useful when the start of a service is impending; for example, in train stations where there is a danger of missing the train. Work by Pruyn and Smidts (1993) indicates that, though people may prefer the single line, the queueing system is of less consequence than the duration of delay and the quality of the waiting environment.

A managerial checklist

Work on CSD should help us to make goods and services better. A very useful paper by Halstead (1993) summarizes the mistakes about consumer satisfaction programmes. The disconfirmation model, by specifying how people become satisfied and dissatisfied, defines the targets for management action. Specific management decisions are required under three headings:

1. Refining the product.
2. Belief management.
3. Damage limitation.

Refining the product

Where the product has physical form, improvements are usually the province of technical specialists. These specialists need clear feedback on customer preference and a mandate to act on the evidence. I have been surprised at the way obvious design weaknesses persist for years. For example, older people lose strength and may not be able to operate depression switches on torches. A torch with a slider switch is suitable for everyone, yet many torches have depression switches.

Where the product is a service its quality depends on the staff who deal with customers and the procedures that they use. Customer care programmes should appraise policy, the way it is put into practice and personnel training so that deficiencies are eliminated. Management should pay attention to:

- *Customer preference.* Provide the service that customers want, rather than the one that it is convenient to give. This requires regular assessment of customer satisfaction, monitoring of complaints, etc. It is not sufficient to provide monitoring forms since most customers will not bother to fill these in. And it may be better to focus on the best and worst aspects of a service rather than taking the customer through all the possibilities.
- *Communication.* Make sure that senior management gets the information on customer perceptions of product quality. Many perceptions of service quality arise in the exchange between customers and (usually) junior staff such as receptionists, so that senior management can easily be unaware of dissatisfactions. Senior managers are responsible for policy on complaint handling, returned goods, compensation and the general quality of exchanges with customers; they must define this policy and communicate it to staff and customers.

  To achieve more direct contact with customers, many firms are now using mass communications, supported by modern database management. Together with bills and bank statements we receive magazines, customer charters and detailed accounts from utilities about how the money is spent. (I received one entitled *Looking after Water, Sewerage and You*, which seemed an unfortunate title.) I have yet to see evidence that this 'close to the customer' material does a useful job in its present form.
- *Competitors.* Customer expectations are set by the market so management should monitor competitor practices.
- *Research.* Managements should search for ways of adding value to the product but also should monitor the customer response to any changes.

Belief management

- *Prime relevant expectations.* People can have several expectations about a product. People may have views about what is fair, ideal, desirable, common, just adequate, and these could all be different. For example, when we go to a bank the ideal may be no queue, the minimum acceptable might be a short queue and the prediction (when going at lunch time) might be a long queue. When a number of expectations are in play, the supplier should try to increase the salience of those expectations that the product can normally meet and to avoid those claims which may be dashed by reality.

  The management of expectation also includes forewarning customers about problems with products, e.g. about price rises, or that ionizers produce dirty deposits on nearby walls. One case noted by Carsky (1989) concerned a Ford model with a sporty T-shaped sunroof which was prone to let rain water through. Dealers were reluctant to sell the model because of later complaints. When customers were warned about the dubious weather proofing of the sunroof the complaints of buyers were reduced. Marketing communications to trade users sometimes identify the limitations of a product; it is possible that suppliers would benefit if they were more open with consumers about product weaknesses, particularly when these deficiencies are quickly discovered by users.

■ *Reveal hidden benefits*. Another aspect of belief management occurs when marketing communications draw attention to benefits that would otherwise go unnoticed, even though they fulfil a need. An example might be the fact that foodstuffs are free of certain preservatives or pesticides that may cause concern. This builds satisfaction and negatively positions competitors who have not made such claims. Information slips in the pack, notices at the checkout and informational advertising can all be used to inform customers.

■ *Cue negative beliefs about competitors*. There are also tactical gains to be made when a competitor upsets customers. In London, Foyles is known as a large but rather eccentrically managed bookshop. Their competitor, Dillons Bookshop, ran the advertisement: 'Foyled again? Try Dillons', which was well understood by London book-buyers. In Britain, comparative advertising is relatively subdued, and there may be large gains to be made by reminding customers of the deficiencies of competitive products. For instance, a manufacturer of dental floss might remind customers that their pack does not come apart like so many of their competitors' packs.

■ *Don't draw attention to the unnoticed*. Do not overreact to minor deficiencies in your product. People may not notice or bother about small discrepancies between expectation and outcome. Apologies or explanations for minor shortfalls may increase dissatisfaction by drawing attention to a problem that customers had ignored.

Damage limitation

Company policy should be designed to reduce dissatisfaction when a brand has fallen short of expectation by:

■ Listening to and responding politely to complaints.
■ Recognizing the deficiency.
■ Apologizing and accepting responsibility to assist customers, but not necessarily responsibility for causing the problem.
■ Explaining what's gone wrong, describing any steps taken by the company to prevent it happening again, and inviting customer comment.
■ Compensating customers where appropriate.
■ Using customers' complaints to improve the product.

Summary

Consumer satisfaction, dissatisfaction, quality perception and complaining behaviour have acquired considerable importance in academic marketing because of their relationship to profit. The need to raise quality is widely recognized, but the willingness of companies to hear complaints is rather less apparent. A particular emphasis in this field has been on the quality of services; this reflects the growing proportion of Gross Domestic Product contributed by services and the fact that services are inherently difficult to standardize.

Consumers are contented when products meet positive expectations and are discontented with goods and services that show expected weaknesses, but this fulfilment of expectations (*the confirmation model*) normally occasions little arousal and, therefore, little behavioural response. Much research has now focused on those occasions where product performance surprises the consumer (*the disconfirmation model*). Surprise is arousing and causes more behavioural response, and therefore more potential impact on profit. There is some variation in the way researchers describe the detail of the disconfirmation model but there is agreement that the discrepancy between expectation and perception creates disconfirmation, and it is also recognized that expectations and perceptions may have independent effects on (dis)satisfaction. In addition, researchers now recognize an interpretive phase in which consumers' explanations of their experience may modify their responses to it.

Work on service quality has focused on an instrument called SERVQUAL which has been developed as a measure of quality in any service field. The instrument has attracted substantial criticism and, although it has been modified, there are continuing concerns about the specific items in the instrument, the dimensions they factor into, and the extent to which the measurement and findings apply across different services. There are also worries that the measurement of quality produced by SERVQUAL may not be sufficiently related to consumer behaviour: SERVQUAL measures what service providers *should* provide whereas consumer satisfaction measures usually relate to expectations by customers of what they *will* receive.

Hirschman (1970) set out the consequences of good and bad product performance. He proposed that the dissatisfaction of consumers led to two sorts of response: *exit* and *voice*. When consumers were pleased they stayed loyal and commended the product to others; when they were dissatisfied they tended to move to other brands and complained to suppliers and other consumers about the product. Subsequent work expanded and modified this initial approach.

Research has related complaining behaviour to the level of dissatisfaction and to outcomes such as redress and time-cost. When all salient factors were measured in a planned behaviour framework, one study revealed that normative factors (the views of others, standing up for rights) and a control factor (confidence about complaining) had strong influences on whether or not a complaint was made; if this work is confirmed, it suggests that outcomes such as redress may have been given too much importance as determinants of complaining.

Delay is a general liability of service provision and has now been extensively studied. Unexpected delay (causing disconfirmation) is more disliked. When it occurs the delay is tolerated better if people understand why they are delayed and how long it will last; if consumers can occupy their time they are less bothered. It is better to start a service and then impose a delay than to begin or end with the delay.

Delay is a transaction cost that may be set against other costs; in post offices it was found that those who wait for benefits object to delay less than those who wait to spend money. Resentment at delay varies quite widely; it is greater among those who attribute blame to management.

Further reading

Kunst, P. and Lemmink, J. (eds.) (1994) *Managing Service Quality*, Vol. 1, London, Paul Chapman Publishing.

Kunst, P. and Lemmink, J. (eds.) (1996) *Managing Service Quality*, Vol. 2, London, Paul Chapman Publishing.

Smith, A.M. (1995) Measuring service quality: Is SERVQUAL now redundant?, *Journal of Marketing Management*, 11, 257–76.

Yi, Y. (1990) A critical review of consumer satisfaction. In Zeithaml, V.A. (ed.) *Review of Marketing*, Chicago, AMA, 68–113.

Part V

Applications

Chapter 9

The consumer as shopper

Introduction

Retailers spend large amounts of capital creating environments that will attract customers and induce them to spend money. The results of their work may be measured at an aggregate level, or more individually in terms of shoppers' actions and motivations. In this chapter the research on aggregate effects is addressed only briefly and more attention is given to the way in which the consumer, as a shopper, uses and evaluates the retail environment. Retailers need to know how shoppers react to stores if they are to offer their services in an attractive form that meets consumer needs. It is also important that policy-makers take account of patterns of use and preference when they regulate retailing. The consumer's use of supermarkets has been a focus of research at Kingston University and, at several points during this chapter, I draw on findings from our surveys and those made collaboratively in the United States by Dr Debra Perkins at Purdue University.

In this chapter you will find:

- A brief review of some of the changes in retailing and a comment on the policy issues that have been raised by retail development.

- A summary of ideas associated with gravity models.

- A report on motivational factors that affect the customer's use of different types of store in the United States and Britain.

- A consideration of customer types including the compulsive shopper.

- A review of evidence on the store-loyal shopper.

- Theories and evidence on the effect of store atmospherics.

- Findings on the responses to crowding.

- Evidence on the way in which the use of supermarkets is spread over time.

Policy issues

Retail changes

Over the last two decades there has been considerable change in retailing (see Kotler and Armstrong, 1994; Sparks, 1993, for fuller reviews). In the United States, we have seen the creation of larger and larger units, the development of regional shopping centres (malls), and a growing emphasis on discount stores and warehouse clubs. In France, as in the United States, the vast hypermarket has evolved with food, furniture, appliances and other merchandise being sold. In Britain, regional shopping centres such as the Metro Centre in Newcastle upon Tyne have been built, while other shopping concentrations, such as Kingston, have evolved from established centres of retailing. Size has increased in Britain too; in the grocery field many of the new stores in the last decade have been out-of-town superstores (defined by Nielsen as 25,000 square feet of selling area or more). One recent development has been counter to the growth in unit size; Tesco has experimented with smaller formats which may capitalize on a local demand for high margin products and defend catchments from competitors, a strategy discussed by Duke (1991). Growth among the main retailers has raised concentration – a larger and larger proportion of shopping is done in the shops of a limited number of retailers; this trend has been clearly visible in the grocery sector in Britain, which now has one of the highest concentrations in the world. Some innovations hover in the wings. Television and telephone shopping and buying through interactive computer systems may develop, but seem unlikely to answer mass demand in the near future.

Alongside these many changes, some aspects of purchasing have stayed much the same. Despite increasing competition from the supermarkets, the small shop remains in all countries because of its convenience, its service and sometimes because it can offer local or specialized products not easily found elsewhere. Similarly, markets persist throughout the world and are particularly effective at supplying more perishable products such as fresh fruit and vegetables. Sales continue to be made through catalogues; though less visible, these are an important part of distribution. And we should not forget second-hand markets; in Britain, these are conducted through specialized shops, auctions, car boot sales and by advertisements in magazines such as *Auto Trader, Exchange and Mart* and *Loot*. Such magazines may come under threat from the Internet which is well suited to second-hand trading.

Controlling development

The growth of retailing has raised issues of public policy in Britain, some of which may become issues in other countries. In Britain, the grocery sector is near saturation in most areas and there is evidence of increased price competition as a result. The new supermarkets have been located mainly on trunk roads and town peripheries, and in some cases centrally located stores have been closed as the new stores are opened. In Britain, concern has mounted about the resulting blight of city centres which may become dismal and inactive and, beginning in 1994, supermarket groups have found it difficult to secure out-of-town planning consents and have had to look again to city centre locations for expansion.

Should out-of-town consents be withheld? This is a complex issue. When they deserted the city centre, the supermarket groups were responding to high rentals, congestion, poor parking and lack of sites of sufficient size; their action helped to remedy these problems. With less pressure on the city centre, services could be improved and new facilities introduced, though there is little sign that this opportunity has been grasped. Many shoppers like the new large out-of-town stores with their easy, open and safe parking. It is also true that the daytime bustle of a city centre devoted to shopping can give way to drab and deserted streets in the evening. An interesting contrast occurs between two nearby towns in Britain, Kingston and Richmond: the latter seethes with life in the evening whereas Kingston, the stronger shopping centre, has less activity after the shops have closed.

A second issue of public policy is associated with saturation. Competition is generally beneficial but there are losers when poorly located supermarkets and small shops close or run inefficiently because of over-provision in retailing space. When assets give a poor return the economy is less efficient and this has consequences for all of us. Thus, there may be a case for some constraint on supermarket development. This may offend the free marketeer, but all markets operate under regulations that restrict modes of business. Against constraint is the fact that British supermarkets have maintained very high margins compared with store groups in other countries, and this indicates that there is scope for more price competition which could be stimulated by excess capacity.

A third issue is associated with supermarket concentration. A few operators control most of the market in Britain and each year their share increases. Should we be worried by these levels of concentration? One reason for the high concentration is that the British supermarket operators are extremely competent and they (and we) are reaping the benefits of their efficiency. A concern about high concentration might be that restraint of trade may develop between the operators when so few store groups control so much of the market. Although this may occur, there is evidence that competition flourishes even in duopolies. Very high concentration has not inhibited competition between Lever Brothers and Procter & Gamble; similarly, in continuous market research, there is fierce competition between Nielsen and IRI in the United States.

Exercise 9.1   Policy issues

As indicated above, supermarket development has become quite controversial. Suppose that you were advising *either* the industry *or* government about further growth. Identify the issues and the evidence that are required for a reasoned response.

Shopper choice

Gravity models

Gravity models look at aggregate demand in relation to population sizes and the accessibility of shopping locations.

The revenue from a retail unit is limited by the number of people who will use it, and this in turn depends upon local population densities, transport access, the size of the store, its product sector and the attractions of adjacent units. This has focused attention on the way shops, centres and cities draw customers from different distances. Early work focused on the attraction exerted on a shopper at different distances from two cities; Reilly (1929) applied a gravity model to this problem and argued that trade was attracted in direct proportion to the population of each city and in inverse proportion to the square of the distance from the city. This model implies that between two cities there will be a *breaking point* where trade is equally attracted to the two cities. The model was tested on thirty city pairs and found to be accurate. This approach does not allow for the strong appeal of some parts of the city or of particular stores. Also, it is clear that distance is not the same as travel and time costs, and that Reilly's model is likely to be compromised where transport facilities make distant locations easily accessible. For these reasons population size and physical distance are crude determinants of shopping use. Other work, called *central place theory* (Christaller, 1933; Losch, 1939), uses the importance of a centre and the economic distance as basic concepts and thus takes some account of the difficulties raised by Reilly's variables. Also, consumers vary in their preferences and spending, and geo-demographic methods can allow for such different types of customer.

Store operators want more specific answers to their location problems. Huff's (1962; 1981) retail gravitation model was developed to describe the pulling power of a retail centre within a city. In this model the attraction of a centre, A_1, is a function of its selling area, (S), divided by a power (λ, lambda) of the travel time (T):

$$A_1 = S/T^\lambda$$

The probability of a consumer using a shopping area is a function of A_1 divided by the sum of the attractions of all the available shopping centres, i.e.

$$p = A_1/\Sigma(A_1 \dots A_n)$$

Wee and Pearce (1985) note that a large number of studies have supported Huff's model and have generally found that the exponent λ is 2, so that the attraction of a location is inversely related to *the square* of the travel time, which supports Reilly's thinking. One of the problems with Huff's approach was that it included *all* the possible shopping centres, although a consumer might rule many of these out. Wee and Pearce modified Huff's model so that the choice set of shopping centres was defined by the shopper. With this adjustment predictions were better, but even the improved model gave an adjusted R^2 of only 0.25 showing that much of the shoppers' behaviour remained unexplained. This is hardly surprising since a gravity model cannot take in any of the detail of a particular shopping environment. One example of detail is provided by Foxall and Hackett (1992), who found that stores that were located at path junctions were better remembered.

For retailers, the gravity model is normative and can be used to estimate the size of a potential market in different locations and, therefore, where retail outlets should be located. Gravity models are also descriptive and indicate how settlements may grow, and how retail units will tend to cluster together so that they each take advantage of the custom generated by the others; even businesses in the same field may benefit from proximity since together they increase the total custom. Another use of the theory is in impact analysis: what happens to sales in existing stores when a new store is opened at a particular location? In practice, gravity models are modified to take account of other measurable variables, and location decisions are likely to be taken after applying these more complex analyses. Some of these issues are reviewed by K. Jones and Simmons (1990) and by McGoldrick (1990).

Store preferences

We may also examine how shoppers come to use stores at an individual level by recording the reasons that they give for their choice. Compared with similarly sized units, particular stores may draw custom from great distances because of their name, range, service or cheapness. In Britain for example, Marks & Spencer, Toys 'R' Us and John Lewis are credited with strong drawing power; they offer a product range or standard of service that is not easily found in other stores. If asked, shoppers will give a range of beliefs and feelings about such stores which are the *store image*, the retail counterpart of brand image.

Store image has a basis in the quality of the goods and service offered, but it also reflects other beliefs about the store. Customers seem to retain images over long periods, even when they are hard to justify; for example, it has taken Tesco many years to lessen its cheap and cheerful image, despite the fact that its product range has been of high quality for a long time. The most important aspect of store image is the part that makes the store attractive to shoppers. Table 9.1 compares the main reasons given for use of supermarkets (respondents were allowed only one reason). The table shows that there are differences in the attractions of the different supermarkets in Britain. Sainsbury is rated high on quality compared to other stores; the same rating has appeared in earlier studies and appears to be a well-sustained advantage. The discount operator, Kwik Save, is chosen almost entirely for good value and could, therefore, be subject to price competition; such competition developed in 1995 and 1996 as the leading operators introduced ranges of tertiary brands that undercut Kwik Save, and Kwik Save has suffered.

Table 9.1 Store users' main reasons for their usual store choice in Britain, 1994

	Sainsbury %	Tesco %	Safeway %	Asda %	Kwik Save %	Somerfield/ Gateway %	Coop %
Near where I live	23	27	37	29	19	36	54
Good value	15	15	7	17	73	34	23
Wide choice	10	19	18	23	0	6	4
Good quality	30	13	8	8	4	12	4
Easy parking	4	9	9	9	0	2	2
Other	18	17	21	14	4	10	13

Source: Consumer Research Unit, Kingston Business School, 1994.

In the grocery sector the largest difference in the way stores are regarded is between convenience stores (local food shops) and supermarkets. Table 9.2 shows how convenience stores and supermarkets were chosen in Britain according to a 1991 survey (East, Lomax and Willson, 1991b). In this work, respondents were allowed to give two reasons. Closeness and convenient opening times were the main attractions of the local shop while the supermarket scored on convenient location, wide choice, good value and easy parking. The small shop is clearly not immune from attack from supermarkets, which often open long hours, are now more numerous than in 1991 and are usually cheaper.

Table 9.2 'Thinking about the last time you went to the supermarket/local food shop, what were your two main reasons for shopping there?'

	Supermarket % all responses	Local food shop % all responses
Quality, wide choice	27	8
Convenient location	25	42
Good value, offers	14	8
Easy parking	14	5
Convenient opening times	9	24
Cleanliness	5	4
Friendly staff	4	10
Can get petrol	3	–

Source: East, Lomax and Willson (1991b).

Evidence of this sort is very much affected by the method by which it is established. People may like a number of features of a supermarket, but this does not mean that they make their store choice using all these criteria. Assumptions about the way factors are used in decisions were considered in Chapters 6 and 7. East, Lomax and Willson assumed that one or two criteria were normally crucial to choice. If, instead, respondents had been invited to check all the factors they liked about a store, they might have obtained data more like Table 9.3 below, which is abridged from *Which?*. Notice that the *Which?* study omits any reference to convenient location, and whereas cleanliness is top of the *Which?* list in Table 9.3, it is a minor criterion in the East *et al.* study in Table 9.2.

Table 9.3 Percentage of respondents stating that
a supermarket feature was important

Clean floors and shelves	86
Well-stocked shelves	79
Wide selection of products	73
A lot of staffed checkouts	70
Helpful, knowledgeable staff	69
Access for disabled people	68
Wide shopping aisles	59
Ample car parking	57
Cash/basket only/express tills	54
Free shopping bags	52
'Environmentally friendly' goods	50

Source: Which? (February 1991).

Table 9.4 shows that the main reason for using a particular store in the British surveys in 1992 and 1994 was nearness to home (83 per cent shopped from home). A separate question asked whether the supermarket which was used most was the easiest to get to; in 1992, three-quarters of the sample in both Britain and the United States usually used the most accessible store. Thus we can see that close location is a very important determinant of store use in both countries.

In the United States, low prices were more important than location in 1992; this probably reflected the scale of the recession which began earlier in the US. However, in 1994, prices were still very important in the United States, and it looks as though US citizens are more price-sensitive than the British. Table 9.4 shows the signs of increased price competition which developed in Britain in 1993; 'good value' moved from fourth place to second as a criterion for supermarket choice. This change in consumer attitudes to price is likely to have been the result of the recession in Britain which began in earnest in 1993. Also, prices in supermarkets became more diverse in 1993, thus justifying more attention being given to them. This evidence shows that supermarket choice criteria can change quite substantially in response to economic conditions; retailers should be alert to such changes and adjust their offering accordingly.

Table 9.4 Shoppers' main reason for going to a supermarket? Four surveys in Britain and the United States

	United Kingdom		United States	
	1992	*1994*	*1992*	*1994*
	%	%	%	%
Near where I live	32	29	25	33
Good value/lowest price/discounts	14	24	34	29
Wide choice	18	13	13	12
Good quality	15	14	15	11
Other	21	20	13	15

Sources: Consumer Research Unit, Kingston Business School; Dr Debra Perkins, Purdue University.

Table 9.5 reveals the percentages of shoppers citing different main reasons for using different types of stores in Britain and the United States. One difference between the two countries is that the users of the large, out-of-town stores are more discount-oriented in the United States. In Britain, the large, out-of-town store is valued a little more for the choice and quality it offers.

In the United States, nearly all supermarket visits are by car. In Britain, 80 per cent of all supermarket visits were by car in 1994, but nearly all those using the large, out-of-town store went by car. About 60 per cent of those using large, out-of-town stores travel more than 2 miles compared with 25 per cent of those using other stores; this shows the power of the larger outlet to draw from a greater distance. Despite the longer journeys, there is little difference in claimed travel time, which shows how well sited most of these stores are.

Table 9.5 Shoppers' main reason for store choice by type of store in Britain and the US, 1994

| | United Kingdom | | United States | |
	Large out-of-town %	Other %	Large out-of-town %	Other %
Near where I live	23	33	25	35
Good value	21	25	33	28
Wide choice	16	11	12	12
Good quality	17	12	10	12
Other	23	19	20	13

Sources: Consumer Research Unit, Kingston Business School; Dr Debra Perkins, Purdue University.

Shopping trip patterns

Consumers go shopping for a great variety of goods, but researchers have learned most about grocery shopping. Groceries constitute a very large part of what we buy so particular attention to grocery shopping is justified (in Britain, the top five supermarket groups took 38 per cent of the total retail spending in 1994).

A number of studies have shown that households have a routine of supermarket shopping which often includes one weekly main trip and one or more secondary 'quick' trips. In the United States, Thompson (1967), Kollat and Willett (1967), McKay (1973) and Frisbie (1980) found this pattern. Kahn and Schmittlein (1989), also in the United States, report similar findings; they were able to distinguish between those who relied principally on the main trip and those whose shopping included more quick trips than main trips. In Britain, Dunn, Reader and Wrigley (1983) also found evidence of weekly trips. Thus many people appear to make a once-a-week main shopping trip, which might be supplemented by secondary trips. Nielsen (1992) reports that expenditure on the main shopping trip is about three times that of a quick trip; thus, by focusing on the main trip, it is possible to cover most of a household's grocery spending.

Exercise 9.2 Supermarket use analysis

The software available in association with this text contains the questionnaire used in the Consumer Research Unit's 1994 study in the file called SU4.TXT. Retrieve this questionnaire and fill it out. As you do so, try to work out what the purposes of the research were and what the answers are likely to be. This will help you to follow the evidence reported in this chapter.

Types of customer

Textbooks sometimes contain classifications of customer types. These may be hypothetical or derived empirically from data. For example, I might hypothesize that shoppers divide into 'prospecting' and 'reluctant' shoppers. The 'prospectors' are generally positive about shopping and see the retail environment as a hunting ground for new ideas, fashions and bargains; these people play a game with retailers in which they win when they get good value for their money, or find just what they wanted. The 'reluctants' have little interest in shopping, seeing it as a necessary means for achieving other goals. With such a hypothesis one may search data for supporting patterns. A more empirical approach is to use the dominant motivations for good value, quality, etc., revealed by surveys; these are partly a characteristic of the person although we also saw that they varied with store preferences and over time.

Alternatively, it is possible to derive types of customer from a factor analysis of survey responses, but this sort of investigation is limited by the focus of the investigation and the particular questions used to generate the data. A principal components analysis of the 1992 supermarket surveys in Britain and the United States showed three factors:

- *The heavy buyer.* Heavy buyers tend to have larger incomes and households, and to be under 45; they prefer large, out-of-town stores, shop later in the day and less often, and tend to have a regular day for shopping.
- *Congestion dislikers.* Such people hold management responsible for delay, more often dislike shopping, claim to avoid busy times and to be busy themselves. This person might fit my concept of the reluctant shopper.
- *Local shoppers.* These people use small local stores more, shop frequently, spend little, are more often old and come from small households.

Of particular interest here is the heavy buyer. According to the 'heavy half' principle, the 50 per cent heaviest buyers make about 80 per cent of all purchases. Retailers should be alert to heavy buyers and should try to target promotions on these shoppers, and this analysis helps to identify them.

Jarratt (1996) reviews different typologies in a useful paper. Many of these divisions include some reference to the cost-saving, economizing customer who searches for cheapness or good value for money. As noted above this seems to be a powerful motivation in shopping. We saw that this factor was involved in the comparison between Kwik Save and other supermarkets and, not surprisingly, it appeared again in a comparison by McGoldrick and Andre (1997) between loyal Tesco shoppers and those who divided their purchasing between Tesco and a discounter.

In the following pages we look at two important sorts of customer: first, the compulsive or addictive shopper, and second the loyal shopper.

Compulsive shoppers

In recent years a new and disturbing type of shopping behaviour has emerged. In the United States, 15 million people are estimated to exhibit a deviant pattern of compulsive purchase, buying clothes, shoes and other goods which they do not need and sometimes never use (Arthur, 1992); Scherhorn, Reisch and Raab (1990) have reported on compulsive shopping in Germany, and Elliott (1993; 1994) has noted the same effect in Britain. This is clearly a serious problem, which often causes financial and psychological distress, and it is now receiving increased attention partly because of publicity from a book called *Shopaholics* by Janet Damon (1988). One reason for compulsive shopping is the more attractive shopping environment of the present day, but, in the search for causes, more attention has been focused on the behaviour and background of the compulsive shopper.

Faber and O'Guinn (1988) saw compulsive shopping as part of a wider range of compulsive behaviour which they describe as:

> a response to an uncontrollable drive or desire to obtain, use, or experience a feeling, substance, or activity that leads an individual to repetitively engage in behaviour that will ultimately cause harm to the individual and/or others.

This behaviour often occurs among people with emotional problems who are unhappy at the time of the shopping. Compulsive shoppers appear to get some emotional release, or mood repair, out of the process of buying. D'Astous (1990) argues that this type of behaviour is the extreme end of a continuum, and that many people have strong urges to buy which they can barely hold in check. If we accept this view, we can learn about compulsive behaviour by examining those who are less extreme. This issue is reviewed by Magee (1994).

Compulsive shoppers more often own credit cards (d'Astous, 1990), are usually women (92 per cent in Faber and O'Guinn's 1992 study), and some research has revealed them to be younger and to have lower self-esteem. Research in this area is by survey, and it is difficult to assign cause and effect; compulsive shoppers may have low self-esteem *because of* their behaviour (Higgins (1987) found that awareness of personal shortcomings can create anxiety) or the compulsive purchase may be a response to low self-esteem.

More about the nature of compulsive shopping emerges in a paper by Elliott, Eccles and Gournay (1996). These researchers interviewed fifty compulsive shoppers and probed their thinking and motivation. The respondents accepted that their behaviour was aberrant, that they could not easily control it and that, though it served purposes of short-term mood repair, it was potentially very damaging. In this respect it functioned rather like a drug dependence and Elliott *et al.* emphasize this by describing the behaviour as addictive. Addictive shopping was associated with emotional disturbances which often arose in unsatisfactory relationships with partners. Women whose partners worked excessively, who ignored them, or who were controlling, were more likely to be compulsive shoppers; in many cases their behaviour was a form of revenge or was deliberately designed to rile their partner.

Store loyalty

Like brand loyalty (Chapter 2), store loyalty has been defined in a number of ways; as a behaviour it may be operationalized as:

- *A sequence* of purchases at the same store.
- The *proportion* of purchase or expenditure that a given store takes in the retail category.
- The *repeat patronage frequency*.
- The *duration of patronage*, or *store allegiance*.

Despite the assumption that they have some common basis, these different measures may show weak associations. For instance, a person may regularly buy at Store A but spend more at Store B; thus the buyer is loyal to Store A on a duration of patronage criterion, but has low loyalty when measured by a proportion of purchase criterion. It would probably be better if we accepted that we are trying to accommodate two different concepts here: one is the proportional use of the store in the shopper's store portfolio, and the second is the duration of patronage. These measures may both be driven by the same motivations, but other factors could make them diverge; as with brand loyalty we do not know how much these two different forms of behavioural loyalty move together.

It is likely that general determinants of the duration of store patronage can be found, but there is little published on this subject. Most allegiance studies relate to customer defections in different industries and relate these to failures in the product (Reichheld, 1996). This is worthwhile practical work but it is *ad hoc* and does little to widen our general understanding of allegiance. Work is required that relates store defection to demographic factors, patronage effort (e.g. distance from store), attitude to store and to the proportional use of the store. In the following section we focus on proportional use concepts of store loyalty.

Research on store loyalty

Like brand loyalty, store loyalty can be investigated in different ways:

- We may search for economic, demographic or psychological *correlates* which may explain or predict individual consumer loyalty to stores. This work is explained further below.

Another approach, which is not developed here, is:

■ Treating loyalty measures such as repeat purchase rate as factors to be *modelled* in relation to other factors such as penetration, purchase frequency and market share (Kau and Ehrenberg, 1984; Uncles and Ehrenberg, 1990a; Uncles and Hammond, 1995). In this approach we can aggregate individual data and report loyalty as a store characteristic. This method of analysis was demonstrated for brands in Chapter 3.

Both academic researchers and marketing practitioners are interested in establishing whether there are characteristics which identify those with high loyalty. In particular we are interested in whether a shopper's store loyalty relates to particular social circumstances, demographic factors, brand loyalty, the number of stores used and the total expenditure in the retail category. Retailers will also be interested in whether different store groups command higher loyalty and whether this relates to the size of the store.

The measurement used in individual studies is usually *first-store loyalty* (Cunningham, 1961), which is the proportion of expenditure devoted to the store most used.[1] Loyalty studies are usually based on consumer panel research because this type of data covers long periods of time with high precision. Cunningham used the early panel established by the Chicago *Tribune*. In Britain, Dunn and Wrigley (1984) used a specially established panel in Cardiff, and Mason (1991) reported on store loyalty using the Nielsen HomeScan panel. Denison and Knox (1993) and East, Harris, Willson and Lomax (1995) used surveys to study store loyalty. Though surveys give less accurate measures of purchase behaviour than panels they do have advantages: they can measure *individual* rather than *household* purchase, and they can include a variety of items (e.g. attitude measures) that may not be available with panel data.

General theories of store loyalty

There may be no overarching explanations of store loyalty. It may be the result of a large number of weak influences that have little in common. However, it is reasonable to look for one or two mobilizing influences that are responsible for much of the effect and here there have been three competing theories about the nature of store loyalty.

---

[1] *British supermarket loyalty.* Average levels of store loyalty depend on the retail category, the market concentration, the average store size, the period of time taken for measurement and the year of measurement. For supermarkets in Britain, AGB (1992), using Superpanel data, reported that over an eight-week period approximately 75 per cent of expenditure took place in the favourite supermarket. Also in Britain, Mason (1991; 1996) reported first-store group loyalty of 75 per cent over one month, and 65 per cent over a year. The decline occurs because shoppers are more likely to switch their primary store allegiance over a longer period and this has the effect of reducing first-store loyalty. It is difficult to compare these figures with earlier ones that included convenience store purchases (e.g. 42 per cent found in Cardiff by Dunn and Wrigley, 1984), but it seems likely that store loyalties have risen as grocery trade concentration and average store sizes have increased.

Resource constraints

The first theory, specified by Charlton (1973) but drawing on earlier work (Enis and Paul, 1970) is that store loyalty is essentially *negative* and is the outcome of limited resources: those who lack money, time and transport, or whose environment lacks choice (Tate, 1961), are forced to use one store much of the time and are therefore obliged to be loyal.

'Non-shopping' lifestyle

Carman (1970) was also negative about store loyalty but emphasized a *lifestyle* that featured commitments outside the home, full-time work, little home entertaining and lack of interest in deals, advertising and shopping. Such people had little interest in shopping, did not experiment and were consequently loyal by default to both brands and stores.

Discretionary loyalty

Dunn and Wrigley (1984), noting that the growth of supermarkets in many countries could have affected patterns of behaviour, suggested that the negative concept of store loyalty needed review. Dunn and Wrigley suggested that some store loyalty arose by choice from one-stop shopping, often in large supermarkets; I call this *discretionary* store loyalty. It differs from the first theory because it implies that resources are used by shoppers to raise rather than to reduce store loyalty. For example, the car is used to do most of the shopping in one outlet and not to diversify shopping across many outlets. Discretionary loyalty differs from Carman's 'non-shopping' lifestyle by implying a more positive approach to brands and shopping. Discretionary loyalty is an adaptation to circumstances which is most likely when people shop by car, are relatively well-off and need to be efficient about shopping because of commitments to work and family. However, different segments of the population could be loyal for different reasons so that all three accounts of loyalty could be supported when different population groupings are examined.

Demographic correlates

Previous research has generally revealed weak associations between store loyalty and demographic measures. In some ways this is not surprising because demographic factors are only loosely connected to the attitudes, beliefs and opportunities that more directly control behaviour. This is shown in Figure 9.1, where geographic, demographic and personal background factors are seen as primary variables which underlie the secondary variables, the attitude and behaviour factors.

Farley (1968), who used Cunningham's (1961) data, found no demographic associations with store loyalty but *low income* appeared as a correlate in studies in the United States by Carman (1970) and Enis and Paul (1970), and in Britain by Dunn and Wrigley (1984); *school age children* in the household were positively associated in Carman's study and, in Britain, Mason (1991) found that *household size and number of*

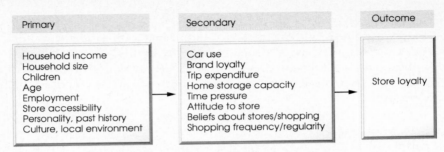

Figure 9.1 Variables influencing store loyalty

children were positively associated. In Mason's work loyalty was higher when the housewife *worked*, but not according to Dunn and Wrigley. Mason also found that the *under 45-year-old* shoppers were more loyal.

These findings have elements that could be consistent with all three theories of store loyalty and research is required which will help to identify any dominant explanation. Evidence that store loyalty is associated with high income and the use of a car supports the discretionary view of store loyalty and conflicts with the idea that store loyalty is based on a lack of resources. Also, Carman's negative lifestyle view of loyalty would be damaged by evidence that the store-loyal shopper enjoys shopping no less than others, or is interested in shopping issues. Support for the idea that store loyalty is an adaptation most common among the busy, hard-pressed groups would come from evidence that the under-45s, the larger households and those with full-time jobs are more loyal.

The small study by East *et al.* (1995) found that there was no difference between high and low loyalty groups in the accessibility of their preferred store, which does not support the resource constraint theory. Shoppers with different loyalty levels gave similar ratings for the pleasantness of supermarket shopping which does not support the 'non-shopper' lifestyle theory. East *et al.* (1995) found, like Dunn and Wrigley (1984), that many in the high loyalty group shopped in large out-of-town stores and that car use raised loyalty. They also found highest loyalty in the 25–44 age group and when the housewife worked.

This work does not invalidate findings that apply to earlier times in the United States and Britain, but it indicates most support for the discretionary loyalty theory that loyal shoppers used their resources to concentrate on fewer stores in Britain in 1993–4. It seems likely that larger incomes, freezers (allowing large quantity storage) and the widespread ownership of cars have combined to produce a new pattern of one-stop supermarket shopping that leads to higher store loyalty in countries with extensive supermarket provision. However, the study was small and restricted to supermarkets; loyalty in other retail categories could be different.

Brand, store and spending correlates

Cunningham (1961) found that store loyalty was *weakly associated with brand loyalty* –

an effect that he thought was due to preferences for store brands; however Rao (1969) found a residual correlation between store and brand loyalty after allowing for store brand effect and this was also found by East, Harris, Willson and Hammond (1995). When people go to fewer stores they restrict the number of brands available to them, and this may explain why their loyalty is higher; alternatively, the association may be due to personal, economic or social factors that focus spending.

Cunningham (1961) found little relationship between a proportion of purchase measure and the number of stores visited. This is because many single trips to different stores can substantially raise the number of stores visited without much affecting the proportion of spending devoted to the favourite store. Dunn and Wrigley (1984), Mason (1991) and East, Harris, Willson and Lomax (1995) showed that, as the number of stores visited increased, so the percentage of expenditure in the primary store decreased but the correlation is quite modest, about -0.4, and Mason notes that even when households visited nine different supermarkets over a three-month period, they still devoted over 50 per cent of their expenditure to their first store.

One potential discriminator between those with high and low store loyalty is *total expenditure* in the retail category. It might be thought that those who spend more would use more shops and therefore have lower loyalty, but Dunn and Wrigley (1984) and Mason (1991) found that first store loyalty did not change with increasing total expenditure in supermarkets. Denison and Knox (1993) found a small *positive* association ($r = 0.24$) between store loyalty and total spending for supermarkets and a negative relationship for other types of retail outlet. If bigger spenders are more loyal, it follows that the high loyalty customers will spend more in their primary store than others. Their first-store spending is boosted because they spend more in total and a higher proportion of this spending goes to their favourite store. A positive relationship between loyalty and primary store expenditure has been noted in several studies (Tate, 1961; Enis and Paul, 1970; Mason, 1991; and East *et al.*, 1995). In unpublished work on 1994 British and US data, we find that high loyalty shoppers spend about 70 per cent more than low loyalty shoppers in the primary store. This makes the recruitment and development of high loyalty customers very attractive to store managements.

The in-store environment

Store layout

Actions occur when the environment presents *opportunities, stimuli* and *rewards*. The store layout is therefore concerned with optimizing spending opportunities, presenting purchase cues and making the store an easy and pleasant place to use. These different considerations do not always coincide. IKEA uses a layout that requires the customer to cover the whole store in order to reach the exit; this may raise impulse purchasing by increasing stimulus, but it can be a near-claustrophobic experience for some customers who find it difficult to get out.

Some aspects of store layout are deliberately chosen to increase the opportunity to buy. In supermarkets, profitable products such as delicatessen and fish are often placed at the back of the store so that they draw traffic through the store. Another popular point is the end-aisle which appears to get more attention and is therefore used for displays. One of the applications of scanner technology is called direct product profitability (DPP); this is the measurement of profit from a given Stock Keeping Unit[2] (SKU) in a specific location. DPP can be used to vary the space and location devoted to an SKU so that profit is optimized. This technology identifies 'hot-spots' in the store, and has been used to assess the average sales from facings at different levels. Eye-level height is most profitable and can give about twice the return of facings at the lowest level.

Atmospherics

The store environment includes the use of space and the choice of fittings, colours, aromas and sound. Laura Ashley stores use wood and give an impression of middle-class solidity, discount stores sell out of cases to emphasize their price-competitive image, shopping centres may create central areas with water displays and other entertaining features, fashion shops use music that suits the age and taste of their clientele. The Body Shop is scented with a rather synthetic dewberry smell. In Britain, the Oddbins wine shops use handwritten prices, enhancing an image of a knowledgeable management, close to the products being sold. Such features are an extension of product display and are chosen to enhance the store image. They are associated signs that help to define the store offering and differentiate it from that of other stores. In this sense store design and the display of goods have parallels with goods packaging.

Kotler (1973) suggested that these store features create an *atmosphere*, modifying the buyer's knowledge and mood and thus affecting behaviour. Kotler also noted that atmospherics could be used to *demarket*; e.g. the state liquor stores in some countries are deliberately deterrent environments. In a preliminary study, Donovan and Rossiter (1982) used a classification of mood states described by Mehrabian and Russell (1974) and found that the environmental factors that make up a store's atmosphere produced emotional responses in consumers which could affect the time and money spent in the store. Figure 9.2 shows this Stimulus → Organism → Response (SOR) model in more detail. Donovan and Rossiter expected arousal to amplify the pleasure–displeasure

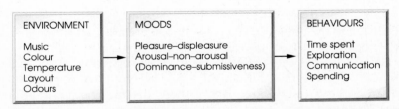

Figure 9.2 The role of moods in mediating atmospheric effects on shopping behaviour

response and to produce more spending only when the latter was positive, but there were too few unpleasant environments to test the interaction. As the researchers expected, the dominance–submissiveness dimension had little effect.

A paper by R.B. Smith and Sherman (1992) showed that store image was associated with mood, which then predicted the amount of time and money spent in the store. German studies of atmospheric effects are discussed by Gröppel (1993); she notes evidence that supermarkets with high novelty and complexity levels (hypothesized by Mehrabian and Russell to affect emotional states) give more pleasure, and that original and attractive stores do better on measures such as time spent in the store and turnover. Swinyard (1993) has examined the impact of mood on shopping intentions in relation to involvement. Swinyard argued that only the more elaborate processing of the highly involved consumer would be affected by mood and that this would impact on shopping intentions; this was supported in a scenario-based experiment in which only the highly involved shoppers modified their shopping intentions.

---

[2] Brands come in different sizes, flavours, etc.; the SKU used by retailers will have a unique combination of attributes.

These studies do not prove convincingly that mood mediates the effects produced by atmospherics. In some cases the environmental conditions may produce store image inferences (Baker, Grewal and Parasuraman, 1994) and these *cognitive* effects may influence behaviour. In other cases the store atmospherics may *directly stimulate* behaviour through an SR mechanism so that any mood responses are incidental and not part of the causal sequence affecting purchase; Figure 9.3 shows this last possibility.

Donovan *et al.* (1994) have now reviewed research in this area. They note weaknesses in their earlier paper and those of others. In particular there is a need to study behaviour and mood *in-store* if this is to be used as an explanation, and to distinguish moods induced by the environment from emotions associated with purchase. Donovan *et al.* conducted a further study which avoided these weaknesses. They found that pleasure did contribute to extra spending and time in the store and that arousal did reduce spending in environments rated as unpleasant (but in this study arousal did not increase spending in pleasant environments).

This work does not dispose of my concern, illustrated by Figure 9.3, that some behaviour may be directly triggered by atmospherics. Many stimuli affect behaviour without much awareness; this is part of our low involvement response to the environment which helps us to cope with the wide variety of stimuli that impinge on our senses. By modifying our behaviour unconsciously, we leave ourselves free to

concentrate on other features of the environment. Some studies where influence may occur by direct SR effects are:

■ Bellizzi, Crowley and Hasty (1983), who noted that people moved closer to red which was more arousing than 'cool' colours such as blue and green. Bellizzi *et al.* suggest that red will speed processes up and might be appropriate where quick decisions benefit the store.

■ Milliman (1982) found that the tempo of music affected the speed of customers through the store; faster music speeded them up and reduced their purchases, while slower music did the reverse, producing expenditures that were 38 per cent above those in the fast music condition; customers had little awareness of these influences.

■ Areni and Kim (1993) found that, compared with popular music, classical background music in a wine store was associated with the choice of more expensive wines so that the customer spent considerably more. The classical music seemed to cue more upmarket purchasing. Another study by Yalch and Spangenberg (1993) showed that music could affect sales in different parts of the same store. The music had to be appropriate for the store department and its type of customer, music in

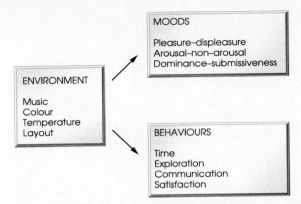

Figure 9.3 Alternative effect of store stimuli on both mood and behaviour

departments for younger customers, for example, needed to be played at high volume.

■ Areni and Kim (1994) found that the lighting level in a retailing wine cellar affected the amount of merchandise handling but had no significant effect on the time spent in the cellar or the amount bought.

This work has policy implications. There are now specialist firms in the United States that will supply aromas for stores, and one company in Britain manufactures synthetic human pheromones that are claimed to make people more relaxed. These new understandings put power into the hands of the retailer to modify the behaviour of the unknowing customer, and this could lead to abuses.

Crowding

A common problem in shops is the level of congestion or crowding. People have a complex response to crowding and, in different contexts, may find it attractive or aversive. Hui and Bateson (1991) found that an important factor in determining whether crowding was liked or disliked is the control that the customer feels that he or she has in the situation. People seek to preserve their control (S.S. Brehm and Brehm, 1981; J.W. Brehm, 1989) and Ajzen (1991) has shown that perceived control consistently contributes to the explanation of discretionary behaviour (Chapter 6). In Hui and Bateson's study, high densities of people were associated with *increased* control in a bar and *reduced* control in a bank. People go to banks for instrumental reasons and bars for recreation, and it seems likely that this different usage is associated with the way crowding affects perceived control; crowding obstructs activity in banks but is less obstructive in bars. In shops, therefore, people are likely to dislike densities that impede action and store designs should aim to reduce perceived crowding. But there may be some people who enjoy store congestion, particularly if they have little time pressure and not much to buy, and for whom shopping is more recreational. It is also likely that people are put off when a store appears empty. Wicker (1984) has suggested that every setting has an optimal number of occupants; for example, many of us feel reluctant to go into a restaurant with few customers.

Another treatment of crowding is to see it as a cause of stimulus overload, or stress, which may affect performance. Milgram (1970) saw crowding as stressful, making people quicker, less exploratory and more inclined to omit purchases. The impact of stress is to narrow concentration; the focal task may be performed better under stress but more complex operations which require a wide range of perceptions or memories for their completion may be performed less efficiently. This means that the key functions of shopping may be done more efficiently under crowded conditions but shoppers may forget items that are peripheral to their needs. Anglin, Stuenkel and Lepisto (1994) found that shoppers scoring high on measures of stress engaged in more comparison shopping and were more price-sensitive, and these behaviours might be seen as central to shopping; this is another reason why stress-reducing atmospheric factors may raise spending.

Harrell, Hutt and Anderson (1980) surveyed store densities, perceived crowding and shoppers' stated responses to the store environment. The results showed that perceived crowding was connected with claimed deviations from the planned shopping routine and resulted in a negative evaluation of the shopping experience. We might infer from this study that people might try to avoid congested times and that some off-peak shopping might occur because of this; this is explored below.

We see from this work that the impact of crowding is complex and depends on the retail setting, the individual and the level of crowding; more work is needed before we can be very confident about findings.

Time of store use

Retail demand over time

As has been noted earlier, the service product is perishable; unlike goods, services cannot be stocked and need a buyer at the time when they are available. Theatres, airlines, hotels and restaurants must match demand and supply by using a reservation system and by enlarging supply at periods of peak demand. Stores also suffer from uneven demand, but have less scope for reducing peak-time pressure since reservation systems cannot be used. The store is little used over much of the day while at other times congestion and delay reduce the quality of service delivered. Off-peak periods are useful for staff relaxation, cleaning, restocking, training and maintenance as Sasser (1976) notes, but smoothing demand remains a desirable managerial objective.

This problem was addressed by East *et al.* (1994). They attempted to identify when supermarkets were used, whether customers avoided congestion, and what their reasons were for using stores at their chosen times. Store use varies over the year

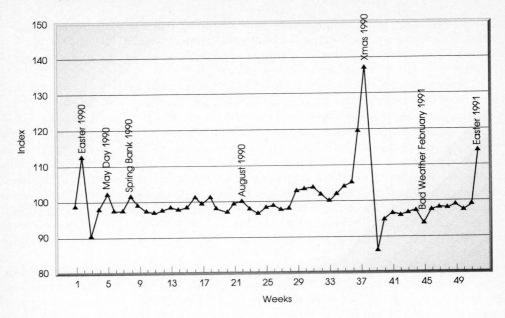

Figure 9.4 Seasonal variation in grocery sales

(illustrated by Figure 9.4), as well as over the week and over the day. Figure 9.4 shows the considerable effect of holidays and some impact of weather. Table 9.6 shows the days when the 1,012 respondents from the 1992 study did their main shopping.

Table 9.6 Percentage of supermarket main shopping trips by day

Mon.	Tues.	Wed.	Thur.	Fri.	Sat.	Sun.	Total
8	10	12	24	29	15	2	100

Source: East et al. (1994).

From Table 9.6 we see that Friday is the most popular day and Monday, Tuesday and Wednesday are much less busy than the end of the week. Table 9.7 shows that there are two main periods of high demand over the day: the first, in the morning, peaking 10–11 am, and the second, in the early evening (which occurs only on Wednesday, Thursday and Friday). The demand on stores fits the 'heavy half' principle with the busiest 50 per cent of shopping hours taking 83 per cent of trips; the busiest 20 per cent of shopping hours takes 47 per cent of all trips East *et al.* (1994).

Table 9.7 Percentage of supermarket main shopping trips by hour

Time	Total
–9 am	3
9–10 am	13
10–11 am	16
11–12 pm	12
12–1 pm	7
1–2 pm	7
2–3 pm	10
3–4 pm	7
4–5 pm	6
5–6 pm	8
6–7 pm	9
7 pm–	2
Total	**100**

Source: East *et al.* (1994).

Segments by time of use

Underlying this distribution of shopping time are two quite distinct patterns of use. Those in full-time employment shop later in the week and later in the day while those without full-time jobs make more use of Monday, Tuesday and Wednesday and the morning shopping times. This is shown in Tables 9.8 and 9.9. Although it is widely accepted that services are time-based products, it is rare to find marketers analyzing segments by time of use, and there seems to be much scope for doing this.

Table 9.8 Day of use of supermarket by employment status

Day	Full-time employed %	Not full-time employed %
Monday	6	9
Tuesday	6	11
Wednesday	9	14
Thursday	19	27
Friday	33	26
Saturday	23	12
Sunday	4	1
Base	**348**	**659**

Source: East *et al.* (1994).

Table 9.9 Hours of use of supermarket by employment status

Hour	Full-time employed %	Not full-time employed %
Before 10 am	10	20
10–12 pm	17	35
12–2 pm	11	15
2–4 pm	16	18
4–6 pm	25	8
After 6 pm	21	6
Base	**350**	**663**

Source: East *et al.* (1994).

The flexibility of shopping times

East *et al.* (1994) were interested in the flexibility of shoppers' times of use of stores and, in particular, whether they deliberately avoided busy times. This was tested in two ways. The first method compared the times of shopping of the 48 per cent who disliked being held up at the checkout with the 52 per cent who minded this less. There was no significant difference in the times when these groups used supermarkets. This fits the idea that checkout delay is a low involvement discontent which has little impact on behaviour. A second method compared those who claimed to often avoid supermarket shopping at busy times ('avoiders') with the rest and found that the avoiders used quiet times slightly more than the rest; however, the investigators judged that, at most, 6 per cent of shoppers were affected and some of these might have chosen quiet times for other reasons, but claimed to have done so to avoid congestion. This evidence indicates little flexibility in shopping times and an explanation for this was sought.

East *et al.* found that in Britain over 60 per cent of consumers had a routine day, and time, for their main grocery shopping, which suggested that their supermarket shopping habits were well established. In this study reasons were only sought from those with regular shopping times, and these reasons were corroborated by the customers' times of use. For example, those who gave as their reason 'day not working' often shopped on Saturday and Sunday, 'near weekend' on Thursday and Friday and those who stated that they 'left work then' often shopped at 5–6 pm. In more recent research conducted in 1994, all respondents were asked the reasons for the time and day of their last main shopping trip; Table 9.10 shows the findings.

These data support the view that many shopping trips are related to situational factors over which shoppers have little or no control. They cannot choose when they are paid or when they have to collect their children from school. Because of this, their shopping times are fairly rigid; shoppers *could* shop at other times, and state this, but they have good reasons for their present practices, and stores would have to offer attractive inducements at off-peak times to change the shopping time pattern. It is also clear that the reasons that shoppers have for their habits are relatively unchanging so that any inducements that a store might offer would have to be sustained. Often the

Table 9.10 'What was your main reason for shopping on this day/at this time of day?'

... on this day?	%	... at this time of day?	%
Near weekend	28	Fitted in with other shopping	25
Day not working	16	Store less busy	25
Store less busy	13	Left work then	15
Ran out of food, needed specific item	13	Car/lift/help available	13
Wages/pension day	12	Ran out of food, needed specific item	6
Car/lift/help available	12	On route to/from work	5
Food fresher/better stocked	5	Taking child to/from school	4
Open late	2	Easier parking	4
		Happened to be passing store	3
		To meet people	1

Source: Consumer Research Unit, Kingston Business School (1995).

natural incentives to use off-peak facilities are impaired by the service operator. East *et al.* (1994) found that customers thought that shelves were often unfilled and that there were still checkout delays at off-peak times. Customers might also use off-peak periods more if these times were advertised. East *et al.* found that customers knew the days when demand was low in supermarkets but had more limited knowledge about the quiet times during the day.

These findings suggested limited scope for redistributing demand to different days and times of day in the whole population, though an individual store group could benefit by recruiting from the off-peak customers of other store groups.

Exercise 9.3   Analysis of store data

In the software available in association with this text there are two files: SU4.DAT and SU4.SPS. The first is the data derived from the questionnaire SU4.TXT, which was Exercise 9.2. The second is the basis of an SPSSX analysis. If you are proficient in the use of SPSS, you can use these files to test your own hypotheses about supermarket use.

Summary

Retail use is explained at the aggregate level by gravity models and at the individual level by identifying the motivations of customers. Shoppers are strongly affected by convenience and price, and to a lesser extent by wide choice and quality. US shoppers are somewhat more discount-oriented than British shoppers.

A number of typologies have been suggested for shoppers, but the most important group for retailers are high spenders. Among grocery shoppers these people are found, not surprisingly, to be wealthier, have larger households and to use a car.

The compulsive shopper is a ubiquitous phenomenon that has raised concern because of the financial devastation that uncontrolled shopping can produce. These people gain temporary comfort from shopping and in some cases their behaviour is related to unsatisfactory relationships with their partner.

Store loyalty, like brand loyalty, has two basic behavioural forms: the proportion of patronage given to a store in the retail category, and the duration of patronage, or store allegiance. Early studies indicated that people were more loyal (measured as a proportion) because they lacked the time, money and transport resources to spread their custom; a second theory was that certain people had no interest in shopping and were loyal by default because they did not experiment. Recent evidence in Britain did not support these theories; the results fitted the idea that people used their resources to do one-stop shopping and as a result they were more loyal. These people were more often in the 25–44 age band and it appeared that high loyalty might be an efficient response among those with busy family lives.

The store environment can be adjusted to affect spending. In supermarkets the profitability of different locations can be measured and goods placed for optimal profit. In all types of store, spending may be affected by *atmospherics* – the management of the sensory impacts of the store environment on shoppers; this may directly stimulate behaviour or may change mood and, as a result of this, affect behaviour.

Crowding in retail environments is usually disliked in non-recreational settings where the crowding limits the customer's freedom of action. Stress from crowding may change the way people shop.

Retail use varies by day and time of day, and stores are underused much of the time. Investigations of the reasons for use at different times shows that many of these reasons concern the shopper's situation: 'pay-day', 'leaving work then', 'near week-end', etc. Shoppers often have routine times for shopping based on these reasons, and, because of this, may not easily change their times of shopping. There are two distinct time-use segments which are based on work: the full-time employed shop later in the day and later in the week compared with those not in full-time employment.

Further reading

Donovan, R.J., Rossiter, J.R., Marcoolyn, G. and Nesdale, A. (1994) Store atmosphere and purchasing behaviour, *Journal of Retailing*, 70: 3, 283–94.

Elliott, R. (1993) Shopping addiction and mood repair, in Davies, M. *et al.* (eds.) *Emerging Issues in Marketing*, Loughborough, Loughborough University Press.

Chapter 10

The response to advertising

Introduction

Advertising uses many different types of appeal and a number of media to achieve a variety of goals. In the light of this complexity, a search for general accounts of how advertising works may seem a fruitless quest. We must accept that different ads may work in different ways and that individuals may respond variously to the same ad. Even so, our knowledge has expanded in recent years and more coherent accounts of the consumer response to advertising are now emerging.

Advertising can act at different levels of consciousness. When we are involved in an issue, ads may change our feelings, thoughts and perceptions, making it more likely that we will want, recall, recognize, like and know how to purchase a brand in relevant contexts. Even when we have little involvement, ads may still affect us by connecting brands with needs and by raising brand awareness and brand attitude. Increased awareness of a brand makes it more likely that we will pick it out from the competition and a more positive attitude about a brand means that we may prefer it and may pay more for it.

Advertising is a business investment, but unlike other investments it has been difficult in the past to demonstrate its effectiveness and therefore the return on money spent on advertising. Because of recent research, this picture is now changing so that we are getting a much better idea of the value of advertising in general and the effects that may be expected from different communication strategies.

This chapter is concerned with four questions:

- What methods are available for investigating advertising?
- In what ways may advertising be effective?
- How do individuals process and respond to advertising messages, and how does this knowledge help us to understand, develop, test and classify advertising?
- What sales effects of advertising are observed over time and what are the implications of this evidence?

The measurement of advertising response

Methods

The value of an investment in advertising depends upon *how much* and *how long* it affects people. In most cases any effect is small and difficult to detect, and this means that we need to give careful attention to the methods of research at our disposal. The techniques that are available for studying the effects of advertising are listed below and some of these are then explained in greater detail.

- *Qualitative research* such as focus groups and individual interviewing are widely used for assessing ads but, as a means of testing ad effectiveness, such methods are neither valid nor reliable. Even so, qualitative research has remained an attractive, quick and relatively cheap method for screening out ads that seem to produce little response, or which produce unintended meanings in an audience.
- *Case studies* illustrate agency practice and the response to advertising but focus on the best outcomes and are not therefore representative of all advertising. In Britain a series of case studies called *Advertising Works* has been published under the editorships of Broadbent (1981; 1983), Channon (1985; 1987), Feldwick (1990; 1991) and Baker (1993; 1995); these cases are well written and interesting, and have made a major contribution to the understanding of how campaigns are developed and what effects advertising can have.
- *Experiments*, which control extraneous influences and allow us to infer causal relationships. Findings from laboratory experiments may not apply in normal settings; experiments in normal situations are more informative about the reality of advertising effects. In the United States, Information Resources Inc. (IRI) conducts experiments on the sales effect of different ads delivered to the home in normal TV transmissions.
- *Surveys*, which reveal facts about advertising and media consumption. Surveys have more value when data are collected at intervals; for instance, Millward Brown regularly repeat their surveys of advertising awareness so that changes can be related to ad schedules. Further value is derived from surveys when consumer characteristics are also collected so that the effects of advertising can be related to particular demographic groups, viewing patterns and product usage habits.
- *Consumer panel data*, which reveal change over time and from which much of our recent knowledge of advertising effects has been derived. Such data used to be collected by diaries kept by panellists, but now most panellists scan the product bar codes (universal product identification, or UPI) at home. In the United States, IRI avoids home scanning by using the store scanning record when the product is bought; this work is explained more fully below.
- *Econometric analyses*. These are mathematical techniques applied to survey and panel data and are discussed below.

■ *Data fusion*. This technique combines the data from two sources by using elements that are common to both sources as a key. Using this procedure it is possible to combine television viewing from one panel with purchases in another. Roberts (1994) reports on a study which fused data from the BARB TV viewing panel with data from AGB's Superpanel using reported viewing habits as the key. Roberts showed that this technique could be used to infer the TV commercial exposure of those making specific purchases.

Advertising terms

The television rating (TVR) is the percentage of the potential audience exposed to a commercial. The sum of the TVRs for each showing of the commercial is a measure of total advertising. In the United States, this is called gross rating points (GRPs).

Advertising weight is the amount of advertising, often measured by GRP or by spend; an *upweight* is an increase in advertising in a period.

Weight tests measure the impact of an upweight on sales.

Copy tests evaluate the effect of the ad on recall, comprehension, attention, arousal, interest, intention to buy or actual purchase.

Opportunities-to-see (OTS) or *exposures* are the occasions when people see the ad (or could see it because the TV is on). Usually expressed for a period.

Reach or *coverage* is a measure of advertising penetration. It is the proportion of a target population exposed to the advertisement once or more.

Media planning objectives are the intended OTS for a stated percentage of the population, e.g. two OTS to 30 per cent of the population.

The analysis of advertising data is sometimes done by the market research agency, often by the client (the advertiser) and sometimes by academic researchers. Inevitably there is some filtering of the findings that are reported by commercial organizations since these firms are concerned to present a positive image of their work; because of this we should be cautious of some of their claims. Research under academic auspices is aided by the high level of cooperation between market research organizations and the academic community so that academic researchers can usually get the data they need for research. As a consequence of this cooperation, we are now answering questions that have concerned us for a long time. Because the findings are so recent, there is inevitably some doubt about them and I have tried to show where the effects of advertising remain uncertain.

Scanner-based developments in research

The introduction of bar codes has greatly improved the data available on the sales of packaged goods. In the United States it is now possible to measure the effects of television advertising very accurately using cable TV, checkout scanners and computing. The most advanced form of this research method is BehaviorScan, developed by IRI in Chicago. The methods employed by IRI are described in detail by Fulgoni and Eskin (1981), and by Malec (1982). Isolated communities are used where off-air TV reception is poor and people therefore rely on cable TV. IRI controls the cable transmission to those who agree to be panel members; it can monitor the TV channel that the main household set is tuned to, and it can switch the advertisements received in panellists' homes. This means that one group of households can receive one advertisement while another equivalent group receives a quite different version; alternatively different households can receive different weights of advertising.

The other half of the system is based in the local stores and records purchases. All stores in the community are equipped with IRI's scanners which read the bar codes on the products purchased. Each household in the panel has an identification card which the panellist shows to the checkout operator; this ties sales to a particular household. Each day purchase data are relayed automatically to Chicago for analysis. This system seems likely to deliver a more complete purchase record than any other method. The whole system depends upon split-second control of advertising transmissions and computer analysis of scanner data. The data analysis can show how much a particular brand was purchased by households receiving a specific advertising copy, weight or schedule. IRI currently runs ad research panels in six communities in the United States. The scanner system gives very good measurement of sales in each community; Eskin (1985) showed that 91 per cent of panel measures were within ± 10 per cent of store sale measures. IRI also records marketing mix variables such as deals.

Nielsen, the largest market research agency in the world and IRI's main competitor in the United States, uses home scanned panels. Nielsen uses national samples, not local communities, so that its findings are more representative, but this approach does not lend itself to experimentation of the form conducted by IRI. In some instances Nielsen has combined sales measures with measures of television viewing so that exposure to commercials and subsequent purchase can be linked. However, there is a difference between naturally occurring exposures and those that are controlled experimentally, using BehaviorScan, and this is discussed later in the context of work by J.P. Jones (1995a).

In Germany, GfK have set up a test panel using IRI technology and some of their findings have been reported by Litzenroth (1991). In Britain, there is no experimental ad testing service like the BehaviorScan procedure. Completed television commercials can be evaluated using an area test (i.e. by using different ads in comparable TV areas), but this procedure is not fully controlled since TV areas may differ in relevant respects, for example, by having different levels of competitor advertising. However the Area Marketing Test Evaluation System (AMTES), originally developed by Beecham (now SmithKline Beecham), has been designed to deal with this situation. Those factors that are not experimentally balanced by the regional comparison are modelled using econometric analysis.

Two other products, Nielsen's ScanTrack and IRI's InfoScan, extract sales from checkout data but these services provide only *aggregate* sales by brand and variety; there is no household identification. We call this *store-level data*.

The validity of IRI's results

Any system of measurement has errors associated with it and a number of limitations attach to the BehaviorScan procedures:

- More than one television may be used in a household and purchasers in the store may not have watched the monitored set when the ad was screened.
- The BehaviorScan system does not pick up out-of-town sales (called outshopping) but these are rare for the packaged goods studied by IRI.
- There are doubts about whether the isolated communities used by IRI are representative of the rest of the United States, particularly when these communities are used as test markets. Eskin (1985) reports that the aggregated scanner data do correspond with nationwide sales but the test communities cannot show the consumption patterns of ethnic minorities which they do not contain.
- Those who commission tests do not select at random and there is likely to be a bias in favour of commercially advantageous studies, e.g. weight tests of ads that are thought either to be very effective or to be worn out, and copy tests on ads which are thought to have lost their effect. Also testing is very expensive so it is likely to be confined to big brands. This means that the general findings on weight or ad tests are not typical of all ads.
- The tests exclude the effect of trade responses. Retailers are more ready to stock an item if it is well advertised so that advertising works in part by priming the distribution system. Although ads in the test area may cause some extra stocking by dealers, this will affect both experimental and control groups which means that its effect is cancelled out in the experimental design. Also competitor response occurs in the real environment (Stewart, 1990) and this effect is also removed by the experimental design. (Competitor response is an important consideration when companies decide about adspend; many firms will refrain from increasing advertising because they fear that competitors will respond by raising their ad budgets which would leave sales little changed but costs increased.)
- The testing process is not validated. When advertising goes nationwide after copy testing, the weaker ad from the copy test is abandoned so that the testing process is never itself evaluated by comparisons in the national market. There must be some awareness of current tests in the communities used by IRI and this could affect sales response. This raises doubt about whether an ad which is 10 per cent better on test would be 10 per cent better outside the test market.

Modelling the sales effects of advertising

When data on seasonal variation, adspend, relative price, etc. are available, *econometric modelling* can be used to estimate the influence of each of these factors on sales. When the econometric model is correctly framed the movement of sales over time should be predicted. Barnard and Smith (1989) have written a useful introduction to this technique.

A merit of econometric models is that they represent all the known influences on sales so that the potential returns from different marketing interventions can be compared. Some marketing departments go to considerable trouble to construct such models but the value of the exercise is always open to doubt. This is because: ad effects are often small and hard to detect, some sales determinants may not be recognized and are therefore omitted from the model, some determinants may be mis-specified and the effect on sales of determinants may change over time. Sometimes more than one model will fit the data and judgement must be used to choose between alternatives. The efficiency of the econometric procedure depends upon the quantity and variability of the data used. Improvements in precision are achieved when variability is increased by delivering different weights of advertising to different areas as was done when sales of Andrex were modelled by O'Herlihy (Baker, 1993). Ideally, some of the data should be held back, the model developed on the remaining data, and then tested on the retained data.

Any model applies to the past and is an uncertain guide to the future where new and unmeasured determinants may appear and changes in the campaign, media schedule or competitor activity may go outside the assumptions of the model.

Adstock

One problem in modelling is that the effect of advertising dies away after each exposure; to deal with this the ad effect is usually represented as *adstock* – a measure of the effect of advertising which has accumulated in people. To compute the adstock figure the contribution of each ad exposure is discounted in relation to the time elapsed since it was shown. This discounting usually assumes a geometric decay, i.e. that the rate of decay is constant but, because it applies to a dwindling quantity, the change becomes less and less as it approaches a base level. Such processes are usually measured by their *half-life*, the time taken for an effect to decay to half its value. Once obtained, adstock can be used alongside other measures in the econometric modelling of sales. There has been some doubt about the speed of ad decay and whether a geometric decay function is appropriate and this subject is revisited in the last section of this chapter when long-term aggregate effects of advertising are considered. A point to note here is that the effect of an exposure may decline more because of external influence from competitive advertising than from any intrinsic decay.

Advertising awareness

Different advertising campaigns can have quite different impacts on sales and this means that gross adspend provides only a crude measure of a campaign's effect on sales; it would be very useful if we had a separate measure of campaign effectiveness. One proposed proxy for the sales effectiveness of a campaign is the measure of advertising awareness which is derived from surveys of advertising recall. It seems plausible that those who can remember ads for a product are more likely to have been influenced to purchase the product by those ads. Unfortunately ad awareness has little relationship with sales; this may be because ads can have an effect on brand purchase without the ad being remembered, or because the ad is remembered but the brand is not part of the purchase repertoire. Channon (1985) observed that the advertising for *Cadbury's Fudge* was very effective on sales but it did not have much effect on ad awareness. Broadbent and Colman (1986) found little relationship between ad awareness and sales effectiveness in a study of eighteen campaigns in the confectionery market. There are also recall differences between media; G. Brown (1994) notes that print ads create more sales than their awareness ratings would imply.

The different effects of advertising

What is effective advertising?

To be effective, commercial advertising must improve the profit trend compared with what would have happened without the advertising. In social contexts ads have many other applications such as reducing accidents, increasing voting and reducing smoking which must be assessed instead of profit. Ads may assist profits by:

- Encouraging people to pay higher prices, supporting margins.
- Encouraging people to buy the advertised brand, supporting sales.

Sales and margins can also be affected indirectly by advertising. This can occur when advertising:

- Increases consumption from stock, leading to more purchases.
- Increases distribution, raising sales by increased opportunity to purchase.
- Improves targeting, reducing costs.
- Restrains market entry by competitors, thereby reducing competition. This may raise sales and margins.

Evidence on these effects is considered below.

Price support
Where supply is limited, the effect of advertising may be to raise price by raising demand. This applies to auctions, and to share markets where corporate advertising may have a small effect on the share price. Evidence on share price effects is sketchy but Moraleda and Ferrer-Vidal (1991) showed rising awareness and intentions to apply for shares in the Spanish oil company Repsol in the run-up to privatization when the offer was being advertised. It seems likely that high levels of interest in a privatization mean that the price of shares can be set a little higher, but the main purpose here is to ensure the take-up of all the shares.

When there is no effective constraint on supply the effect of advertising on price is more equivocal. Some advertising is, of course, directly related to price claims and here there is clear evidence that it is associated with lower prices (Popkowski and Rao, 1989). Less specific advertising is thought to be positively related to brand price because it increases the acceptability of that price. Broadbent (1989) illustrates this with a case where improved advertising increased the proportion of purchasers who were tolerant of the brand's price. Adding value to a brand often amounts to this, i.e. raising the reference price for the brand so that a higher price can be charged without loss of sales. King (1984) noted that the market share of *Andrex*, a well-advertised brand of British toilet paper, had scarcely changed over two decades yet the price premium against comparative brands rose from 10 per cent to 35 per cent, suggesting that the advertising support had contributed to brand equity, and that this benefit had been taken in higher margins.

Andrex

This is a brand that appears to have benefited from advertising. The performance of this brand up to the start of 1992 has been evaluated by Baker (1993); despite recession and competition from 'green' brands it achieved a price premium of about 25 per cent in 1990–91. Baker reports that when the *Kleenex Velvet* toilet tissue was introduced in the early 1980s, consumers preferred it to *Andrex* on blind test; in 1992 the two brands were equally rated on blind test but *Andrex* was much preferred when the name was visible, showing the strength of the brand. Andrex, with 25 per cent of the market, consistently outsold *Kleenex* on 10 per cent share. A share of 25 per cent is high compared with other European markets; in France, the market leader, *Lotus*, has only 16 per cent share and a price premium of 19 per cent. This example indicates that advertising can create brand equity, which can then be used to raise either margins or sales, or both.

Subsequently *Andrex* has suffered. The competition from high-quality private label at lower prices in a recession was more than it could withstand, and from 1992 to mid-1994 Andrex lost one third of its sales. Even this scale of loss might be seen as indicating the strength of the brand – it could have been worse.

It is generally argued that advertising can do little for a poor product; this may be so, but it does appear that advertising can help a sound product gain an advantage in pricing and sales. There was a period when *Kleenex Velvet* was technically superior to *Andrex* (see box) but the *Andrex* price premium and sales advantage were unaffected. Another example might be the establishment of Australian lagers such as *Castlemaine XXXX* and *Fosters* in the British market; this achievement is probably based more on excellent advertising than on any special quality of the product. *Häagen-Daz* ice-cream (Baker, 1993) also shows the power of advertising to turn a sound product into a leader.

Here we have a combination of high adspend coupled with high factory and retail price; Farris and Reibstein (1991) have argued that this is a common pattern for leading brands.

Stella Artois

The interaction between advertising and price has also been demonstrated by the success of *Stella Artois* in Britain (Baker, 1993). On blind test *Stella* is not significantly preferred, but in Britain it is premium priced and advertised as 'reassuringly expensive', implying high quality. *Stella* attracts a large proportion of lager drinkers and secures a trade price premium of 7.5 per cent which finances the adspend; publicans more than recover this premium when they sell *Stella* at its higher retail price.

Sales support

Advertising may often be effective without any obvious change in sales because, without it, sales would have fallen back. In mature markets most categories are fairly static so that brand gains tend to be at the expense of other brands in the category; advertising then becomes a requirement for a brand to hold its own. Broadbent (1989) has compared advertising to an aeroplane's engines. When the engines are working the aeroplane maintains its height. If the engines fail the aeroplane does not crash directly but it does start to lose height – more rapidly in the case of some aeroplanes. The analogy with the aeroplane implies that advertising is continuous but it is often concentrated into bursts and then discontinued or run at low level; this is more like the firing of a hot air balloon than the steady thrust of aeroplane engines. Just as you can see a hot air balloon rising with each firing, and then falling back, so we might expect to see sales rise a little with a burst of advertising and then fall back again after the burst has finished. We now have more sensitive measures of sales and such movements may be detectable (e.g. J.P. Jones, 1995a).

The modest impact of advertising is because most sales in repetitively bought markets are sustained by brand loyalty, but sometimes the combination of a clever campaign and high adspend does produce substantial sales shifts. Some major successes have been reported in the case studies described in the *Advertising Works* series, for example, a campaign for *Levi 501s* in Britain raised sales fifteen times in one year (Feldwick, 1990) and in other European countries a similar campaign has produced impressive sales gains and has re-established Levi as the leading jean manufacturer (Baker, 1993).

Reducing adspend

Sales effects have been tested by reductions in adspend and Aykac, Corstjens and Gautschi (1984) found that reduced adspend on several products had no immediate impact on sales. This may be because the advertising was poor and was having no effect. One famous study by Ackoff and Emshoff (1975) showed *increased* sales of *Budweiser* beer when adspend was cut; this strange effect has never been satisfactorily explained but it suggests that over-advertising is possible.

Although they are a selected sample, the IRI ad weight tests are one of the most substantial accumulations of evidence on the sales effects of ads; Lodish and Lubetkin (1992) have reviewed much of IRI's findings and have reported on these weight tests. Out of 293 tests, 49 per cent showed a significant increase in sales on upweight (usually 50–100 per cent increase in adspend); when an upweight produced an effect, the gain was on average 23 per cent by volume. This research confirmed evidence from Eastlack and Rao (1989) that, if there was an increase in sales with upweight, the size of the upweight made little difference; this suggests rapidly diminishing returns from extra advertising and helps to explain why increased share of voice has been found to have no effect on sales (Lodish *et al.*, 1995).

It is interesting that half the tests had no effect. In Fulgoni's (1987) view, many weight test failures were due to bad copy; ads that have no effect remain ineffective even when they are shown twice as often. Usually the idea behind weight tests is to identify situations where increased advertising can bring extra sales so that more profit is made. But even a significant increase in sales may not make enough profit to justify the extra adspend. IRI found that a case could be made for increasing the adspend in only about 20 per cent of the test cases. Stewart (1990) points out that if the increased adspend makes competitors react by increasing their advertising, the money may still be wasted. Thus it will be quite rare that weight tests show convincing evidence that extra spend is worthwhile. It seems better to look at weight tests from the opposite standpoint: when extra weight brings no extra sales there is a case for reducing adspend or for bringing forward new copy.

Increasing consumption from stock

Wansink and Ray (1992) have focused attention on the frequency of consumption of goods that are normally kept in the home. If the consumption of everyday consumables such as cereals and canned soups can be raised, sales will eventually increase. We see attempts to raise consumption in some campaigns, either by getting people to consume more frequently, e.g. drinking more tea and having cereal for other meals than breakfast, or by finding new uses for products, e.g. putting Hellman's on different foods, kitchen towelling to absorb fat from fried food and using bleach in drains.

Supporting distribution

Distribution creates the opportunity to purchase and sales usually rise when a brand appears on more shelves. Thus wide stocking and good facings in the stores are important determinants of sales volume. Distribution is a rather unexciting aspect of the marketing mix but it frequently has the strongest effect on the sales of supermarket goods; if a given brand is not available, people will buy another brand – there are few brands where people are loyal to the point that they refuse to buy an alternative. Distribution increases are reported in relation to advertising effects in some of the *Advertising Works* papers, e.g. the success of the *Mangers Sugar Soap* campaign was partly due to wider distribution (Broadbent, 1983); here the retailers were more willing to stock the product because they knew that it was the subject of an advertising campaign. Similarly, part of the success of *Häagen-Daz* ice-cream in Britain was due to increased stocking by retailers.

Supporting promotions

It is generally believed that advertising and promotion act synergistically to raise sales. For example, if a promotion adds 100 per cent and advertising adds 20 per cent to sales, the joint effect will be greater than 120 per cent because each component in the promotion mix amplifies the effect of the other component. Synergistic effects are found when the advertising is price-related (see Chapter 4). However the picture is more complicated when general media advertising is run as well as in-store deals and display. Lodish *et al.* (1995) report that the strong effects of in-store promotion appear to swamp any gains that might have come from increased brand advertising. There is synergy between media advertising and discounts delivered through coupons (which are partly advertising). Jones (1995a) reports evidence that promotions and advertising act synergistically, but does not distinguish between point-of-sale discounts and coupons. Much of the US promotions are delivered by coupon and therefore his findings may be consistent with Lodish and Lubetkin, but clarification is required in this area.

Improving targeting

When enquiries use up the time of skilled personnel it is important that the enquirers are good prospects, so that time is not wasted on those who will not buy. This is particularly true for industrial marketing and personnel recruitment and it is therefore crucial that the advertising copy communicates effectively with the right groups and discourages those who are unsuited to the product. Broadbent (1981) illustrated how improvements in advertising raised both the number and the quality of those applying for commissions in the RAF.

Restraining market entry

Big brands advertise more, but their ad budgets may be a smaller *proportion of sales* than those of smaller brands. Since ads often appeal to existing buyers they work better for a brand with more buyers. It is part of the benefit of being large that advertising shows economies of scale along with other benefits of size on distribution, margin and management. To get into a market a new brand may need to advertise heavily and, while the brand remains small, the proportionate costs are high. Because of this the US Federal Trade Commission sees excessive advertising as a restraint of trade. This is certainly a matter that affects the consumer interest. In many established markets the only new brands to be seen are retailer brands.

The wider impact of advertising

Although heavy advertising for single brands is associated with higher prices the effect of advertising on whole categories is less clear. McDonald (1992, ch. 3) summarizes the evidence on this more general effect of advertising and concludes that higher levels of advertising usually exert a downward pressure on prices, probably because consumers are better informed. Steiner (1973) found that prices fell in the toy industry with growth in advertising and Polyani (1972) claimed that consumers benefited from lower prices as a result of intense advertising in the British detergent industry. This subject has been reviewed by Farris and Albion (1980) who found that more advertising tended to raise prices to the retailer but lower them to the consumer, an effect predicted by Steiner (1973). The advertising increases demand for the product and raises the power of the manufacturer to charge the retailer more, but it increases consumer knowledge about prices, brand variants, etc. so that consumers become price-sensitive and exert more pressure on the retailer. This forces retailers to lower prices across the category even though some heavily advertised brands secure a premium. The impact on category price levels will be more marked when the product category is less familiar to the consumer, when the retailer is weak and when advertising emphasizes price comparisons and cheapness. Such conditions do not apply to fmcg products in British supermarkets and the study by Hamilton, East and Kalafatis (1997) found that heavily advertised category groupings had somewhat lower price elasticities, contrary to Steiner's thesis.

The individual response to advertising

Exercise 10.1   Your ideas about ad effect

You will understand the arguments in this section better if you start by trying to frame your own explanations for the ways in which advertising works. Answer the following questions:

1. How are brand awareness, attitude, beliefs and purchase related?

2. How do these relationships change when we pass from high involvement purchases to low involvement purchases?

3. You see an ad at one time and place, but you buy the advertised product later in a different place. How is ad reception linked to the later purchase?

Early theories of advertising influence came from practitioners. In any field practitioners need to act and, in order to act coherently, they form ideas, classifications and theories about their subject matter. Such theories may lack supporting evidence, but they provide a useful starting point and introduce some of the issues with which we are concerned.

Much of practitioner theory is based on ideas about how consumers choose. A prevailing theme of this book has been that accounts of consumer behaviour tend to overemphasize rational cognitive processes and we see this again in practitioner theories that place emphasis on an intelligent assimilation of the advertising message. Rosser Reeves (1961) was a well-known exponent of this approach with his idea of the 'unique selling proposition' (USP), which was a feature of the brand, real or assumed, that differentiated it from the opposition. For Reeves a good ad was one which successfully implanted knowledge of the USP. This new information must be processed in some way and connected with purchase. Thus the Reeves approach implies an active cognitive processing of messages dealing with frequently purchased goods. Although the USP approach can be criticized as too cognitive, the focus on a single selling feature has merit. Inspection of modern television and magazine ads for low involvement goods shows that there are few that offer more than one or two ideas for the receiver to accept; this suggests that practitioners have found that simple appeals work better, perhaps *because* people generally give ads little attention or thought.

Hierarchy of effects models

Practitioners have also developed theories about stages in the process of influence which are again based on rational principles. The earliest, credited to St Elmo Lewis in the late nineteenth century, was a sequence with the acronym AIDA, that ads persuade people to go through the stages:

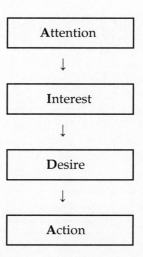

Hierarchy of effects (or more briefly, *sequential*) models like AIDA rest on an analysis of what is necessary for influence to be achieved. Also well known is the Lavidge and Steiner (1961) model:

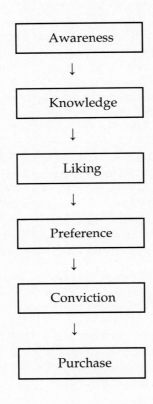

Some models include comprehension, acceptance and modification of beliefs before action but, whatever the sequence, all these models are based on the assumption that each stage is a precondition to the next. A benefit of the sequential model is that it suggests a programme of copy evaluation; if each stage is required, then ads can be tested to see whether they secure the changes needed at each stage, in particular whether they are understood and recalled. Such tests can be applied early on in the development of advertising before too much money has been spent. Colley (1961) developed this approach with DAGMAR (Defining Advertising Goals for Measured Advertising Results), which, even today, is an influence on copy design and testing. In DAGMAR, effective advertising is believed to take recipients down the ACCA path:

Awareness

↓

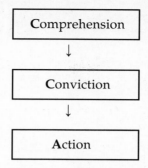

The DAGMAR model was accompanied by tests for recall, understanding and acceptance of the message which were used for the development of advertising. These models combine a *logical* aspect of necessary precondition with a less explicit implication of *psychological* process which is more contentious. Logically, it is necessary that individuals must be aware of an ad if they are to comprehend the message, but this does not mean that they have to recall the ad for any influence to occur. Much of the early recall testing focused on the ad itself, but it is clearly much more important to remember the brand than the vehicle that presented it. Ideally, tests would check directly on the eventual action – usually purchase – but this is only feasible when the ad is finally used; decisions are required on alternative ad contents well before this time and tests are needed to establish the likely effects of these alternatives.

Models like DAGMAR are related to the work of social psychologists such as Hovland, Janis and Kelley (1953) in the Yale Communication and Attitude Change Program. Their work was designed to answer the questions:

■ Who said what?
■ Via which medium?
■ To whom?
■ With what effect?

Within the Yale Program, research was conducted on the credibility of sources, the design of persuasive communications, attention to and comprehension of messages, and acceptance by recipients. The approach of the Yale School, in common with the sequential models, emphasizes cognitive processing. The conclusions of the researchers sometimes gave rules of good practice, but did not give much understanding of the mechanisms underlying the effect of ads on purchase. We need to understand what processes are at work within people when they respond to a communication; rational accounts may give an overview but they do not tell us about the role of information processing mechanisms as discussed in Chapter 7.

Conversion and reinforcement

There are a number of criticisms of sequential models. One of the most fundamental (Ehrenberg, 1974) is that the proposed sequence of effects is not appropriate for the repetitive advertising of established brands.

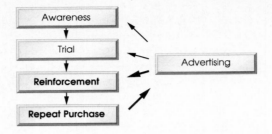

Figure 10.1 The ATR model

Most purchases are repeat purchases by people who are fully aware of the brands that they buy; indeed they are aware of many brands that they do not normally buy. Because of this, awareness and knowledge of the brand is not at issue. Ehrenberg treats consumption as mainly a matter of habit and in his **A**wareness → **T**rial → **R**einforcement (ATR) account, awareness and trial are exceptional and the main effect is the reinforcement of established purchase, as shown in Figure 10.1. Here the advertising amplifies the reinforcement from product usage, and usage makes consumers responsive to the advertising.

Thus, for Ehrenberg, advertising works mainly on existing buyers and induces them to maintain their purchases and sometimes to buy a brand a little more often; thus buyers are rarely *converted* or *persuaded* (via awareness and trial) because they are already knowledgeable about the brand. A feature of this analysis is that advertising mostly acts *after* purchase to justify buying and to firm up later repeat purchase, rather than *before* purchase to inform buyers about where their needs might be satisfied and thereby to convert them to the advertised brand.

Ehrenberg's description of the way advertising functions rests on an assumption that buyers rarely change their purchase portfolios. Advertising is defensive and serves to *maintain* the brand share. Ehrenberg is opposed to the idea that advertising works by shifting brand allegiance, which he describes as the *leaky bucket theory* of consumption. According to this theory, advertising maintains the level in the bucket by converting buyers of other brands and non-buyers of the category to the advertised brand. In this account, advertising has a strong offensive role in the battle to maintain share as consumers switch from brand to brand. Instead of this, Ehrenberg offers a 'weak theory of advertising' – ads are defensive and have a modest effect in reinforcing existing purchase tendencies, rather than a dramatic effect in converting people. For Ehrenberg advertising is just one of the influences supporting continued consumption; the quality of the product is often the most important factor.

Even in the case of consumer durable purchase, advertising may be more effective after the purchase; people often search for useful or reassuring information after buying, and ads, or written material supplied with the product, may provide this reassurance. If they are reassured about the product, people are more likely to recommend it to others and they may eventually buy the brand again themselves. (There are repeat purchases in durables markets; as was noted in Chapter 2, most durable purchases are replacements or additional purchases.)

However, as we also saw in Chapter 2, a stationary market can conceal quite a large buyer churn – the bucket does leak. East and Hammond (1996) found that, each year, about 15 per cent of buyers left a market and were replaced by the same percentage of new buyers if the market was stationary. This leaves considerable scope for both the offensive and the defensive functions of advertising. But even the new buyers of an established brand may not really be converted. Most of them will be familiar with the brand and the category in low involvement markets so that the way in which the advertising acts on recruits to a brand could be the same as the way in which it supports existing purchase. Thus real conversion will be quite rare.

Ehrenberg (1974) speculated on the mechanisms that might be involved in effective reinforcement and suggested that selective perception may operate so that people notice ads for the brands that they buy. In this account the use of the term 'reinforcement' may be confusing. What is claimed is that advertising has the *outcome* of reinforcing behaviour; it is not claimed that this is achieved by a direct conditioning mechanism. If the advertising works by raising the salience of the brand name (stimulus control), it would still fit Ehrenberg's use of the term reinforcement. Later we consider some of the other mechanisms that may be involved in advertising effect.

It seems likely that the ad appeal may need to vary, depending on the weight of purchase. The downside potential of a brand's heavy buyers (i.e. the 20 per cent responsible for about 50 per cent of sales) seems much larger than the upside and this implies that they should be treated defensively with the object of retaining their custom. The buyers of other brands and the light buyers of your own brand who may also be heavy buyers of competitor brands, require a different, more offensive pitch, since these people have more potential to increase sales.

Conversion or reinforcement?

The strapline 'No FT, no comment' has become familiar to British audiences. It tells them that those who do not take the *Financial Times* are poorly informed and ill-equipped to deal with business life at the higher levels. This ad may convert some readers of other papers, but it also reinforces current buying by telling existing readers of the *FT* (in a slightly smug, self-satisfied way) that they are wise and well informed.

A second approach to sequential models is empirical. The most extensive tests have been reported by Information Resources Inc.; they compared the standard ad recall and persuasion (shift of preference) scores with sales effects for established brands in test markets; there was a tenuous relationship at best (Lodish *et al.*, 1995). By contrast a paper at the Advertising Research Foundation Workshop (Haley and Baldinger, 1991) showed that when a small sample of successful ads was compared with an equivalent number of unsuccessful ads the former scored higher on brand recall, persuasion and liking for the ad (see McDonald, 1992). A problem with this work is the design of the study – working backwards from success – which has limited *predictive* value; in order

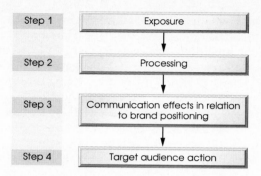

Figure 10.2 The buyer response sequence

to predict we need the relative frequencies of, say, ad likeability across a selection of ads before their effect on psychological measures is tested. If most ads are liked, then the finding that successful ads are liked has less importance. There are cases where an ad is disliked but is effective (e.g. the advertising for *Charmin* toilet tissue in the United States, and the *Radion* advertising in Britain (Feldwick, 1991)).

Improving the sequential model

Despite the problems with the hierarchy of effect models it is difficult to abandon them. We must accept the logical aspect of such models that there are preconditions to audience changes. And there are clearly some psychological processes involved. Advertising and purchasing occur at different times and in different places (except for direct and point-of-sale advertising). Thus, when it affects the later buying response, the advertising must have been received, processed, stored and then have been activated again; this is implied in Rossiter and Percy's (1997) buyer response model (Figure 10.2), which is a general expression of the sequential model approach. The problem is to give this general hierarchy more precision in the different contexts to which it applies.

Here we focus particularly on the human responses that are implied in Steps 2 and 3 of this sequence. In particular we want to know:

■ How involvement affects processing.
■ What advertising effects are required if the ad is to support existing purchase or persuade the audience to adopt new purchase practices when they next have the opportunity to buy, i.e. the relationship between ad, the brand properties and the purchase context.
■ How some ads gain attention and understanding while others do not.

These issues are addressed below.

Involvement and processing

The way in which ads are processed is affected by the degree of audience involvement. When the purchase is important and the decision not easily reversed, it is likely that people will give more thought and will decide more consciously about the products they buy.

An example of a successful campaign in a high involvement field is provided by the advertising that encouraged British households to fit and maintain smoke detectors (Baker, 1995); this was founded on the communication of a number of key beliefs: how quickly fires spread and kill, the cheapness of alarms and their value in waking people before they are asphyxiated in their sleep. By contrast, the increased purchase of *Peperami* (a salami snack) was achieved with much more fanciful ads, which probably raised the salience of the product in the minds of those familiar with salami but which communicated a much less specific set of ideas (Baker, 1995). As a result consumers were more likely to buy *Peperami* when they saw it in the shops, even though they might never have come to a conscious decision to do this.

The high involvement decision is more likely to fit a sequential model where new information is received and consciously processed, while the low involvement situation usually enhances existing responses and affects information-processing mechanisms which may be scarcely apprehended by the consumer. Successful advertising in a high involvement context may result in persuasion, while in the low involvement situation it is likely that reinforcement of established responses will be the norm. The two following subsections indicate two ways of describing high and low involvement processes, together with some of the criticisms that might be made of these approaches.

Three types of process

One classification used by Batra and Ray (1983) proposes three different types of response to advertising which are related to involvement in the purchase.

1. The most common form is a low involvement process where the ad affects brand salience and increases purchase disposition without any direct change in attitude. In this process attitude change follows rather than precedes changes in purchase disposition. Batra and Ray thought that such advertising worked mainly by enhancing brand salience relative to competitors.
2. A high involvement sequence, following Ajzen and Fishbein's theory (Chapter 6), in which changes occur in the order: belief, attitude, intention, action. This was found in a study of political advertising and was most often conveyed through the print medium.
3. A high involvement sequence called *dissonance-attribution*, in which the behaviour occurs first and is followed by changes in attitude and then belief. This sequence occurred when there were few apparent differences between important alternatives, e.g. cars. It was more common when personal influence was the factor that precipitated purchase.

Batra and Ray find that repetition has little effect under high involvement; here people 'get the point' so that further exposures produce no more change. Thus, for this sort of influence, a wide coverage strategy is required. By contrast, low involvement learning is facilitated by repetition so that a high exposure strategy may be better.

The elaboration–likelihood model

Another account of the differences between high and low involvement responses is offered by the elaboration–likelihood model (Petty, Cacioppo and Schumann, 1983; Petty and Cacioppo, 1985; Cacioppo and Petty, 1985). When people respond to a message that is important to them they are more likely to review the arguments, think of contrary and supporting propositions, and reflect on the implications of these different ideas: in short, they elaborate on the message. Eiser and Ross (1977) found that persuasion occurred more often when people had to generate their own arguments compared with conditions in which they were given ready-made arguments.

Petty and Cacioppo distinguish between the central and peripheral routes to persuasion. The central route involves elaboration and here any changes are thought to be more long-lived, resistant to counter-argument and predictive of future behaviour. The peripheral route is based on associations of feeling and simple responses to cues; since there is no elaboration, this route does not generate the arguments that will anchor attitudes and protect a person from change. According to this theory, involvement will increase the amount of elaboration and, supporting this, Petty and Cacioppo (1979) found that there was more persuasion when messages were made personally relevant. Eiser (1986: 44–9) reviews this topic, which is rather more controversial than is indicated by this brief account; much of the controversy is related to the precise mechanisms that are initiated by different sorts of message. Chaiken (1980), for example, argues that the peripheral influence is likely to occur through the agency of heuristic mechanisms such as those discussed in Chapter 7.

Also in question is the extent to which beliefs have priority in the process of change. In Chapters 5 and 6 work by Powell and Fazio (1984) and Fazio (1986; 1990) was described. These researchers define a process in which attitude has a central role in the coordination of beliefs and behaviour. The process starts when an object or situation is perceived, stimulating an appropriate attitude, which then selectively activates related beliefs, and sometimes behaviour. Thus, in this account, attitude is causally prior to beliefs. Fazio divides between the spontaneous processing that occurs in this way and the deliberate processing that occurs under Ajzen's (1985; 1991) planned behaviour model, but Bargh et al. (1992) have shown that most objects evoke attitudes so that spontaneous processing could also occur in high involvement situations. This implies that the cognitions that are elaborated depend on the attitudes that are activated by the ad.

Another qualification of the elaboration–likelihood model is the idea that beliefs that are established by the peripheral route have less durability than those established by the direct route. Beliefs established by the peripheral route may be less anchored, but they are also less likely to be subjected to strong arguments since competitive advertising is likely to use the peripheral route too. In these circumstances there can be no assumption that one type of belief will last longer than the other. None the less

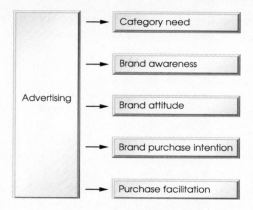

Figure 10.3 The five communication effects

the elaboration–likelihood model suggests that many everyday consumer habits may be founded on simple mechanisms that could not withstand strong counter-arguments. Returning to our earlier examples, it is easy to see that propositions on smoke alarms are important and self-involving and could generate many additional arguments – the safety of one's children and the censure of others if smoke alarms are not fitted. By contrast, a salami snack is likely to be accommodated within an existing pattern of thinking and, if strong counter-arguments to eating *Peperami* were produced, the behaviour could easily be dropped. Interestingly, a strong case against *Peperami* did occur when, in Britain, a major TV news broadcast reported that there was a danger of salmonella infection from the product. Unfortunately, the effect on consumers could not be judged because *Peperami* was quickly withdrawn; some time later it was returned to the market in a pasteurized form.

Advertising and the purchase context

Rossiter and Percy (1997) have introduced some welcome clarity into the discussion of what advertising needs to do. Their basic list of communication objectives is shown in Figure 10.3. The way in which advertising may be used to address these objectives is discussed below.

Category need
Need may be aroused by forging connections between the category and audience values; it is not hard to imagine suitable ways of arousing need in respect of a smoke alarm, while *Peperami* requires a more creative approach. A brand may also be linked to non-category groupings. Barsalou (1985) has distinguished between taxonomic groupings such as product categories and goal-derived groupings such as 'things for camping', which spread response across categories. A well-designed ad associates any

relevant needs with the brand. Usually the need–brand association cannot be immediately satisfied but may be rekindled later in a buying context.

Brand awareness

The next level, brand awareness, is more complicated. Brand awareness of, say, the Black and Decker smoke alarm requires either *recall* of the brand name or *recognition* of the product, depending on the circumstances of purchase. For Rossiter and Percy, brand awareness is *cued memory*. When the brand is not present a person is aware of a brand if he or she can recall it when the category is named. When the brand is present brand awareness is shown by ease of recognition of the brand. Thus recall is *category → brand*, and recognition is *brand → category*. For purchase decisions based on recall, for example when you ask an electrician to purchase and fit a particular brand of smoke alarm, the ad should help you to think of the brand name when asking the electrician to do the work. For decisions based on recognition, for example when the smoke alarm is purchased in a DIY store, the ad should increase the speed and accuracy of brand recognition; here the advertising needs to ensure that the buyer knows the look of the pack and logo as well as the brand name.

It is the purchase context that defines whether recall or recognition is required. In the case of smoke alarms, two different contexts may apply so that both recall and recognition could be important; similarly the wine decision in a restaurant is affected both by recognition of wine names on the list and also by recall, since one may recall a wine and then search the list for it. In other cases only one type of brand awareness is required and thus we have a basis for classifying ads by the purchase context. Products that are selected on recognition are usually goods, and here the awareness is usually visual, making logo, colour, pack shape, etc. an important part of consumer memory. Products that are selected via recall include most services and goods that are bought through intermediaries, and here awareness of the brand *name* is key; since packaging and logo are less important, visual media such as magazines and television are less useful for recall advertising. An ad may fail because it is inappropriate to the mode of purchase or presented in the wrong medium.

This distinction means that detergent is better promoted using visual stimuli on TV or by pictures in print which aid recognition by conveying size, shape, colour and logo, while courier services, based more on recall, benefit from strong emphasis on brand name in the copy. Radio is good for brand name emphasis, and thus recall, and it is interesting that the courier company DHL did very well with this medium in Britain.

Exercise 10.2   Classifying advertising

1. Identify a number of ads for goods and services.
2. Is purchase dependent on recognition, recall, or both?
3. On what media are these mainly advertised?
4. Does the advertising reflect the dominant form of brand awareness?

The effects of ads must be retrieved in the purchase context. Holden and Lutz (1992) point out that a range of cues are present in this context. Benefits, physical context features, the product category, other brands and attributes of the brand can all cue the brand and the importance of these different factors depends on the strength of association between them and the brand. Holden (1993) makes the point that since features of the purchase situation may aid brand awareness it is wise to try to engineer such features into the purchase environment and to use them in advertising, the McDonalds sign is an example. In this way it is possible to produce a crosstalk between ad and purchase context by appropriate pack symbols and slogans. From this analysis, a major role of advertising is to establish brand awareness and to do so in particular by showing the moment of recognition or recall in the appropriate context and with appropriate indication of need; then, when the recipient of the ad is next in a relevant purchase context, the advertised brand will be more salient.

The power of the pack

Leo Burnett offered Campbell's soup to customers in two forms: one kept the name and design except that the red and white can was changed to green and white; the second kept the colour and design but changed the name from 'Campbell's' to 'Gongdote'. Customers avoided the first and bought the second, showing that recognition uses the overall visual features and does not involve the detail. The change of letters for the brand name did not have much effect on its stylistic form and therefore did not interfere with recognition.

Brand attitude

There are brands such as the Lada car that have little public esteem but are, none the less, well known. Most of us can think of stores and brands that we know quite well, but which we avoid because we do not like them. Thus a further purpose of advertising is to enhance the liking of a brand so that it is preferred to other brands. Rossiter and Percy see brand attitude as the outcome of the perceived benefits conferred by the brand, and benefits are the satisfaction of needs. Aspirin may be liked because it eases a headache and specific brands must claim to ease headaches better; this benefit is the removal of a negative condition. On the positive side, products such as cars offer a raft of useful features directed to different needs and the manufacturers of specific models have to find ways of stating how their models meet these needs more effectively.

Purchase intention

Rossiter and Percy point out that advertising should encourage people to instruct themselves to buy. Most purchase is conditional on a range of factors and, when it can be communicated, the self-instruction may therefore take the form of 'I will buy that when ...'. The conditions might be times and places which may then act as cues to buy when they are next encountered. For direct response advertising it is essential to generate a purchase intention; in other cases the ad may work without the formation of intention since people may recall their need when they are next in the purchase context; this is a routine matter for frequently purchased goods but much less common for durables where self-instructions are therefore more important.

Purchase facilitation

Work using the theory of planned behaviour (Chapter 6) has revealed how often behaviour depends on facilitating factors. Thus an important part of advertising for some products must take the form of communicating answers to questions such as 'How much does it cost? What stores sell it? How can I pay?'

Evaluating the Rossiter and Percy approach

The Rossiter and Percy approach is presented as a logical, cognitively-based account, which probably fits high involvement rather better than low involvement purchase. Rossiter and Percy support the sequence:

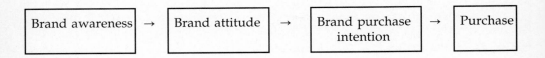

In this sequence brand awareness is a prerequisite of brand attitude. Against this account, attitude might be prior to thoughts (Fazio, Powell and Herr, 1983; Fazio, 1986). Also, brand attitude might be directly enhanced by classical conditioning when it is associated with positively evaluated stimuli such as music (Gorn, 1982) or an attractive ad (Biel, 1990). However, a study by Madden and Ajzen (1991) indicates that a positive attitude to an ad had no significant effect on the attitude to the brand. In general Rossiter and Percy give little attention to mechanisms such as dissonance reduction, framing, availability and the impact of exposure on affect. The main account is by the formation of stimulus–response connections in awareness and the apprehension of benefits.

However, Rossiter and Percy are primarily addressing a management audience which is concerned with a logically coherent basis for advertising practice. Their analysis clearly relates advertising and purchase context. Advertising in one time and place must be 'carried over' to a later purchasing context, and Rossiter and Percy specify in general terms how to incorporate purchasing conditions into the ad. When people find themselves in the purchase context, responses should be triggered by features of the context. It follows that good advertising begins with a close look at the different circumstances of brand/category purchase. We shall return to this later.

Securing attention and understanding

The subtle ways in which different ads may draw attention and deliver meaning help us to explain why equal expenditures on different campaigns can produce different sales results. Differences between campaigns have been noted by G. Brown (1985) in his review of advertising for Cadbury's *Dairy Milk* and Fry's *Turkish Delight*. Eastlack and Rao (1986) also note that a new creative approach can have more effect than an increase in advertising weight.

In extreme cases, advertising campaigns can catch the public mood and produce startling results. For example, the British advertising for *Levi 501s* (Feldwick, 1990) was very much more successful than US campaigns. In this case it was easy to see that the creativity of the British advertising was largely responsible for the different results. But it is rare that advertising has such strong effects; some guide to the effect of different advertising comes from TV copy research in which the sales effects of alternative advertisements are compared. Fulgoni (1987) found that after four months three-quarters of the copy tests done by IRI showed differences in the sales response to the two copy versions of at least 10 per cent.

Advertising can have no effect unless people notice it, but this is not enough. It is easy to grab attention by using startling material; the problem for the copywriter, however, is to find a format that demands attention but remains on the subject. If the message that is received is unrelated to the brand, it is unlikely that there will be any useful impact on sales. This issue was explored in the dissonance work of Fazio and Zanna (1978), discussed in Chapter 7, where effective attitude change required both arousal and relevant information. Copywriters therefore have to use their creative skills to draw the attention of the audience to specific matters which will assist the brand. In particular they must find ways of expressing the message within the understandings and value structures of those who see the ad.

The meaning of advertising images

Advertising is not an instruction to the recipient but a conversation, which will founder in the absence of shared meanings; for this reason the ad must be framed using ideas that make sense to the recipient. Bullmore (1984) has expressed this view most eloquently. Ads use typefaces, colours, symbols, types of people, humour, accents, contexts, etc., and these all have associated meanings which may be evoked in the recipient of the advertising. Successful ads must present a coherent set of meanings and, more than this, a message with enough interest to get through the barriers that we set up in a world prone to an excess of information.

We are all familiar with the way that evocative words and phrases catch our interest and stay with us. Poetry supplies the best examples. Andrew Marvell's lines

> But at my back I always hear
> Time's wingèd chariot hurrying near

evoke feelings of relentless time pressure far more eloquently than ordinary prose and do so very economically, a requirement of successful advertising. Similarly, snatches of music may arouse feelings and particular associations. Ads may be seen as a form of art, often aesthetically weak but sometimes subtle and stimulating. Some ads have been shot by famous film directors such as Fellini and Scorsese.

Culturally shared meanings

Poetry, like any communication, achieves its effect by touching chords in the reader and it is therefore appropriate to look at the culturally shared meanings that can be used in the communication process. Lannon and Cooper (1983) have been influential in agency circles for their redefinition of the way in which advertising works (see also Lannon, 1985). They argue that models like DAGMAR have sidetracked us into treating people as passive receivers; as a result we have neglected the way in which people process and make sense of ad messages. I think that they overstate their case here; effective advertising must leave traces in some of the individual recipients and a sensible programme of research sets out to detect these traces which must exist whether the consumer is active or passive.

In place of sequential models Lannon and Cooper (1983) have promoted the idea that advertising is culturally situated, and that it makes sense and influences people because it reflects the shared meanings in social groups and societies. They ask 'What do people do with advertising?' rather than 'What does advertising do to people?', and they argue that a person-centred anthropology of advertising is much more use to the staff who create advertisements. Lannon and Cooper argue that much advertising draws heavily on shared cultural experience. Referring to British advertising they state:

> After Eight uses the myth of the upper class, an enduring archetype; Hovis uses the myth of the industrial working class sentimentalities combined with Yorkshire stubbornness; Mr. Kipling Cakes are made by an imaginary prototypical bespoke master baker living in a bespoke calendar art cottage; Courage recreates the pub of the 1920s/1930s as the preserve of the working class male; Campari uses a modern Eliza Doolittle figure.

To someone familiar with life in Britain this quotation still makes sense, years after it was made, and shows how advertising draws on long-lived shared meanings.

More recently Lannon (1994) has noted that brands have themselves become part of everyday life and have a role in industrialized society that is similar to the symbolic meanings (e.g. about status) invested by simpler societies in shells, animals and other property. In some ways this is not new and reflects the emphases of Veblen (1899) and Goffman (1959).

The Lannon and Cooper approach has raised the importance of qualitative research in Britain because this type of investigation explores the ways in which brands are used and thought about by different social groups. It also bodes ill for attempts to produce advertisements that work well across several cultures. Because different societies place different emphases on different cultural forms, transnational advertising is forced to use the most general ideas, witness the appeals to simple human sentiment made in *Coca-Cola* ads; this restriction of advertising to the most general of feelings and ideas is likely to stifle range and creativity.

Lannon and Cooper's approach to advertising is essentially qualitative; it demands a case-by-case treatment, defends the role of creativity in advertising, and does not easily provide us with generalizations. One point of contact should be noted between Lannon and Cooper's ideas and the research reported in Chapter 7. The 'culturally shared archetype' is a *schema* which aids recognition and thought.

Semiotics

Semiology is an approach that identifies the signs used in a communication, and gives each their own set of meanings. A Barbour jacket and green wellies are not simply outdoor clothing, but convey meanings of masculinity, conservatism and a rugged love of field sports to the user, while to some non-users such items may convey the image of 'upper-class prat'. The sets of meanings inferred by semiologists draw upon psychoanalytic and political theory as well as sociology and cultural studies. We may accept that signs have residual meaning beyond their denotation and that the deliberate use of appropriate signs is therefore part of the skill of the copywriter. But this does not support the particular meanings identified in semiotics. My question to semioticians is: 'How would you know if you were wrong?' Unless they have a means of detecting and discarding mistaken interpretations of signs, their approach is intuitive and unscientific.

An intuitive approach is acceptable as a creative exercise or as a critical judgement; but if semiologists want to claim more than this and prescribe appropriate ad content, they must employ a standardized system of measurement for the meaning of signs. My guess is that this would be unhelpful. Signs do not exist on their own but in association with other signs, so that ads convey complex meanings, depending on the *mix* of signs used. Creative people combine signs in original ways to create meanings that are more than the simple addition of the meanings of individual signs; this means that the range of alternative meanings is enormous, defying systematic analysis.

Classifying ads

Effective and ineffective ads

A prevailing concern has been to find ways in which good advertisements differ from the bad. For example, Stewart and Furse (1984) found that brand differentiating factors were most important to successful advertising, while Moldovan (1984) found that credibility was most important followed by stimulation, taste, empathy and clarity. G. Brown (1986) reviewed many studies and argued that the advertisement had to be arresting to secure attention and he argued that the creative features of the ad must embrace the brand name. Brown thinks that the ad must convey the idea that experience with the brand will justify the claims in the advertisement. More recently Brown (1991) has extended this thinking and argues that good ads *involve* the potential purchaser with the brand and that this brand-linkage remains dormant until it is recalled by a relevant need or because it is recognized in the store. This does not tell us how to achieve this involvement and the suggestion is not that radical; he is stating that good

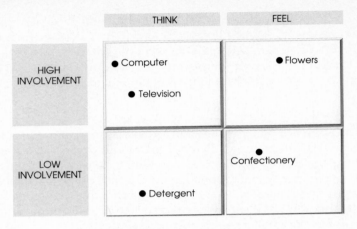

Figure 10.4 The FCB grid

advertising should make the product attractive and personally relevant; this is not a contentious proposition.

Classification grids
The comparison of good and bad ads can scarcely take account of all the different features that differentiate one market from another: target response, market concentration, brand awareness, price versus quality, novelty, range of purchasers, etc. can all vary and demand rather different emphases in copy and execution. For this reason it seems that any classification of good and bad ads must be made *within* divisions of the market since otherwise there is too much variety. In this context ad agencies have used one classification, the Foote, Cone, Belding (FCB) grid, to divide the market on a 2 × 2 cross-tabulation.

The Foote, Cone, Belding (FCB) grid (Vaughn, 1980; 1986; Ratchford, 1987) is based on the assumption that it should fit the consumer decision-making process that occurs when the product is bought. The grid uses an X-axis which divides thinking-centred decisions from feeling-centred ones, and a Y-axis that expresses high and low involvement; the two axes produce four quadrants. The grid is illustrated in Figure 10.4. Confectionery purchases might be feeling-related and low involving, while the purchase of a new television set will appear diagonally opposite as highly involving and thoughtful.

Typologies like this are needed to direct the efforts of ad agency staff but the FCB grid contains a number of confusions (Rossiter, Percy and Donovan, 1991):

■ The grid does not distinguish brand and product.
■ Thought is involved in the definition of both axes.
■ Thought and feeling are not necessarily alternatives.

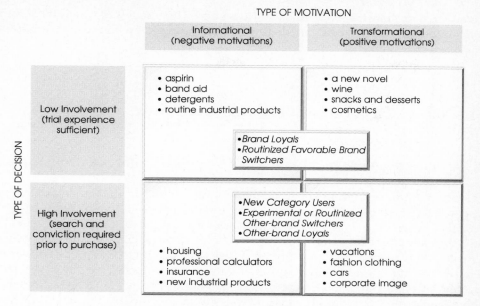

Figure 10.5 The brand attitude component of the Percy–Rossiter grid (examples are tentative and depend on specific market conditions)

■ It is not clear how the purchase type defines the ad type; just because a purchase is low involvement and feeling based does not mean that the ad must have this pattern. In Britain, cars are advertised on television with quite strongly feeling-related ads despite the fact that many people would see the car purchase decision as more thoughtful.

Rossiter and Percy (1997) offer an alternative classification to the FCB grid; Figure 10.5 shows its main features. They divide by level of involvement and argue that, typically, low involvement products appeal to those who regularly buy them as their only brand or as part of their portfolio. Thus low involvement is habitual and fits the reinforcement pattern whereas there is more scope for persuasion with the high involvement products. Rossiter and Percy also divide by whether consumers seek to reduce or turn off negative conditions such as pain and thirst, or whether they seek to enhance their lives with positive gains – for example, to enjoy an interestingly flavoured beer, master a new computing skill or achieve more personal self-expression by choice of clothes. This latter positive motivational basis is called *transformational*, a term borrowed from Wells (1984). Informational and transformation motivations make different assumptions about consumer knowledge and will therefore have a rather different content.

Rossiter and Percy's grid captures the main differentiating factors of how people choose; it can be used by practitioners to select the right content and targeting of advertising, so that it is more efficient. Kover and Abruzzo (1993) tested the Rossiter–Percy grid and found that advertising which was congruent with the grid implications was more successful.

The sales effects of advertising over time

Is the sales response to ad exposures S-shaped or downwardly concave?

The profitability of investment in advertising is dependent on the amount of sales response to an exposure. Of particular interest is the shape of the sales response of an *individual* when ad exposures are increased in a short period, such as a week. Does each exposure have less effect than the one before, producing diminishing marginal returns? Or is there a *frequency* threshold that must be crossed before the advertising achieves its full effect? In the first case the response to increments in advertising is *downwardly concave* and in the second *S-shaped*. Figure 10.6 illustrates these alternatives. This issue is very important because it relates to media variety, ad scheduling and to the price that should be paid for extra exposures. A concave shape, i.e. diminishing gains in sales with increments in exposure, means that it is better to get one exposure per buyer than two exposures to half the number of buyers. This generally means spreading advertising over time and across media. If the curve is S-shaped, advertising is most profitable when exposures exceed the threshold frequency, though in practice some consumers will receive more, and others less, than this frequency.

Early work on ad frequency by Pomerance and Zielske (1958) and Zielske (1959) compared mailings of different numbers of ads at different intervals and J.L. Simon (1979) reanalyzed their data and found that increased exposures gave diminishing returns, implying a concave response. McDonald conducted the first individual study

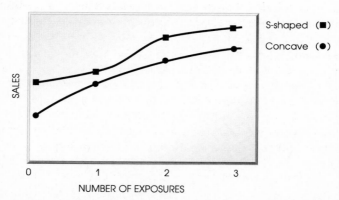

Figure 10.6 Possible relationships between sales and advertising exposures

of the effect of advertising exposure on *purchase* in a consumer panel and his data appeared to show an S-shape, though later it became apparent that the shape of the response arose from data aggregation and was not a true picture. Broadbent (1986) conducted an analysis of IRI data and found that the response to exposures was S-shaped when no allowance was made for ad decay, but linear when exposures were converted to adstock. McDonald (1995a) and Jones (1995a; 1995b; 1995c) now agree that the true pattern is concave for mature brands and that the S-shape arose from artifacts in the original study; however, the basis for their beliefs may be questioned. The problem, explained by Broadbent (1995), is that the exposure studies used by Jones (1995a) are naturally occurring and not experimental. In an experiment, two equivalent groups can be subjected to different exposure levels and, because the groups are equivalent, any difference in sales of the advertised brands can only be attributed to the exposure difference. When a difference in exposures occurs naturally between two households it is likely to be associated with different levels of television watching, as Garrick (1986b) showed. Garrick found that heavy viewers were more deal-prone and one might add that they are also more likely to be unemployed or retired, full-time housewives and belong to particular age groups. These group differences are confounded with the effects of exposure and make any inferences unreliable. Jones inferred from his data that there are diminishing marginal returns as exposures increase but this does not follow from the design of his study since the people who had two or more exposures were a different group of people from those who had one exposure.

Following Broadbent's criticism both Jones (1995d) and McDonald (1995b) replied and the reader is directed to this controversy. This matter is not resolved by other studies. Simon and Arndt (1980) reviewed laboratory experiments, field experiments and less controlled studies of ad effects. The lab experiments mostly used recall as a criterion of effect and for this reason are suspect; actual sales are a much better test so that field studies using purchase orders as the criterion are of more interest. These studies were mainly direct mail; one of the best was the earliest by Shryer (1912) who found sharply diminishing sales returns with each mail shot. In all Simon and Arndt examined thirty-seven response curves of which the great majority showed diminishing returns and only one case showed an S-shape.

Simon and Arndt concluded that the response to advertising exposures diminished with each exposure but they were at pains to point out the considerable methodological problems of research in this field. There is a problem posed by ad decay since a lapse of time diminishes the ad effect, and more exposures tend to take more time to deploy; and there is a further problem of data aggregation since individual response curves could change their shape when put together. In aggregated data we do sometimes see evidence of S-shaped response curves; e.g. an S-shaped curve was obtained for *Swan Vestas* matches (Broadbent, 1981) and for *V-8* vegetable juice (Eastlack and Rao, 1986). For commercial purposes it is very important to know the aggregate sales response to media spend, but this does not tell us much about the individual response to advertising.

There are two special circumstances that favour the S-shaped sales response:

1. When interest snowballs after the initial exposure. This would apply if the ads

were the subject of public concern, e.g. Benetton's use of shocking pictures, but we lack evidence here.

2. When the product is unfamiliar or complex and cannot easily be understood. It seems likely that new products are good candidates for threshold effects in advertising exposure, particularly when the product really does have novelty and consumers are unfamiliar with its form and function. O'Herlihy (1976) has claimed that S-shaped responses were more likely to be found with new products.

Some work at Kingston showed increased response to the second mailing of postal surveys. Postal surveys where two or more waves are used have similarities to direct mail studies of ad effect. In mail surveys the appeal associated with the first wave differs from the appeal at the second wave so that a two-wave survey is more like the presentation of two different ads for the same product. Three surveys conducted at Kingston University recorded response rates to the first and second waves. In these surveys the second wave *excluded initial responders* and gave percentage response rates which exceeded those obtained on the first wave. Table 10.1 shows the returns from the three mail studies. If the response to the second wave is calculated on the initial numbers the figures (in brackets) show a linear response pattern and if the depletion of the sample is allowed for the response is accelerating. The parallels between the survey response and media advertising response are limited but this evidence should make us wary about assuming that increments in advertising exposure always have a diminishing effect.

Table 10.1 Response rates to first and second waves in three mail surveys

Subject	Wave 1	Wave 2
Supermarkets and post offices	23	33 (25)
Banks and building societies	16	24 (20)
Supermarkets	31	36 (25)
Mean	**23**	**31** (23)

Such work does not reveal the psychological mechanisms that operate when successive exposures have either more or less effect, but it seems likely that habituation is at work when exposures produce diminishing returns; we alert to the new and not to the familiar. This is illustrated by a study by Adams (1916) which showed diminishing returns with repetition of the same ad, but increasing returns when different ads were used. Supporting this, Burnkrant and Unnava (1987) found that three different advertisements had more effect than the same advertisement presented three times. One way of varying the ads is to turn them into a 'serial'; this technique has been used in Britain and the United States to promote instant coffee.

There are also explanations for threshold effects. Krugman (1972) argued that the first exposure creates curiosity, the second recognition and the third clinches the decision, but these stages are irrelevant to buyers of established products who are already familiar with the brands. More plausibly, McDonald (1970) suggested that the main virtue of multiple exposures was to exceed the exposure rates of competitive brands and this implies that the appropriate frequency will be contingent on the level of advertising in the category.

The effect of different exposures has been reviewed by McDonald (1995c). In the advertising industry the idea of *effective frequency* (first used by Naples, 1979) has been widely held. Sometimes this refers to the impact of different numbers of ads delivered in a short period of time, discussed above, and at other times the notion covers the optimal frequency of advertising for the average inter-purchase interval of the category. There has been support for two or three exposures in an inter-purchase interval among advertising practitioners, but it is difficult to see much rationale for this.

Scheduling, media and copy implications

If extra exposures usually bring diminishing sales gains, as Jones (1995a) and others contend, then ads will be more effective if they are spread out in time. This raises doubts about the practice of beginning campaigns with heavy bursts of advertising. Simon (1979) reanalyzed some data gathered by J.B. Stewart (1964) and found that a given number of exposures worked better when spread over a longer period. However, the major analysis reported by Lodish and Lubetkin (1992) and Lodish *et al.* (1995) failed to confirm this. These authors found, as expected, that new products do well when extra advertising is concentrated rather than spread, but they also found that this pattern worked better for sales of established products and this is not easily explained.

An implication of diminishing marginal returns is that advertising money is better used when it is spread across media to give more coverage and fewer exposures per person, though sometimes this will make the targeting less accurate. In general the greater the variety of media the wider the coverage; as well as spreading coverage, the use of different media probably helps to reduce habituation effects among those who see communications on more than one medium. O'Herlihy (1983) reported that diversifying the adspend across media helps to defer the onset of saturation. Other evidence comes from nine studies in different countries, which show that it is better to spend a proportion of the budget on print rather than devote it all to television (Confer, 1992); this has been labelled the *media multiplier effect*. Lodish and Lubetkin (1992) also provide evidence that better results are obtained when schedules are designed to reach a wider audience. However, the reader should remember that more concentrated schedules may often be purchased at lower unit prices and any saving in cost may compensate for reductions in effectiveness. Also, the use of more than one medium raises the production costs of a campaign.

Lodish *et al.* (1995) also suggest that refreshing the advertising copy may bring benefits; again we can see that this may help to overcome habituation. They suggest that advertisers should run their advertising in test markets some six months ahead of the main schedule. If an upweight fails to deliver, they could try a reduction in advertising weight in the test market; after six months, if there are no sales losses the reduction can be made national whilst being maintained in the test market. Advertising can then be raised again nationally if sales start to fall in the test market. Similar advance testing can be done on new copy.

Longer-term effects of advertising

There has been a degree of agreement that advertising may have both a short-term and a longer-term effect. There is less agreement about how long these effects last and how they are related. We start with evidence gathered by IRI on the effects of extra advertising over a three-year period.

Initially, the details of the IRI research were very limited and earlier reports produced very critical comments from Bloom (1989; 1990) and Stewart (1990), which were countered by East (1991). A more recent report is given by Lodish and Lubetkin (1992). Groups of consumers were compared in an experimental format. Two groups were initially matched in terms of brand purchasing and one of the groups was then exposed to an upweight in advertising for a year (the test year). In all, forty-four brands were studied in this way (cases where there was no response to the upweight were excluded). In the following two years the groups received equal levels of advertising. This meant that differences in sales could only be attributed to the different level of advertising in the test year (or to chance fluctuations). Table 10.2 shows the results.

Table 10.2 Sales response to an upweight in test year: forty-four brands

	Test year %	Year 2 %	Year 3 %
Sales gain	22	14	7

Table 10.2 shows that sales gains were extended over a long period of time and that about the same number of extra sales occurred after the upweight had finished as during the test year. Note that these gains are secured by an upweight in established advertising; this means that the sales effect arises from increased exposures. A new product, advertised for the first time, or an old product, re-advertised after a period without advertising, would probably be more responsive to advertising.

There are two points about the figures in Table 10.2 that are at odds with assumptions that have previously been made; first, after the test year, the decline in sales effect seems to be linear rather than exponential, and second, the effect of the upweight lasts longer than had previously been supposed. In earlier work the decay in sales effect has usually been treated as exponential, falling to half its value in a specific period of time called the half-life. Broadbent (1984) stated that the half-life was usually between 3 and 11 weeks and was frequently in the narrower band of 4–6 weeks. Examples of half-lives can be found in advertising cases; e.g. *Oxo* has a half-life of four weeks while for *Andrex* the half-life is about ten weeks (Baker, 1993). Clarke (1976) reviewed seventy econometric studies and concluded that 90 per cent of the extra sales generated by the advertising of established products occurred within 3–9 months of the advertisement; this is consistent with half-lives in the range 4–12 weeks. Clearly, it is difficult to square such findings with the IRI results. Part of the problem arises from the very small effects being modelled in econometric studies of advertising, but it does seem that the way in which we have previously thought about ad effect may be mistaken. Previously adstock, the accumulated effect of advertising, was thought to be composed of two parts: a rapidly decaying short-term component and a base level that might be altered by campaigns but which was relatively constant. In his new thinking, Broadbent retains the short-term effect on sales but considers another way of conceptualizing the base level sales.

Broadbent and Fry (1995) propose a *floating base* model as an alternative way of thinking about ad effect. In this model the base is not constant, but moves up or down according to two forces: first, there are negative forces derived from the marketing support for other brands, and second, counteracting the first influence, there is an adstock with a long half-life (e.g. six months to several years). Together these forces may give the impression of a relatively stable base but, under closer scrutiny, we see that this base is floating up and down – like a hot air balloon – under the influence of the changing forces. In addition to these effects there will be an influence from short-term adstock, as before. In econometric tests this model has worked rather better than one in which a single, longer-term ad decay is postulated, but Broadbent and Fry argue that more than one model may be required to cover different market conditions. The floating base model has one clear merit. Previous thinking tended to treat adstock decay as the property of the single brand, rather like an isotope decaying, but there is no *intrinsic* reason why adstock should decay given the habitual nature of much consumer behaviour. The principal reason for decline in adstock is *extrinsic*, and occurs as a result of the marketing support for other brands; the floating base model recognizes this and could be extended to encompass all the brands in a category.

A second approach to short- and long-term ad effects is to be found in Jones' (1995a) work. You will recall that Jones used measurements of ad exposure and purchases by household. A key measure was based on household purchases of a brand over seven days in which the purchases of those who have seen an ad are compared with those who have not. The difference gives the Short Term Advertising Strength (STAS) Differential, which is indexed on 100. For seventy-eight brands the average STAS differential was 24 (i.e. a 24 per cent increase in brand purchase if households had received the ads). Thus Jones claims to demonstrate a substantial and rapid effect of advertising, but because of the non-experimental nature of this work the people who see the ad are likely to be different from those who do not, and this makes the STAS measure questionable.

Jones then relates this STAS differential to long-term growth in the brand, which he defines as share gain over a year. Overall the 24 per cent STAS gain is related to a 6 per cent annual share gain and it is the relatively few brands with large STAS differentials that see most of this gain; their advertising has allowed them to break out from the situation experienced by most brands in which their gains are cancelled out by losses to other brands. More specifically Jones finds that, of the 70 per cent cases where there is a short-term effect, 46 per cent show a long-term effect and that a long-term gain does not occur unless there is a short-term gain. In this way he claims to show that advertising can contribute to sales over a longer period (though a year is quite a short period in this context).

Jones' data could be subjected to more sophisticated analysis; until this is done his claims remain poorly substantiated, but we may speculate on one basis for short-

and long-term effects suggested by work by Givon and Horsky (1990). Advertising may produce cognitive and affective changes which have a direct effect on purchase propensity; this may be the short-term effect. Then the effect of purchasing the brand may raise the probability of subsequent repeat purchase – this is called *purchase reinforcement* and could produce a longer-term effect. (Do not confuse this purchase reinforcement – the effect of *ad-induced purchase* on later purchase – with the use of the term reinforcement by Ehrenberg (1974) and others to mean the general effect of advertising on purchase.) Thus, there may be a two-step process in which advertising gets people to make a purchase that they would not otherwise have made, and then this purchase has an effect on subsequent purchase, which will be a longer-term effect if it occurs. Givon and Horsky (1990) find that the main effect of advertising is via purchase reinforcement, but further work is required to confirm this study. Such further work may show whether purchase reinforcement does produce long-term effects but it must be noted that the concept of purchase reinforcement raises two particular problems:

1. It conflicts with sales promotion research (Chapter 4) showing little evidence of purchase reinforcement when the increased purchase occurs as a result of a sales promotion.
2. It seems unlikely that this account can work for durables where the purchase cycle is long and the trial purchase would usually be delayed, yet durables are advertised and show benefit.

Responsiveness to advertising

An understanding of how advertising works should help us to decide which brands, categories or buyers are worth supporting in this way. We note:

■ *The size of the user group.* The work by Lodish *et al.* (1995) indicates that among established brands it is the ones with large numbers of purchase occasions that benefit strongly from advertising; these are brands with high purchase frequency and penetration such as leading brands in the bread market. This fits Ehrenberg's contention that such advertising reinforces existing purchase. This does not mean that big brands show large percentage gains but it is the extra volume for a given expenditure that is important.

   This leads to further questions about the subgroup most likely to give increased sales: frequent buyers or infrequent buyers? Heavy buyers are relatively few in number and therefore may not present much potential for increased sales even if, per person, they respond more. On Lodish and Lubetkin's (1992) evidence the large tail of infrequent buyers are a good target because of their numbers; also, as we noted before, some light buyers are heavy buyers of other brands and could therefore buy much more if they shifted allegiance.

■ *Proportionate loyalty.* A study by Raj (1982) looked at gains induced by advertising in different loyalty segments; the highest gains occurred among those who were around average loyalty at 50–70 per cent. It might be thought that these gains would have been at the expense of competitors, but there was no evidence that this occurred in this study.

- *New products.* These have no user base but seem to be very responsive to advertising, perhaps because of novelty effects. The novelty of the advertising and the product means that ads are more likely to be noticed compared with more familiar ads and products.
- *The flexibility of total category consumption.* In some categories such as detergent and toothpaste there can be little variation in total category consumption; this means that brands in these fields can only gain at each other's expense. In contrast most food and confectionery brands can gain at the expense of other categories. Unpublished work by Lever Brothers in the United Kingdom has supported this assumption; the sales response to advertising was generally higher for food products than for household cleaners. Lever Brothers also found that new brands, and brands in expanding markets, tended to do well, emphasizing the scope for gains in categories without fixed limits on consumption.

Media ads versus sales promotions

In the 1980s more emphasis was placed on trade promotions than media advertising in Britain and America. Schultz (1987) reported that many US companies devoted as much as 70 per cent of expenditure to sales promotion. Broadbent (1989) quoted British trade sources to show that from 1976 to 1986 there was an increase in promotions and a reduction in the proportion of media advertising; this has worried the advertising industry and the shift of emphasis has been hotly debated. However, trade promotions are effectively price reductions imposed by retailers (see box below) and it is questionable whether these should be seen as an alternative to media spending. Also some coupon promotions are at least partly advertising.

Practitioner views

Fulgoni (1987) noted that one reason for the growth in promotion was that retailers demanded point-of-sale support as a condition for stocking a brand. He pointed out that manufacturers who accede to such pressure weaken their control over the brand and enhance the retailer's power. By comparison media advertising may build demand for a brand so that retailers need to stock it if they are to meet consumer needs. Trade discounts suit retailers; they reduce prices at the supplier's expense and the retailer may be able to stockpile brands at trade discount for later sale at a higher price. In the store, discounts may build traffic when they are a regular feature, but Walters and Rinne (1986) found no evidence that the sales of non-promoted items were affected by promotions for other goods in the store.

Schultz (1987) suggested that short-term thinking favoured discounts because they deliver rapid increases in sales, albeit at reduced margins. He also noted that difficulty in demonstrating the effect of advertising made it less attractive to managers.

Ogilvy (1987), in characteristically trenchant style, castigated the same short-term thinking and argued that the reduction in media advertising meant that brand equity would languish to the long-term detriment of sales and market control. There is a danger that repeated price promotions will diminish the perceived value of the brand and eventually reduce market share.

In their favour, discounts do help managers to fine-tune sales in the short term and thus avoid overstocking and staff layoffs, but the best justification for sales promotions would be that they give a better return than media advertising. At one time this was widely believed, but now evidence is taking the place of guesswork. As reported above, Lodish and Lubetkin (1992) have shown that media advertising can bring extra sales in the years following the campaign and this raises the attractiveness of ads. By contrast, the effect of sales promotions seems to be largely restricted to the period when they operate, as discussed in Chapter 4. Lodish and Lubetkin refer to work on the profitability of trade promotions; they did not have full data on these operations but their available information suggested that less than 20 per cent of trade promotions gave a greater return than their cost. When we couple this work with the new evidence on the substantial long-term effects of advertising, we see a considerably stronger case for investment in advertising. Thus research has begun to reinforce the case for media spending.

Summary

The varied nature of advertising makes the search for explanation difficult. Ads take a variety of forms and so do the relevant products, purchase situations and target groups. When a number of processes are in play explanation will inevitably be complex. However a rather clearer account of ad effects is emerging, particularly because of developments in measurement using panel data.

In the United States and Germany the effect of advertising on sales can be measured with techniques that control the transmission of commercials and use the scanner records of purchase in local stores. This system has shown that many ads fail to influence sales. In other countries pure experiments on copy, ad weight and scheduling are not possible but effects can be evaluated using regional comparisons and econometric analysis.

Effective advertising raises profit in comparison with the level that would have been achieved without the advertising. Often this means that sales are largely static since one brand's advertising cancels the effect of advertising for other brands. When sales movements do occur they are usually modest, but occasionally campaigns catch the interest of their audience and large gains occur. Profit is also raised by the maintenance of price margin; advertising may assist here by raising brand reference price so that consumers are less price-sensitive. High levels of advertising in the category are thought to make consumers better informed about the market which may raise price sensitivity and lower prices.

Explanations of how advertising achieves its effect have tended to emphasize the rational, cognitive and persuasive aspects and to understate the impact of associative processes such as brand name repetition, mere exposure and classical conditioning, which probably play a large part in low involvement purchase. Early sequential models show a number of flaws, but some sequence must occur between exposure in one context and purchase in another. Sequential models focus concern on the *processing* of ads and the securing of *attention*. Petty and Cacioppo (1985) have suggested two different information processing routes corresponding to the high and low involvement situations. Ehrenberg (1974) has argued that ads mainly influence those already purchasing (in fmcg markets). Rossiter and Percy (1997) have emphasized the building of brand awareness and the forging of brand associations with category need and purchase context cues; this last approach helps to specify ad content and is of much value to practitioners.

Attention to an ad depends on the creativity of the copywriter who has to arrest attention in a relevant and succinct way. Creativity is by definition innovative and rule-breaking, and therefore difficult to study, but Lannon and Cooper have emphasized the way in which copywriters draw on cultural forms for conveying ideas and feelings, while semioticians have drawn attention to components of the ad which have 'residual meanings' for people.

There have been efforts to refine the classification of purchase decisions (and by implication copy design) beyond the dimension of involvement. The FCB grid divides the purchase decision by degree of involvement and by reference to whether it is primarily cognitive or affective. Rossiter and Percy also use involvement and divide the decision further by reference to the type of motivation involved – positive or negative (avoidance). There are some problems with these grids – for example, it might be asked why the ad, delivered in one context, has to reflect the character of a purchase decision made in another context. However, there is some support for the idea that ads that fit the Rossiter–Percy classification perform better.

A prevailing concern in advertising has been the optimum number of exposures in a short period. Is there a threshold number of exposures that must be exceeded before the ads have much impact on sales? The research on this matter has been confused. It requires evidence on the response of *individuals* (not groups) to different numbers of ads delivered over a short period of time. Early work was untypical of the sales response to media advertising and more recent work has not compared equivalent samples. It seems likely that there are circumstances in which there is a threshold of effect (e.g. for new or complex products), but that for many familiar products there is no threshold and the response to advertising diminishes with each exposure. This work has important implications for media spending; if there is no threshold, advertising is best spread over media and over time. There is evidence to support widening the media range but, inexplicably, Lodish and Lubetkin (1992) found that a *concentration* of exposures generally worked better in the United States.

Another issue with major cost implications is the duration of effect of advertising. It used to be thought that the ad impact on sales was relatively short-term with decay half-lives not exceeding three months. Recent research on upweights has indicated that the effect of advertising can still be observed a year later and that decay is more linear than exponential; this indicates that advertising has a longer effect and is a better investment than had been supposed.

Some brands respond more to advertising than others. It seems likely that brands with large user bases benefit more. Also new brands often do well.

Spending on trade promotions has been rising for many years and there have been worries about the impact of this trend on media advertising. Recent evidence has tended to favour media spending, particularly the evidence of longer-term effects.

Further reading

Lodish, L.M., Abraham, M., Kalmansen, S., Livelsberger, J., Lubetkin, B., Richardson, B. and Stevens, M.E. (1995) How T.V. advertising works: A meta-analysis of 389 real world split cable T.V. advertising experiments, *Journal of Marketing Research*, 32:2, 125–39.

Lodish, L.M., Abraham, M.M., Livelsberger, J., Lubetkin, B. and Stevens, M.E. (1995) A summary of fifty-five in-market experimental estimates of the long-term effect of TV advertising, *Marketing Science*, 14, 3, Part 2 of 2, G133–G140. This paper updates the forty-four brand study and adds further technical analysis.

A series of papers in *Admap* over 1995 by Jones, McDonald and Broadbent, respectively.

McDonald, C. (1992) *How Advertising Works*, Henley-on-Thames, The Advertising Association and NTC Publications, is a very readable book though already a little out of date.

The Rossiter–Percy model is described in Rossiter, Percy and Donovan (1991) and at greater length in Rossiter and Percy (1997) *Advertising Communications and Promotion Management*. Read Chapters 5 and 6.

The *Advertising Works* series is of great interest (Broadbent, 1981; 1983; Channon, 1985; 1987; Feldwick, 1990; 1991; Baker, 1993; 1995).

Chapter 11

Postscript: Some policy implications of consumer behaviour

Overemphasis on the cognitive model

Throughout this book I have drawn attention to the weakness of 'the cognitive model'. By this I mean the explanation of consumer and other forms of behaviour as the outcome of processes that assemble all alternatives, apply logical rules of self-interest, use careful cognitive processing, and give equal attention to each option. In contrast, I have emphasized that people often do not appraise alternatives and may simply act in accordance with established habit; when they do consider alternatives, they usually consider only one at a time and usually take the first alternative that is adequate; thought processes are often better explained as heuristic mechanisms rather than as logical processes, and behaviour is often rooted in the consumer's environment which initiates many of the cognitive processes that do occur.

When we look at consumer behaviour we find that people:

- Often do not know the price of the goods that they are buying.
- Leave money in investment accounts that offer low and uncompetitive interest rates.
- Do not reclaim tax rebates to which they are entitled.
- Do not use relevant information from Consumer Associations, newspapers, etc. about products or investments.
- Remain loyal to brands over long periods, even when there are better brands, or when they rate their brand poorly in a blind test.
- Are constrained by the views of others and by limited knowledge about how to acquire products.
- Often do not complain to the supplier, or switch to another, when their purchases are unsatisfactory.
- Can be swayed by descriptions that 'frame' an issue in different ways.
- Are enticed by advertising that contains little descriptive content on product benefits.

Some people will see this catalogue of consumer practice as diminishing the powers of human beings. I take an opposite view: our control of our outcomes is low if we misunderstand how our behaviour comes about, and it is increased by a realistic understanding of the bases of human action. Once we recognize how we and others come to decide and act as we do, we have more scope for change – both individually and collectively. We see this gain in control in behaviour therapy where people are taught to manage their environment and thereby to control their behaviour. Instead of struggling against the desire to overeat, smoke or spend compulsively, the self-therapist alters the contextual stimuli and reinforcers that control his or her behaviour so that the desire is less strong. Many of those who have used such techniques find them liberating; by understanding how they and others act, people gain control because they can then see what to do in order to bring about change. If people overestimate the extent to which actions are carefully thought through, they will miss the real causes of behaviour and have less power to influence themselves and others.

Instigating change

Although everyday purchasing is routine, predictable and much controlled by environmental cues, it is not irrational; people have reasons for acting habitually. These reasons are not rehearsed each time people buy; instead they economize on their time by buying fairly automatically. In so doing, they often meet their needs quite well but may miss innovations and may not notice defects in the products that they consume because they have become so used to them. Suppliers benefit from such loyal behaviour when it is their product that is being bought but, conversely, consumer loyalty makes it difficult for other suppliers to break into markets with a technically superior product.

A worthwhile objective of consumer policy is to encourage the adoption of beneficial innovations but this is frustrated if consumer habits create resistance to new products. The problem is all the greater if policy-makers blithely assume that competitive processes are swift and sure and easily lead to the dominance of the better product. Consumers do not beat a pathway to your door when you make a better product unless you can somehow cause them to reappraise their existing pattern of purchasing. Perhaps it is in the public interest to disrupt loyalty and cause people to question their behaviour more?

There are arguments on both sides of this issue. On the one hand, we need a discriminating consumer public so that genuine product improvements are rewarded by shifts in consumption, and poor products are pushed off the market by lack of interest; on the other hand, manufacturers want to see a return on the capital that they have invested in product development, and volatile consumers could reduce returns and make manufacturers reluctant to invest. This problem focuses our attention on the extent to which consumers are volatile; we know (Chapter 2) that perhaps about 15 per cent lose allegiance to a brand in a year so change does occur, but there are a great many reasons for these changes and in many cases consumers will not be moving purposively to a product that is believed to be better. Competitive processes do not usually work strongly in favour of the better product and there is a case for measures which *enhance* the operation of competition.

The belief that competition resolves market-place problems to the advantage of consumers is part of our culture. It is preferred on the political right, and arguments in its favour can be found in the writings of many economists. But although economists must take some large measure of blame for this aspect of the 'cognitive model' of consumer behaviour, I do not wish to lay simplistic charges at their door. Many of them are just as interested in reckoning with the realities of consumer behaviour as I am. None the less, the discipline does use assumptions about rational choice that only too easily become articles of faith. Consider the introduction to a text on the economic theory of choice:

> Apples or pears? Guns or butter? Liberty or death? We experience life as a series of choices, large and small. (Heap *et al.*, 1992)

To my mind this is fanciful; we do not think like this. Displaced from the choice situation we may describe behaviour in this way, but we should not confuse such descriptions with the mechanisms that direct behaviour.

The main thrust of economics is normative. The subject specifies what a rational planner would do, given knowledge about the alternatives and some order of preference about outcomes. Usually predictions from such assumptions are tested at an aggregate level but this provides a poor test of the truth of the assumptions at an individual level since a variety of conditions could produce the aggregate outcomes. It is argued that selection processes favour the more calculating agents in a society, for example, arbitrageurs in share markets, and this leads to their behaviour becoming the dominant form; however, there is evidence from framing research that suboptimal biases persist. Rational choice models are of use as norms against which actual behaviour is compared. This comparison helps us to see what factors guide behaviour but it would be a mistake to suppose that actual behaviour is somehow deficient if it differs from the rational assumption. We saw in the treatment of planned behaviour (Chapter 6) that intentions and behaviour were often associated with social reference and with perceived control – factors that may be left out of a rational analysis. Also prospect theory and the concept of framing (Chapter 7) have helped to explain discrepancies between human behaviour and economic assumptions.

Taking a wider perspective

The enlargement of the economic perspective has become the province of *economic psychologists*, who have taken an interest in the way in which psychological research illuminates economic issues. These people share the theories of consumer behaviour researchers but tend to focus on rather different problems. Economic psychologists such as Lewis, Webley and Furnham (1995) have cast light on gambling, compulsive shopping, the impact of poverty and unemployment, tax evasion and on the way money is perceived. Their agenda is set by economic and social problems and they do not address the more trivial (but profit related) low involvement behaviours that have concerned many consumer behaviour researchers.

Academic disciplines permeate and help to form the thinking of policy-makers. In social welfare, for example, social scientists have had an influence and political thinkers may occasionally affect decisions on the form of political institutions. However the dominant discipline in policy-making has been that of economics. Keynesian ideas and more recently those of the monetarists have held sway over economic policy; as emphases change in economics the ascendant thinking touches the lives of most members of society. By general reckoning the Keynesian revolution in the 1930s helped to develop the West; rather more doubt may be felt about the monetarist regimes of the 1980s – perhaps these were a necessary retrenchment, or maybe they were a lost opportunity as more people were thrown out of work and ceased to contribute to the development of the economy.

Economists differ in their willingness to support intervention in the working of the economy by government. For some, the free market decides; intervention is likely to be ineffectual, or distorting, and governments should do little but set central bank interest rates and tax levels; even attempts to control exchange rates produce artificialities and may in any case be swamped by market forces. For other economists, there is no such thing as a free market since governments control the legal and institutional environments which circumscribe economic activity. From this standpoint, governments may intervene usefully in job training, regional development and in a host of other ways that provide a degree of central planning to the economy. Well-educated, thoughtful people may be able to anticipate economic needs rather better than a market that operates on a much shorter timescale. For example, the growth of France in the 1980s and 1990s probably owed much to the earlier improvements in the infrastructure of roads, rail, telephone, water and power which had been overseen by a civil service of notable quality.

In recent years the beliefs of free market economists have been dominant, and many economies have moved away from central planning and towards market-driven provision. One consequence of this thinking has been the movement of state assets from the public sector to the private sector; in Britain, most of the possible transfers from public ownership have been completed while in other countries programmes are just beginning, and there has been a widespread acceptance that this is the way forward. These transfers of ownership provide revenue for governments and weaken the hold of unions, but the principal justification has been that the private sector is more responsive to market forces and is better driven by consumer preference than any state institutions. This argument was given force by the spectacular collapse of the USSR and Eastern European centrally planned economies which manifestly failed to serve the economic interests of their peoples. It is not my wish to reverse this trend but rather to note some of the problems, and to relate the new order to consumer behaviour.

More competition

When public services are unsatisfactory, or inefficient, the problem of effective control can be approached by freeing the market, increasing competition and facilitating switching between suppliers. A problem here is that there are areas of public activity that are not amenable to competition so that transfers of ownership in such areas may not help much.

One example is transport deregulation; in Britain, a survey by the Metropolitan Authorities showed that the policy was associated with substantial increases in fares and a 12.5 per cent reduction in patronage (*The Independent*, 2 September 1988). Transport systems are interdependent with one part of the system providing passengers to other parts; because of this, they may work better when parts of the system are subsidized by other parts. Deregulation can produce piecemeal competition that destroys cross-subsidy. In other circumstances the competition becomes an episode that leads the way to monopoly. This has occurred between bus companies where the stronger firm has destroyed the business of the weaker and taken control. Similarly in hospital cleaning the winning tender gains a monopoly for a period of time, and when this has elapsed some of the original competitors are no longer around.

Another difficult area has been the requirement that hospitals compete for referrals. Although this applies a pressure to provide medical services efficiently it is also necessary to create marketing departments to sell these services; this is a function that sits uneasily with health provision and is an additional cost to the hospital.

In Britain, the transfer to private ownership has often occurred before break-up in the monopoly status of the industry and this has required more state control with regulators being appointed to police the more profit-conscious private enterprises that are created. Downward pressure on prices has been effected for the most part through regulation, not competition. In Britain, these private monopolies have created more profit by substantial workforce reduction; the cost of this, in unemployment benefits, then falls on the taxpayer.

Even when the industry is open to competition the established player appears to have a major advantage. After twelve years of competition, British Telecom still had 90 per cent of the market. When British Gas had to compete in South-West England, and its rivals offered 25 per cent discounts, there were few takers (*The Guardian*, 23 April 1996). Some of this lack of competition relates to the power of the large incumbent company, but it also indicates the advantage of having consumer inertia on your side. The more effective route to competition is to break up the incumbent – this was the US strategy in telecommunications.

So, the benefits of privatization vary from application to application and may have costs that can make this approach less attractive as a means of stimulating competition.

Competition in private industry

Even those markets that are supposed to be competitive may not be so. In Britain, the prices of white goods appear to be artificially maintained by restrictions on distribution. In Europe, most air travel is expensive compared with trans-Atlantic flights, in large measure because of inter-government agreements. In other areas prices are supported by implicit agreements among suppliers and these unofficial arrangements are only exposed when interlopers step in and create real competition – for example, the entry of the supermarkets to petrol retailing has pushed prices down in France and Britain. The supply of housing finance in Britain also appears to have been uncompetitive; a stockbroking analyst, Rob Thomas, claimed that, in the early 1990s, building societies were charging borrowers about 1 per cent more than they needed, given the cost of money (*The Guardian*, 3 February 1996). In the United Kingdom, mortgages are provided by a mix of building societies and banks, and there seemed no good reason why their rates were not more competitive.

The virtues of competition are twofold: it exerts a downward pressure on prices and an upward pressure on quality; extra quality can be a competitive advantage to a company, allowing it to maintain higher prices than competitors. The pressure for quality leads to better products which can compete in wider markets, give greater consumer satisfaction and probably produce more jobs. It is more attractive to raise quality than to lower prices. A narrow price perspective can lead to price wars that leave no resources free for developing the product. Heil and Helsen (1995) suggest that such price wars are generally damaging to companies and it could be argued that, in the long run, they do not serve consumer interests.

This brief review is intended to show that competition often does not occur, either because monopolies continue, or because implicit trade agreements and consumer inertia restrict it. The implication of this thinking is that much more attention needs to be given to:

- Driving competitive processes so that consumers take advantage of opportunities more readily.
- Producing the effects of competition in organizations, whether or not these organizations operate in a free market.

Management and organization

Competition puts organizations and their employees in a position in which individual rewards and costs are more often related to performance. In non-competitive organizations it is also possible to create the same regime by designing the organizational structure appropriately, ensuring that the customer voice is heard and that employee performance is related to the quality and quantity of the product provided. Goods and services that are inadequate can be improved when providers consult their users and know when their products are unsatisfactory. This approach uses regulation, targets, feedback on performance and incentives within the organization to ensure that employee standards are high. In this field total quality management has helped to define good organizational procedures. Critics of this approach can point to budgetary constraints that prevent management action in state monopolies, but these also occur in private industry. And it is clear that some state enterprises can improve.

Often there is a reluctance to change, and the rigidities that are found in management and the workforce have the same origins as the inertia that can be detected in consumer behaviour. Both involve limitations of thinking and the settled acceptance of habitual practice. Both can be changed. If managers ensure direct feedback about products, and individual careers depend in part on the satisfaction of customers, an organization that is not technically competitive (post office, passport office, local government department) can operate very effectively. This thinking requires some fairly direct relationship between pay, promotion and performance.

More regulation

Governments and their agencies frame the rules within which public activity takes place and this can have an effect on efficiency. Government legal enactions and administrative changes often affect consumer opportunities: freer trade by the elimin-ation of border restrictions, rules against monopolies and restrictive agreements, control of interest and exchange rates, the resourcing of the public sector, privatization of public assets, laws on labelling and shop hours; all of these impact upon the choices available to the citizen.

Despite the views of the free market purist, there is an important role for government regulations that will *raise* competition. Rules against cartels are a well-established example of this (though their effectiveness may be questioned). Competition can be raised by other regulations; for example by:

- Price displays using standardizing notices in all sales contexts where display is feasible. French cafés, which show the prices of what they sell on a board behind the bar, are a good example of this.
- Prohibiting business practices that capitalize on consumer inertia; e.g. payment orders that are not date-restricted, or building society accounts where the interest is reduced without publicity.
- Requiring that the procedure for redress is printed on the reverse of receipt notes and that medium and large firms keep records of complaints, detail them in annual reports and specify the company response to identified problem areas.
- Insisting that service-switching costs are minimized by cooperation between the loser and gainer in a switch, e.g. that banks make transfer of bank accounts easy.
- Making the charges of financial agencies such as unit trusts, and the bonuses of staff in all profit-making organizations, relate to the long-term investment per-formance of the firm (compared with other firms in the same field).
- Restricting the level of charges when consumer choice is limited, e.g. on rail transport, cable services.
- Raising access to information. Increasingly, state organizations such as schools and hospitals are publishing data on their performance. In other areas the state has a role in specifying comparison standards and requiring standardized information (such as the annual interest for hire purchase agreements).

There is also a case for controlling practices which add to total manufacturing costs. For example, everyday low pricing is reckoned to save on costs such as management time that raise average prices paid by the consumer. Restrictions on price promotions might be of general benefit. Against such a proposal is the claim that promotions allow those with little money to stretch their resources by buying only on deal. This neglects the fact that those with little income may not be able to take advantage of cheap offers by buying ahead, as Andreasen (1991) points out. Generally, the poor get a raw deal on their purchases compared to those who are better off and a predictable environment might be of more use to them than one with unpredictable benefits that they cannot easily use. There may also be a case for restricting loyalty schemes that tend to be copied by competitors and, in the end, just add to costs.

Even more radical might be the removal of brands from the market in certain areas. In financial investment, people would benefit if the instruments that consistently performed poorly in their investment categories were barred and the assets transferred to those with better investment skills. Unfortunately, the control of financial organizations has usually been seen as a legal field where emphasis is placed on the prevention of fraud rather than the promotion of efficiency. In Britain, the legal requirements attaching to the sale of financial products have added to costs and there is little evidence that they have reduced malpractices such as insider dealing.

Using advertising

It is also possible to influence consumers so that they are more price vigilant and quality conscious; changes here will exert pressure on suppliers with the most receptive firms profiting from the changes while consumers benefit from better value for money. In addition to this, there is a potential benefit to the economy as a whole. Western nations have seen rising unemployment in the 1990s as governments struggle to contain inflation and state spending. Their principal weapon has been high interest rates, which add to the cost of borrowing by industry and individuals. Often, younger members of society at a productive stage in their careers are heavily burdened while older citizens with investment income benefit from rising interest rates. Control on interest rates is a blunt instrument in the battle against inflation. Those with capital may spend more, so that the effect on the economy of an interest rate rise is mixed, even though it is predominantly deflationary.

A direct approach to consumers, influencing them to consume more advantageously, is a strange idea for economists and others who are used only to macro-controls. My proposal is to advertise to consumers (and industrial buyers), and to urge them to look for quality and good value, to assert their rights and demand redress when a product fails. It is likely that if more people were more demanding in this way there would be some impact on prices and therefore on inflation. This suggestion simply extends an already established use of advertising in the social sphere. If we can use ads to improve health, raise safety and limit energy waste, surely we can also use ads to encourage price and quality competitiveness? And why should a method that is well accepted in business not have a use in the management of the national economy? The reluctance to try such methods is itself a kind of habit; we have become used to the idea that the control of economies is achieved through tax and interest changes and it seems bizarre to suggest that a population could respond to such advertising;

my own view is that such advertising would be pushing on an open door, that it would make consumers significantly more critical, and could have appreciable effects on the economy as a whole. But we will not find out unless we try it.

Further reading

A.R. Andreasen (1991) Consumer behavior research and social policy. In T.S. Robertson and H.H. Kassarjian (eds.) *Handbook of Consumer Behavior*, Englewood Cliffs, NJ, Prentice Hall, 459–506.

Appendix

Research: Issues and methods

The dissertation

Many first degrees and most higher degrees require students to present a dissertation or long report. Often a proposal of intended work is required before the dissertation proper. This type of work forces the student to be more pro-active; it can be very demanding and stressful, but it is also very satisfying for some students and gives them an opportunity to establish an area of expertise that they may later apply in their work.

There are a number of books that assist students to manage this type of work but these are detailed and may carry more than students require. Initially, students want something more succinct, which applies to their particular concerns but, since they are all doing different studies, it is hard to standardize. None the less I have found that certain elements of advice are frequently needed and the material below, in note form, seems to be generally helpful. Much of it is about managing the work and writing it up but I have also included notes on questionnaire design since this type of research is often used by students.

Proposal

Often an initial proposal of work is required. This should cover:

- the question(s) you seek to answer,
- the main research findings so far,
- the topics your proposed research relates to,
- proposed research methods and analysis,
- sponsors, necessary cooperation, resources,
- timings for the work that take realistic account of your time.
- supervisor's agreement.

Finding the research question

This is a substantial part of the work, so do not get too agitated if it is hard to establish a topic. Try to:

- Think of more than one possibility.
- Search for evidence, talk to people, anticipate problems, *write down* what you want to do, go through it with your supervisor.
- If your initial idea is too sweeping, look for sub-questions.
- Part-time students should be careful about using narrow work problems as their object of study. What is the wider issue?

As you settle on a question:

- Search for the 'key paper': a recent study that summarizes the research in the field (ACR Proceedings, not available through computer searches, are often useful here).
- Are there related problems? What is the theory? What methods should be employed for investigation?
- Distinguish between trade hype and objectivity. Trade articles are good for showing the marketing relevance of the problem, but are not sound evidence.

Some check questions

- Is the topic interesting?
- Does it lead to specific hypotheses or questions?
- Is it useful (e.g. as expertise in your career)?
- Can good cooperation be expected from the work organizations involved?
- Is it related to course work?
- Is there a suitable supervisor?
- How long will the work take? (Usually underestimated.)
- How accessible is the existing research? Is it confidential?
- Has the topic already been explored? This could be a good sign, but you need to know about it.
- If you are prone to stress, how will you handle this? Realistic programming of your time helps.
- Do you want to use non-standard formats such as video or computer programs in the presented work? Discuss this with your supervisor.

Writing up

Good work rises above the level of factual accuracy and:

- Identifies focal issues.
- Employs novel methods and interesting applications.
- Shows deficiencies in other work.

- Is open about weaknesses in presented work.
- Draws connections between different bodies of work and proposes further research.
- Is clearly and interestingly expressed.

Often you need a 'dialogue with your data'; sometimes it is not apparent what to make of findings from surveys and you may need to give yourself time to reflect on the evidence.

- Start early, you will need the time.
- Think out the structure of your report, but be willing to change.
- Try to relate the empirical work and the literature review, often the first is not effectively introduced by the second.
- Go for brevity, clarity, interest.
- Cite references properly (avoid numerals in text, use author, date).
- Present tables properly (see below).
- Use your spellchecker.

Figures and tables

Ehrenberg (1986) has made useful suggestions about using tables in reports:

- Give marginal averages or comparison norms to provide a visual focus.
- Make comparisons by column.
- Order rows and columns by key factors or averages and retain this order across a series of tables.
- Round to two effective digits.
- Use the layout to guide the eye and help comparisons.
- Give brief verbal summaries to the main patterns and exceptions.

Also:

- Simplify by aggregation, and by leaving out. It is much easier to compare two columns than three or more.
- Tables versus charts. Practitioners are devoted to pie charts and histograms which add nothing that is not given by a clear table. Temporal trends need graphical presentation for best effect though.
- Use diagrams to assist the reader's comprehension; you may also scan in pictures if they are relevant.

Making the prose readable

- Use short, common words, present tense where appropriate, bold type and italics.
- Avoid negatives, long and compound sentences.
- Do use quotations, examples, illustrations if they are *relevant*.
- Sometimes repetition and agenda-setting help. Be wary of humour, you and the reader may not see things the same way.

■ Get the order right – in sentences and in the whole work.
■ If in doubt, cut.
■ When revising, try to leave it for a while, try reading it aloud or get someone else to read it.
■ You may find that the grammar checkers in wordprocessing packages are useful.
■ Your prose may be clear but a bit 'dead'. Good style is not within the scope of these notes but try to give special attention to summaries and opening paragraphs, which are so much more important than the rest. I give below two openers, one of which elicits far more interest than the other:

> I went down yesterday to the Piræus with Glaucon the son of Ariston, that I might offer up my prayers to the goddess; and also because I wanted to see in what manner they would celebrate the festival, which was a new thing. (Plato, *The Republic*)

> In writing this brief discussion of some problems of the philosophy of social science, I have addressed those who may have a special interest in appropriate areas of philosophy, as well as those who have some technical interest in substantive problems of theory construction and validation in any of the social sciences. (Rudner, *Philosophy of Social Science*)

■ The following is Ehrenberg's (1982) example of prose that could be made more readable:

> In the UK and throughout the western world a rapidly growing proportion of young people appears to be faced with the almost certain prospect of periods of prolonged unemployment, brought about by fundamental changes in the structure of industry and commerce. However, many young people currently in employment find that a lack of initial basic educational skills, together with a lack of access to training facilities at work, means that their ability to adapt to these changes is also very restricted.

> How would you improve this passage? You can compare your changes with those suggested by Ehrenberg (1982).

Investigation

Questions

(Comments on these questions are found in later pages.)

■ Why do you have more confidence in a finding that you predicted than one which you discovered when searching through data? Can you explain why a predicted finding is of more value than one derived from *post hoc* analysis?
■ The forty-four brand experiment reported by Lodish and Lubetkin used only those brands that showed a positive sales response to advertising. Was this good practice? Can you explain why more random error is found at the extremes of a distribution?
■ In a survey it was found that people who shop at out-of-town supermarkets buy 25 per cent more than those who go to other supermarkets. It was suggested that the larger out-of-town stores carry a wider range of merchandise and induce more spending. Have you any other explanations?

Experiments

■ The experimental design allows you to infer causal relationships by holding constant all factors except the independent variable, X. O_1, O_2 are measures of the dependent variable which may be affected by X.

■ Simple experiment:

$$\text{Group 1} \qquad X \qquad O_1$$
$$\text{Group 2} \qquad \qquad O_2$$

If the samples are drawn from the same population $O_1 - O_2$ must be due to X or to chance variation in the samples. The statistical analysis identifies the probability that it is chance variation.

■ What is wrong with the pre-test post-test design using one group?

$$O_1 \qquad X \qquad O_2$$

The problem here is that O_1 may affect responses to X so that you effectively have two independent variables: X and X after O_1.

■ Experiments can be used in business research to test alternatives in advertising, direct mail, packaging, product alternatives, etc.

Problems with experiments

■ Often you cannot do them; sometimes a quasi-experiment is possible – i.e. the sampling is not random or other aspects of control are lacking.

■ Problem of representativeness, particularly if done under unrealistic conditions: will the results generalize to other populations, variables and situations?

■ Experiments give few findings. Appropriate when predictions can be made. Often preliminary investigations are best made with surveys which give lower grade results but more of them.

Surveys

■ Sometimes described as the method of the amateur but actually a very demanding procedure.

■ Define the target group and the objectives.

■ How can this group be approached? Will this meet the research objectives?

■ Remember the limitations of:
  – non-response,
  – comprehension of items,
  – cost.

■ Some surveys are exploratory, but you have to anticipate the use that you will be making of the findings and make sure that you have the right questions. If questions do not cover alternative interpretations of results there is little that can be concluded. For example, the extra spend in out-of-town supermarkets (reported above) may not be due to the store range but may relate to car use, frequency of shopping and the proportion of heavy shoppers drawn to such stores. If measures of these factors are included it is possible to disentangle the alternative explanations.

■ If you conduct a survey, start the analysis using frequencies. Using the output, you may aggregate some values and can see whether responses are adequately spread. Next it is likely that you will cross-tabulate using certain key variables. Then, when you have a good idea of the main findings, discuss the results with your supervisor and consider other tests.

Using questionnaires

Questionnaire delivery

The alternatives are:

■ *Mail*: self-administered, response rates can be good for popular subjects but the questions must be simple. This method is cheap, slow and quite easily programmed. A second wave is advised (to those who have not responded to the first wave) and this may give as many responses as the first. In Britain, the Postcode Address File or the Electoral Register can be used for sample selection from the general population. A mail questionnaire should look quite short, even if it is not, by careful use of space, fonts, columnization, etc.

■ *Street, mall*: interviewer administered, difficult to secure representativeness, suitable only for short questionnaires with limited response range, flash cards aid response, quick.

■ *Home visit*: Expensive, time-consuming, suitable for long questionnaires and ones where the responses cannot be pre-listed, interviewer security problems.

■ *Conference, hall*: Can be cheap and quick and may catch many members of the target group at once. Group administration can be used to present products, ads, etc., which are being investigated but social influence between respondents can be a problem.

■ *Telephone*: Fast, cheap, omits those without telephone but random digit dialling gets the ex-directory subscribers, CATI (computer assisted telephone interviewing) is now standard in commercial work.

Computer advantages

Computers using proprietary software can rotate item orders to reduce order effects in responding. The computer checks that the response is within the range, uses earlier responses to particularize later items, does skips automatically, computes individual scores and can produce a running tally of results. It saves on coding and punching, and speeds up the survey; it may be interviewer applied, usually on the telephone but can also be self-administered.

Computer interviewing reduces errors in the interview and processing but has hazards of its own, particularly programming errors and lost data on computer crashes.

Structuring the questionnaire

There are two sorts of statement in a questionnaire:

1. *Directions* such as 'tick one', 'If YES, go to question 7' and 'Please turn over'.
2. *Items* such as 'Do you own a sun bed? Yes [1] No [2]'.

Directions need careful phrasing. Do not forget:

- 'Please answer *every* question'.
- 'Tick box', 'tick one only', 'circle number'.
- 'Your answers will be treated in confidence'.
- 'Thank you for your help'.
- 'When completed please send to ...' (even when a return envelope is supplied).

Items have two parts:

1. The *question*, such as 'Are you worried about skin cancer?'; and
2. The *response format* such as 'Yes [1] No [2]'.

- Response formats are usually pre-coded with numbers or letters to make data entry easy.
- The *sequence* of questions. The questionnaire should show a progression that interests the respondent so that he/she is motivated to answer further questions. Sudden jumps should be avoided or prefaced e.g. 'Now could you give us the following information about yourself?'

Framing questions

Questions fail because they are:

Ambiguous

- 'Do you use the sun bed often?' Use specific time periods in a response format such as 'Once a month'. Try to avoid 'usually', 'only', 'often' and 'all'.
- 'Is skin cancer a risk?' Risks vary – so be more specific.
- 'Have you ever felt bad because you were unfaithful to your partner?' Two questions in one.

Leading

- 'Do you agree with the expert finding ...?'
- 'Do you agree that a person has the right to smoke?'
- 'Wouldn't you say ...?'

Not understood

Because they are too long, or contain long or unfamiliar words, negatives, subjunctives. Try to avoid long and complex sentences employing 'and', 'or', 'unless'. Generally make items short, words simple, use the positive form and the present tense.

Understood in different ways

Items may mean different things to different people and are not then a valid measure of the concept. This may be revealed when you test out the questionnaire with potential respondents.

Response formats

These should be familiar and predictable. People get into a rhythm when they fill out a questionnaire and you should not break this rhythm. So, where possible, instruct people to respond in the same way for each question, e.g. don't go from 'tick one' to 'tick two' and then back to 'tick one'.

Open formats (allowing free expression) should be used for:

- Getting salient thoughts, e.g. What is the most important thing about a holiday in Australia?
- When there are too many responses to itemize them.
- Letting people have their say, sometimes at the end.
- Quotations for the research report.

Often questions that require categorical answers will be the result of substantial initial testing, e.g.:

What was your
main reason
for shopping
on *this* day?
(*Tick one only*)

Wages/pension day [1]
Near weekend [2]
Food fresher/better stocked [3]
Car/lift/help available [4]
Day not working [5]
Supermarket less busy [6]
Ran out of food, needed something specific [7]
Open late [8]
Other (please state) .... [9]

Sometimes questions will apply to only some of the respondents. Use two questions and a skip, e.g.:

23. Have you changed your usual
brand of toothpaste in the *last*
twelve months?   Yes [1] No [2]
If 'No' go to Q.25

24. What is the main reason for   Better value [1]
changing your usual   Better quality, taste, pack [2]
brand of toothpaste?   More easily available [3]
                                              Dentist's recommendation [4]
                              Other (please specify) .... [5]

Questions should *spread* responses where possible; sometimes the pilot work will show
that people are responding at one end of the scale (change verbal referents to spread
responses out) or using only the extremes of the scales (use fewer points on the scale).
One rule of thumb is to double the number with each jump in a numeric response
format, e.g.:

> How much   £5 or less [1]
> did you spend on   £5–£10 [2]
> the *last main trip*   £10–£20 [3]
> to a supermarket?   £20–£40 [4]
>   £40–£80 [5]
>   £80–£160 [6]
>   Over £160 [7]

Two common scales are:

1. The Likert, e.g.:

> Going shopping   Strongly agree [1]
> with young children   Agree [2]
> is an enjoyable   Neither agree nor disagree   [3]
> experience.   Disagree [4]
> *Do you?* . . . .   Strongly disagree   [5]

2. The semantic differential scale, e.g.:

Going shopping with young children is:

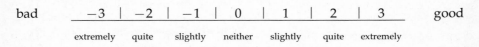

bad   −3 | −2 | −1 | 0 | 1 | 2 | 3   good

    extremely quite slightly neither slightly quite extremely

Keep the degrees of response down to the minimum; when the interviewer asks the
question never exceed five degrees of response, and use flash cards.

Checking and piloting

■ Ask people to paraphrase items to see whether they understood them in the intended way. Substantial amendments need retesting. Questionnaire development takes time and should not be rushed, so start early.
■ Pilot the questionnaire by applying it to a sample of the appropriate population, noting problems of response, etc. Where the questionnaire is intended to reveal differences between social groups, see whether these are likely to be significant with the proposed sample sizes. Recast the questionnaire after assessing difficulties in the pilot. Do not use pilot respondents in the main study.

Other points

There are some standardized ways of collecting data, e.g.

■ *Age bands.* Use 15–24, 25–44, 45–64 and 65+ (or 25–34, 35–44, 45–54, 55–64).
■ *Income.* As with age, people are happier to give a band than a specific figure.
■ *Socio-economic status (SES).* Self-assigned status is best avoided. When SES is collected you should follow a standard classification, for example in UK marketing: A, B, C1, C2, D and E.
■ *Sensitive issues.* Care is required investigating personal habits, income. Generally such items are put late in the questionnaire after rapport has been established.
■ *Interviewers* affect respondents:
  (a) by getting them to talk,
  (b) by affecting their responses.

Remember that most interviewers are female and may produce different results from males on some topics. Where interviewer effect is suspected, and more than one interviewer is employed, a comparison of results by interviewer can be made.

Measurement

The concept of measurement

Research methods courses sometimes leave out the idea of measurement. I introduce it with an example.

Suppose that you were asked to taste ten beers and then to rate how much you liked them on a scale from 1 to 100. A little while later (Time 2) you rate them again. In Table A.1 below we put the average ratings (hypothetical) from a group of people for the beers they rated first, second, etc. at Time 1 and the second set of ratings at Time 2.

What do we see? First, the second measurement is close to the first; clearly we are measuring something that endures. Second, we see a small tendency for the extreme measurements to move toward the mean and the central measurements to move away from it. How do we explain this?

Table A.1 Repeated measurement of an ordered sample

Order of preference at Time 1	Time 1 Mean rating for each order	Time 2 Mean rating for each order	Measurement shift
1	83	79	↓ Towards
2	81	78	↓ the mean
3	71	71	–
4	65	67	↑ Away
5	60	63	↑ from
6	55	54	↓ the
7	47	46	↓ mean
8	39	39	–
9	30	31	↑ Towards
10	29	32	↑ the mean
Mean:	**56**	**56**	

The explanation for these movements lies in the nature of measurement itself which is well described by Kish (1959). He argued that a measurement has three parts:

1. true measurement,
2. random error,
3. systematic bias.

True measurement is what you are seeking and we would have failed here if the measurements at Time 2 had borne no relation to those at Time 1. Random error and systematic bias can be explained with an example. Suppose that you are trying to measure the length of a room with a ruler; the room is exactly 3 metres long and you try several times and get a slightly different answer each time. The spread of the answers indicates the random error in the measurement system (you and the ruler). *All* measurements have this sort of problem and it can be quite large when human beings are a part of the measurement process.

Now suppose that the ruler that you used was defective and showed 29.9 cm as 30 cm. Again you can see that *all* measurements are going to suffer from this systematic bias and it will have the effect of spreading the measurements around the wrong mean, in this case 2.99 instead of 3 metres. So:

■ Random error produces measurement spread; and
■ Systematic bias displaces the mean of measurements. In some cases the systematic bias means that something different is measured.

In the beer-tasting example the reason for the movements in measurement at Time 2 lies in the random error. After the measurements have been made, some will have more error than others. When the error is positive the measurement will tend to be more positive and when the error is negative the measurement will be more negative. This means that, when you put measurements in order, the higher ones will tend to have more positive error and the lower measurements more negative error. You can see this most clearly if you assume that all the true measurements are the same, and roll a die to provide the random error component; in this case all the measurement spread is provided by the random error so that when you put the measurements in order from high to low you know that repeating the 'measurement' for the high or low scores would be likely to bring the extremes back to the mean. Central measurements tend to disperse away from the mean because they will receive normal error on remeasure instead of the below average error that helped to keep them central at Time 1.

Earlier we asked what would be the effect of taking only those brands that showed a positive response to advertising in the forty-four brand study. It is likely that some of these positive results arose because of positive random error; therefore, the measured effect of advertising (in its first year when these brands were selected) probably overstated the effect but this would not be true in later years.

The beer-tasting example could also show bias. We might have found that the measurements at Time 2 were all higher or lower than at Time 1, indicating the effect of inebriation which can be seen as a systematic bias.

Good measurement reduces both forms of error. Of the two it is systematic bias that gives more problem; random error makes the picture fuzzy but multiple measurement and statistical analysis help us to resolve this. In the case of systematic bias there is uncertainty about what it is that you have measured; it is therefore good practice to use procedures that create random error rather than systematic error. For example, when drawing groups for an experiment it is better to assign people to their groups on the toss of a coin than on any systematic criterion such as order of arrival which could bias the study.

Random error is reduced when we can take several measurements of the same thing. I might, for example, have got you to rate the quality of the beer first and then how much you like it. If you agree with me that the second is much the same as the first, then we can average the two measurements to reduce random error. Alternatively we may measure twice but with an interval between measurements. In the beer example the average of the two measurements would normally give a better measurement than one of them. When several measures are to be averaged we normally check that they are intercorrelated using a reliability test called Cronbach's Alpha; scores above 0.7 are usually taken to justify averaging.

Systematic bias is also reduced by using several different measures so that the different biases associated with each method have less impact on the total measurement and may cancel each other out. In the beer example there may be a systematic effect related to order of presentation so that different orders are desirable to cancel out this bias. Another technique might be to have the beers ranked as well as rated but this technique is usually too cumbersome with ten alternatives.

Applications

1.   You can see student assessment as a measurement procedure with random and systematic biases as well as true measurement. By assessing frequently the random error is reduced. By using different types of assessment, and different examiners, the systematic bias is reduced.

2.   Random error may also be used to advantage in programmed share trading. High and low share prices reflect in part the operation of random error so that selling on highs and buying on lows (derived from normal share price movements) may capitalize on random fluctuation.

The presence of systematic biases limits the conclusions that can be made from research. In particular, we can be confident about making causal inferences only from experiments where such biases are ruled out by randomly assigning individuals to the different conditions of the experiment. When it is not possible to control the groups in this way, as in cross-sectional studies, it is always possible that some unmeasured associated bias is responsible for observed effects.

Reliability and validity

When a measure consistently returns the same findings we call it reliable but, as we have seen, this is true for measures with systematic biases. A short ruler or a misphrased question can both be reliable but they are not valid, i.e. they do not measure what they purport to measure. We want measures to be valid; measures which are high on validity must be high on reliability.

Hindsight and foresight

Random error is also at work when we use hindsight to explain findings. Why should we attach less importance to a result that is found in data, after the data have been gathered, than a result which is predicted and then found in data? Sociology, economics and history are among the subjects where the explanation usually comes after the data have been gathered. In the physical sciences and much of psychology the results are often predicted before they happen – why do we feel more confident about such results? Most of us know that hindsight explanations are of less consequence than finding a predicted outcome but it is difficult to explain why.

We have to look at the play of chance. How many interesting findings might have been possible before the research was done? Suppose the research involves twenty correlations. At a 0.05 significance level it is likely that one of these correlations will be 'significant' because there are twenty chances. But if, with foresight, you had predicted that one of the twenty correlations would be significant, and only that one, then you could be much more confident in the result if this specific prediction was found to hold. This is why hypotheses are important in research. If you have anticipated a specific outcome you can have much greater confidence if you later find that it occurs.

References

Ehrenberg, A.S.C. (1986) Reading a table: an example, *Applied Statistician*, 35: 3, 237–44.

Ehrenberg, A.S.C. (1982) Writing technical papers or reports, *The American Statistician*, November, 36: 4, 326–9.

Kish, L. (1959) Some statistical problems in research design, *American Sociological Review*, 24, 328–38.

Bibliography

Aaker, D.A. (1991a) *Managing Brand Equity: Capitalizing on the Value of a Brand Name*, New York, The Free Press.

Aaker, D. (1991b) Are brand equity investments really worthwhile? *Admap*, Sept, 14–17.

Aaker, D.A. and Keller K.L. (1990) Consumer evaluations of brand extensions, *Journal of Marketing*, 54, 27–61.

Abelson, R.P. (1972) Are attitudes necessary? In King, B.T. and McGinnies, E. (eds.) *Attitudes, Conflict and Social Change*, New York, Academic Press, 19–32.

Ackoff, R.L. and Emshoff, J.R. (1975) Advertising research at Anheuser-Busch Inc. 1963–68, *Sloan Management Review*, Winter, 1–15.

Adams, H.F. (1916) *Advertising and its Mental Laws*, New York, Macmillan.

AGB (1992) Revealed: the nation's shopping habits, *SuperMarketing*, 14 August.

Ajzen, I. (1971) Attitude vs. normative messages: an investigation of the differential effects of persuasive communications on behavior, *Sociometry*, 34, 263–80.

Ajzen, I. (1985) From intentions to actions: a theory of planned behavior. In Kuhl, J. and Beckmann, J. (eds.) *Action-control: From Cognition to Behavior*, Heidelberg, Springer, 22–39.

Ajzen, I. (1988) *Attitudes, Personality and Behavior*, Chigago, Dorsey Press.

Ajzen, I. (1991) The theory of planned behavior. In Locke, E.A. (ed.) *Organizational Behavior and Human Decision Processes*, 50, 179–211.

Ajzen, I. and Driver, B.L. (1992) Application of the theory of planned behavior to leisure choice, *Journal of Leisure Research*, 24: 3, 207–24.

Ajzen, I. and Fishbein, M. (1969) The prediction of behavioral intentions in a choice situation, *Journal of Experimental Social Psychology*, 5, 400–16.

Ajzen, I, and Fishbein, M. (1972) Attitudinal and normative variables as factors influencing behavioral intentions, *Journal of Personality and Social Psychology*, 27, 41–57.

Ajzen, I. and Fishbein, M. (1977) Attitude–behavior relations: a theoretical analysis and review of empirical research, *Psychological Bulletin*, 84, 888–918.

Ajzen, I. and Fishbein, M. (1980) *Understanding Attitudes and Predicting Social Behavior*, Englewood Cliffs, NJ, Prentice Hall.

Ajzen, I. and Madden, T.J. (1986) Prediction of goal-directed behavior: attitudes, intentions and perceived behavioral control, *Journal of Experimental Social Psychology*, 22, 453–74.

Ajzen, I., Nichols, A.J. and Driver, B.L. (1995) Identifying salient beliefs about leisure activities: frequency of elicitation versus response latency, *Journal of Applied Social Psychology*, 25: 16, 1391–1410.

Allais, M. (1953) Le comportement de l'homme rationel devant le risque: critique des postulats et axiomes de l'école américaine, *Econometrica*, 21, 503–46.

Allport, G.W. (1935) Attitudes. In Murchison, C. (ed.) *A Handbook of Social Psychology*, Worcester, MA. Clark University Press, 798–844.

Ambler, T. (1996) Marketing: *From Advertising To Zen*, London, FT Pitman Publishing.

Anand, P., Holbrook, M.B. and Stephens, D. (1988) The formation of affective judgements: the cognitive–affective model versus the independence hypothesis, *Journal of Consumer Research*, 15, 386–91.

Anand, P. and Sternthal, B. (1991) Perceptual fluency and affect without recognition, *Memory and Cognition*, 19: 3, 293–300.

Andreasen, A.R. (1988) Consumer complaints and redress: what we know and what we don't know. In Maynes, E.S. (ed.) *The Frontier of Research in Consumer Interest*, Columbia, University of Columbia and American Council of Consumer Interest, 675–721.

Andreasen, A.R. (1991) Consumer behavior research and social policy. In Robertson, T.S. and Kassarjian, H.H. (eds) *Handbook of Consumer Behavior*, Englewood Cliffs, NJ, Prentice Hall, 459–506.

Andreasen, A.R. and Manning, J. (1990) The dissatisfaction and complaining behavior of vulnerable consumers, *Journal of Consumer Satisfaction, Dissatisfaction and Complaining Behavior*, 3, 12–20.

Anglin, L.K., Stuenkel, J.K. and Lepisto, L.R. (1994) The effect of stress on price sensitivity and comparison shopping. In Allen, C.T. and John, D.R. (eds) *Advances in Consumer Research*, 21, 126–31.

Areni, C.S. and Kim, D. (1993) The influence of background music on shopping behavior: classical versus top-forty music in a wine store. In McAlister, L. and Rothschild, M.L. (eds.) *Advances in Consumer Research*, 20, 336–40.

Areni, C.S. and Kim, D. (1994) The influence of in-store lighting on consumers' examination of merchandise in a wine store, *International Journal of Research in Marketing*, 11, 117–25.

Arthur, C. (1992) Fifteen million Americans are shopping addicts, *American Demographics*, March, 14–15.

Assael, H. (1994) *Consumer Behavior and Marketing Action*, Boston, PWS-Kent Publishing Co.

Aykac, A., Corstjens, M. and Gautschi, D. (1984) Is there a kink in your advertising? *Journal of Advertising Research*, 24: 3, 27–36.

Babacus, E. and Boller, G.W. (1992) An empirical assessment of the SERVQUAL scale, *Journal of Business Research*, 24, 253–68.

Bagozzi, R.P. (1981) Attitudes, intentions and behavior: a test of some key hypotheses, *Journal of Personality and Social Psychology*, 41, 607–27.

Bagozzi, R.P. (1984) Expectancy-value attitude models: An analysis of critical measurement issues, *International Journal of Research in Marketing*, 1, 295–310.

Bagozzi, R.P. (1992) The self-regulation of attitudes, intentions and behaviors, *Social Psychology Quarterly*, 55, 178–204.

Bagozzi, R.P. and Kimmel, S.K. (1995) A comparison of leading theories for the prediction of goal directed behaviours, *British Journal of Social Psychology*, 34: 4, 437–61.

Bagozzi, R.P. and Warshaw, P.R. (1990) Trying to consume, *Journal of Consumer Research*, 17, 127–40.

Baker, C. (1993) *Advertising Works 7*, Henley-on-Thames, Institute of Practitioners in Advertising, NTC Publications.

Baker, C. (1995) *Advertising Works 8*, Henley-on-Thames, Institute of Practitioners in Advertising, NTC Publications.

Baker, J., Grewal, D. and Parasuraman, A. (1994) The influence of store environment on quality inferences and store image, *Journal of the Academy of Marketing Science*, 22, 4, 328–39.

Baldwin, M.W. and Holmes, J.G. (1987) Salient private audiences and awareness of the self, *Journal of Personality and Social Psychology*, 52, 1087–98.

Bales, R.F. and Strodtbeck, F.L. (1951) Phases in group problem solving, *Journal Abnormal and Social Psychology*, 46, 485–95.

Bandura, A. (1977) Self-efficacy: toward a unifying theory of behavioral change, *Psychological Review*, 84, 191–215.

Bargh, J.A., Chaiken, S., Govender, R. and Pratto, F. (1992) *Journal of Personality and Social Psychology*, 62, 6, 893–912.

Barker, R.G., Dembo, T. and Lewin, K. (1941) Frustration and regression: an experiment with young children, *University of Iowa Studies in Child Welfare*, 18, 1.

Barnard, N.R. (1987) Presentation to *Centre for Marketing and Communication*, London Business School.

Barnard, N.R., Barwise, T.P. and Ehrenberg, A.S.C. (1986) Reinterviews in attitude research, *MRS Conference*, Brighton.

Barnard, N.R. and Smith, G. (1989) *Advertising and Modelling: An Introductory Guide*, London, Institute of Practitioners in Advertising.

Barsalou, L.W. (1985) Ideals, central tendency and frequency of instantiation as determinants of graded structure in categories, *Journal of Experimental Psychology: Learning, Memory and Cognition*, 11: 4, 629–53.

Bartlett, F.C. (1932) *Remembering*, Cambridge, Cambridge University Press.

Barwise, T.P. (1993) Brand equity: Snark or Boojum? *International Journal of Research in Marketing*, 10: 1, 93–104.

Barwise, T.P. and Ehrenberg, A.S.C. (1985) Consumer beliefs and brand usage, *Journal of the Market Research Society*, 27, 81–93.

Barwise, P. and Ehrenberg, A.S.C. (1987) Consumer beliefs and awareness, *Journal of the Market Research Society*, 29: 1, 88–94.

Bass, F.M., Givon, M.M., Kalwani, M.U., Reibstein, D. and Wright, G.P. (1984) An investigation into the order of the brand choice process, *Marketing Science*, 3, 267–87.

Bass, F.M., Jeuland, A.P. and Wright, G.P. (1976) Equilibrium stochastic choice and market penetration theories: derivation and comparisons, *Management Science*, 22, June, 1051–63.

Bass, F.M. and Talarzyk, W.W. (1972) An attitude model for the study of brand preference, *Journal of Marketing Research*, 9, 93–6.

Bateson, J.E.G. (1989) *Managing Services Marketing*, London, Dryden.

Batra, R. and Ray, M.L. (1983) Advertising situations: the implications of differential involvement and accompanying affect responses. In Harris, R.L. (ed.) *Information Processing Research in Advertising*, London, Lawrence Erlbaum Associates, 127–51.

Bayus, B.L. (1991) The consumer durable replacement buyer, *Journal of Marketing*, 55, January, 42–51.

Beale, D.A. and Manstead, A.S.R (1991) Predicting mothers' intentions to limit frequency of infants' sugar intake, *Journal of Applied Social Psychology*, 21: 5, 409–31.

Beales, H., Mazis, M.B., Salop, S.C. and Staelin, R. (1981) Consumer search and public policy, *Journal of Consumer Research*, 8, June, 11–22.

Beatty, S.E. and Smith, S.M. (1987) External search effort: an investigation across several product categories, *Journal of Consumer Research*, 14, June, 83–95.

Beck, L. and Ajzen, I. (1990) Predicting socially undesirable behaviors: the sufficiency of the theory of planned behavior and the validity of self-reports. Unpublished manuscript. Dept of Psychology, University of Massachusetts. Cited by Ajzen (1991).

Bellizzi, J.A., Crowley, A.E. and Hasty, R.E. (1983) *Journal of Retailing*, 59: 1, 21–44.

Belson, W. (1988) Major error from two commonly used methods of market and social research, *Market Research Society Newsletter*, August, 33.

Bem, D.J. (1967) Self-perception: an alternative explanation of cognitive dissonance phenomena, *Psychological Review*, 74, 183–200.

Bemmaor, A.C. (1995) Predicting behavior from intention-to-buy measures: the parametric case, *Journal of Marketing Research*, 32: 2, 176–91.

Bemmaor, A.C. and Mouchoux, D. (1991) Measuring the short-term effect of in-store promotion and retail advertising on brand sales: a factorial experiment, *Journal of Marketing Research*, 28, May, 202–14.

Benterud, T. and Stø, E. (1993) TV shopping in Scandinavia: Consumer satisfaction, dissatisfaction and complaining behavior, *Journal of Consumer Satisfaction, Dissatisfaction and Complaining Behavior*, 6, 196–203.

Bentler, P.M. and Speckart, G. (1979) Models of attitude–behavior relations, *Psychological Review*, 86: 5, 452–64.

Bentler, P.M. and Speckart, G. (1981) Attitudes 'cause' behaviors: a structural equation analysis, *Journal of Personality and Social Psychology*, 40, 226–38.

Berlyne, D.E. (1954) A theory of human curiosity, *British Journal of Psychology*, 45, 180–91.

Berlyne, D.E. (1965) *Structure and Direction in Thinking*, London, Wiley, 1965.

Berlyne, D.E. and Borsa, M. (1968) Uncertainty and the orientation reaction, *Perception and Psychophysics*, 3, 1B.

Berlyne, D.E. and McDonnell, P. (1965) Effects of stimulus complexity and incongruity on duration of EEG desynchronisation, *Electroencephalography and Clinical Neurophysiology*, 18: 2, 156–61.

Bernoulli, D. (1738) Specimen Theoriae novae de mensura sortis. *Comentarii Academiae Scientiarum Imperiales Petropolitanae*, 5, 175–92. Translated by L. Sommer, in *Econometrica*, 1954, 22, 23–36.

Bettman, J.R. (1977) Data collection and analysis approaches for studying consumer information processing. In Perreault W.D. Jr (ed.) *Advances in Consumer Research*, 4, 342–48.

Bettman, J.R. and Park, C.W. (1980) Implications of a constructive view of choice for analysis of protocol data: a coding scheme for elements of choice processes. In Olson, J.C. (ed.) *Advances in Consumer Research*, 7, 148–53.

Bettman, J.R. and Zins, M.A. (1977) Constructive processes in consumer choice, *Journal of Consumer Research*, 4, 75–85.

Biel, A.L. (1990) Love the ad, buy the product? Why liking the advertising and preferring the brand aren't such strange bedfellows after all, *Admap*, 26: 9, 21–5.

Biel, A.L. (1991) The brandscape: converting brand image into equity, *Admap*, October, 41–6.

Bird, M. and Ehrenberg, A.S.C. (1966) Intentions-to-buy and claimed brand usage, *Operational Research Quarterly*, 17, 27–46.

Bitner, M.J., Booms, B.H. and Tetreault, M.S. (1990) The service encounter: diagnosing favourable and unfavourable incidents, *Journal of Marketing*, 54, January, 71–84.

Blattberg, R.C., Briesch, R. and Fox, E.J. (1995) How promotions work, *Marketing Science*, 14, 3, Part 2 of 2, G122–G132.

Blodgett, J.G., Granbois, D.H. and Walters, R.G. (1993) The effects of perceived justice on complainants' negative word-of-mouth behavior and repatronage intentions, *Journal of Retailing*, 69: 4, 399–428.

Bloemer, J. and Poiesz, T.B.C. (1989) The illusion of consumer satisfaction, *Journal of Consumer Satisfaction, Dissatisfaction and Complaining Behavior*, 43–8.

Bloom, D. (1989) Do we need to worry about long-term effects? *Admap*, October, 49–52.

Bloom, D. (1990) Modelling beyond the blip – rejoinder, *Journal of the Market Research Society*, 32: 3, 465–67.

Boldero, J. (1995) The prediction of household recycling of newspapers – the role of attitudes, intentions and situational factors, *Journal of Applied Social Psychology*, 25: 5, 440–62.

Boldero, J., Moore, S. and Rosenthal, D. (1992) Intentions, context and safe sex, *Journal of Applied Social Psychology*, 22: 17, 1374–96.

Bornstein, R.F. (1989) Exposure and affect: overview and meta-analysis of research, *Psychological Bulletin*, 106, 2, 265–89.

Boutillier, J. Le, Boutillier, S.S. Le and Neslin, S.A. (1994) A replication and extension of the Dickson and Sawyer price-awareness study, *Marketing Letters*, 5: 1, 31–42.

Brehm, J.W. (1956) Post-desisional changes in the desirability of alternatives, *Journal of Abnormal and Social Psychology*, 52, 384–9.

Brehm, J.W. (1989) Psychological reactance: Theory and applications. In Srull, T.K. (ed.) *Advances in Consumer Research*, 16, 72–5.

Brehm, J.W. and Cohen, A.R. (1962) *Explorations in Cognitive Dissonance*, New York, Wiley.

Brehm, S.S. and Brehm, J.W. (1981) *Psychological Reactance*, New York, Academic Press.

Broadbent, S. (1981) *Advertising Works*, Institute of Practitioners of Advertising, London, Holt Rinehart Winston.

Broadbent, S. (1983) *Advertising Works 2*. Institute of Practitioners of Advertising, London, Holt Rinehart Winston.

Broadbent, S. (1984) Modelling with adstock, *Journal of the Market Research Society*, 26: 4, 295–312.

Broadbent, S. (1986) 'Two OTS in a purchase interval' – some questions. *Admap*, 22: 11, 12–6.

Broadbent, S. (1989) *The Advertising Budget: The Advertiser's Guide to Budget Determination*, Henley, NTC Publications.

Broadbent, S. (1992) Using data better – a new approach to sales analyses, *Admap*, January, 48–54.

Broadbent, S. (1995) Single source – the breakthrough? *Admap*, June, 29–33.

Broadbent, S. and Colman, S. (1986) Advertising effectiveness: across brands, *Journal of the Market Research Society*, 28: 1, 15–24.

Broadbent, S. and Fry, T. (1995) Adstock modelling for the long term, *Journal of the Market Research Society*, 37, 4, 385–403.

Brown, G. (1985) Tracking studies and sales effects: a UK perspective, *Journal of Advertising Research*, 25, 1, 52–64.

Brown, G. (1986) Monitoring advertising performance, *Admap*, 22: 3, 151–3.

Brown, G. (1991) *How Advertising Affects the Sales of Packaged Goods Brands: A working hypothesis for the 1990s*, Millward Brown International plc.

Brown, G. (1994) The awareness problem, *Admap*, January, 15–20.

Brown, G.H. (1952) Brand loyalty – fact or fiction? *Advertising Age*, 23, 19 June, 53–5; 23, 30 June, 45–7; 23, 14 July, 54–6; 23, 28 July, 46–8; 23, 11 August, 56–8; 23, 1 September, 76–9.

Brown, G.H. (1953) Brand loyalty, *Advertising Age*, 24. Reproduced in Ehrenberg, A.S.C. and Pyatt, F.G. (eds.) *Consumer Behaviour*, Harmondsworth, Penguin Books, 28–35.

Brown, T.J., Churchill Jr, G.A. and Peter, J.P. (1993) Improving the measurement of service quality, *Journal of Retailing*, 69: 1, 127–39.

Bucklin, R.E. and Lattin, J.M. (1992) A model of product category competition among grocery retailers, *Journal of Retailing*, 68: 3, 271–93.

Buday, T. (1989) Capitalizing on brand extensions: lessons of success and failure, *Journal of Consumer Marketing*, 6: 4, 27–30.

Budd, R. (1986) Predicting cigarette use: the need to incorporate measures of salience in the theory of reasoned action, *Journal of Applied Social Psychology*, 16, 663–85.

Bullmore, J. (1984) The brand and its image revisited, *International Journal of Advertising*, 3, 235–8.

Burnkrant, R.E. and Page, T.J. (1988) The structure and antecedents of the normative and attitudinal components of Fishbein's theory of reasoned action, *Journal of Experimental Social Psychology*, 24, 66–87.

Burnkrant, R.E. and Unnava, H.R. (1987) Effects of variation in message execution on the learning of repeated brand information. In Wallendorf, M. and Anderson, P. (eds.) *Advances in Consumer Research*, 14, 173–6.

Burns, D.J. and Perkins, D. (1996) Accounts in post-purchase behavior: excuses, justifications and meta-accounts, *Journal of Satisfaction, Dissatisfaction and Complaining Behavior*, 9, 144–57.

Buzzell, R.D. and Gale, B.T. (1987) The PIMS Principles: *Linking Strategy to Performance*, New York, The Free Press.

Cacioppo, J.T. and Petty, R.E. (1985) Central and peripheral routes to persuasions: the role of message repetition. In Mitchell, A.A. and Alwitt, L.F. (eds.) *Psychological Processes and Advertising Effects*, Hillsdale, NJ, Lawrence Erlbaum Associates, 91–112.

Campbell, D.T. (1963) Social attitudes and other acquired behavioral dispositions. In Koch, S. (ed.) *Psychology: A Study of a Science*, 6, New York, McGraw-Hill, 94–172.

Caplovitz, D. (1967) *The Poor Pay More*, 2nd edn, New York, The Free Press.

Cardozo, R.N. (1965) An experimental study of consumer effort, expectation and satisfaction, *Journal of Marketing Research*, 2, August, 244–9.

Carman, J.M. (1970) Correlates of brand loyalty, *Journal of Marketing Research*, 7, 67–76.

Carman, J.M. (1990) Consumer perceptions of service quality: an assessment of the SERVQUAL dimensions, *Journal of Retailing*, 66, 33–55.

Carsky, M.L. (1989) Moderating the effects of point-of-sale information and consumer satisfaction, *Journal of Consumer Satisfaction, Dissatisfaction and Complaining Behavior*, 2, 111–19.

Castleberry, S.B., Ehrenberg, A.S.C. and England, L.R. (1989) Price parity for very close substitutes: an exploratory result, *Marketing and Research Today*, 17, 84–8.

Chaiken, S. (1980) Heuristic versus systematic information processing and the use of source versus message cues in persuasion, *Journal of Personality and Social Psychology*, 39, 752–66.

Chan, D.K.S. and Fishbein, M. (1993) Determinants of college women's intention to tell their partners to use condoms, *Journal of Applied Social Psychology*, 23, 18, 1455–70.

Channon, C. (1985) *Advertising Works 3*, London, Holt, Rinehart and Winston.

Channon, C. (1987) *Advertising Works 4*, London, Cassell.

Charlton, P. (1973) A review of shop loyalty, *Journal of the Market Research Society*, 15: 1, 35–51.

Chatfield, C. and Goodhardt, G. (1975) Results concerning brand choice, *Journal of Marketing Research*, 12, 110–13.

Chebat, J.C. and Filiatrault, P. (1993) The impact of waiting in line on consumers, *International Journal of Bank Marketing*, 11: 2, 35–40.

Christaller, W. (1933) *Central Places in Southern Germany*. Translated by Baskin, C.W. (1966) Englewood Cliffs, NJ, Prentice Hall.

Churcher, P.B. and Lawton, J.H. (1987) Predation by domestic cats in an English village, *Journal of Zoology*, 212, 439–55.

Churchill, G.A. Jr and Surprenant, C. (1982) An investigation into the determinants of customer satisfaction, *Journal of Marketing Research*, 19, November, 491–504.

Churchill, H. (1942) How to measure brand loyalty, *Advertising and Selling*, 35, 24.

Clare, J.E. and Kiser, C.V. (1951) Preference for children of a given sex in relation to fertility. In Whelpton, P.K. and Kiser, C.V. (eds.) *Social and Psychological Factors Affecting Fertility*, New York, Milbank Memorial Fund, 621–73.

Clarke, D.G. (1976) Econometric measurement of the duration of advertising effect on sales, *Journal of Marketing Research* 13: 4, 345–57.

Clemmer, E.C. and Schneider, B. (1987) Toward understanding and controlling customer dissatisfaction with waiting during peak demand times, *Service Customer*, 1.

Cohen, J.B., Fishbein, M. and Ahtola, O.T. (1972) The nature and uses of expectancy-value models in consumer attitude research, *Journal of Marketing Research*, 9, 456–60.

Colley, R.H. (1961) *Defining Advertising Goals and Measuring Advertising Results*, New York, Association of National Advertisers.

Collins, B.E., Ashmore, R.D., Hornbeck, F.W. and Whitney, R.E. (1970) Studies in forced compliance: 13 and 15. In search of a dissonance producing forced compliance paradigm, *Representative Research in Social Psychology*, 1.

Collins, M. (1971) Market segmentation – the realities of buyer behaviour, *Journal of the Market Research Society*, 13: 3, 146–57.

Condiotti, M.M. and Lichtenstein, E. (1981) Self-efficacy and relapse in smoking cessation programs, *Journal of Consulting and Clinical Psychology*, 49, 648–58.

Confer, M.G. (1992) The media multiplier: nine studies conducted in seven countries, *Journal of Advertising Research*, 32: 1, RC4–RC10.

Cooper, J., Zanna, M.P. and Taves, P.A. (1978) Arousal as a necessary condition for attitude change following compliance, *Journal of Personality and Social Psychology*, 36, 1101–6.

Copeland, M.T. (1923) Relation of consumer's buying habits to marketing methods, *Harvard Business Review*, 1, 282–9.

Cotton, B.C. and Babb, E.M. (1878) Consumer response to promotional deals, *Journal of Marketing* (July), 109–13.

Courneya, K.S. (1995) Understanding readiness for regular physical activity in older individuals: an application of the theory of planned behavior, *Health Psychology*, 14: 1, 80–7.

Crocker, J., Fiske, S.T. and Taylor, S.E. (1984) Schematic bases of belief change. In Eiser, J.R. (ed.) *Attitudinal Judgement*, New York, Springer-Verlag.

Cronin, J.J. Jr. and Taylor, S.A. (1992) Measuring service quality: a re-examination and extension, *Journal of Marketing*, 56, 55–68.

Cronin, J.J. Jr. and Taylor, S.A. (1994) SERVPERF versus SERVQUAL: reconciling performance-based and perceptions-minus-expectations measurement of service quality, *Journal of Marketing*, 58, January, 125–31.

Cunningham, R.M. (1956) Brand loyalty – what, where, how much? *Harvard Business Review*, 34, Jan./Feb., 116–28.

Cunningham, R.M. (1961) Customer loyalty to store and brand, *Harvard Business Review*, 39, Nov./Dec., 127–37.

Curtin, R.T. (1984) Consumer attitudes for forecasting. In Kinnear, T.C. (ed.) *Advances in Consumer*

Research, 11, 714–17.

Dabholkar, P.A., Thorpe, D.I. and Rentz, J.O. (1996) A measure of service quality for retail stores, *Journal of the Academy of Marketing Science*, 24, 1, 3–16.

Dacin, P.A. and Smith, D.C. (1993) The effect of adding products to a brand on consumer's evaluations of new brand extensions. In McAlister, L. and Rothschild, M.L., *Advances in Consumer Research*, 20, 594–8.

Damon, J. (1988) *Shopaholics: Serious Help for Addicted Spenders*, Los Angeles, CA, Price, Stern, Sloan Inc.

D'Astous, A. (1990) An inquiry into the compulsive side of normal consumers, *Journal of Consumer Policy*, 13, March, 15–32.

Davidson, A.R. and Jaccard, J.J. (1975) Population psychology: a new look at an old problem, *Journal of Personality and Social Psychology*, 31, 1073–82.

Davis, R. (1992) *Death on the Streets*, Worcester, MA, Ebenezer Baylis.

Davis, S., Inman, J.J. and McAlister, L. (1992) Promotion has a negative effect on brand evaluation – or does it? Additional disconfirming evidence. *Journal of Marketing Research*, 29, 143–8.

Dawar, N. and Anderson, P.F. (1993) *Determining the order and direction of multiple brand extensions*, INSEAD Working Paper 93/17/MKT.

Day, D., Gan, B., Gendall, P. and Esslemont D. (1991) Predicting purchase behaviour, *Marketing Bulletin*, 2, May, 18–30.

Day, G.S. (1969) A two-dimensional concept of brand loyalty, *Journal of Advertising Research*, 9, 29–35.

Day, R.L. (1984) Modeling choices among alternative responses to dissatisfaction. In Kinnear, T.C. (ed.) *Advances in Consumer Research*, 11, 496–9.

Day, R.L. and Ash, S.B. (1979) Consumer reponses to dissatisfaction with durable products. In Wilkie, W.L. (ed.) *Advances in Consumer Research*, 6, 438–44.

Day, R.L. and Landon, E.L. (1976) Collecting comprehensive complaint data by survey research. In Anderson, B.B. (ed.) *Advances in Consumer Research*, 3, 263–8.

Day, R.L. and Perkins, D.S. (1992) The satisfaction construct: a folk history, *Journal of Satisfaction, Dissatisfaction and Complaining Behavior*, 5, 223–7.

Denison, T. and Knox, S. (1993) Pocketing the change from loyal shoppers: the double indemnity effect, *Proceedings of the Marketing Education Group Conference*, Loughborough, 1993, 221–32.

Dennison, C.M. and Shepherd, R. (1995) Adolescent food choice: an application of the theory of planned behavior, *Journal of Human Nutrition and Dietetics*, 8: 1, 9–23.

DeSarbo, W.S., Huff, L., Rolandelli, M.M. and Choi, J. (1994) On the measurement of perceived service quality. In Rust, R.T. and Oliver, R.L. *Service Quality: New Directions in Theory and Practice*, London, Sage Publications, 201–22.

De Soto, C. and Albrecht, F. (1957) Cognition and social orderings. In Abelson, R.P., Aronson, E., McGuire, W.J., Newcomb, T.M., Rosenberg, M.J. and Tannenbaum, P.H. (eds.) *Theories of Cognitive Consistency: A Sourcebook*, Chicago, Rand-McNally, 531–8.

Desroches, J.J.Y. and Chebat, J.C. (1995) Why Quebec businesses go public: attitudes and the decision-making process, *Revue Canadienne des Sciences De L'Administration*, 12: 1, 27–37.

Devries, H. and Backbier, E. (1994) Self-efficacy as an important determinant of quitting among pregnant women who smoke: the phi pattern, *Preventive Medicine*, 23: 2, 167–74.

Dewit, J.B.F. and Teunis, G.J.P. (1994) Behavioral risk reduction strategies to prevent HIV-infection among homosexual men, *Aids Education and Prevention*, 6: 6, 493–505.

Dick, A.S. and Basu, K. (1994) Customer loyalty: towards an integrated framework, *Journal of the Academy of Marketing Science*, 22: 2, 99–113.

Dickson, P.R. and Sawyer, A.G. (1990) The price knowledge and search of supermarket shoppers, *Journal of Marketing*, 54, July, 42–53.

Dobni, D. and Zinkhan, G.M. (1990) In search of brand image: a foundation analysis. In Goldberg, M.E., Gorn, G. and Pollay, R. (eds.) *Advances in Consumer Research*, 17, 110–19.

Dollard, J., Doob, L.W., Miller, N.E., Mowrer, O.H. and Sears, R.R. (1939) *Frustration and Aggression*, New Haven, CT, Yale University Press.

Donovan, R.J. and Rossiter, J.R. (1982) Store atmosphere: an environmental psychology approach, *Journal of Retailing*, 58, 34–56.

Donovan, R.J. and Rossiter, J.R., Marcoolyn, G. and Nesdale A. (1994) Store atmosphere and purchasing behaviour, *Journal of Retailing*, 70: 3, 283–94.

Doob, A.N., Carlsmith, J.M., Freedman, J.L., Landauer, T.K. and Tom, S. (1969) The effects of initial selling price on subsequent sales, *Journal of Personality and Social Psychology*, 1, 345–50.

Doyle, P. (1989) Building successful brands: the strategic options. *Journal of Marketing Management*, 5: 1, 77–95.

Dubé, L., Schmitt, B.H. and Leclerc, F. (1991) Consumers' affective response to delays at different phases of a service delivery, *Journal of Applied Social Psychology*, 21: 10, 810–20.

Dubé-Rioux, L., Schmitt, B.H. and Leclerc, F. (1989) Consumers' reactions to waiting: when delays affect the perception of service quality. In Srull, T.K. (ed.) *Advances in Consumer Research*, 16, 59–63.

Duke, R. (1991) Post-saturation competition in UK grocery retailing, *Journal of Marketing Management*, 7: 1, 63–75.

Dunn, R.S., Reader, S. and Wrigley, N. (1983), An investigation of the assumptions of the NBD model as applied to purchasing at individual stores, *Applied Statistics*, 32: 3, 249–59.

Dunn, R.S. and Wrigley, N. (1984) Store loyalty for grocery products: an empirical study, *Area*, 16: 4, 307–14.

Eagly, A.H. and Chaiken, S. (1993) *The Psychology of Attitudes*, Orlando, FL, Harcourt Brace Jovanovitch.

East, R. (1972) *Uncertainty and Attention Before Choice*. Doctoral thesis, University of Sussex.

East, R. (1973) The duration of attention to alternatives and re-evaluation in choices with two and three alternatives, *European Journal of Social Psychology*, 3: 2, 125–44.

East, R. (1991) Beyond the blip: the 15 brand experiment, *Journal of the Market Research Society*, 33: 1, 57–9.

East, R. (1992) The effects of experience on the decision making of expert and novice buyers, *Journal of Marketing Management*, 8: 2, 167–76.

East, R. (1993) Investment decisions and the theory of planned behaviour, *Journal of Economic Psychology*, 14, 337–75.

East, R. (1996) Redress seeking as planned behavior, *Journal of Consumer Satisfaction, Dissatisfaction and Complaining Behavior*, 9, 27–34.

East, R. and Hammond, K.A. (1996) The erosion of repeat purchase loyalty, *Marketing Letters*, 7: 2, 163–72.

East, R., Harris, P., Willson, G. and Hammond, K. (1995) Correlates of first-brand loyalty, *Journal of Marketing Management*, 11: 5, 487–97.

East, R., Harris, P., Willson, G. and Lomax, W. (1995) Loyalty to supermarkets, *International Review of Retail, Distribution and Consumer Research*, 5: 1, 99–109.

East, R., Lomax, W. and Willson, G. (1991a) Factors associated with service delay in supermarkets and post offices, *Journal of Consumer Satisfaction, Dissatisfaction and Complaining Behaviour*, 4, 123–28.

East, R., Lomax, W. and Willson, G. (1991b) *Demand over Time: Attitudes, Knowledge and Habits that Affect When Customers Use Supermarkets*, Kingston Business School.

East, R., Lomax, W., Willson, G. and Harris, P. (1992a) *Demand over Time: Patterns of Use and Preference Among Post Office Users*, Kingston Business School.

East, R., Lomax, W., Willson, G. and Harris, P. (1992b) *Demand Over Time: Attitudes, Knowledge and Habits that Affect When Customers Use Banks and Building Societies*, Kingston Business School.

East, R., Lomax, W., Willson, G. and Harris, P. (1994) Decision making and habit in shopping times, *European Journal of Marketing*, 28: 4, 56–71.

East R., Whittaker, D. and Swift, A. (1984) *Measuring the Factors that Affect Product Take-up: Key Beliefs about Breakfast TV in Britain*, Working paper, Kingston Business School.

Eastlack, J.O. and Rao, A.G. (1986) Modeling response to advertising and pricing changes for 'V–8' cocktail vegetable juice, *Marketing Science*, 5: 3, 245–59.

Eastlack, J.O. and Rao, A.G. (1989) Advertising experiments at the Campbell Soup Company, *Marketing Science*, 8: 1, 57–71.

Edwards, W. (1954) The theory of decision making, *Psychological Bulletin*, 51: 4, 380–417.

Ehrenberg, A.S.C. (1959) The pattern of consumer purchases, *Applied Statistics*, 8, 26–41.

Ehrenberg, A.S.C. (1969) The discovery and use of laws of marketing, *Journal of Advertising Research*, 9: 2, 11–17.

Ehrenberg, A.S.C. (1974) Repetitive advertising and the consumer, *Journal of Advertising Research*, 14, 25–34.

Ehrenberg, A.S.C. (1986) Pricing and brand differentiation, *Singapore Marketing Review*, 1, 5–15.

Ehrenberg, A.S.C. (1988) *Repeat Buying: Theory and Applications*, 2nd Edition, London, Charles Griffin & Co. (first published in 1972 by North Holland).

Ehrenberg, A.S.C. (1993) If you're so strong why aren't you bigger? *Admap*, October, 13–14.

Ehrenberg, A.S.C. and England, L.R. (1990) Generalising a pricing effect, *The Journal of Industrial Economics*, 39: 1, 47–68.

Ehrenberg, A.S.C and Goodhardt, G.J. (1979) *Essays on Understanding Buyer Behavior*, New York, J. Walter Thompson Co. and Market Research Corporation of America.

Ehrenberg, A.S.C., Goodhardt, G.J. and Barwise, T.P. (1990) Double jeopardy revisited, *Journal of Marketing*, July, 82–90.

Ehrenberg, A.S.C., Hammond, K.A. and Goodhardt, G.J. (1994) The after-effects of price-related consumer promotions, *Journal of Advertising Research*, 34: 4, 11–21.

Ehrenberg, A.S.C. and Uncles, M.D. (1996) *Dirichlet-type Markets: A Review*, Working Paper, South Bank University Business School.

Eiser, J.R. (1986) *Social Psychology: Attitudes, Cognition and Social Behaviour*, Cambridge, Cambridge University Press.

Eiser, J.R. and Ross, M. (1977) Partisan language, immediacy and attitude change, *European Journal of Social Psychology*, 7, 477–89.

Elliott, R. (1993) Shopping addiction and mood repair. In Davies, M. *et al.* (eds.) *Emerging Issues in Marketing, Proceedings of the Marketing Education Group*, Loughborough, Loughborough University Press, 287–96.

Elliott, R. (1994) Addictive consumption: function and fragmentation in postmodernity, *Journal of Consumer Policy*, 17, 159–79.

Elliott, R., Eccles, S. and Gournay, K. (1996) Man management? Women and the use of debt to control personal relationships, *Marketing Education Group Proceedings*, Strathclyde. Available on compact disk, Buyer Behaviour Track.

Elliott, R. and Jobber, D. (1990) Understanding organizational buying behaviour: the role of cognitions, norms and attitudes, *Proceedings of The 23rd Marketing Education Group Conference*, Oxford Polytechnic, 402–23.

Elliott, R., Jobber, D. and Sharp, J. (1995) Using the theory of reasoned action to understand organizational behaviour: the role of belief salience, *British Journal of Social Psychology*, 34: 2, 161–72.

Engel, J.F., Blackwell, R.D. and Miniard, P.W. (1995) *Consumer Behavior*, 8th edn, New York, The Dryden Press.

Engel, J.F., Kollat, D.T. and Blackwell, R.D. (1968) *Consumer Behavior*, New York, Holt, Rinehart and Winston.

Enis, B.M. and Paul, G.W. (1970) Store loyalty as a basis for market segmentation, *Journal of Retailing*, 46: 3, 206–8.

Eskin, G.J. (1985) Tracking advertising and promotion performance with single source data, *Journal of Advertising Research*, 25: 1, 31–9.

Etgar, M. and Malhotra, N.K. (1981) Determinants of price dependency: personal and perceptual factors, *Journal of Consumer Research*, 8, September, 217–22.

Evans, J.St B.T. (1980) Current issues in the psychology of reasoning, *British Journal of Psychology*, 71: 2, 227–39.

Faber, R.J. and O'Guinn, T.C. (1988) Compulsive consumption and credit abuse, *Journal of Consumer Policy*, 11, 97–109.

Faber, R.J. and O'Guinn, T.C. (1992) A clinical screener for compulsive buying, *Journal of Consumer Research*, 19, 459–69.

Farley, J.U. (1964) Why does 'brand loyalty' vary over products? *Journal of Marketing Research*, 9–14.

Farley, J.U. (1968) Dimensions of supermarket choice patterns, *Journal of Marketing Research*, 5, May, 206–8.

Farris, P.W. and Albion, M.S. (1980) The impact of advertising on the price of consumer goods, *Journal of Marketing*, 44: 3, 17–35.

Farris, P.W. and Reibstein, D.J. (1991) How prices, ad expenditures, and profits are linked, *Harvard Business Review*, 173–84.

Fazio, R.H. (1986) How do attitudes guide behavior? In Sorrentino, R.M. and Higgins, E.T. (eds.) *The Handbook of Motivation and Cognition: Foundations of Social Behavior*, New York, Guildford Press, 204–43.

Fazio, R.H. (1990) Multiple processes by which attitudes guide behavior: the mode model as an integrative framework. In Zanna, M.P. (ed.) *Advances in Experimental Social Psychology*, 23, 75–109.

Fazio, R.H. and Zanna, M. (1978) Attitudinal qualities relating to the strength of the attitude–behavior relationship, *Journal of Experimental Social Psychology*, 14, 398–408.

Fazio, R.H. and Zanna, M. (1981) Direct experience and attitude-behavior consistency. In Berkowitz, L. (ed.) *Advances in Experimental Social Psychology*, 14, New York, Academic Press, 161–202.

Fazio, R.H., Powell, M.C. and Herr, P.M. (1983) Toward a process model of the attitude–behavior relation: accessing one's attitude on mene observation of the attitude object, *Journal of Personality and Social Psychology*, 44, 723–35.

Fechner, G.T. (1860) *Elemente der Psychophysik*, Leipzig, Breitkopf and Hartel.

Feinberg, R.A. and Smith, P. (1989) Misperceptions of time in the sales transaction. In Srull, T.K. (ed.) *Advances in Consumer Research*, 16, 56–8.

Feinberg, R.A., Widdows, R., Hirsch-Wyncott, M. and Trappey, C. (1990) Myth and reality in customer service: good and bad service sometimes lead to repurchase, *Journal of Consumer Satisfaction, Dissatisfaction and Complaining Behavior*, 3, 112–13.

Feinberg, R.A., Widdows, R., and Steidle, R. (1996) Customer (dis)satisfaction and delays, *Journal of Consumer Satisfaction, Dissatisfaction and Complaining Behavior*, 9, 81–5.

Feldwick, P. (1990) *Advertising Works 5*, London, Institute of Practitioners in Advertising, Cassell.

Feldwick, P. (1991) *Advertising Works 6*, Henley-on-Thames, Institute of Practitioners in Advertising, NTC Publications Ltd.

Feldwick, P. (1996) What is brand equity anyway, and how do you measure it? *Journal of the Market Research Society*, 38, 2, 85–104.

Ferber, R. (1954) The role of planning in consumer purchase of durable goods, *American Economics Review*, 44, 854–74.

Festinger, L. (1957) *A Theory of Cognitive Dissonance*, IL, Evanston, Row Peterson.

Festinger, L. (1964) *Conflict, Decision and Dissonance*, Stanford, CA, Stanford University Press.

Festinger, L. and Carlsmith, J.M. (1959) Cognitive consequences of forced compliance, *Journal of Abnormal and Social Psychology*, 58, 203–10.

Finn, D.W. and Lamb, C.W. Jr (1991) An evaluation of the SERVQUAL scale in a retail setting. In Holman, R.H. and Solomon, M.R. (eds.) *Advances in Consumer Research*, 18, 483–90.

Fishbein, M. (1963) An investigation of the relationships between beliefs about an object and attitudes to that object, *Human Relations*, 16, 233–40.

Fishbein, M. (1966) *Sexual Behavior and Propositional Control*. Paper read to the Psychonomic Society.

Fishbein, M. (1972) Some comments on the use of 'models' in advertising research, *Proceedings of the ESOMAR Madrid Seminar on Advanced Advertising Theories and Research*, Amsterdam, ESOMAR, 297–318.

Fishbein, M. (1976) Extending the extended model: some comments. In Anderson, B.B. (ed.) *Advances in Consumer Research*, 3, 491–7.

Fishbein, M. (1977) *Consumer Beliefs and Behavior with Respect to Cigarette Smoking: A Critical Analysis of the Public Literature*. A report to the U.S. Federal Trades Commission.

Fishbein, M. and Ajzen, I. (1974) Attitudes towards objects as predictors of single and multiple behavioral criteria, *Psychological Review*, 81, 59–74.

Fishbein, M. and Ajzen, I. (1975) *Belief, Attitude, Intention and Behavior*, Reading, MA, Addison-Wesley.

Fishbein, M. and Ajzen, I. (1976a) Misconceptions about the Fishbein model: reflections on a study by Songer-Nocks, *Journal of Experimental Social Psychology*, 12, 579–84.

Fishbein, M. and Ajzen, I. (1976b) Misconceptions revisited: a final comment, *Journal of Experimental Social Psychology*, 12, 591–3.

Fishbein, M.F. and Ajzen, I. (1981) On construct validity: a critique of Miniard and Cohen's paper, *Journal of Experimental Social Psychology*, 17, 340–50.

Fletcher, W. (1992) *A Glittering Haze*, Henley, NTC Publications Ltd.

Folkes, V.S. (1984) Consumer reactions to product failure: an attributional approach, *Journal of Consumer Research*, 10, March, 398–409.

Folkes, V.S. (1988) The availability heuristic and perceived risk, *Journal of Consumer Research*, 15, 13–23.

Folkes, V.S., Koletsky, S. and Graham, J.L. (1987) A field study of causal inferences and consumer reaction: the view from the airport, *Journal of Consumer Research*, 13, 534–9.

Fornell, C. (1992) A national customer satisfaction barometer: the Swedish experience, *Journal of Marketing*, 56, 1–18.

Fornell, C and Wernerfelt, B. (1987) Defensive marketing strategy by customer complaint management: a theoretical analysis, *Journal of Marketing Research*, 24: 4, 337–46.

Fornell, C and Wernerfelt, B. (1988) A model for customer complaining management, *Marketing Science*, 7, Summer, 187–98.

Fornell, C. and Westbrook, R.A. (1984) The vicious circle of consumer complaints, *Journal of Marketing*, 48, Summer, 68–78.

Foxall, G.R. (1990) *Consumer Psychology in Behavioural Perspective*, London and New York, Routledge.

Foxall, G.R. (1992a) The consumer situation: an integrative model for research in marketing, *Journal of Marketing Management*, 8, 383–404.

Foxall, G.R. (1992b) The behavioral perspective model of purchase and consumption: from consumer theory to marketing practice, *Journal of the Academy of Marketing Science*, 20: 2, 189–98.

Foxall, G. and Hackett, P.M.W. (1992) Consumers' perception of micro-retail location: wayfinding and cognitive mapping in planned and organic shopping environments, *International Review of Retail, Distribution and Consumer Research*, 2: 3, 309–27.

Frank, R.E. (1967) Correlates of buying behavior for grocery products, *Journal of Marketing*, 31, 48–53.

Fredricks, A.J. and Dossett, K.L. (1983) Attitude–behavior relations: A comparison of the Fishbein–Ajzen and the Bentler–Speckart models, *Journal of Personality and Social Psychology*, 45, 501–12.

Frisbie, G.A. Jr (1980) Ehrenberg's negative binomial model applied to grocery store trips, *Journal of Marketing Research*, 17, 385–90.

Frost, W.A.K. and Braine, R.L. (1967) The application of the repertory grid technique to problems in marketing research, *Market Research Society Conference Proceedings*.

Fulgoni, G.M. (1987) The role of advertising – is there one? *Admap*, 262, 54–7.

Fulgoni, G.M. and Eskin, G.J. (1981) Use of the BehaviorScan research facility for studying retail shopping patterns. In Lusch, R.F. and Carden, W.R. (eds.) *Retail Patronage Theory – 1981 Workshop Proceedings*, University of Oklahoma.

Gabor, A. (1977) *Pricing, Principles and Practices*, Aldershot, Gower.

Gabor, A. (1988) Pricing, *Concepts and Methods for Effective Marketing*, 2nd edn, Vermont, Gower Publishing Co Ltd.

Gabor, A. and Granger, C.W.J. (1961) On the price consciousness of consumers, *Applied Statistics*, 10: 3, 170–88.

Gabor, A. and Granger, C.W.J. (1972) Ownership and acquisition of consumer durables: report on the Nottingham consumer durables project, *European Journal of Marketing*, 6: 4, 234–48.

Gardner, A.G. and Levy, S.J. (1955) The product and the brand, *Harvard Business Review*, 33, March/April, 33–9.

Garrick, G. (1986a) *Spend Better Advertising Dollars, Not More*. Paper presented to the Advertising Research Foundation Electronic Media Workshop, Hilton, New York, 11 December.

Garrick, G. (1986b) *What Will Copy Research be Like in 1990?* Paper presented to the Third Annual ARF Copy Research Workshop, Hilton, New York, 28 May.

Gerard, H.B. (1967) Choice difficulty, dissonance and the decision sequence, *Journal of Personality and Social Psychology*, 35, 91–108.

Gigerenzer, G. (1991) How to make cognitive illusions disappear: beyond 'heuristics and biases'. In Stroebe, W. and Hewstone, M. (eds.) *European Review of Social Psychology*, 2, Chichester, Wiley & Sons, 83–115.

Gijsbrechts, E. (1993) Prices and pricing research in consumer marketing: some recent developments, *International Journal of Research in Marketing*, 10, 115–51.

Giles, M. and Cairns, E. (1995) Blood donation and Ajzen's theory of planned behaviour, *British Journal of Social Psychology*, 34: 2, 173–88.

Gilly, M. and Gelb, B. (1982) Post-purchase consumer processes and the complaining consumer, *Journal of Consumer Research*, 9, December, 323–8.

Givon, M. and Horsky, D. (1990) Untangling the effects of purchase reinforcement and advertising carryover, *Marketing Science*, 9: 2, 171–87.

Godin, G., Valois, P. and Lepage, L. (1993) The pattern of influence of perceived behavioral control upon exercising behavior: an application of Ajzen's theory of planned behavior, *Journal of Behavioral Medicine*, 16: 1, 81–102.

Godin, G., Valois, P., Lepage, L. and Desharnais, R. (1992) Predictors of smoking behavior: an application of Ajzen's theory of planned behaviour, *British Journal of Addiction*, 87: 9, 1335–43.

Goffman, E. (1959) *The Presentation of Self in Everyday Life*, New York, Doubleday.

Goodhardt, G.J., Ehrenberg, A.S.C. and Chatfield, C. (1984) The Dirichlet: a comprehensive model of buying behaviour, *Journal of the Royal Statistical Society*, A: 147, 621–55.

Goodhardt, G.J., Ehrenberg, A.S.C. and Collins, M.A. (1975) *The Television Audience: Patterns of Viewing*, Aldershot, Saxon House.

Goodhardt, G.J., Ehrenberg, A.S.C. and Collins, M.A. (1987) *The Television Audience: Patterns of Viewing, An Update*, Aldershot, Gower.

Gorn, G.J. (1982) The effects of music in advertising on choice behavior, a classical conditioning approach, *Journal of Marketing*, 46: 1, 94–101.

Granbois, D., Summers, J.O. and Frazier, G.L. (1977) Correlates of consumer expectation and complaining behavior. In Day, R.L. (ed.) *Consumer Satisfaction, Dissatisfaction and Complaining Behavior*, Bloomington, Indiana University Press, 18–25.

Grønhaug, K. (1977) Exploring complaining behavior: a model and some empirical results. In Perreault, W.D. Jr. (ed.) *Advances in Consumer Research*, 4, 159–63.

Grønhaug, K. and Zaltman, G. (1981) Complainers and noncomplainers revisited: another look at the data. In Monroe, K.B. (ed.) *Advances in Consumer Research*, 8, 83–7.

Grönroos, C. (1978) A service-oriented approach to marketing service, *European Journal of Marketing*, 12: 8, 588–601.

Grönroos, C. (1984) A service quality model and its marketing implications, *European Journal of Marketing*, 18: 4, 35–44.

Grönroos, C. (1990) *Service Management and Marketing: Managing the Moments of Truth in Service Competition*, Lexington, MA, Lexington Books.

Gröppel, A. (1993) Store design and experience orientated consumers in retailing: comparison between United States and Germany. In Raaij, W.F. van and Bamossy, G.J. (eds.) *European Advances in Consumer Research*, 1, 99–109.

Grunert, K.G. and Grunert, S.C. (1995) Measuring subjective meaning by the laddering method: theoretical considerations and methodological problems, *International Journal of Research in Marketing*, 12: 3, 209–25.

Guadagni, P.M. and Little, J.D.C. (1983) A logit model of brand choice calibrated on scanner data, *Marketing Science*, 2, Summer, 203–38.

Haley, R.I. (1968) Benefit segmentation: a decision oriented research tool, *Journal of Marketing*, 32, 30–5.

Haley, R.I. and Baldinger, A.L. (1991) The ARF copy research validation project, *Journal of Advertising Research*, April/May, 11–32.

Halstead, D. (1993) Five common myths about consumer satisfaction programs, *Journal of Services Marketing*, 7: 3, 4–12.

Hamilton, W., East, R. and Kalafatis, S. (1997) The measurement and utility of brand price elasticities, *Journal of Marketing Management*, 13, 4.

Hammond K.A. and Ehrenberg, A.S.C. (1994) How important is the favourite brand? *Proceedings of the Marketing Education Group*, University of Ulster, 444.

Hammond K.A. and Ehrenberg, A.S.C. (1995) Heavy buyers: How many do you have? How important are they? In Bergardaá, M. (ed.) *Marketing Today and for the 21st Century. 24th EMAC Conference Proceedings*, Essec, Paris 1651–6.

Hammond K.A., Ehrenberg, A.S.C. and Goodhardt, G.J. (1996) Market segmentation for competitive brands, *European Journal of Marketing*, 30, 12.

Harrell, G.D., Hutt, M.D. and Anderson, J.C., (1980) Path analysis of buyer behavior under conditions of crowding, *Journal of Marketing Research*, 17, 45–51.

Harrison, A.A. (1968) Response competition, frequency, exploratory behavior and liking, *Journal of Personality and Social Psychology*, 9: 4, 363–8.

Harrison, D.A. and Liska, L.Z. (1994) Promoting regular exercise in organisational fitness programs: health related differences in motivational building-blocks, *Personnel Psychology*, 47: 1, 47–71.

Hartman, C.L., Price, L.L. and Duncan, C.P. (1990) Consumer evaluation of franchise extension products. In Goldberg, M.E., Gorn, G. and Pollay, R. (eds.) *Advances in Consumer Research*, 17, 110–27.

Heap, S.H., Hollis, M., Lyons, B., Sugden, R. and Weale, A. (1992) *The Theory of Choice*, Blackwell, Oxford.

Heath, T.B., Chatterjee, S. and France, K.R. (1995) *Journal of Consumer Research*, 22, June, 90–7.

Heider, F. (1944) Social perception and phenomenal causality, *Psychological Review*, 51, 358–74.

Heider, F. (1958) *The Psychology of Interpersonal Relations*, New York, Wiley.

Heil, O.P. and Helsen, K. (1995) Price wars: a definition, a propositional inventory using early warning signals to understand the emergence of price wars. In Bergardaá, M. (ed.) *Marketing Today and for the 21st Century. 24th EMAC Conference Proceedings*, Paris, ESSEC, 437–50.

Helson, H. (1964) *Adaptation Level Theory*, New York, Harper and Row.

Helsen, K. and Schmittlein, D.C. (1992) How does a product market's typical price promotion pattern affect the timing of a household's purchases? *Journal of Retailing*, 68: 3, 316–38.

Higgins, T. (1987) Self-discrepancy: a theory relating self to affect, *Psychological Review*, 94, 319–40.

Hilgard, E.R. and Marquis, D.G. (1940) *Conditioning and Learning*, New York, Appleton Century.

Hirschman, A.O. (1970) *Exit, Voice and Loyalty: Responses to Decline in Firms, Organizations and States*, Cambridge, MA, Harvard University Press.

Hjorth–Anderson, C. (1984) The concept of quality and the efficiency of markets for consumer products, *Journal of Consumer Research*, 11: 2, 708–18.

Holbrook, M.B. (1994) The nature of customer value: an axiology of services in the consumption experience. In Rust, R.T. and Oliver, R.L. (eds.) *Service Quality: New Directions in Theory and Practice*, London, Sage Publications, 21–71.

Holden, S.J.S. (1993) Understanding brand awareness: let me give you a c(l)ue! In McAlister, L. and Rothschild, M.L. (eds.) *Advances in Consumer Research*, 20, 383–8.

Holden, S.J.S. and Barwise T.P. (1995) An empirical investigation of what it means to generalize. In Bergardaá, M. (ed.) *Marketing Today and for the 21st Century. 24th EMAC Conference Proceedings*, Cergy, France, 1677–7.

Holden, S.J.S. and Lutz, R.J. (1992) Ask not what the brand can evoke; ask what can evoke the brand. In Sherry, J.F. and Sternthal, B. (eds.) *Advances in Consumer Research*, 19, 101–7.

Homans, G.C. (1961) *Social Behavior: Its Elementary Forms*, London, Routledge and Kegan Paul.

Horst, L. and Jarlais, D.C. (1984) Naturally occurring attitude and behavior changes: content and duration of the change process, *Quarterly Journal of Human Behavior*, 21: 2, 36–42.

Hovland, C.I., Janis, I.L. and Kelley, H.H. (1953) *Communication and Persuasion*, New Haven, CT, Yale University Press.

Howard, J.A. (1994) *Consumer Behavior in Marketing Strategy*, Englewood Cliffs, NJ, Prentice Hall.

Howard, J.A. and Sheth, J.N. (1969) *The Theory of Buyer Behavior*, New York, Wiley.

Huefner, J.C. and Hunt, H.K. (1994) Extending the Hirschman model: when voice and exit don't tell the whole story, *Journal of Satisfaction, Dissatisfaction and Complaining Behavior*, 7, 267–70.

Huff, D.L. (1962) *Determination of Intra-Urban Retail Trade Areas*, Los Angeles, University of California, Real Estate Research Program.

Huff, D.L. (1981) Retail location theory. In Stampfl, R.W. and Hirschman, E.C. (eds.) *Theory in Retailing: Traditional and Non-Traditional Sources*, Chigago, American Marketing Association, 108–21.

Hui, M.K. and Bateson, J.E.G. (1991) Perceived control and the effects of crowding and consumer choice on the service experience, *Journal of Consumer Research*, 18, 174–84.

Hunt, H.K. (1991) Consumer satisfaction, dissatisfaction and complaining behavior, *Journal of Social Issues*, 47: 1, 107–17.

Hunt, H.K., Hunt, D. and Hunt, T. (1988) Consumer grudge holding, *Journal of Consumer Satisfaction, Dissatisfaction and Complaining Behavior*, 1, 116–18.

Infosino, W.J. (1986) Forecasting new product sales from likelihood of purchase ratings, *Marketing Science*, 5: 4, 372–84.

Inman, J.J., McAlister, L. and Hoyer, W.D. (1990) Promotion signal: proxy for a price cut? *Journal of Consumer Research*, 17, June, 74–81.

IRI (1989) Larger sample, stronger proof of P-O-P effectiveness. Reprint from IRI which enlarges on a report that first appeared in *P-O-P Times*, March/April, 28–32.

Jaccard, J.J. and Davidson, A.R. (1972) Toward an understanding of family planning behaviors: an initial investigation, *Journal of Applied Social Psychology*, 2: 3, 228–35.

Jacobson, R. and Obermiller, C. (1990) The formation of expected future price: a reference price for forward-looking consumers, *Journal of Consumer Research*, 16, March, 420–32.

Jacoby, J. and Chestnut, R.W. (1978) *Brand Loyalty Measurement and Management*, New York, Wiley.

Jacoby, J. and Olson, J.C. (1970) An attitudinal model of brand loyalty: conceptual underpinnings and instrumentation research. Purdue Paper in Consumer Psychology, No. 159.

Jarratt, D.E. (1996) A shopper typology for retail strategy development, *The International Journal of Retail, Distribution and Consumer Research*, 6: 2, 196–215.

Jones, E.E. and Nisbett, R.E. (1972) The actor and observer: divergent perceptions of the causes of behavior. In Jones, E.E., Kanouse, D.E., Kelley, H.H., Nisbett, R.E., Valins, S. and Weiner, B. (eds.) *Attribution: Perceiving the Causes of Behavior*, Morristown, NJ, General Learning Press, 79–94.

Jones, K. and Simmons, J. (1990) The Retail Environment, London and New York, Routledge.

Jones, J.P. (1995a) *When Ads Work: New Proof that Advertising Triggers Sales*. New York, Lexington Books.

Jones, J.P. (1995b) Single source research begins to fulfil its promise, *Journal of Advertising Research*, 35: 3, 9–16.

Jones, J.P. (1995c) Advertising exposure effects under a microscope, *Admap*, February, 28–31.

Jones, J.P. (1995d) We have a breakthrough, *Admap*, June, 33–5.

Jöreskog, K.G. and Sörbom, D. (1989) *LISREL 7: A Guide to the Program and its Applications*, 2nd edn, Chicago, SPSS.

Juster, F.T. (1966) Consumer buying intentions and purchase probability: an experiment in survey design, *Journal of the American Statistical Association*, 61, September, 658–96.

Kahle, L.R. and Berman, J.J. (1979) Attitudes cause behaviors: a cross-lagged panel analysis, *Journal of Personality and Social Psychology*, 37: 3, 315–21.

Kahn, B.E., Morrison, D.G. and Wright, G.P. (1986) Aggregating individual purchases to the household level, *Marketing Science*, 5, 260–8.

Kahn, B.E. and Schmittlein, D.C. (1989), Shopping trip behavior: an empirical investigation,

Marketing Letters, 1: 1, 55–69.

Kahneman, D. and Tversky, A. (1972) Subjective probability: a judgement of representativeness, *Cognitive Psychology*, 3, 430–54.

Kahneman, D. and Tversky, A. (1973) On the psychology of prediction, *Psychological Review*, 80, 237–51.

Kahneman, D. and Tversky, A. (1979) Prospect theory: an analysis of decision under risk, *Econometrica*, 47, 263–91.

Kahneman, D. and Tversky, A. (1984) Choices, values and frames, *American Psychologist*, 39: 4, 341–50.

Kalyanaram, G. and Little, J.D.C. (1994) An empirical analysis of latitude of price acceptance in consumer package goods, *Journal of Consumer Research*, 21, December, 408–18.

Kamakura, W.A. and Russell, G.J. (1993) Measuring brand value with scanner data, *International Journal of Research in Marketing*, 10: 1, 9–22.

Kapferer, J.-N. (1991) *Les Marques, Capital de l'Enterprise*, Paris, Les Editions d'Organisation.

Kashima, Y., Gallois, C. and McCamish, M. (1993) The theory of reasoned action and cooperative behaviour: it takes two to use a condom, *British Journal of Social Psychology*, 32: 3, 227–39.

Katona, G. (1947) Contribution of psychological data to economic analysis, *Journal of the American Statistical Association*, 42, 449–59.

Katz, K., Larson, B. and Larson, R. (1991) Prescription for waiting-in-line blues: entertain, enlighten, and engage, *Sloan Management Review*, 32, 44–53.

Kau, A.K. and Ehrenberg, A.S.C. (1984) Patterns of store choice, *Journal of Marketing Research*, 21, 399–409.

Keller, K.L. and Aaker, D.A. (1992) The effects of sequential introduction of brand extensions, *Journal of Marketing Research*, 29, 35–50.

Kelly, C. and Breinlinger, S. (1995) Attitudes, intentions and behavior: a study of women's participation in collective action, *Journal of Applied Social Psychology*, 25: 16, 1430–45.

Kelly, G.A. (1955) *The Psychology of Personal Constructs*, New York, Norton.

Kimiecik, J. (1992) Predicting vigorous activity of corporate employees: comparing the theories of reasoned action and planned behavior, *Journal of Sport and Exercise Psychology*, 14: 2, 192–206.

King, S. (1984) Setting advertising budgets for lasting effects, *Admap*, 20, August, 335–9.

Kish, L. (1959) Some statistical problems in research design, *American Sociological Review*, 24, 328–38.

Kitchen, P.J. (1986) Zipping, zapping and nipping, *International Journal of Advertising*, 5: 4, 343–52.

Klein, G.A. (1989) Recognition-primed decisions. In Rouse, W.B. (ed.) *Advances in Man-Machine System Research*, 5, Greenwich, CT, JAI Press Inc., 47–92.

Klein, N.M. and Oglethorpe, J.E. (1987) Cognitive reference points in consumer decision making. In Wallendorf, M. and Anderson, P. (eds.) *Advances in Consumer Research*, 14, 183–87.

Klobas, J.E. (1995) Beyond information quality: fitness for purpose and electronic information resource use, *Journal of Information Science*, 21: 2, 95–114.

Knox, S.D. and de Chernatony, L. (1994) Attitude, personal norms and intentions. In Jenkins, M. and Knox, S. (eds.) *Advances in Consumer Marketing*, London, Kogan Page, 85–98.

Koelemeijer, K. (1992) Measuring perceived service quality in retailing: a comparison of methods. In Grunert, K. (ed.) *Marketing for Europe – Marketing for the Future*, Proceedings of the 21st Annual Conference of the European Marketing Academy, Aarhus, Denmark, 729–44.

Koepp, S. (1987) Pul-eeze! Will someone help me? *Time*, 2 February, 28–34.

Kollat, D.T. and Willett, R.P. (1967) Customer impulse purchasing behavior, *Journal of Marketing Research*, 4, 21–31.

Korgaonkar, P.K., Lund, D. and Price, B. (1985) A structural equations approach toward examination of store attitude and store patronage behavior, *Journal of Retailing*, 61: 2, 39–60.

Kotler, P. (1973) Atmosphere as a marketing tool, *Journal of Retailing*, 49, Winter, 48–64.

Kotler, P. and Armstrong, G. (1994) *Principles of Marketing*, 6th edn, Englewood Cliffs, NJ, Prentice Hall.

Kover, A.J. and Abruzzo, J. (1993) The Rossiter–Percy Grid and emotional response to advertising:

an initial evaluation, *Journal of Advertising Research*, 33: 6, 21–7.

Kristiansen, C.M. (1987) Salient beliefs regarding smoking: consistency across samples and smoking status, *Journal of the Institute of Health Education*, 25, 73–6.

Krugman, H.E. (1965) The impact of television advertising: learning without involvement, *Public Opinion Quarterly*, 29, Fall, 349–56.

Krugman, H.E. (1972) Why three exposures may be enough, *Journal of Advertising Research*, 12: 6, 11–14.

Kuehn, A.A. (1962) Consumer brand choice as a learning process, *Journal of Advertising Research*, 2, December, 10–17.

Kunst, P. and Lemmink, J. (eds.) (1994) *Managing Service Quality*, Vol. 1, London, Paul Chapman Publishing.

Kunst, P. and Lemmink, J. (eds.) (1996) *Managing Service Quality*, Vol. 2, London, Paul Chapman Publishing.

Kunst-Wilson, W.R. and Zajonc, R.B. (1980) Affective discrimination of stimuli that cannot be recognised, *Science*, 207, 557–8.

Lannon, J. (1985) Advertising research: new ways of seeing, *Admap*, October, 520–4.

Lannon, J. (1994) Mosaics of meaning: anthropology and marketing, *Journal of Brand Management*, 2: 3, 155–68.

Lannon, J. and Cooper, P. (1983) Humanistic advertising: a holistic cultural perspective, *International Journal of Advertising*, 2, 195–213.

Lapersonne, E., Laurent, G. and Le Goff, J.-J. (1995) Consideration sets of size one: an empirical investigation of automobile purchases, *International Journal of Research in Marketing*, 12: 1, 55–66.

LaPiere, R.T. (1934) Attitudes vs. actions, *Social Forces*, 13, 230–7.

LaTour, S.A. and Peat, N.C. (1979) Conceptual and methodological issues in consumer satisfaction research. In Wilkie, W.L. (ed.) *Advances in Consumer Research*, 6, 431–7.

Lattin, J.M. and Bucklin, R.E. (1989) Reference effects of price and promotion on brand choice behavior, *Journal of Marketing Research*, 26, August 299–310.

Lavidge, R.J. and Steiner, G.A. (1961) A model for predictive measurements of advertising effectiveness, *Journal of Marketing*, 25, October, 59–62.

Leclerc, F., Schmitt, B.H. and Dubé, L. (1995) Waiting time and decision making: is time like money? *Journal of Consumer Research*, 22: 1, 110–9.

Lee, A.Y. (1994) The mere exposure effect; is it a mere case of misattribution? In Allen, C.T. and John, D.R. (eds.), *Advances in Consumer Research*, 21, 270–5.

Lewis, A., Webley, P. and Furnham, A. (1995) *The New Economic Mind: The Social Psychology of Economic Behaviour*, London, Harvester Wheatsheaf.

Lichtenstein, S., Slovik, P., Fischoff, B., Layman, M. and Combs, B. (1978) Judged frequency of lethal events, *Journal of Experimental Psychology: Human Learning and Memory*, 4, 551–78.

Liljander, V. (1994) Modeling perceived service quality using different comparison standards, *Journal of Consumer Satisfaction, Dissatisfaction and Complaining Behavior*, 7, 126–42.

Linder, D.E., Cooper, J. and Jones, E.E. (1967) Decision freedom as a determinant of the role of incentive magnitude in attitude change, *Journal of Personality and Social Psychology*, 6, 245–54.

Litzenroth, H. (1991) A small town in Germany: single source data from a controlled micromarket, *Admap*, 26: 5, 23–7.

Lodish, L.M., Abraham, M.M., Livelsberger, J., Lubetkin, B., Richardson, B. and Stevens, M.E. (1995) A summary of fifty-five in-market experimental estimates of the long-term effect of TV advertising, *Marketing Science*, 14, 3, Part 2 of 2, G133–G140.

Lodish, L.M., Abraham, M.M., Kalmansen, S., Livelsberger, J., Lubetkin, B., Richardson, B. and Stevens, M.E. (1995) How T.V. advertising works: a meta-analysis of 389 real world split cable T.V. advertising experiments, *Journal of Marketing Research*, 32: 2, 125–39.

Lodish, L.M. and Lubetkin, B. (1992) How advertising works. General truths? Nine key findings from IRI test data, *Admap*, February, 9–15.

Loken, B. (1983) The theory of reasoned action: examination of the sufficiency assumption for a television viewing behavior. In Bagozzi, R.P. and Tybout, A.M. (eds.) *Advances in Consumer*

Research, 10, 100–5.

Lomax, W., Hammond, K., Clemente, M. and East, R. (1996) New entrants in a mature market: an empirical study of the detergent market, *Journal of Marketing Management*, 12, 281–95.

Losch, A. (1939) *The Economics of Location*. Translated by Woglom, W.H. and Stolper, F. (1954) New Haven, CT, Yale University Press.

Lutz, R.J. (1977) An experimental investigation of causal relations among cognitions, affect, and behavioral intentions, *Journal of Consumer Research*, 3, 197–208.

Lutz, R.J. (1978) Rejoinder, *Journal of Consumer Research*, 4, 266–71.

McAlister, L. (1985) *The Impact of Price Promotions on a Brand's Sales Pattern, Market Share and Profitability*. Sloan School Working Paper No. 1622-85, MIT, Cambridge, MA.

McAlister, L. (1986) *The Impact of Price Promotions on a Brand's Sales Pattern, Market Share and Profitability*. Sloan School Working Paper No. 86–110, MIT, Cambridge, MA.

McAlister, L. and Totten, J. (1985) *Decomposing the Promotional Bump: Switching, Stockpiling, and Consumption Increase*. Paper presented at the ORSA/TIMS Joint Meeting, 4 November.

McArdle, J.B. (1972) *Positive and Negative Communications and Subsequent Attitude and Behavior Change in Alcoholics*. Doctoral Dissertation, University of Illinois. Reported in Ajzen, I. and Fishbein, M. (1980) *Understanding Attitudes and Predicting Social Behavior*, Englewood Cliffs, NJ, Prentice Hall.

McCaul, K.D., Sandgren, A.K., O'Neill, H.K. and Hinsz, V.B. (1993) The value of the theory of planned behavior, perceived control and self-efficacy expectations for predicting health-protective behaviors, *Basic and Applied Social Psychology*, 14: 2, 231–52.

McDonald, C. (1970) What is the short term effect of advertising? *Proceedings of the ESOMAR Congress*, Barcelona, 463–85.

McDonald, C. (1992) *How Advertising Works*, Henley-on-Thames, The Advertising Association and NTC Publications.

McDonald, C. (1995a) Where to look for the most trustworthy evidence. Short-term advertising effects are the key, *Admap*, February, 25–7.

McDonald, C. (1995b) Breakthrough or bun fight, *Admap*, June, 35–8.

McDonald, C. (1995c) *Advertising Reach and Frequency*, Chicago, NTC Business Books.

McGoldrick, P.J. (1990) *Retail Marketing*, Maidenhead, McGraw-Hill.

McGoldrick, P.J. and Andre, E. (1997) Consumer misbehaviour: promiscuity or loyalty in grocery shopping, *Journal of Retailing and Consumer Services*, 4.

McGoldrick, P.J. and Marks, H. (1987) Shoppers' awareness of retail grocery prices, *European Journal of Marketing*, 21: 3, 63–76.

McGuiness, D., Brennan, M. and Gendall, P. (1995) The effect of product sampling and couponing on purchase behaviour: some empirical evidence, *International Journal of Advertising*, 14: 3, 219–30.

McIntyre, K.O., Lichtenstein, E. and Mermelstein R.J. (1983) Self-efficacy and relapse in smoking cessation: a replication and extension, *Journal of Consulting and Clinical Psychology*, 51: 4, 632–3.

McKay, D.B. (1973) A spectral analysis of the frequency of supermarket visits, *Journal of Marketing Research*, 10, 84–90.

McPhee, W.N. (1963) *Formal Theories of Mass Behavior*, Glencoe, IL, Free Press.

McQuarrie, E.F. (1988) An alternative to purchase intentions: the role of prior behaviour in consumer expenditure on computers, *Journal of the Market Research Society*, 30: 4, 407–37.

McQueen, J. (1992) Stimulating long-term brand growth, *Admap*, April, 43–7.

McWilliam, G. (1993) The effect of brand typology on the evaluation of brand extension fit: commercial and academic research findings. In Van Raaij, W.F. and Bamossy, G.J. (eds.) *European Advances in Consumer Research*, 1, 485–91.

Madden, T.J. and Ajzen, I. (1991) Affective cues in persuasion: an assessment of causal mediation, *Marketing Letters*, 2: 4, 359–66.

Madden, T.J., Ellen, P.S. and Ajzen, I. (1992) A comparison of the theory of planned behavior and the theory of reasoned action, *Personality and Social Psychology Bulletin*, 18: 1, 3–9.

Magee, A. (1994) Compulsive buying tendency as a predictor of attitudes and perceptions. In Allen, C.T. and John, D.R. (eds.), *Advances in Consumer Research*, 21, 590–4.

Maister, D.H. (1985) The psychology of waiting lines. In Czepiel, J.A., Solomon, M.R. and

Surprenant, C.F. (eds.) *The Service Encounter*, Lexington, MA, D.C. Heath, 113–24.

Malafi, T.N., Cini, M.A., Taub, S.L. and Bertolami, J. (1993) Social influence and the decision to complain: investigations on the role of advice, *Journal of Consumer Satisfaction, Dissatisfaction and Complaining Behavior*, 6, 81–9.

Malec, J. (1982) Ad testing through the marriage of UPC scanning and targetable TV, *Admap*, May, 273–9.

Manstead, A.S.R., Proffitt, C. and Smart, J.L. (1983) Predicting and understanding mothers' infant-feeding intentions and behavior: testing the theory of reasoned action. *Journal of Personality and Social Psychology*, 44, 657–71.

Marcel, J. (1976) *Unconscious Reading: Experiments on People Who Do Not Know They Are Reading*. Paper presented at the British Association for the Advancement of Science, Lancaster.

Markus, H. and Zajonc, R.B. (1985) The cognitive perspective in social psychology. In Lindzey, G. and Aronson, E. (eds.) *Handbook of Social Psychology*, 1, 3rd edn, New York, Random House, 137–230.

Marsh, A. and Matheson, J. (1983) *Smoking Attitudes and Behaviour: An Enquiry Carried out on Behalf of the Department of Health and Social Security*, London, HMSO.

Marsh, P., Barwise, P., Thomas, K. and Wensley, R. (1988) *Managing Stategic Investment Decisions in Large Diversified Companies, Working Paper, London Business School reviewed in The Economist*, 9 July.

Mason, N. (1991) *An Investigation into Grocery Shopping Behaviour in Britain*, Headington, Oxford, Nielsen.

Mason, N. (1996) Store loyalty – that old chestnut. In *Customer Loyalty – The Issue for the 90s, The Researcher*, 1, Headington, Oxford, Nielsen, 6–15.

Mazis, M.B., Ahtola, O.T. and Klippel, R.E. (1975) A comparison of four multi-attribute models in the prediction of consumer attitudes, *Journal of Consumer Research*, 2, 38–52.

Mehrabian, A. and Russell, J.A. (1974) *An Approach to Environmental Psychology*, Cambridge, MA, MIT.

Meyers-Levy, J. and Tybout, A.M. (1989) Schema congruity as a basis for product evaluation. *Journal of Consumer Research*, 16, 39–54.

Milgram, S. (1970) The experience of living in cities, *Science*, 167, 1464–8.

Milgram, S., Liberty, H.J. and Toledo, R. (1986) Response to intrusion into waiting lines, *Journal of Personality and Social Psychology*, 51: 4, 683–9.

Miller, N. (1959) Liberalisation of basic S–R concepts: extensions to conflict behavior, motivation and social learning. In Koch, S. (ed.) *Psychology: The Study of a Science*, 2, New York, McGraw-Hill, 196–292.

Milliman, R.E. (1982) Using background music to affect the behavior of supermarket shoppers, *Journal of Marketing*, 46, Summer, 86–91.

Miniard, P.W. and Cohen, J.B. (1979) Isolating attitudinal and normative influences in behavioral intentions models, *Journal of Marketing Research*, 16, 102–10.

Miniard, P.W. and Cohen, J.B. (1981) An examination of the Fishbein–Ajzen behavioral-intentions model's concepts and measures, *Journal of Experimental Social Psychology*, 17, 309–39.

Miniard, P.W. and Cohen, J.B. (1983) Modeling personal and normative influences on behavior, *Journal of Consumer Research*, 10, 169–80.

Mintzberg, H. (1979) *The Structuring of Organizations*, New York, Prentice Hall.

Moldovan, S.E. (1984) Copy factors related to persuasion scores, *Journal of Advertising Research*, 24: 6, 16–22.

Monroe, K.B. (1979) *Pricing: Making Profitable Decisions*, New York, McGraw-Hill Book Co.

Moore, C.M.J., Maxwell, G.A. and Barron, P.E. (1996) UK retail customers – are they being served? *Journal of Consumer Satisfaction, Dissatisfaction and Complaining Behavior*, 9, 229–39.

Moraleda, P. and Ferrer-Vidal, J. (1991) Proceedings of the 1990 ESOMAR Conference, Monte Carlo.

Morgan, R.P. (1987) Ad hoc pricing research. In Bradley, U. (ed.) *Applied Marketing and Social Research*, Chichester, Wiley, 207–21.

Morojele, N.K. and Stephenson, G.M. (1992) The Minnesota model in the treatment of addictions:

a social psychological assessment of changes in beliefs and attributions, *Journal of Community and Applied Social Psychology*, 2: 1, 25–41.

Morrison, D. and Schmittlein, D.C. (1981) Predicting future random events based on past performances, *Management Science*, 27, 1006–23.

Morrison, D. and Schmittlein, D.C. (1988) Generalizing the NBD model for customer purchases: what are the implications and is it worth the effort? *Journal of Business and Economic Statistics*, 6: 2, 145–66.

Morrison, D.M., Gillmore, M.R. and Baker, S.A. (1995) Determinants of condom use among high-risk heterosexual adults: a test of the theory of reasoned action, *Journal of Applied Social Psychology*, 25: 8, 651–76.

Motes, W.H. and Woodside, A.G. (1984) Field test of package advertising effects on brand choice behavior, *Journal of Advertising Research*, 24: 1, 39–45.

Naples, M.J. (1979) *Effective Frequency: The Relationship between Frequency and Advertising Effectiveness*, New York, Association of National Advertisers.

Neslin, S.A. and Stone, L.G.S. (1996) Consumer inventory sensitivity and the postpromotion dip, *Marketing Letters*, 7: 1, 77–94.

Netemeyer, R.G., Andrews, J.C. and Durvasula, S. (1993) A comparison of three behavioral intentions models: the case of Valentine's Day gift-giving, *Advances in Consumer Research*, 20, 135–41.

Newcomb, M.D. (1984) Sexual behavior, responsiveness, and attitudes among women: a test of two theories, *Journal of Sex and Marital Therapy*, 10: 4, 272–86.

Nielsen (1992) *The British Shopper, 1992/93*, Henley-on-Thames, Nielsen in association with NTC Publications Ltd.

Nisbett, R.E. and Wilson, T.D. (1977) Telling more than we can know: verbal reports on mental processes, *Psychological Review*, 84, 231–59.

Norman, P. and Smith, L. (1995) The theory of planned behavior and exercise: an investigation into the role of prior behavior, behavioral intentions, and attitude variability, *European Journal of Social Psychology*, 25: 4, 403–15.

Nuttin, J.M. Jr (1975) *The Illusion of Attitude Change; Towards a Response Contagion Theory of Persuasion*, London, Academic Press.

Ogilvy, D. (1987) Sound the alarm! *International Journal of Advertising*, 6: 1, 81–4.

O'Herlihy, C. (1976) Making advertising profitable for the advertiser, *Admap*, August, 360–9.

O'Herlihy, C. (1983) How econometrics work in practice: 10 years of measuring the sales effects of advertising, *Admap*, 19, March, 146–52.

Oliver, R.L. (1980) Cognitive model of the antecedents and consequences of satisfaction decisions, *Journal of Marketing Research*, 17, November, 460–9.

Oliver, R. L. (1981) Measurement and evaluation of satisfaction processes in retail settings, *Journal of Retailing*, 57: 3, 25–48.

Oliver, R.L. (1987) An investigation of the interrelationship between consumer (dis)satisfaction and complaint reports. In Wallendorf, M. and Anderson, P. (eds.) *Advances in Consumer Research*, 14, 218–22.

Oliver, R.L. (1989) Processing of the satisfaction response in consumption: a suggested framework and research propositions, *Journal of Consumer Satisfaction, Dissatisfaction and Complaining Behavior*, 2, 1–16.

Oliver, R.L. and Bearden, W.O. (1985) Disconfirmation processes and consumer evaluations in product usage, *Journal of Business Research*, 13, 235–46.

Oliver, R.L. and Swan, J.E. (1989) Consumer perceptions of interpersonal equity and satisfaction in transactions: a field survey approach, *Journal of Marketing*, 53, 21–35.

Olshavsky, R.W. and Granbois, D.H. (1979) Consumer decision making – fact or fiction? *Journal of Consumer Research*, 6, September, 93–100.

Osgood, J.F., Suci, G.J. and Tannenbaum, P.H. (1957) The Measurement of Meaning, Urbana, IL, University of Illinois Press.

Ostlund, L.E., Clancy, J.C. and Sapra, R. (1980) Inertia in copy research, *Journal of Advertising Research*, 20: 1, 17–23.

Parasuraman, A., Berry, L.L. and Zeithaml, V.A. (1991) Refinement and reassessment of the SERVQUAL scale, *Journal of Retailing*, 67, 420–50.

Parasuraman, A., Berry, L.L. and Zeithaml, V.A. (1993) More on improving service quality measurement, *Journal of Retailing*, 69: 1, 140–7.

Parasuraman, A., Zeithaml, V.A. and Berry, L.L. (1985) A conceptual model of service quality and its implications for future research, *Journal of Marketing*, 49, 41–50.

Parasuraman, A., Zeithaml, V.A. and Berry, L.L. (1988) SERVQUAL: a multiple-item scale for measuring consumer perceptions of service quality, *Journal of Retailing*, 64, 12–40.

Parasuraman, A., Zeithaml, V.A. and Berry, L.L. (1994) Reassessment of expectations as a comparison standard in measuring service quality, *Journal of Marketing*, 58, January, 111–24.

Park, C.W. (1976) The effect of individual and situation related factors on consumer selection of judgmental models, *Journal of Marketing Research*, 13, 144–51.

Parker, D. and Manstead, A.S.R. (1996) The social psychology of driver behaviour. In Semin, G.R. and Fiedler, K. (eds.) *Applied Social Psychology*, London, Sage Publications, 198–224.

Parker, D., Manstead, A.S.R. and Stradling S.G. (1995) Extending the theory of planned behaviour: the role of the personal norm, *The British Journal of Social Psychology*, 34: 2, 127–37.

Parker, D., Manstead, A.S.R., Stradling S.G., Reason, J.T. and Baxter, J.S. (1992) Intention to commit driving violations: an application of the theory of planned behavior, *Journal of Applied Psychology*, 77: 1, 94–101.

Patterson, P.G. and Johnson, L.W. (1993) Disconfirmation of expectations and the gap model of service quality: an integrated paradigm, *Journal of Satisfaction, Dissatisfaction and Complaining Behavior*, 6, 90–9.

Pavlov, I.P. (1927) *Conditioned Reflexes*, translated by Anrep, G.V. London, Oxford University Press.

Payne, J.W., Bettman, J.R. and Johnson, E.J. (1993) *The Adaptive Decision Maker*, Cambridge, Cambridge University Press.

Pederson, R.A. (1977) Consumer perceptions as a function of product colour, price and nutrition labeling. In Perrault, W.D. (ed.) *Advances in Consumer Research*, 4, 61–3.

Peltzman, S. (1983) The effects of automobile safety regulation, *Journal of Political Economy*, 75, 681.

Perkins, D.S. (1993) An update on the CS/D&CB bibliography: revolution and evolution, *Journal of Satisfaction, Dissatisfaction and Complaining Behavior*, 6, 217–79.

Petkova, K.G., Ajzen, I. and Driver, B.L. (1995) Salience of anti-abortion beliefs and commitment to an attitudinal position: on the strength, structure and predictive validity of anti-abortion attitudes, *Journal of Applied Social Psychology*, 25: 6, 463–83.

Petty, R.E. and Cacioppo, J.T. (1979) Issue-involvement can increase or decrease persuasion by enhancing message-relevant cognitive responses, *Journal of Personality and Social Psychology*, 37, 1915–26.

Petty, R.E. and Cacioppo, J.T. (1985) The elaboration likelihood model of persuasion. In Berkowitz, L. (ed.) *Advances in Experimental Social Psychology*, 19, New York, Academic Press.

Petty, R.E., Cacioppo, J.T. and Schumann, D. (1983) Central and peripheral routes to advertising effectiveness: the moderating role of involvement, *Journal of Consumer Research*, 10, September, 135–46.

Pickering, J.F. (1975) Verbal explanations of consumer durable purchase decisions, *Journal of the Market Research Society*, 17: 2, 107–13.

Pickering, J.F. (1984) Purchase expectations and the demand for consumer durables, *Journal of Economic Psychology*, 5: 4, 342–52.

Pickering, J.F., Greatorex, M. and Laycock, P.J. (1983) The structure of consumer confidence in four EEC countries, *Journal of Economic Psychology*, 4: 4, 353–62.

Pickering, J.F. and Isherwood, B.C. (1974) Purchase probabilities and consumer durable buying behaviour, *Journal of the Market Research Society*, 16: 3, 203–26.

Polyani, G. (1972) *Detergents: A Question of Monopoly*, Institute of Economic Affairs Research Monograph No. 24, London, Monopolies Commission.

Pomerance, E. and Zielske, H. (1958) How frequently should you advertise? *Media/Scope*, 2: 9, 25–7.

Popkowski, P.T.L. and Rao, R.C. (1989) An empirical analysis of national and local advertising effect on price elasticity, *Marketing Letters*, 1: 2, 149–60.

Powell, M.C. and Fazio, R.H. (1984) Attitude accessibility as a function of repeated attitudinal expression, *Personality and Social Psychology Bulletin*, 10, 139–48.

Progressive Grocer (1974) What shoppers know and don't know about prices, November, 39–41.

Pruyn, A.Th.H. and Smidts, A. (1993) Customers' evaluations of queues: three exploratory studies. In Van Raaij, W.F. and Bamossy, G.J. (eds.) *European Advances in Consumer Research*, 1, 371–82.

Raats, M.M., Shepherd, R. and Sparks, P. (1995) Including moral dimensions of choice within the structure of the theory of planned behavior, *Journal of Applied Social Psychology*, 25: 6, 484–94.

Raj, S.P. (1982) The effects of advertising on high and low loyalty segments, *Journal of Advertising Research*, 9, June, 77–89.

Rajecki, D.W. (1982) *Attitudes: Themes and Advances*, Sunderland, MA, Sinaur Associates Inc.

Raju, P.S. (1977) Product familiarity, brand name and price influences on product evaluation. In Perrault, W.D. (ed.) *Advances in Consumer Research*, 4, 64–71.

Randall, D.M. and Wolff, J.A. (1994) The time interval in the intention–behaviour relationship, *British Journal of Social Psychology*, 33: 4, 405–18.

Rao, T.R. (1969) Consumer's purchase decision process: stochastic models, *Journal of Marketing Research*, 6, 321–9.

Rao, A.R. and Monroe, K.B. (1988) The moderating effect of prior knowledge on cue utilization in product evaluations, *Journal of Consumer Research*, 15, September, 253–63.

Rao, A.R. and Sieben, W.A. (1992) The effect of prior knowledge on price acceptability and the type of information examined, *Journal of Consumer Research*, 19, September, 256–70.

Ratchford, B.T. (1987) New insights about the FCB Grid, *Journal of Advertising Research*, 27: 4, 24–38.

Reeves, R. (1961) *Reality in Advertising*, London, MacGibbon.

Regan, D.T. and Fazio, R.H. (1977) On the consistency between attitudes and behavior: look to the method of attitude formation, *Journal of Experimental Social Psychology*, 13, 28–45.

Reichheld, F.F. (1993) Loyalty-based management, *Harvard Business Review*, 71: 2, 64–73.

Reichheld, F.F. (1996) Learning from customer defections, *Harvard Business Review*, March/April, 56–69.

Reichheld, F.R. and Sasser, W.E. (1990) Zero defections: quality comes to services, *Harvard Business Review*, Sept./Oct., 301–7.

Reilly, W.J. (1929) *Methods for the Study of Retail Relationships*, Austin, TX, Bureau of Business Research Studies in Marketing, No. 4.

Resnik, A.J. and Harmon, R.R. (1983) Consumer complaints and managerial response: a holistic approach, *Journal of Marketing*, 47, Winter, 68–78.

Richard, L., Dedobbeleer, N., Champagne, F. and Potvin, L. (1994) Predicting child restraint device use: a comparison of two models, *Journal of Applied Social Psychology*, 24: 20, 1837–47.

Richins, M.L. (1981) An investigation of the consumer's attitudes towards complaining. In Mitchell, A. (ed.) *Advances in Consumer Research*, 9, 502–6.

Richins, M.L. (1983) Negative word-of-mouth by dissatisfied consumers: a pilot study, *Journal of Marketing*, 47, 68–78.

Richins, M.L. (1985) The role of product importance in complaint initiation, *Proceedings of the Eighth and Ninth Conferences on Consumer Satisfaction and Complaining Behavior*, Baton Rouge, Louisiana and Phoenix, Arizona, 50–3.

Richins, M.L. (1987) A multivariate analysis of responses to dissatisfaction, *Journal of the Academy of Marketing Science*, 15, 24–31.

Riley-Smith, P. (1984) Do shoppers look at prices? *Proceedings of the Market Research Conference*, March, 235–51.

Rip, P. (1980) The informational basis of self-reports; a preliminary report. In Olson J.C. (ed.) *Advances in Consumer Research*, 7, 140–5.

Roberts, A. (1980) Decision between above and below the line, *Admap*, June, December, 588–92.

Roberts, A. (1994) Media exposure and consumer purchasing: an improved data fusion technique, *Marketing And Research Today*, 22: 3, 159–72.

Robertson, K. (1989) Strategically desirable brand name characteristics, *Journal of Consumer*

Marketing, 6: 4, 61–71.

Rosenberg, M.J. (1956) Cognitive structure and attitudinal affect, *Journal of Abnormal and Social Psychology*, 53, 367–72.

Rosenberg, M.J. (1968) Discussion: impression processing and the evaluation of new and old objects. In Abelson, R.P. *et al.* (eds.) *Theories of Cognitive Consistency: a Sourcebook*, Chicago, Rand McNally, 763–8.

Rosenberg, M.J. and Hovland, C.I. (1960) Cognitive, affective and behavioral components of attitudes. In Hovland, C.I. and Rosenberg, M.J. (eds.) *Attitude Organization and Change*, New Haven, CT, Yale University Press, 1–14.

Rossiter, J.R. (1987) Comments on 'Consumer beliefs and brand usage' and on Ehrenberg's ATR model, *Journal of the Market Research Society*, 29: 1, 83–8.

Rossiter, J.R. and Percy, L. (1997) *Advertising Communications and Promotion Management*, New York, McGraw-Hill.

Rossiter, J.R., Percy, L. and Donovan, R.J. (1991) A better advertising planning grid, *Journal of Advertising Research*, Oct./Nov., 11–21.

Rothschild, M.L. and Gaidis, W.C. (1981) Behavioral learning theory: its relevance to marketing and promotions, *Journal of Marketing*, 45, 70–8.

Russo, J.E. and Leclerc, F. (1994) A eye-fixation analysis of choice processes for consumer non-durables, *Journal of Consumer Research*, 21: 2, 274–90.

Rust, R.T. and Oliver, R.L. (1994) Service quality: insights and managerial implications from the frontier. In Rust, R.T. and Oliver, R.L. (eds.) *Service Quality: New Directions in Theory and Practice*, London, Sage Publications, 1–20.

Rutter, D.R., Quine, L. and Chesham, D.J. (1995) Predicting safe riding behavior and accidents: demography, beliefs and behavior in motorcycling safety, *Psychology and Health*, 10: 5, 369–86.

Ryan, M.J. (1982) Behavioral intention formation: the interdependency of attitudinal and social variables, *Journal of Consumer Research*, 9, 263–78.

Ryan, M.J. and Etzel, M.J. (1976) The nature of salient outcomes and referents in the extended model. In Anderson, B.B. (ed.) *Advances in Consumer Research*, 3, 485–90.

Saegert, S.C. and Jellison, J.M. (1970) Effects of initial level of response competition and frequency of exposure on liking and exploratory behavior, *Journal of Personality and Social Psychology*, 16: 3, 553–8.

Sahni, A. (1994) Incorporating perceptions of financial control in purchase prediction: an empirical examination of the theory of planned behavior, *Advances in Consumer Research*, 21, 442–8.

Samelson, F. (1980) J.B. Watson's Little Albert, Cyril Burt's twins, and the need for a critical science, *American Psychologist*, 35: 7, 619–25.

Sandell, R. (1981) *The Dynamic Relationship between Attitudes and Choice Behavior in the Light of Cross-lagged Panel Correlations*. Department of Psychology, University of Stockholm, December, Report no. 581.

Sasser, W.E. (1976) Match supply and demand in the service industries, *Harvard Business Review*, 54: 6, 133–8.

Schachter, S. and Singer, J.E. (1962) Cognitive, social and physiological determinants of emotional state, *Psychological Review*, 69, 379–99.

Scherhorn, G., Reisch, L.A. and Raab, G. (1990) Addictive buying in West Germany: an empirical study, *Journal of Consumer Policy*, 13, 355–87.

Schifter, D.B. and Ajzen, I. (1985) Intention, perceived control and weight loss: an application of the theory of planned behavior, *Journal of Personality and Social Psychology*, 49: 3, 843–51.

Schlegel, R.P., Davernas, J.R. and Zanna, M.P. (1992) Problem drinking: a problem for the theory of reasoned action, *Journal of Applied Social Psychology*, 22: 5, 358–85.

Schmitt, B.H., Dubé, L. and F. Leclerc (1992) Intrusions into waiting lines: does the queue constitute a social system? *Journal of Personality and Social Psychology*, 63: 5, 806–15.

Schmittlein, D.C., Bemmaor, A.C. and Morrison, D.G. (1985) Why does the NBD model work? Robustness in representing product purchases, brand purchases and imperfectly recorded purchases, *Marketing Science*, 4: 3, 255–66.

Schmittlein, D. C., Cooper, Lee G. and Morrison, Donald G. (1993) Truth in concentration in the land of (80/20) laws, *Marketing Science*, 12: 2, 167–83.

Schugan, S.M. (1994) Explanations for the growth of services. In Rust, R.T. and Oliver, R.L. (eds.) *Service Quality: New Directions in Theory and Practice*, London, Sage Publications, 223–40.

Schultz, D.E. (1987) Above or below the line? Growth in sales promotion in the United States, *International Journal of Advertising*, 6: 1, 17–27.

Schuman, H. and Johnson, M.P. (1976) Attitudes and behavior, *Annual Review of Sociology*, 2, 161–207.

Sears, D.O. (1968) The paradox of *de facto* selective exposure without preferences for supportive information. In Abelson, R.P., Aronson, E., McGuire, W.J., Newcomb, T.M., Rosenberg, M.J. and Tannenbaum, P.H. (eds.) *Theories of Cognitive Consistency: a Sourcebook*, Chicago, Rand-McNally, 777–87.

Seiders, K. and Costley, C.L. (1994) Price awareness of consumers exposed to intense retail rivalry: a field study. In Allen, C.T. and John, D.R. (eds.) *Advances in Consumer Research*, 21, 79–85.

Shapiro, B.P. (1973) Price reliance: existence and sources, *Journal of Marketing Research*, 10, Aug, 286–94.

Sheppard, B.H., Hartwick, J. and Warshaw, P.R. (1988) The theory of reasoned action: a meta-analysis of past research with recommendations for modifications and future research, *Journal of Consumer Research*, 15, 325–43.

Sheth, J.N. (1972) Reply to the comments on the nature and uses of expectancy-value models in consumer research, *Journal of Marketing Research*, 9, 462–5.

Sheth, J.N. and Talarzyk, W.W. (1972) Perceived instrumentality and value importance as determinants of attitudes, *Journal of Marketing Research*, 9, 6–9.

Shimp, T.A. and Kavas, A. (1984) The theory of reasoned action applied to coupon usage, *Journal of Consumer Research*, 11, December, 795–809.

Shoemaker, R.W. and Shoaf, F.R. (1977) Repeat rates of deal purchases, *Journal of Advertising Research*, 17, April, 47–53.

Shoemaker, R.W. and Tibrewala, V. (1985) Relating coupon redemption rates to past purchasing of the brand, *Journal of Advertising Research*, 25: 5, 40–7.

Shryer, W.A. (1912) *Analytical Advertising*, Detroit, Business Service Corporation.

Simon, H.A. (1957) *Administrative Behavior*, New York, Macmillan.

Simon, J.L. (1979) What do Zielske's real data show about pulsing? *Journal of Marketing Research*, 16: 3, 415–20.

Simon, J.L. and Arndt, J. (1980) The shape of the advertising response function, *Journal of Advertising Research*, 20: 4, 11–28.

Singh, J. (1990) Voice, exit, and negative word-of-mouth behaviors: an investigation across three categories, *Journal of the Academy of Marketing Science*, 18, 1–15.

Singh, J. and Howell, R. (1985) Consumer complaining behavior: a review and prospectus. In Hunt, H.K. and Day, R.L. (eds.) *Consumer Satisfaction, Dissatisfaction and Complaining Behavior*, Bloomington, Indiana University Press, 41–9.

Skinner, B.F. (1938) *The Behavior of Organisms*, New York, Appleton-Century-Crofts.

Skinner, B.F. (1953) *Scientific and Human Behavior*, New York, Macmillan.

Smith, A.M. (1995) Measuring service quality: is SERVQUAL now redundant? *Journal of Marketing Management*, 11, 257–76.

Smith, D.C. and Park, C.W. (1992) The effects of brand extensions on market share and advertising efficiency, *Journal of Marketing Research*, 29, 296–313.

Smith, E.R. and Miller, F.D. (1978) Limits on perception of cognitive processes: a reply to Nisbett and Wilson, *Psychological Review*, 85, 355–62.

Smith, R.B. and Sherman, E. (1992) Effects of store image and mood on consumer behavior: a theoretical and empirical analysis. In McAlister, L. and Rothschild, M.L. (eds.) *Advances in Consumer Research*, 20, 631.

Smith, R.E. and Swinyard, W.R. (1983) Attitude–behavior consistency: the impact of product trial versus advertising, *Journal of Marketing Research*, 20, August, 257–67.

Solnick, S.J. and Hemenway, D. (1992) Complaints and disenrollment at a health maintenance organization, *Journal of Consumer Affairs*, 26: 1, 90–103.

Songer-Nocks, E. (1976a) Situational factors affecting the weighting of predictor components in the Fishbein model, *Journal of Experimental Social Psychology*, 12, 56–69.

Songer-Nocks, E. (1976b) Reply to Fishbein, *Journal of Experimental Social Psychology*, 12, 85–90.

Sparks, L. (1993) The rise and fall of mass marketing? Food retailing in Great Britain since 1960. In Tedlow, R.S. and Jones, G. (eds.), *The Rise and Fall of Mass Marketing*, Routledge, London.

Speed, R. (1995) Similarity of positioning and branding decisions in line extensions. In Bergardaá, M. (Ed) *Marketing Today and for the 21st Century*. 24th EMAC Conference Proceedings, Cergy, France, 2003–7.

Sproles, G.B. (1986) The concept of quality and the efficiency of markets: issues and comments, *Journal of Marketing*, 13, June, 146–7.

Steiner, R.L. (1973) Does advertising lower consumer prices? *Journal of Marketing*, 37, 4, 19–27.

Stewart, D.W. and Furse, D.H. (1984) Analysis of executional factors on advertising performance, *Journal of Advertising Research*, 24, 6, 23–6.

Stewart, J.B. (1964) *Repetitive Advertising in Newspapers: A Study of Two New Products*, Boston, MA, Harvard University, Graduate School of Business Administration and Research.

Stewart, M.J. (1990) A comment on 'Modelling beyond the blip', *Journal of the Market Research Society*, 32: 3, 457–62.

Stø, E. and Glefjell, S. (1990) The complaining process in Norway: five steps to justice, *Journal of Consumer Satisfaction, Dissatisfaction and Complaining Behavior*, 3, 92–9.

Stoetzel, J. (1954) Le prix comme limite, in Reynaud, P.L. (ed.) *La Psychologie Economique*, Paris, Librarie Marcel Rivière et Cie, 183–8.

Sunde, L. and Brodie, R.J. (1993) Consumer evaluations of brand extensions: further empirical results, *International Journal of Research in Marketing*, 10: 1, 47–53.

Sutton, S., Marsh, A. and Matheson, J. (1987) Explaining smokers' decisions to stop: test of an expectancy-value approach, *Social Behaviour*, 2: 1, 35–50.

Svenson, O. (1974) *Coded Think Aloud Protocols Obtained when Making a Choice to Purchase One of Seven Hypothetically Offered Houses*. Report, University of Stockholm.

Swan, J.E., Powers, T.L. and Hansen, S.W. (1995) The industrial buyer complaint process: an ethnography of finding and fixing vendor mistakes, *Journal of Consumer Satisfaction, Dissatisfaction and Complaining Behavior*, 8, 1–10.

Swan, J.E. and Trawick, I.F. (1980) Satisfaction related to predicted versus desired expectations. In Hunt, H.K. and Day, R.L. (eds.) *Refining Concepts and Measures of Consumer Satisfaction and Complaining Behavior*, Bloomington, School of Business, Indiana University, 7–12.

Swan, J.E. and Trawick, I.F. (1981) Disconfirmation of expectations and satisfaction with a retail service, *Journal of Retailing*, 57: 3, 49–67.

Swinyard, W.R. (1993) The effects of mood, involvement and quality of store experience on shopping intention, *Journal of Consumer Research*, 20, September, 271–80.

TARP (1979) *Consumer Complaint Handling in America: a Summary of Findings and Recommendation*, Washington, DC, US Office of Consumer Affairs.

Tate, R.S. (1961) The supermarket battle for store loyalty, *Journal of Marketing*, 25, October, 8–13.

Tauber, E.M. (1975) Predictive validity in consumer research, *Journal of Advertising Research*, 15: 5, 59–64.

Tauber, E.M. (1981) Brand franchise extension: new product benefits from existing brand names, *Business Horizons*, 24, 36–41.

Tauber, E.M. (1988) Brand leverage: strategy for growth in a cost conscious world, *Journal of Advertising Research*, 31, 26–30.

Taylor, S. (1994) Waiting for service: the relationship between delays and evaluations of service, *Journal of Marketing*, 58, April, 56–69.

Taylor, S. (1995) The effects of filled waiting time and service provider control over the delay on evaluations of service, *Journal of the Academy of Marketing Science*, 23: 1, 38–48.

Taylor, S. and Todd, P. (1995) An integrated model of waste management behavior: a test of household recycling and composting intentions, *Environment and Behavior*, 27: 5, 603–30.

Taylor, S.A. (1996) Consumer satisfaction with marketing education: extending services theory to academic practice, *Journal of Satisfaction, Dissatisfaction and Complaining Behavior*, 9, 207–20.

Teas, R.K. (1994) Expectations as a comparison standard in measuring service quality: an assessment of a reassessment, *Journal of Marketing*, 58, January, 132–9.

Tellis, G.J. (1988) The price elasticities of selective demand: a meta-analysis of econometric models of sales, *Journal of Marketing Research*, 331–41.

Tellis, G.J. and Wernerfelt, B. (1987) Competitive price and quality under asymmetric information, *Marketing Science*, 6, 240–53.

Telser, L.G. (1962) The demand for branded goods as estimated from consumer panel data, *Review of Economics and Statistics*, 44, August, 300–24.

Thaler, R. (1985) Mental accounting and consumer choice, *Marketing Science*, 4, Summer, 199–214.

Thaler, R. (1987) The psychology of choice and the assumptions of economics. In Roth, A.E. (ed.) *Laboratory Experiments in Economics: Six Points of View*, Cambridge, Cambridge University Press, 99–130.

Theil, H. and Kosobud, R.F. (1968) How informative are consumer buying intentions surveys? *Review of Economics and Statistics*, 50, 50–9.

Thibaut, J.W. and Kelley, H.H. (1959) *The Social Psychology of Groups*, New York, Wiley.

Thompson, B., (1967) An analysis of supermarket shopping habits in Worcester, MA, *Journal of Retailing*, 43: 3, 17–29.

Thorndike, E.L. (1911) *Animal Intelligence*, New York, Macmillan.

Tom, G. and Lucey, S. (1995) Waiting time delays and customer satisfaction in supermarkets, *Journal of Services Marketing*, 9: 5, 20–9.

Totten, J.C. (1986) *Measuring Retail Sales Response to Retail Sales Promotion*. Paper presented at the ORSA/TIMS Marketing Science Conference, March.

Totten, J.C. and Block, M.P. (1987) *Analyzing Sales Promotion: Text and Cases*, Chicago, Commerce Communications Inc.

Trafimow, D. and Fishbein, M. (1995) Do people really distinguish between behavioural and normative beliefs? *British Journal of Social Psychology*, 34: 3, 257–66.

Treasure, J. (1975) How advertising works. In Barnes, M. (ed.) *The Three Faces of Advertising*, London, The Advertising Association, 48, 52.

Triandis, H.C. (1977) *Interpersonal Behavior*, Monterey, CA, Brooks Cole.

Trout, J. and Ries, A. (1972) Positioning cuts through chaos in the marketplace, *Advertising Age*, 1 May. Also in Enis, B.M. and Cox, K.K., *Marketing Classics*, 7th edn, Boston, MA, Allyn and Bacon, 216–33.

Tse, D.K. and Wilton, P.C. (1988) Models of consumer satisfaction formation: an extension, *Journal of Marketing Research*, 25, May, 204–12.

Tuck, M. (1977) *How Do We Choose?* London, Methuen.

Tucker, W.T. (1964) The development of brand loyalty, *Journal of Marketing Research*, 1, 32–5.

Tversky, A. (1972) Elimination by aspects: a theory of choice, *Psychological Review*, 79, 281–99.

Tversky, A. and Kahneman, D. (1974) Judgement under uncertainty: heuristics and biases, *Sciences*, 185, 1124–31.

Tversky, A. and Kahneman, D. (1980) Causals schemas in judgements under uncertainty. In Fishbein, M. (ed.) *Progress in Social Psychology*, 1, 49–72.

Tversky, A. and Kahneman, D. (1981) The framing of decisions and the psychology of choice, *Science*, 211, 453–58.

Tversky, A. and Kahneman, D. (1986) Rational choice and the framing of decisions, *Journal of Business*, 59: 4, S251–78.

Uncles, M.D. (1988) BUYER: Buyer Behaviour Software, available from Kathy Hammond, London Business School, Sussex Place, Regent's Park, London, NW1 4SA.

Uncles, M.D. and Ehrenberg, A.S.C. (1990a) The buying of packaged goods at US retail chains, *Journal of Retailing*, 66: 3, 278–96.

Uncles, M.D. and Ehrenberg, A.S.C. (1990b) Brand choice among older consumers, *Journal of Advertising Research*, 30: 4, 19–22.

Uncles, M.D. and Hammond, K.A. (1995) Grocery store patronage, *International Journal of Retail, Distribution and Consumer Research*, 5: 3, 287–302.

Urbany, J.E., Bearden, W.O. and Weilbaker, D.C. (1988) The effect of plausible and exaggerated reference prices on consumer perceptions and price search, *Journal of Consumer Research*, 15, June, 95–110.

Van der Plight, J. and van Schie, E.C.M. (1990) Frames of reference, judgement and preference. In Stroebe, W. and Hewstone, M. (eds.) *European Review of Social Psychology*, 1, Chichester, Wiley and Sons, 61–80.

Vanhuele, M. (1994) Mere exposure and the cognitive-affective debate revisited. In Allen, C.T. and John, D.R. (eds.), *Advances in Consumer Research*, 21, 264–9.

Van Raaij, W.F. (1977) Consumer information processing for different information structures and formats. In Perreault, W.D. Jr (ed.), *Advances in Consumer Research*, 4, 176–84.

Van Raaij, W.F. and Schoonderbeek, W.M. (1993) Meaning structure of brand names and extensions. In Raaij, W.F. van and Bamossy, G.J. (eds.) *European Advances in Consumer Research*, 1, 479–84.

Vaughn, R. (1980) How advertising works: a planning model, *Journal of Advertising Research*, 20: 5, 27–33.

Vaughn, R. (1986) How advertising works: a planning model revisited. *Journal of Advertising Research*, 26: 1, 57–66.

Veblen, T. (1899) *The Theory of The Leisure Class*, London, Macmillan (New Library Edition, 1963).

Viscusi, W.K. (1984) The lulling effect: the impact of child resistant packaging on aspirin and analgesic ingestions. *American Economic Review*, 74, 324–7.

Vroom, V.H. (1964) *Work and Motivation*, New York, Wiley.

Walters, R.G. and Rinne, H.S. (1986) An empirical investigation into the impact of price promotions on retail store performance, *Journal of Retailing*, 62: 3, 237–66.

Wansink, B. and Ray, M. (1992) Estimating an advertisement's impact on one's consumption of a brand, *Journal of Advertising Research*, May/June, 9–16.

Warland, R.H., Herrmann, R.O. and Willits, J. (1975), Dissatisfied customers: who gets upset and what they do about it, *Journal of Consumer Affairs*, 9, Winter, 152–62.

Watson, J.B. and Rayner, R. (1920) Conditioned emotional reactions, *Journal of Experimental Psychology*, 3, 1–14.

Wee, C.H. and Pearce, M.R. (1985) Patronage behavior toward shopping areas: a proposed model based on Huff's model of retail gravitation. In Hirschman, E.C. and Holbrook, M.B. (eds.) *Advances in Consumer Research*, 12, 592–7.

Weigel, R.H. and Newman, L.S. (1976) Increasing attitude–behavior correspondence by broadening the scope of the behavioral measure, *Journal of Personality and Social Psychology*, 33, 793–802.

Weiner B. (1980) *Human Motivation*, New York, Holt, Rinehart and Winston.

Weiner B. (1990) Searching for the roots of applied attribution theory. In Graham, S. and Folkes, V.S. (eds.) *Attribution Theory: Application to Achievement, Mental Health and Interpersonal Conflict*, Hillsdale, NJ, Lawrence Erlbaum, 1–16.

Wellan, D.M. and Ehrenberg, A.S.C. (1988) A successful new brand: Shield, *Journal of the Market Research Society*, 30: 1, 35–44.

Wellan, D.M. and Ehrenberg, A.S.C. (1990) A case of seasonal segmentation, *Marketing Research*, 1, 11–13.

Wells, W.D. (1984) Informational and transformational advertising: the differential effects of time. In Kinnear, T.C. (ed.) *Advances in Consumer Research*, 11, 638–43.

Westbrook, R.A. (1980) Intrapersonal affective influences upon consumer satisfaction, *Journal of Consumer Research*, 7, June, 49–54.

Westbrook, R.A. and Oliver, R.L. (1991) The dimensionality of consumption emotion patterns and consumer satisfaction, *Journal of Consumer Behavior*, 18, June, 84–91.

Wheatley, J.J. and Chiu, J.S.Y. (1977) The effect of price, store image, product and respondent characteristics on perceptions of quality, *Journal of Marketing Research*, 14, May, 181–6.

White, K.M., Terry, D.J. and Hogg, M.A. (1994) Safer sex behavior: the role of attitudes, norms and control factors, *Journal of Applied Social Psychology*, 24: 24, 2164–92.

White, P.A. (1988) Knowing more than we can tell: 'introspective access' and causal report accuracy 10 years later, *British Journal of Psychology*, 79, 13–45.

Wicker, A.W. (1969) Attitude vs actions: the relationship of verbal and overt behavioral responses to attitude objects, *Journal of Social Issues*, 25, 41–78.

Wicker, A.W. (1984) *An Introduction to Ecological Psychology*, Monterey, CA: Brooks/Cole.

Wilkie, W.L. and Dickson, P.R. (1985) *Shopping for Appliances: Consumers' Strategies and Patterns of Information Search*, Cambridge, MA, Marketing Science Institute Research Report No. 85–108.

Winer, R.S. (1988) Behavioral perspectives on pricing: buyers' subjective perceptions of price revisited. In Divinney, T.M. (ed.) *Issues in Pricing*, Lexington, MA, Lexington Books, 35–57.

Woodruff, R.B., Cadotte, E.R. and Jenkins, R.L. (1983) Modeling consumer satisfaction processes using experience-based norms, *Journal of Marketing Research*, 20, August, 296–304.

Wright, P. and Rip, P. (1980) Retrospective reports on consumer decision processes: 'I can remember if I want to but why should I bother trying?' In Olson, J.C. (ed.) *Advances in Consumer Research*, 7, 146–7.

Yalch, R. and Spangenberg, E. (1993) Using store music for retail zoning: a field experiment. In McAlister, L. and Rothschild, M.L. (eds.) *Advances in Consumer Research*, 20, 632–6.

Yi, Y. (1990) A critical review of consumer satisfaction. In Zeithaml, V.A. (ed.) *Review of Marketing*, Chicago, AMA, 68–113.

Zaichkowsky, J.L. and Vipat, P. (1993) Inferences from brand names. In Van Raaij, F.W. and Bamossy, G.J. (eds.) *European Advances in Consumer Research*, 1, 534–40.

Zajonc, R.B. (1968) Attitudinal effects of mere exposure, *Journal of Personality and Social Psychology Monograph Supplement*, 9, 2 (Part 2), 1–27.

Zajonc, R.B. (1980) Feeling and thinking: preferences need no inferences, *American Psychologist*, 35, 151–75.

Zajonc, R.B. and Markus, H. (1982) Affective and cognitive factors in preferences, *Journal of Consumer Research*, 9: 2, 123–32.

Zajonc, R.B. and Rajecki, D.W. (1969) Exposure and affect: a field experiment, *Psychonomic Science*, 17, 216–17.

Zanna, M.P. and Cooper, J. (1974) Dissonance and the pill: an attribution approach to studying the arousal properties of dissonance, *Journal of Personality and Social Psychology*, 29, 703–9.

Zeithaml, V. (1988) Consumer perceptions of price, quality and value: a means–end model and synthesis of evidence, *Journal of Marketing*, 52: 3, 2–22.

Zielske, H. (1959) The remembering and forgetting of advertising, *Journal of Marketing*, 23: 3, 239–43.

Subject index

Author index